The Deacon
and the Schoolmaster

ALSO BY ROBERT PEYTON WIGGINS

*Jungle Combat with the 112th Cavalry:
Three Texans in the Pacific in World War II* (McFarland, 2011)

Chief Bender: A Baseball Biography (McFarland, 2010)

*The Federal League of Base Ball Clubs: The History of an
Outlaw Major League, 1914–1915* (McFarland, 2009)

The Deacon and the Schoolmaster
*Phillippe and Leever,
Pittsburgh's Great
Turn-of-the-Century Pitchers*

ROBERT PEYTON WIGGINS

McFarland & Company, Inc., Publishers
Jefferson, North Carolina, and London

LIBRARY OF CONGRESS CATALOGUING-IN-PUBLICATION DATA

Wiggins, Robert Peyton.
　　The Deacon and the Schoolmaster : Phillippe and Leever, Pittsburgh's great turn-of-the-century pitchers / Robert Peyton Wiggins.
　　　p.　　cm.
　　Includes bibliographical references and index.

　　ISBN 978-0-7864-5842-4
　　softcover : 50# alkaline paper ∞

　　1. Pittsburgh Pirates (Baseball team)—History—20th century.
2. Pitchers (Baseball)—Pennsylvania—Pittsburgh—History.
3. Phillippe, Charles, 1872–1952.　4. Leever, Samuel, 1871–1953.
I. Title.
　　GV875.P5W54　2011
　　796.357'640974886—dc23　　　　　　　　　　2011027367

BRITISH LIBRARY CATALOGUING DATA ARE AVAILABLE

© 2011 Robert Peyton Wiggins. All rights reserved

No part of this book may be reproduced or transmitted in any form or by any means, electronic or mechanical, including photocopying or recording, or by any information storage and retrieval system, without permission in writing from the publisher.

On the cover: Charles Phillippe and Sam Leever, Pittsburgh Pirates, baseball card portraits, 1911 (Library of Congress)

Manufactured in the United States of America

McFarland & Company, Inc., Publishers
　Box 611, Jefferson, North Carolina 28640
　　www.mcfarlandpub.com

To the memory of my grandfather
Walter Wiggins
who experienced the major league game
through the words of the great broadcasters
in the golden age of radio

Table of Contents

Acknowledgments ix
Preface 1

- ONE • Charles Louis Phillippe — 7
- TWO • The Goshen Schoolmaster — 26
- THREE • A New Era in Pittsburgh — 45
- FOUR • A Pennant Comes to Pittsburgh — 63
- FIVE • The Best Pitching in Baseball — 85
- SIX • Three in a Row — 114
- SEVEN • The First World Series — 133
- EIGHT • Mugsy McGraw's Giants — 148
- NINE • Transition — 178
- TEN • World Series Champions — 197
- ELEVEN • Swan Song — 221
- TWELVE • With the Outlaws — 236
- THIRTEEN • Life After Baseball — 251

Appendix: Career Pitching Summaries 259
Chapter Notes 261
Bibliography 275
Index 277

Acknowledgments

There are several things to keep in mind when selecting a subject for a book. It has to be someone or something that would hold an author's interest, there must be sufficient source material, and the subject should be of interest to a publisher.

Little has been written about Deacon Philippe and Sam Leever after they left baseball, so most of my research was focused on contemporary sources. At the turn of the twentieth century, the city of Pittsburgh had several newspapers in circulation that provided a wealth of information about the pair's playing careers. Alfred R. Cratty's columns in *Sporting Life* supplied numerous tidbits about the two pitchers' personal lives during their time as Pirates.

This book would not have been possible without the support of my wife, Deborah Gholson Wiggins. I would like to express my appreciation to the National Baseball Hall of Fame and Museum in Cooperstown, New York, for access to player files and copies of photographs from their extensive archives; the staff of the Pennsylvania State Library in Harrisburg for pulling numerous microfilm reels of historic Pittsburgh newspapers; staff of Hobbs Microfilm Room, Minnesota Historical Society; and Jim Trdinich, Director of Media Relations, Pittsburgh Pirates Baseball Club, for several photographs included in this volume. Also thanks go to Steve Steinberg and Dennis Goldstein for their assistance in the acquisition of photographs. And a special thanks to fellow SABR member Rich Arpi for his research on the years Phillippe played independent baseball in Minnesota and for shepherding me through the microfilm holdings of the Minnesota Historical Society.

The completion of this project was expedited by home computer access to several online sites including ProQuest Historical Newspapers through the Society for American Baseball Research; Bob Huggins' "Paper of Record" for early issues of *The Sporting News*; the Library of Congress website

"Chronicling America" for several pre–1910 newspapers; and "LA84" for free access to the historic *Sporting Life*. These sources decreased the number of tedious hours required to scan microfilm reel by reel. Also important to note were the contributions of the Allegheny County Department of Court Records for official documents on Charles and Belle Phillippe, the University of Virginia Library System for digitized newspapers as well as census information on the Leever and Phillippe families, and the National Archives for several baseball photographs from the early 1900s. Finally, the 1960 Pittsburgh Pirates must receive notice for tweaking my interest in this subject matter by defeating the New York Yankees in the World Series that year.

The origin of this book oddly began with the boyhood hobby of collecting baseball cards and a fondness for Pirate lore — not the baseball Pirates but the swashbuckling type. I began collecting baseball cards even before I became a fan of professional baseball, because at the time that's what pre-teen boys did. By skimping on my lunch money, I was able to save a few pennies a week to buy individually wrapped Topps baseball cards which came with a hard sheet of stale bubble gum that would shatter if dropped on a hard surface. As a young boy in remote Northwest Texas, I became intrigued by books and movies of far-flung adventures so it seemed natural to me that a novice baseball fan would gravitate to the Pirates baseball club rather than a team named for the color of their socks or small ornamental birds.

Though my adopted team from Pittsburgh had nothing do with marauders of the Spanish Main other than their nickname and logo, the very year I began to follow the team on television and the newspapers Pittsburgh played in the World Series for the first time since 1927. Among the Buccaneer heroes of that dramatic fall classic were Roberto Clemente, Harvey Haddix, Hal Smith, Vern Law, Elroy Face, and of course Bill Mazeroski, my favorite player because I aspired to be a second baseman.

Back then school kids could only watch the games of the World Series on weekends because the weekday contests were always played in the afternoon. So when the deciding seventh game came around, I was in a classroom listening to instruction on boring subjects I deemed far less important.

The World Series was the biggest sports event throughout the country at that time and several classmates brought transistor radios to school the day of the final game. We listened to the game in the school cafeteria as Pittsburgh built up a 4 to 0 lead. However, by the first break between classes that afternoon, the radio hounds announced that the Pirates had fallen behind the Yankees by three runs.

I was dejected that "my" Pirates were doomed to lose to the heavily favored Yankees and moped through the next class. The final session of the afternoon was Mrs. Barnes' class, my favorite hour not only because English was my best subject but she was also the prettiest teacher in the ninth grade.

She and her husband, the superintendent, were Pirates fans and when we walked into her classroom that afternoon Mrs. Barnes had written on the chalkboard: "Pittsburgh 10, New York 9!" I don't remember what we studied that day, if anything at all, but it was one of my most memorable days at school.

Finally, I would like to acknowledge the late Fred Lieb, whose book *The Pittsburgh Pirates* I discovered in the school library some 50 years ago. Through Lieb's book there emerged the storied history of the Pirates, and I was especially intrigued with Pittsburgh's three consecutive National League championship teams in the early years of the twentieth century.

My home state finally secured a major league baseball team in 1962 and my allegiance to the Pirates gradually faded. Still, I've always been interested in those Pirates of yesteryear in the age of the dead ball. I was particularly drawn to Deacon Phillippe and Schoolmaster Leever, who never seemed to get their due as the unassuming aces of those powerful Pittsburgh Pirates teams from the dead ball era.

When making the decision on the subject of my third baseball book, I decided to use the opportunity to revisit Leever, Phillippe and the rest of the Pirates from the early 1900s. When one reads about those Pirates teams, one naturally thinks of Honus Wagner — but without the Deacon and the Schoolmaster three of Pittsburgh's National League championships would not have been attainable.

Preface

Why write a book about the baseball careers of Sam Leever and Charles Phillippe, a pair of unheralded Pittsburgh* Pirates pitchers from the turn of the twentieth century? Neither is a member of the National Baseball Hall of Fame. They were not flamboyant on or off the baseball field, nor were they controversial or involved in scandal. The pair just went about their business in a workmanlike manner and became two of the most successful pitchers in the history of the Pittsburgh National League Baseball Club.

Charles "Deacon" Phillippe and Sam Leever, the "Goshen Schoolmaster," were the foundation of the Pittsburgh Pirates' pitching staffs that frustrated National League batters in the early 1900s. Models of consistency, the pair posted a combined record of 261 victories against 131 losses for a won-loss percentage of .666 from 1900 through 1906.

Though Leever and Phillippe are connected because of their pitching art, they were not necessarily close except for an occasional hunting excursion together. They did respect one another, as Alfred R. Cratty, a long-time observer of Pirates baseball, attested in 1903: "These vets formed a close corporation when they joined the Pittsburghs, and it has been on ever since."[1]

Deacon and the Schoolmaster experienced their first full major league season in the same year, 1899. That time was the heyday of Honus Wagner, Cy Young, Kid Nichols, Ed Delahanty, Wee Willie Keeler, and John McGraw. In 1899, the baseball diamond was the same as today; the bases were 90 feet apart and the pitcher's plate was 60 feet 6 inches from home base. Four balls meant a walk and three strikes were an out. The ball was the same size, though the inner components and winding changed with time. All restrictions on a

---

*In 1890 the United States Board of Geographic Names decided that the names of all American cities ending in "burgh" must drop the "h." Newspapers and official records conformed to the ruling, but after protests, the board reversed its decision in 1911 and affected cities restored the "h." For the sake of this volume, the modern spelling will be used.

pitcher's delivery had long since been removed, and once the foul strike rule was introduced prior to the 1901 season the rules used by the National League became essentially the same as today.

Though Phillippe was not a church deacon, Samuel Leever actually was a school teacher before he became a professional baseball player and plied that trade during the off-season in the early years of his career with the Pirates. He won 20 or more games four times with Pittsburgh from 1899 through 1906, enjoying his most productive season in 1903 when he notched 25 victories to help the Pirates to the first World Series. The Schoolmaster is second in Pirates franchise history for career wins (194) and is third in career earned run average (2.47). In October, 1999, Ohio native Leever was named as the right-handed pitcher on the *Cincinnati Enquirer's* all-century Cincinnati area baseball team.

Leever pitched at a time when won-loss percentage was the criterion by which the top pitcher in each league was judged. In the era of Christy Mathewson and Three-Finger Brown, Schoolmaster Sam finished first in winning percentage among National League pitchers in 1901, 1903 and 1905 — and was third in 1906. Among major league pitchers with 200 or more decisions since the distance from the pitcher's box to home plate was increased by five feet to the current length, Leever's winning percentage of .660 is good enough to rank sixth (1893–2010). The five pitchers ahead of him are Whitey Ford, Pedro Martinez, Lefty Grove, Christy Mathewson, and Roy Halladay.

Leever and Phillippe pitched in an era when a major league pitcher was expected to finish what he started. Of the 299 games that Leever started in his career, he completed 241 of them. Leever utilized his curve ball, emphasized control, and relied on his fielders to make plays rather than going for strikeouts. The Schoolmaster had low strikeout totals even for that period. In 1908 he won 15 games, including four shutouts, but struck out only 28 batters in 193 innings pitched. During his 13 years in the major leagues, he averaged less than three strikeouts per nine innings pitched.

Tommy Leach played behind Phillippe for 13 major league seasons and said in 1915 that Deacon was one of the best pitchers in the history of the National League. "He had a fast ball that was as fast as (Grover Cleveland) Alexander's and a bigger breaking curve. It was more effective against strong left-handed hitters than Alexander's for this reason. Phillippe threw his bender with an overhand motion and had it breaking straight down or away from a left-handed batsman. Alexander is a side-arm twirler and his curve usually shoots in, which makes it easier to hit."[2] At the time Leach spoke, Alexander had supplanted Mathewson as the premier pitcher in the National League.

Jack O'Connor caught Phillippe in Pittsburgh from 1900 through 1902

Sam Leever, warming up prior to a game at West Side Grounds, Chicago, in 1905 (Chicago History Museum, SDN-003027; photography by *Chicago Daily News*).

and declared, "His ball would not curve in toward the (left-handed) batter. He always had a little something on it that made it jump up or down."[3]

Phillippe described the difference between his style of pitching and the side-wheeling motion of Sam Leever: "He is one of the best twirlers in the business and has just as good control as I have, but his style and mine are as different as day and night. I pitch a speedy ball straight for the plate, but my curves aren't aimed for the rubber. If they were I would have a catcher digging up the ground with his fists for three or four feet around the plate hunting balls. He pitches his speedy ones straight for the plate the same as I do, but he doesn't differ his mode of delivery in the least for his curve balls, but aims them straight for the catcher's mitt."[4]

Deacon and the Goshen Schoolmaster played baseball at a time when pitchers truly dominated the game. Pitchers had a distinct advantage over batters because a fresh white ball was only in play for a short time. Umpires were not allowed to replace a banged-up ball, so pitchers had the advantage of working much of a game with a dirty baseball rough-hewed by purposeful and accidental scrapes. As the innings wore on, balls turned soft and dark from the repeated beating. Although pitchers benefited from the "deadened" ball, the misshapen spheres often took odd bounces on the way to an infielder.

Furthermore, the infields of that day were not the manicured rugs of today but were full of rocks, pebbles and divots.

The strategy employed by baseball teams in the first decade of the twentieth century featured singles, bunts, sacrifices, hit-and-runs and stolen bases. Batters choked up on the bat and attempted to punch a pitch between the infielders. Outfielders played very shallow so they could throw baserunners out on force plays. Attempts by runners to steal home were a common occurrence and, with men on first and third, the double steal was frequently employed. A home run hit over the outfield fence was a rare occurrence.

Speaking in the early 1960s, Tommy Leach explained the reason for the large number of errors at the time he played; "We had little gloves that would just fit over your hand. Now, they have those big nets, and they catch the ball in the webbing. But we had to catch the ball with our hands. And the fields. Now the lowest minor leagues have better fields to play on than we had in the major leagues. You never knew how a ball was going to bounce in those days. Lots of times we'd get a rake and go out and rake the ground around our own positions."[5]

Charles Louis Phillippe broke into the majors with Louisville of the National League in 1899 and won 21 games, including a no-hitter against the New York Giants. When the National League pared to eight teams the next year, the tall right-hander was one of the players former Louisville owner Barney Dreyfuss took to Pittsburgh after he took over the Pirates.

Called Charley or Phil by his friends, Phillippe earned the nickname "Deacon" early in his baseball career. Though not particularly devout,[6] he acquired the nickname during his minor league days in Minneapolis for his humble demeanor and a solemn countenance whether he won or lost.

Deacon won 22, 20, and 25 games for the Pittsburgh National League champions of 1901, '02 and '03. After a slump in 1904 due to illness and injury, he came back to win 20 in 1905. In 1910, after two years battling a sore arm, he won 13 straight games and compiled a 14–2 record. He did not have a losing season in his 13 years of major league baseball, compiling a 189–109 lifetime record with a 2.59 earned run average. He completed 242 of the 289 games he started during his career, but is most famous for his iron-man performance in the 1903 World Series when he pitched 44 innings in the eight-game series, completing five games, winning three.

Deacon was also one of the stingiest pitchers with the home run ball, permitting no four-baggers in 1905 and only one in each of the 1902 and 1904 seasons, remarkable numbers considering the fact that half his games were in spacious Exposition Park, haven of the inside-the-park homer.

In the mid–1890s, Phillippe utilized the underhand pitch, but it was

Deacon Phillippe completing a throw prior to a game at West Side Grounds, Chicago, in 1909 (Chicago History Museum, SDN-054855; photograph by *Chicago Daily News*).

after the adoption of an overhand delivery that he achieved the great command for which he is most recognized. Phillippe was perhaps the greatest control artist of all time, averaging just 1.25 walks per nine innings over his career, the lowest ratio by any pitcher after the current pitching distance was established in 1893. When the National League considered reducing the number of balls for a walk to three, Phillippe just shrugged it off: "It is a cold day when I get three balls on a man. I seldom give more than one or two bases on balls in a game. This is not said boastfully, but merely to show that this change would not have much effect on me."[7]

He explained to *The Sporting News* that his pitching success was due to "keeping the batters guessing. I study the batsman in every way: his position in the box, his general attitude, the way he holds the bat, and any other individual characteristics he may have... I generally give my catcher the kind of ball he signs for, but use my own judgment as to how high or how near the batter to put it. I try to some extent to work corners — that is, to anywhere as it goes over."[8]

Many pitchers of what was called the "dead ball era" employed a wide array of trick pitches allowed at that time. However, Sam Leever distained the spitball even as it increasingly gained popularity during the first decade of the century. Deacon Phillippe did experiment with it during the 1905 season and even employed it in a game against Chicago. Phillippe continued to tinker with the spitball in practice and planned to add it to his repertory for 1908, but a hand injury doomed his plans for that season.[9]

Phillippe felt sore arms were just part of his trade that a pitcher had to work through. "The care of a pitcher's arm I regard as a simple, though important matter," he said. "I begin active training by merely going through the motions, adding a little more effort each day, but never 'cutting loose' until the opening game. When my arm gets sore, I massage it with my left hand and sometimes resort to electricity. If these do not help it, rest is the only alternative. I do not believe in liniments. A pitcher's arm should always have enough soreness to indicate that it is alive, but this soreness should disappear during the warming-up process before the game."[10]

On the other hand, fellow right-hander Sam Leever treated each sore arm as a potential career-ending injury. During his first full major league season, when he pitched 379 innings for the Pirates, William H. Locke wrote of Leever in the *Sporting News*, "He is the most willing worker ever connected with the Pittsburgh Club and when in form he is one of the grandest pitchers that ever donned a National League uniform."[11]

Leever had an outstanding fastball when he came to the National League, but due to overwork and poor training habits he was annually bothered by problems with his pitching wing. However, he learned how to dominate batters with control and a devastating breaking ball to become one of baseball's top pitchers in the first decade of the twentieth century. Nearly every spring, he would procrastinate on signing his contract and declare that he might not be fit to pitch any more. Pirates owner Barney Dreyfuss and Manager Fred Clarke would reassure him and eventually he would come to spring training.

Despite his idiosyncrasies, Leever is always mentioned in any discussion about the all-time best pitchers that have played for the Pittsburgh Pirates. Renowned historian Bill James has suggested the Schoolmaster was more deserving of enshrinement than several players that have been inducted into the National Baseball Hall of Fame.

Among the great pitchers in baseball history, Charles Phillippe and Samuel Leever are hardly remembered at all. But during the first decade of the twentieth century, Deacon and the Schoolmaster were among the most celebrated pitchers in the major leagues. During the years the pair toiled on the mound in Pittsburgh, the Smoky City club did not finish out of the first division, won four National League pennants, and came in second four times.

♦ ONE ♦

Charles Louis Phillippe

Charles Louis Phillippe came to the Pittsburgh Pirates at a time when the moniker "Deacon" was used throughout baseball to describe players who didn't drink or gamble when those vices were popular pastimes among professional athletes, especially when they were on the road. A dignified and humble man, Deacon Phillippe went about the business of playing baseball without flare and left the spotlight to his teammates. Not one to celebrate or display emotion on the baseball field, before perhaps the most important game of his career in the 1903 World Series, the unassuming hurler simply remarked, "It's up to me, I guess. Well, I feel like a winner, but you can never tell until it's over."[1]

Honus Wagner, arguably the greatest Pittsburgh Pirate of all time, said of his teammate, "Charles 'Deacon' Phillippe was another great pitcher who always wanted to be sent in against the star of the opposing team. He reveled in a hard fight. His greatest quality was that he never in his life complained about errors being made back of him. He took it all as part of the game. He was ready to pitch in any kind of weather and was always anxious to be selected. Phillippe had everything a pitcher ought to have and he used the Mathewson system of pitching to his fielders. That is, he would figure to make a batter hit in a certain direction and let the outfield do the big share of the work until he got into a tight pinch."[2]

Phillippe was popular among his teammates, accommodating to the press and kept his personal life close to the vest. Though he rarely if ever said anything negative about anyone, especially teammates, he did defend the pitchers of his era against detractors. In a *Sporting News* article in 1903 Phillippe supported his contemporaries when they were compared to the underhand flingers of the 1800s. "You hear a great deal said these days about the great pitchers of the olden times. Their speed is touted as being something phenomenal and the way they could keep batsmen from getting hits was simply a wonder.

Until a few years ago the twirlers stood just 50 feet from the home plate and even then they had a six-foot long box to pitch from. You put one of the present day pitchers in the same position and I have money to wager that there isn't a man in the business that can make a hit off them. They would speed balls in there so fast that the batter would think he was up against a streak of greased lightning and he would fan wildly and never touch anything but the atmosphere."[3]

Charles Louis Phillippe was born on a farm near the southwest Virginia town of Rural Retreat, on May 23, 1872. Life for the early residents there was primarily centered on the family, the Lutheran religion and a nearby tavern. Nestled in the Blue Ridge Mountains just to the northeast of the Wythe County line with Smyth County, the village of Rural Retreat grew from a frontier settlement to become a commercial center for a burgeoning farming community.

Charles was the fourth of eight children born to Andrew Jackson Phillippe[4] and Margaret Jane (Hackler) Phillippe. Charles' father was the fourth generation of his family to make Wythe County their home. Charles' grandparents and great-grandparents had lived just south of Rural Retreat at Phillippi Springs, named for a large spring that supplied the village with water.[5] The family name was spelled 'Phillippi' or 'Phillippie' in some early Virginia records, but Andrew used the French and Germanic Phillippe, pronounced Phil'uh-pea, rather than the Anglicized version of the Italian name Filippi.

Although "Phillippi" was the spelling most often used by the newspapers for Charley when he began playing professional baseball, it wasn't until around 1900 that the pitcher insisted his last name be spelled with an "e." Although that spelling was used for the most part in Pittsburgh, many national newspapers continued to print "Phillippi." During the 1903 season, he publically commented about the incorrect spelling of his name by many of those newspapers. "My name is misspelled more than any other player's in the country," he complained. "They persist in putting an 'i' on the end when it should be an 'e.'"[6]

Before Charles' third birthday, Andrew Phillippe and his family left Wythe County for a farm in neighboring Carroll County, Virginia. They lived in the Coulson-Five Forks area for a short time before moving on to Dixon Ferry near the New River.

Charles' nephew, Sidney Floyd Landreth, who would one day be a Virginia State Senator, said his mother told him that Uncle Charles laid the groundwork for his baseball career by spending his spare time throwing rocks on the family's river hill farm. When Charles was 12, Andrew Phillippe left

Virginia with his large family excepting the oldest daughter, Missouri Clementine Landreth, who remained in Carroll County.[7]

The Phillippes lived in Oklahoma Territory for a time before settling near the town of Athol in Dakota Territory around 1886.[8] It was there on the prairies of Spink County that young Charles matured into a tall, athletic, young man. He played baseball for amateur teams in the area and became the star pitcher for Redfield's Rose Post Office town team.

W. E. Briggs was an elderly gentleman living in Florida when he recalled playing ball against Charles Phillippe in South Dakota. "It was about 1895 or 1896 that the Deacon was a farm boy living in Spink County, South Dakota, and played on a team backed by the two villages of Ashton and Mellette. I was playing first base for the Warner team (and) I well recall the curves Phillippe fed us in those games we played out in the sticks. I don't remember much about his speed, but I do know it was awfully hard to get a hit off him."[9]

It was in the spring of 1896 that Phillippe went to Mankato, Minnesota, to seek a position with the professional baseball club there. He watched from the grandstand as the Maroons scrimmaged and upon their game's conclusion sought out Captain Jack Messerly, formerly of the St. Paul Western League club, and proceeded to make his case. When Messerly looked Phillippe over he must have smiled. The prospective pitcher that was going to make "the other fellows look like monkeys" wore a blue flannel shirt, cut-off blue jeans, a slouch hat and a pair of cowhide boots.

The tall rube's confidence convinced Messerly to give Phillippe a shot. According to the story as related by Barney Dreyfuss, the farm boy was given a tryout the next day and "sent overdrops, benders and twisters that almost made the players break their backs trying to get near them with their bats."[10]

The Mankato Maroons were not part of a league and played a loose schedule with several independent professional teams in the southern part of the state. The Mankato team took on all comers, from professionals from the Western League and top African-American clubs to semi-pro or amateur teams like the Minnesota Packing and Provision Company team of St. Paul and the United States Army nine from Fort Snelling.

Newspaper accounts from 1896 routinely referred to Mankato's latest pitching recruit as "Phillips." A contemporary analysis of the Maroons noted that "Chas. Phillips of Ashton, South Dakota, has played for several years in South Dakota, where his reputation as a ball player is good. He is an excellent pitcher, and while a trifle sore yet he will soon work that out."[11]

On April 26, Harry Howe and Phillippe pitched in the Maroons' 12–6 victory over St. Peter. Howe was not effective from the pitcher's box so the new man, "Phillips," was brought in and "pitched a speedy ball and had good control of it" in holding the Saints scoreless for the final four innings.[12]

A day later the Maroons played their official home opener against the Page Fence Giants, the top African-American professional team in the country. The Giants traveled in their own private railroad car advertising the Page Woven Wire Fence Co., marched through towns dressed in baseball uniforms with fire hats, and played local ball teams to defer expenses.

Mankato's new grandstand was said to hold 700 people comfortably and the bleachers had room for an additional 300, though a majority of these seats were rarely occupied during the summer of 1896. The price of admission was set at "25 cents for adults, 10 cents for ladies, and 15 cents extra for the grand stand," a hefty amount for any level of professional baseball in 1896.[13] Mankato lost to the Giants, 5–0, but the next day's game against the same club went down to the final inning.

Against the Page Fence Giants Phillippe again displayed a good fast ball and control. In the seventh inning, he slapped a pitch from Kid Miller "down Graham Avenue for three bases" to score the run that knotted the contest at 3–3. The game was decided in the ninth frame after consecutive errors landed Giants runners on first and third with no outs. The lead run shortly scored on Phillippe's wild pitch. He got out of the inning without further damage by striking out Home Run Johnson and William Binga to retire the side. However, the Maroons went down meekly in the bottom half of the inning to give the Giants a 4–3 victory.[14]

Up to that time, Phillippe was with the club on a trial basis, but his work against the Page Fence Giants guaranteed that he would be signed to a Maroons contract for the season when the team pared its roster to ten men on the first of May. The day after he signed his first professional contract he "played a splendid game" in the victory over St. Peter. He would win most of the games he pitched for Mankato and in mid-June was the winning pitcher on successive days against the Winnebago City Clippers.

Mankato's most serious rival was the team from Winona, Minnesota. In recounting Winona's victory over the Maroons on May 20, the *Winona Daily Herald* referred to the visitors as "babies" who refused to play any more when fairly beaten, then tried to blame the umpire. "Of all the visiting teams that ever came to Winona to play ball, this one from Mankato exhibited the meanest possible spirit," noted the reporter.[15]

By July the Mankato club was in dire financial difficulty and Captain Messerly was approached by the citizens of Winona with a proposal to move the Maroons to their riverside city where there was a greater population.

On July 9 the Maroons won their 59th game (vs. 18 losses) of the season over the visiting team from LeMars, Iowa. Phillippe found himself in an early hole to the best amateur team in Iowa, but allowed only one run in his final eight innings. His teammates overcame a four-run deficit to win in 11 innings, 6–5. Unfortunately, only a small number of the locals came out to see him strike out 13 of the amateurs. Seven days later, the Maroons abandoned Mankato to play in Winona, 120 miles to the east.

As it turned out, Captain Messerly had entered into negotiations with the rival city to hijack the Mankato team. At a meeting of the Winona baseball club the evening of Tuesday, July 14, the current Winona players were given their release and the former Mankato nine would play in their stead against Fort Snelling that weekend.

On Thursday evening, the backers of a new Mankato Base Ball Association made plans to place another team in their city. Instead of "Maroons" the new club would be referred to as the Mankato Base Ball Club. Though the Maroons were to depart the city on Saturday morning for two weekend games in Winona, five players, including Phillippe, signed new contracts with the Mankato Association and promised to return on Monday and join two other players who did not defect.

The *Winona Republican* reported, "The Mankato ball team came to town Saturday morning, took dinner with Proprietor Tarbell, donned the uniforms of the defunct baseball team, and thereby became a full-fledged Winona ball team."[16]

After the Winonas' destruction of the Fort Snelling team, the local newspaper declared that "Phillips" was "almost invincible" during his three-hitter and struck out nine of the soldiers, three of the whiffs coming in the eighth inning.[17] That one game was the only time Phillippe would pitch for Winona.

The new Mankato team had enough players under contract to play their first game on Saturday, July 28. The team's new management also reduced the price of grandstand seats to ten cents and forthwith a banner would span Front Street on the day of a game indicating the start time and opponent for the day.

The new Mankato club went to Winona for the first time in early August and lost two out of three hard-fought games. Again the Winona newspaper complained about the visitors' sportsmanship, but had only kind things to say about Phillippe: "He is a true sportsman and not a whimper was heard from him during the game."[18]

On the evening of September 2, the Detroit Tigers Club of the Western League arrived in Mankato by train and spent the night in a local hostelry. Prior to their departure for Kansas City the following afternoon, the third-place Bengals participated in a morning exhibition game with Mankato. Phillippe was opposed by Detroit's Rip Egan, owner of 15 Western League wins. Although the *Mankato Daily Free Press* noted that "the Detroits had great difficulty in understanding his curves and drops," Phillippe trailed the Western Leaguers 7 to 6 when the contest moved into the ninth inning. The locals scored three runs in the top of the ninth to take the lead, and he preserved the win. With two outs and two runners on base, the final batter he faced was Tigers catcher Art Twineham, who earlier in the game was heard to say, "Phillips (sic) couldn't pitch hay." When Twineham hit to Phillippe's third baseman, who stepped on the bag for the final out, "the crowd could not restrain itself."[19]

Following the 1896 baseball season, the Western League's participation in the National Agreement led to the draft of the Minneapolis Millers' best players by the National League. Phillippe's work with the Mankato team attracted the attention of Manager Walter Wilmont of the Millers, and he was offered the opportunity to play for the defending Western League champions in 1897. Wilmot had learned the inner workings of baseball from the legendary Cap Anson when he played in the Chicago White Stockings' outfield between 1890 and 1895. When Phillippe joined the Millers at Hot Springs, Arkansas, in the spring, Manager Wilmot faced a major rebuilding job due to the loss of several players, including ex-major league pitcher Wild Bill Hutchinson who was drafted by the St. Louis Browns.

Spring workouts were hampered by rain for the first few days of camp. When the rains abated, the Millers played several exhibition games against the National League's Chicago Colts, who also trained at Hot Springs. Phillippe did not appear in any of the games against Cap Anson's Colts or the single game with St. Louis. It was evident Manager Wilmot did not expect much out of the raw rookie from South Dakota, but the Millers were bereft of pitching and he was able to stick with the club when the regular season began.[20]

Phillippe pitched in his first Western League game on May 17 against St. Paul. Wilmot summoned him to the pitcher's slab in the fourth inning after St. Paul scored two runs to increase their total to 11 verses only three for Minneapolis. He retired the side without further scoring and threw four more innings in the Millers' loss.

The first time he saw Phillippe, a *St. Paul Globe* reporter wrote, "Phillippi had not been in the box a minute before he was nicknamed 'Philopene.' He gives promise of future success, however, in spite of his unusual, even classical cognomen.... It was one, two, three with the Saints after he got in and the Saints only got two back, making it 11 to 3."[21]

Three days later, Phillippe pitched the first five innings of a game against Indianapolis on a cold afternoon and was touched for nine runs on nine hits, two of them four-baggers. A sportswriter noted, "A few of the fans who bear no scars from the three battles the Millers have fought and lost, three policemen and the usual contingent of newspaper men sat and shivered in the cold yesterday afternoon as the Hoosiers made it three straight from the home team."[22]

Twenty-four-year-old Charles Phillippe would not pitch in his third Western League game for over seven weeks. A five-game losing streak by the Millers prompted *Sporting Life's* Minneapolis correspondent to write, "The champions have not won a game since Sunday and Wilmot's men are fast going down the toboggan. The cause is we are weak in the box, desperately weak. Figgemeir and Baker are the only pitchers we have."[23] No mention was made of young Phillippe. Wild Bill Hutchinson allowed 41 runs in 40 innings with St. Louis and was returned to the Millers in a deal that precipitated Phillippe's transfer to the Fargo club of the Red River Valley League.

Phillippe arrived in Fargo on June 22 and a day later he pitched the last-place Senators to a 5–1 victory over Moorhead. The *Moorhead Independent* observed, "Phillippi, the 'newly acquired phenom' from Wilmot's aggregation, was in the box for the 'Divorcees.' His delivery was of the '84' vintage when the under-handed ball was in its prime."[24] Phillippe pitched five games for Fargo before Manager Wilmot recalled his pitcher on July 16.

The day after Phillippe's return to the Millers, he started the game against Columbus. The Senators sported a formidable lineup, including former major leaguers Bill Hulen, Sam Mertes, and Patsy Tebeau. The Millers' raw midwesterner finished the game strong, but lost 5–3, leading the *Minneapolis Journal* to note, "Phillippi put up a fine game yesterday which is evident from the fact that none of the five runs secured by the antique Columbians was earned."[25]

Phillippe won his first game for Minneapolis when he threw a complete-game 3 to 2 victory against Indianapolis on July 23. In his next outing four days later, Minneapolis built up a big lead at their home grounds against Grand Rapids and he picked up his second victory, 11 to 5. He would remain in the Minneapolis club's starting rotation until the end of the 1898 season. Though he was a hard thrower, Charles didn't strike out many batters because in those days hurlers pitched to contact whereby his fielders would handle the outs and minimize the number of pitches.

After winning a couple of games, Phillippe suffered a thrashing at the hands of first-place Indianapolis. In his earlier victory over the same club, he had held the Indians to five hits, but three weeks later the Western League's best team got its revenge. Phillippe allowed two runs in the first inning and seven more in the second. While pitching the entire game, he allowed 22 hits and 13 earned runs in the 17 to 1 defeat. The only positive result for him was only one base on balls allowed, and he could take some small consolation in the fact that the newspapers credited the loss to "Phillips."

A week later in Detroit, Phillippe relieved Hutchinson after "Wild Bill" was pounded for 12 runs in the third inning. Phillippe finished the game, a 23 to 3 disaster. The two bad outings culminated the worst week in his career and it was said the losses almost finished him. However, the Millers kept sending the quiet hurler to the box until he worked things out. On September 3, Phillippe allowed only a single and a double to beat Columbus, 1–0. The Millers scored the game's only run in the bottom of the eighth on a single, a sacrifice and another single after the Columbus catcher muffed a foul fly.

"Phillippi was a wizard," beamed the *Minneapolis Journal*. "The slugging Senators came up one after the other and swung with all their might, but there was too much 'english' on the shoots and their hits were clinky little pop-ups or easy little infield rollers."[26]

Manager Wilmot wasn't around to see Phillippe's masterpiece as he was released in mid–July, supposedly because the manager "was altogether too free and easy with the players."[27] By mid-season, rumors of Manager Wilmot's demise were well circulated and on July 21 the inevitable happened. The announcement was made that the new manager-captain of the seventh-place Millers was the team's veteran right fielder, George "Doggie" Miller.

By this time the tall, unassuming hurler had acquired a nickname that would stick with him for the rest of his life. Following Phillippe's 8 to 3 win over the Kansas City Blues on September 9, a Twin Cities correspondent wrote, "One Deacon Phillippi tossed the little Spalding for Doggie's team, and the Kaws could not introduce themselves to the intricacies of his delivery. He had them completely at his mercy, and they got but five hits off him, three of which were inside the diamond, and very, very punky. In addition to his superb twirling, Phillippi fielded his position brilliantly.... His stop of Gear's hit in the fourth was sensational. It knocked him down, but he threw the runner out at first."[28]

The Millers were a woeful club in 1897, winning only 43 games and losing 95. Charles Phillippe won 8 and lost 13 for the seventh-place Millers. However, the rookie called "Deacon" had shown plenty of promise to be reserved for the 1898 season. Despite his record, *Sporting Life* correspondent B. M. Stuart felt Phillippe should have been drafted by a National League club. "There are two men in Western League clubs that have been overlooked ... and it is a matter of great surprise to me. I refer to Pyle, of St. Paul, and Phillippi, of Minneapolis. These are the best pitchers in class 'A' excepting Goar and Hahn."[29]

After two postponements because of rain, Minneapolis opened the 1898 season in Kansas City. Phillippe drew the opening day starting assignment, but the Millers lost 6 to 1. Minneapolis had twice as many errors as hits, eight to four.

The Millers lost four of their first five games on the road before going home to open the season there on April 28. The *St. Paul Globe* reported, "It was 2 o'clock when Watson's band rode away from the Nicollet Hotel, followed by ten of the swellest traps to be found, containing the visitors and Millers in uniform. They paraded the principal downtown streets of the city for an hour, and then drove to the ball park."[30] Two thousand spectators showed up at Millers Park and saw Phillippe scatter seven hits in the 10 to 2 victory over Omaha. In the sixth inning he sent a fly to the Lake Street fence that brought in three men.

"Phillippi covered himself with glory," the *Minneapolis Tribune* bragged, then predicted, "There is a record in store for him this season.... They simply could not find him and his remarkable speed was a revelation to the fans."[31]

During the fourth inning of the game in Columbus on May 23, a finger on Phillippe's right hand was split when he attempted to snare a hard-hit ball. He remained in the game and persevered to win 4 to 3. He did suffer a lapse in the seventh when he hit two batters and gave up a pair of bases on balls to force in a run, but his effort was nonetheless excusable because of his damaged finger.[32]

Before a large crowd of around 5,000 in Milwaukee a week later, Phillippe pitched a four-hit, 3–1 victory; a balk cost him a shutout. On June 16, he went to the mound and stopped a Millers' six-game losing streak at Nicollet Park. In his 6 to 2 victory over Detroit, he allowed only one hit over the first six innings, and both runs off him scored as a result of errors.

Five days later, Kansas City pounded Phillippe for 26 runs on 25 hits and six walks. Kansas City scored ten times in the first inning and added five more in the second, but Manager Reilly left him in for the entirety of the game. Minneapolis scored a couple of late runs to make the final tally 26 to 2. Minneapolis made six errors so "only" 16 of the runs were earned. Although there was no question Phillippe was the best pitcher on the Millers, he occasionally suffered disastrous melt-downs. That September he pitched a complete game against Milwaukee in which he gave up 21 runs on 19 hits. His fielders did their part by committing eight errors.

One of Phillippe's best efforts was a game he ultimately lost. On July 3, he pitched no-hit ball for seven innings against St. Paul and took a 2–0 lead into the ninth. However, an error by third baseman Reilly allowed the game to be tied at two and St. Paul won with three runs in the 11th, 5 to 2.[33]

The Millers were almost as bad as the previous season and again finished seventh in 1898. Predictably the fans responded by staying away from the park. *Sporting Life* reported the Millers' total home attendance for the season was only 40,000, a drop of 50,000 from the previous year.[34]

During a meeting of the Western League magnates that July, the Millers' Clarence Saulpaugh convinced Walter Wilmot to return as the Minneapolis manager. Charles Reilly was informed that Wilmot would replace him as manager on the 27th.[35] On the day Wilmot agreed to rejoin the team, July 23, Deacon Phillippe's 3 to 2 victory over Detroit left the Millers' record at 24 wins and 59 defeats.

The *St. Paul Globe* wrote that in the Detroit victory at Nicollet Park, "Phillippi was invincible ... Dillard was about the only man who could find him, he getting three of the six hits secured by the Tigers." However, the verdict was not settled for the 400 faithful in attendance until the ninth inning. Phillippe was ahead to start the final frame, 3 to 1. Dillard tripled and scored one out later on a single, but that was all the opposition got.

Phillippe was far and above the Millers' best pitcher in 1898, throwing 339 innings, and was responsible for nearly half of his club's 48 victories. The official records of the Western League as compiled by President Ban Johnson credited Phillippe with 22 victories, 18 defeats and one tie.[36] That September, Phillippe was drafted by the National League's Louisville Colonels, and he was to join them in the spring of 1899.

Along with Phillippe, the Colonels signed a number of players that fall that would have a significant impact on the major leagues for over a decade. There were the two undersized outfielders, Tully "Topsy" Hartzell (5'5") of Grand Rapids and Tommy Leach (5'6½") from Auburn of the New York State League. However, the consensus among the experts held that the big prizes among the rookies were pitchers Rube Waddell of Columbus and Deacon Phillippe of Minneapolis.[37]

An observer of the Western League wrote in *Sporting Life*, "Phillippi undoubtedly is one of the greatest pitchers the league has ever turned out, and I believe I am capable of judging a player's ability. I wrote a certain League manager a few years ago and gave him a tip on Chic Frazier (Fraser).... I do not consider him nearly as good a pitcher as Phillippi. This fellow has demonstrated the fact that he can pitch gilt-edge ball with a losing team. This is something few pitchers could do. Keep your eye on him, He's a great one."[38]

The star players for the Colonels at that time were right fielder Honus Wagner of Carnegie, Pennsylvania, and manager-outfielder Fred Clarke from Winfield, Kansas. Rookie Phillippe was actually four months older than Manager Clarke, a Louisville regular since 1894, and two years senior to Wagner, the team's best player.

Though only in his third season, Wagner, the son of German-speaking immigrants, was beginning to draw recognition as one of the National League's premier players. Phillippe and Wagner would be teammates for the next 13 years, and friends for the rest of their lives. Neither Phillippe nor Wagner was a womanizer or a night owl; Wagner too came from a Lutheran background, and both ballplayers were avid hunters and outdoorsmen. When the pair moved on to Pittsburgh, they would add an Ohio Methodist named Samuel Leever to their little group of huntsmen.

Charles Louis Phillippe, photograph from around 1900 (National Baseball Hall of Fame Library, Cooperstown, New York).

German ballplayers dominated professional baseball's ranks in the late nineteenth century and second generation Irish were not far behind. Many other classes and geographical regions were barely represented when compared to the general population. Of course, players of color, mostly those of African descent, were not allowed to play for teams in Organized Baseball, a ban that existed until 1946.

Few Southerners were found among National League players before the turn of the century. In the first decade of the twentieth century, the emergence of stars like the Georgian, Ty Cobb, and future stars like Texan Tris Speaker and South Carolina's Shoeless Joe Jackson gave the South a prominent presence in the major leagues. Often described as a Southerner, Phillippe had Virginia roots and is a member of the Virginia Sports Hall of Fame though he spent the majority of his teenage years in South Dakota and most of his adult life in Pennsylvania.

Although the Louisville Colonels baseball club had been a member of the National League since the American Association folded in 1891, it never finished above ninth place in the 12-team league before a German immigrant named Barney Dreyfuss purchased controlling interest in the club prior to the 1899 season. Seventeen years earlier, Bernhard Dreyfuss was working at a bank in Karlsruhe, Germany, when he decided to immigrate to America. Dreyfuss, who was Jewish, feared the prospect of being drafted into the German army, which was known to deal a harsh hand to persons of his persuasion. He immigrated to Paducah, Kentucky, at age 17, became known as Barney, and worked as a mud clerk on a steamboat. "It is not an exalted position as the one holding it is supposed to do all the work not relished by the two clerks over him," he said. "And I guess that is why they have given it the title of mud."[39]

Soon after his arrival in America, Barney became fascinated with the game of baseball and played on an amateur team in Paducah as a second baseman. Another member of that team was George Dovey, who would one day own the Boston National League Club.

In 1881, Dreyfuss went to work in the accounting office for Bernheim Brothers Distillery in Louisville, owned by his cousins Bernard and Isaac Bernheim. Bernard also happened to be married to Barney's sister, Rosa. Barney continued to study English while working his way up to credit manager at the distillery.

About 1888 Dreyfuss acquired a small block of stock in the Louisville American Association club. In 1890 Barney was elected club treasurer, and Harry C. Pulliam was named president upon the club's entry into the National League a year later. He and Pulliam switched jobs after Dreyfuss obtained majority control of the club with the purchase of Colonels stock for a reported $50,000.

Henry Clay Pulliam was described by one biographer as an eccentric dresser and fabled story teller who put all at ease. The son of a Scottsburg, Kentucky, tobacco farmer, Harry attended public schools in Louisville and graduated from the University of Virginia School of Law before becoming a reporter with The *Louisville Commercial*. In that position he met Barney Dreyfuss and soon was in the smallish immigrant's employ, as secretary and president of the Louisville Colonels baseball club. While still with the city newspaper and also working for the Colonels, Harry went into politics and served in the Kentucky Assembly.[40]

Despite employing several promising players, the Louisville National League club that Dreyfuss purchased was in a dismal state although the city hoped to reverse the team's attendance woes with the restoration of Sunday baseball at Eclipse Park for 1899. Prior to Dreyfuss and Pulliam taking over the club, the Colonels had lost about $36,000 over the previous seven seasons, including $13,000 in 1898 alone.[41]

When Phillippe was drafted by the Colonels, Barney Dreyfuss offered his pitcher $1,200 for the upcoming season. After returning the Colonels' contract unsigned, Phillippe left Minneapolis the evening of February 20 for his farm in Ashton. He felt he was worth more than what the Louisville owner was offering, so he rejected the offer. "I can make more money by organizing an independent team than by taking the terms I was offered by Louisville," he declared, "and I will not sign with them under any other conditions than those I have named."[42]

Dreyfuss informed Phillippe that he was the worst-looking pitcher he had ever bought and reminded him about the score of the Kansas City game earlier that year in which he was tagged for 26 runs.[43] A short time later, the barn on Phillippe's South Dakota farm burned down and he was suddenly in need of ready cash. He really had no recourse than to join the Colonels, because Dreyfuss would not give up the rights to the 26-year-old rookie. Charles wrote to Dreyfuss and was again informed that he would be paid $1,200 for a season's work.

"Sign with me and you will never regret it," Dreyfuss promised. Phillippe relented on his salary demand and would spend his entire major league career playing for the same owner.[44] His trust in Dreyfuss paid off. Following the end of his fourth season in the major leagues, *The Sporting News* wrote, "Phillippe is one of the most prosperous players in the league today and there is not a dirty dollar in his collection."[45]

By the final decade of the nineteenth century, most pitchers were becoming throwers as opposed to the under-handed flingers of the past. Pitchers were expected to finish what they started and mound men emphasized ball control and relied on their fielders to make plays rather than going for strikeouts. By saving wear and tear on their arms, pitchers reserved their "best stuff" for critical points during a game. After the pitcher's box was replaced by a pitcher's plate (later termed "the rubber") at the same time the distance to the foul side of home base was extended to 60 feet six inches, hurlers discovered they could get more speed on the ball if they were able to step downhill during their delivery. Groundskeepers were told to create mounds of earth in the middle of the infield from which the pitchers worked. The height of these "mounds" was not regulated until 1903, when 15 inches was set as the maximum.

Phillippe spent his first major league spring training with the Colonels in Thomasville, Georgia. At just shy of six feet one inch, he was the tallest player on the club. The rookie's best pitch was a devastating curve ball and he also had a good fast ball. He was said to possess an excellent underhand delivery and when in trouble he was not averse to using it with good results.

The highlight, or low-light, of the Colonels' pre-season was a game against the "Bloomer Girls," an all-female baseball team that toured the country. The National Leaguers thoroughly thrashed the females. This led *Sporting Life* to comment, "While at Thomasville the Louisvilles played a female ball team and just about the same time the Senators were contesting with a colored team in Virginia. What is the National League coming to?"[46]

Louisville opened the season with 18 players on its roster: six pitchers, an extra catcher, and three utility players besides the regulars. Manager Clarke predicted a sixth-place finish for his team.[47]

The Colonels opened the 1899 season on April 14 against Chicago. The season opener introduced Phillippe to the overflow crowd practice, whereby fans, or cranks as they were sometime called in those days, stood behind roped-off areas in the deepest environs of the outfield.

The Colonels played their games at Louisville's League Park (also called "Eclipse Park") at South 28th Street and West Broadway. A major source of income for the Louisville club came from well-attended home games on Sunday, outlawed in most eastern cities.

Phillippe made his major league debut six days into the season in relief after Billy Magee's wildness led to four early runs by the visitors from Cleveland. Phillippe held the Spiders scoreless the remainder of the game and earned the first of his 189 major league victories after Louisville batted its way to an 11 to 4 triumph before 1,200 local fans. He also got his first two major league hits, a single and a double against the Spiders' Harry Maupin.

"Phillippi has come to play," wrote Louisville sports scribe C. C. Moore. "In all the exhibition games he had splendid control and good speed. He pitched seven innings in one of the Cleveland games, and was a stumbling block to the Forest City boys, only allowing them to make one hit in the seven innings. Besides having a good stock of speed and curves, he has an underhand ball that he

Early card of Charles Phillippe in uniform of the Louisville Colonels (E107 Breisch Williams Deacon Phillipi [collection R. Cav]).

uses to good advantage. If I am not mistaken, Phillippi will be one of the Colonels' best pitchers before the season is half over."[48]

Unfortunately, highlights for the Colonels early in the season were few apart from the pitching of Phillippe and batting of third baseman Honus Wagner. Much of the blame for the club's bad start fell on veteran pitcher Bert Cunningham. After winning 28 games for Louisville in 1898, Cunningham reported to the team out of condition the following spring and lost his first ten games. There also were disruptive influences among the veterans on the team until the new owner and boy manager Fred Clarke released the disaffected players and brought in new players from the minor leagues to take their places.

Phillippe beat the hapless Spiders of Cleveland for his second win, then pitched against Pittsburgh for the first time on May 5, 1899. His mound opponent at Exposition Park that afternoon was Sam Leever, in his first full season with the Pirates. Some 1,500 Pirates cranks watched as the two pitchers who would become stars in that city struggled to a 5–5 tie after seven innings. With two out in the bottom of the eighth, Louisville's shortstop Billy Clingman couldn't field Leever's grounder and the Pittsburgh pitcher made it safely to first. The next batter, right fielder Patsy Donovan, followed the error with a home run off Phillippe to make Pittsburgh and Leever 7 to 5 winners.[49]

The Colonels were still in Pittsburgh three days later when Leever replaced Pirates starter Tully Sparks in the eighth inning with an 8 to 5 lead. The first man he faced was Billy Clingman, a fellow Buckeye. His third pitch struck the Colonels batter flush on the head. The shortstop dropped to the ground and remained motionless for some time. Eventually, he regained consciousness and was helped to the dressing room.[50]

The disability of their shortstop severely hampered the Colonels. Several players auditioned at the position, including pitcher Walt Woods and manager Fred Clarke, but none proved sufficient. Clingman eventually returned to the lineup, then was disabled again with a case of "typhoid malaria." No one apparently thought to try third baseman Honus Wagner in the hole at short.

Two days following his 27th birthday, Saturday, May 25, 1899, Phillippe took the mound before 1,100 local patrons against the New York Giants in only his seventh National League game. That day, he spun his only major league no-hitter, winning 7 to 0. The game itself was never in doubt as Louisville led 3–0 after two innings and added a four-spot in the fifth. The Colonels collected just four hits off Ed Doheny, but the Giants committed six errors that largely contributed to the Colonels' seven runs. Phillippe's catcher for the historic game was journeyman backstop Malachi Kittredge, who was in his ninth season of a 16-year major league career.

No Giant made it further than first base and there was only one batted ball off Phillippe that was close to being a hit. That was Doheny's hard grounder at Claude Ritchey, who fumbled the ball in his haste to get a force play on Tom O'Brien at second base. Though the New Yorkers had difficulty getting solid wood on Phillippe's deliveries, he struck out only one and that was the final batter he faced. He did walk three hitters, but he would eventually become baseball's best control pitcher.[51]

"The feat of Phillippi in shutting out the New York Club without a hit or run equals any pitcher's best record and stamps that young man at once as a star," wrote John J. Saunders in *Sporting Life*. "Phillippi is deservedly popular in Louisville, and his good work is sure to be appreciated. He has been able to show the club owners that his claims made before his joining the team were substantial."[52]

Three days after his no-hitter, the Giants got their revenge in Louisville when three triples led to three runs in the fifth inning and Phillippe suffered the 4–3 loss. No matter, the no-hitter established him as one of the rising young stars of the National League. A two-column photograph of Phillippe was prominently displayed on the front page of the June 10 edition of *Sporting Life*.

On June 10 Phillippe lost to Sam Leever for the second time during the 1899 season. Charles lost 5 to 4, but he should have won. After the Colonels tagged Leever for three runs in the top of the first, the Pirates got one back in the bottom of the frame when third baseman Wagner threw McCreedy's tapper all the way to the right field bleachers for a three-base error. The Bucs narrowed the lead to one in the third on a double steal that succeeded after second baseman Ritchey dropped the catcher's throw when he had ample time for a return throw to get the runner at the plate.

Louisville regained the lead, but lost the game in the bottom of the seventh. Pirates baserunners were on second and third when Jimmy Williams smacked a sharp grounder to shortstop Leach and Tommy heaved the ball wildly past the first baseman to allow the runner on third to scamper home. The second base runner scored on a sacrifice fly to give Pittsburgh the lead, and Leever retired the final six batters to secure the victory. Although Pittsburgh's Jimmy Williams reached base on a walk and an error, Phillippe stopped the third baseman's consecutive game hitting streak at 26.

Early that summer, rumors suggested the National League would downsize to eight teams after the Fourth of July holiday. Cleveland, Baltimore, Washington and Louisville were named as the franchises that were in jeopardy. Independence Day came and went without any action being taken.

In the early morning hours of Saturday, August 12, an electrical storm caused a fire at Louisville's League Park. Within hours the entire grandstand was destroyed. Dreyfuss rebuilt the damaged fences and arranged for the rental of 2,500 circus seats to be used on an interim basis. The team's home white uniforms were destroyed in the fire so the players completed the season wearing their road grays. The club's temporary seating arrangements proved inadequate, and attendance at Louisville games plummeted.

On August 16, Deacon shut out the powerful Boston club, 3–0. He allowed but three hits to the star-laden lineup that included Billy Hamilton, Fred Tenney, Herman Long, Jimmy Collins, Hugh Duffy, Bobby Lowe and Vic Willis.

"It was a young man by the name of Phillippi that turned the trick yesterday," reported the *Boston Globe*, "and shut out the champions in the first game of a double-header at the South End Grounds. He was a fair haired fellow who threw graceful curves, had fine command and a knack of annoying his opponents until they looked upon him with as much disgust as if he was a midnight piano player at the seashore."[53]

A year later Phillippe said of that game, "The best game I ever pitched in my life was against Boston at a time when I felt sick as a man at sea. I didn't want to beg off, and started in, expecting to be killed, but I shut the Hubbites out without a run. There have been days when I've had everything — speed and control — and feeling great, and they hit all over the lot. Baseball is a mystery. The longer I'm in it the stronger grows my belief that it is a game in which luck cuts the biggest figure."[54]

Following the shutout of the Boston fence breakers, Phillippe went into a slump. Fred Clarke started him again against the Beaneaters with only one day's rest and he lost 5 to 2. Four days later, he was knocked out of a game in the fourth inning by the Quakers of Philadelphia in a 12–0 thrashing.

On September 1, the day the Colonels' management announced the team would play the remainder of its 1899 schedule on the road, Phillippe lost his fifth consecutive decision "in a listless — half hearted sort of fashion" 5 to 3 in Washington.

The fans who attended the 25 to 4 destruction of the Washington club the following afternoon were unaware they were watching the last major league baseball game the Colonels would play in the city of Louisville. The editor of the *Sporting News* surmised that instead of rebuilding the ballpark, Dreyfuss decided to pocket the insurance money and put the locals off with the promise of a pretentious structure for next season. "This, coupled with the transfer of games," he wrote, "leads to the conclusion that the owners of the Louisville club will not invest another dollar on improvements. The twelve-club agreement has only two more years to run and there is little prospect of Louisville being a member of the National League after 1901."[55]

Phillippe broke out of his losing ways in St. Louis on September 4 with an unlikely victory over Cy Young, who was on an eight-game winning streak that included three shutouts. The Colonels drove Young from the mound in the fourth inning and Phillippe coasted in Louisville's 14 to 2 cakewalk. Four days later in Pittsburgh, Phillippe beat the Pirates 5–3 after Jack Chesbro's four walks in the first inning led to four Louisville runs. Furthermore, he shut out the Pirates' outstanding rookie, Jimmy Williams, ending the third baseman's streak of 27 consecutive games with a hit. An earlier 26-game hitting streak was also ended by Phillippe on June 10.

Phillippe adjusted well to pitching on the road for he won eight of his final nine decisions in 1899. One of those victories came in another Louisville blow-out against the St. Louis Perfectos' Cy Young. In this one the Clarkemen tagged the game's best pitcher for 13 hits, two of them by Phillippe, and the Colonels also received the benefit of six bases on balls. Louisville won, 16 to 3.

Phillippe won his 20th victory of the season in Chicago on September 30. The *Chicago Daily Tribune* reported, "It was too cold for baseball and the noble 400 who froze to the bleachers beat upon the boards and applauded the Colonels more through desire to keep warm." With five runs already on the tally sheet in the third inning, Phillippe inherited three base runners when Cunningham was chased from the diamond. He walked his first batter to force home a sixth run, then got out of the jam when he induced Bill Everett to ground one to shortstop Clingman whose throw just beat the runner to first base. Louisville began to hit Chicago's Ned Garvin at will and Charles blanked Chicago for the next five innings. After the Orphans batted in the eighth, Umpire Tom Connolly mercifully called time with Louisville on top, 12 to 6, and "dismissed the freezing congregation."[56]

The final day of the season saw the strange scenario of a doubleheader in Chicago where the home team played games against different visiting teams, St. Louis and Louisville. Phillippe defeated Chicago 9 to 5 in the second game to cost the Orphans a position in the standings as Pittsburgh squeaked past Chicago by .003 percentage points.

The Colonels posted a road record of 24 wins and only 13 losses after September 2 largely due to the pitching of Phillippe and Rube Waddell. The pair combined for a won-lost record of 15 and 3 over the final six weeks of the season. The Louisville correspondent to the *Sporting News* bragged, "Dreyfuss knew what he was doing when he secured Phillipi and Waddell, both young twirlers competent to stand among the best pitchers in the league."[57]

Phillippe started a career-high 38 games in 1899, completed 33, and led the Colonels with 21 victories. Despite pitching 321 innings, he struck out only 68 batters although that was partially due to the rule that dictated a foul ball on any count did not count as a strike. He would not be pitching in Louisville a year later.

Late in the 1899 season, the Colonels' secretary, Harry Pulliam, convinced Barney Dreyfuss that the National League was going to retract to eight franchises for 1900 and Louisville was targeted for elimination. Dreyfuss also learned the Pittsburgh club's owners were receptive to the introduction of fresh capital in their club. Once the decision to drop Louisville was made by the league's owners, Dreyfuss made a deal with Pittsburgh's president, William W. Kerr, in which the Louisville owner would purchase 47.3 percent interest in the Pirates for just under $47,000.[58] The Colonels' best players would come to Pittsburgh as part of the deal.

The Pittsburgh club's offer was presented to the Louisville stockholders at their annual meeting on December 4, and it was accepted the next day. Since the Louisville franchise was not officially dropped, Dreyfuss transferred the Colonels' best players to Pittsburgh by means of a trade on December 7, 1899. The deal consummated in the office of President Kerr at the Arbuckle Building in Pittsburgh was one of the largest in league history. Pittsburgh "traded" Jack Chesbro, George Fox, John O'Brien, Arthur Madison, William Gould and $25,000 to the Colonels for player-manager Fred Clarke, Honus Wagner, Claude Ritchey, Tommy Leach, Charles "Chief" Zimmer, Cliff Latimer, George "Rube" Waddell, Charles Phillippe, Walter Woods, Patsy Flaherty, Elton Cunningham, Mike Massitt, and Conny Doyle. Chesbro and O'Brien were later returned to the Pirates roster. The $25,000 cash in the deal would be turned over to the Louisville club to settle the affairs of that franchise.

In the merger that brought the Louisville players to Pittsburgh, Colonels owner Barney Dreyfuss not only acquired a near half-ownership in the Pirates, he also assumed the presidency of the Pittsburgh Base Ball Club. Harry Pulliam became secretary.

Before Barney departed for the annual National League meeting later that month, he told the press, "I am going to move my family to Pittsburgh at once and will be a Pittsburgher from this time on.... I think the base ball deal is without doubt the most important in the history of the game."[59]

Dreyfuss' goal for his new club was to make the Pirates a perennial first-division team. Four of the former Louisville players (outfielder-turned-shortstop Honus Wagner, outfielder-manager Fred Clarke, third baseman Tommy Leach, and pitcher Deacon Phillippe) plus one holdover from the old Pirates, pitcher Sam Leever, remained with Pittsburgh long enough to help the club to four pennants and, in 1909, their first World Series championship.

♦ Two ♦

The Goshen Schoolmaster

Samuel Leever, "The Goshen Schoolmaster," is the forgotten star of the great Pittsburgh clubs of the early 1900s. The right-hander with a sharp-breaking curve ball won 194 games for the Pittsburgh Pirates between 1898 and 1910.

Quiet, stubborn, and sometimes grouchy, Leever was a mainstay for the Pirates' pitching staff during the club's most successful decade. The former schoolteacher was not colorful, just consistent, posting 11 consecutive winning seasons for the Pirates, beginning in 1900. Leever could throw hard in his early years with Richmond and Pittsburgh, but he came to rely on control, movement on his pitches and a devastating curve. Leever's large hands allowed him to throw an assortment of breaking pitches variously known as outcurves, inshoots and drop balls, all thrown out of a sweeping sidearm delivery.

Leever was called "Professor" or "Schoolmaster" as much for his disposition as for his off-season vocation. On occasion, he also was referred to as "Deacon," an appellation he detested. In a game filled with practical jokers Leever was no prankster, and he quickly gained a reputation as being tight-fisted with his money. Though well respected by his teammates, he appears to have had only a few close friends on the Pirates, among that number Ginger Beaumont, Harry Smith and Honus Wagner. After he left the Pirates, Leever rarely returned to Pittsburgh for special occasions at the ballpark or reunions with former teammates.

Although not as gregarious or accommodating with the press as Deacon Phillippe, Leever was more animated on the mound when in a tough situation. Often manager Clarke would come in from left field, "call Leever off to one side for a few moments, chat cheerily with him, after which the old boy would go in and do better than ever."[1]

At just over five foot ten, Leever was taller than the average hurler at the time. He had intense blue eyes but his most obvious physical trait was a noticeable hair loss even when he was pitching for Richmond in his mid-twenties. He became so self-conscious about his receding hairline that he refused to sit for the official photograph of the 1901 National League champions, thus the picture went out missing the league's leader in winning percentage.[2]

Samuel Leever was born on December 23, 1871, on a farm near Goshen, Ohio, about 20 miles northeast of Cincinnati. Like many of their neighbors, the Leevers were descendants of Pennsylvania German immigrants. Sam was the fourth of the nine children of Edward and Amerideth Ardelia Leever.[3] His younger brother William also aspired to be a professional baseball player and had a trial with Dayton, Ohio, of the Central League in the spring of 1907.

Samuel Leever. Credited as 1900 but may have been taken earlier (courtesy Pittsburgh Pirates).

Young Samuel was a good student and passed the teacher's certification following high school. He became a teacher at his old school and taught in Goshen for seven years before signing his first baseball contract at the age of 25, old for a beginner in the professional game.

During his early years as an aspiring pitcher, Leever taught school during the week and on Sundays played baseball on the field beside the schoolhouse. It was said that he would have the boys from his class try to hit his curves and fast ones during recess.[4] The school teacher from Goshen became a legend pitching for club teams and independent semi-pro clubs in southwestern Ohio and northern Kentucky. In May of 1895, 23-year-old Sam Leever joined the accomplished Maysville, Kentucky, baseball team. The star of the Maysville nine was second baseman and captain Dan McGann, a future major league player with Cincinnati and the New York Giants.

Leever made his pitching debut with the Maysville team in the inaugural game at their new ballpark. The mayor gave a speech before the contest and Captain McGann accepted a bouquet of roses. A short time later, McGann walloped a ball off the left field fence that went for a home run to help send the home team to a 10 to 6 victory over the club from the Cincinnati Y.M.C.A. The grounds were sloppy after a drenching rain the previous day, and Leever's fielders committed five errors so only two of the visitors' runs were earned.

The Maysville *Daily Public Ledger* reported that Leever displayed "more speed than a streak of lightning on a greased track backed up by a Missouri cyclone, and when he settled down to work he made his opponents look like a lot of bargain-counter remains."[5]

Before 250 spectators at East End Park a week later, Leever's four-hit, seven-inning 10 to 0 shutout of Asland prompted the local paper to rhyme:

> When Sammy used his "whizzing in"
> He had the "Wonders" guessin'
> And when he worked his "jump ball"
> They learned a wholesome lesson.[6]

Leever didn't linger in Maysville very long before he jumped to the team from Norwood, a suburb of Cincinnati. The captain of the Norwood Maroons was future major league infielder Norman "Kid" Elberfield, who was referred to by one biographer as "the dirtiest, scrappiest, most pestiferous, most cantankerous, most rambunctious ball player that ever stood in spikes." [7]

Leever returned to Maysville on July 10 to pitch against his former club. He went the distance and despite striking out 13, lost, 11 to 10. The Maysville newspaper called the Norwoods "a set of gentlemen who don't know how to play the game" and noted that "Sammy" Leever "was the whole club" as he hit two singles and a triple in addition to the mound duties.[8]

Leever seriously wrenched his knee on a play at second base during the Maysville game and went home to recuperate. A few days later it was suggested that he was healing slowly and it would be weeks before he would be able to rejoin his team.[9]

Leever would not play another game with the Norwoods in 1895. The day he sent a letter to the manager of the Maroons explaining that he was ill and would not be able to pitch for at least a month, Sam pitched for New Richmond in a game against a team from Bativia, Ohio.[10] Before that game he met Billy Earle, a journeyman catcher for several major league clubs (including Pittsburgh 1892–93), who would claim credit for "discovering" Leever.

"I ran up from Clarksville, Tennessee, to catch a game for New Richmond in a little Clermont County town," recalled Earle. "We played on a diamond laid out in a cornfield and I caught Leever for the first time. He was a country schoolteacher. He looked so good to me I coaxed him to go to Clarksville with me, and I paid his fare. I took Norman Elberfield at the same time."[11]

Sam spent the rest of the summer pitching for the semi-pro Clarksville team managed by part owner Earle. Upon his return to Ohio in late September, Leever again joined the New Richmond team and pitched them to a 15 to 5 win over the Manhattans of Cincinnati.[12]

Billy Earle wanted Leever to join him and Elberfeld in the Texas Southern League, but Sam wanted to stay near home the following spring. On Saturday, May 16, 1896, Sam pitched two games for the New Richmond team, winning them both. In the first game he struck out 14 batters.

It was after he rejoined the Maysville club late that May that Sam began to attract attention from the leagues of mainstream baseball. According to Earle, Maysville sought to forestall Leever's team-hopping during 1895 when the team's bosses swore not to play games against any club Leever pitched for or any club that played Sam's new team.[13]

Once the weather warmed up, Leever was way ahead of the opposition. On July 8, he shut out the Knoxville club on two hits and walked only one batter. On July 21, he pitched ten innings of shutout baseball against Lexington, then won it himself in the bottom of the tenth when he leaned into a slow pitch with the bases loaded to force home the winning run. During his four-hit shutout, he struck out 16 Lexingtons.[14]

Only two days later Leever was even more dominant in the game against Portsmouth, Ohio. "Three hits were all (Portsmouth) got and Leever broke the record by striking out eighteen men," reported the *Portsmouth Times*. "He hasn't lost a game this season. At the bat he was as effective as in the box, getting four hits out of the five times he faced Dunham."[15]

That evening the opposing fans, said to number 2000, celebrated the star Maysville pitcher. Leever and catcher "Punch" Keliner "were cheered when they came upon the field and every time they came to the bat," reported the *Portsmouth Blade*. "Lever (sic) and Keliner were given a royal time during their stay in the city. The cream of Portsmouth's population called on them last evening. They were fairly worshiped."[16]

Always on the search for new talent, Manager Jake Wells of the Virginia State League's Richmond club scouted the Maysville players while his team was playing in the midwest that summer. Wells liked what he saw in pitcher Leever and offered him a job with the Richmond Blue Birds since the right-hander was not on the reserve list of any club subscribing to the National Agreement. Leever wanted more than the Richmond club was willing to pay, so Wells dropped the offer.[17]

Leever's baseball season of 1896 was put on hold that August. According to an article in the Maysville newspaper, "The sad feature of the last trip was coming away from Knoxville and having to leave Sam Lever (sic) on a bed of fever."[18] Leever's sister traveled to Tennessee to attend the stricken ball player until he was able to return home in late August. Newspaper reports indicated that Sam suffered from typhoid.

That September, Leever wrote to his friends in Maysville that he weighed 161 pounds and his arm was as good, if not better, than before he became sick. He said he might pitch at the county fair and would have rejoined the Maysville team except he had to teach school. The *Daily Public Ledger* printed the letter and added, "The scores of friends of Sam's in this city will be pleased to hear that he is in such a fine condition and we hope to have him with us next season."[19]

While Leever was battling typhoid fever, the pitching staff of Manager Wells' Richmond club sustained a serious blow when one of its two best pitchers, John Malarkey, was awarded to Syracuse in the Eastern League. Plus, Richmond's little lefty, Jesse Tannehill, the best pitcher in the Virginia League for two consecutive seasons with won-lost records of 20–7 and 23–17, was sure to be drafted by the National League following the end of the 1896 season.

The Cincinnati and the Louisville National League clubs were interested in Leever, and the Kentucky club's owner, Barney Dreyfuss, instructed Harry Pulliam to get Leever's signature on a contract for 1897. Before entering into salary negotiations with the pitcher, Pulliam sent Leever a National League contract. After Leever perused the contract filled with line after line of legal terminology he balked at signing "so long and voluminous a document."[20]

Meantime, Jake Wells increased his earlier offer and the less complex Richmond contract was more to Leever's liking, even at a lower salary. In Virginia Leever would be reunited with his old "Maroons" teammate Kid Elberfield. The day after Leever signed the contract to twirl for Wells, the *Richmond Dispatch* introduced the city to "the greatest minor league pitcher now on the market ... Captain Jake met Leever in Cincinnati recently, and says he is a great twirler in every sense of the word. He is a strapping big fellow, with a quick, clean delivery, lots of speed, and a clear, cool head. He is 24 years of age, stands 5 feet 10 inches in his stocking feet, and weighs 185 pounds. He is a school teacher by profession, and is at present engaged in teaching the young idea how to shoot, at Newtonville, O. He plays ball for the love of the sport, and incidentally for the money there is in it. He is a good fielder and an excellent hitter, and is a first-class, all-around man. He will prove a valuable acquisition to the Richmond club."[21]

The Richmond club would have a new ball field for their inaugural season in the Atlantic League. Club owner W. B. Bradley built Broad Street Park on land leased from the Richmond, Fredericksburg and Potomac Railroad near where Allen Avenue ends at Broad Street. The field was enormous, with straightaway center field measuring 560 feet from home plate. The left-center field wall incorporated the wall of a house, and the occupants of the building had a good view of games from the windows.

Wells' club began the season wearing the "Blue Bird" uniforms of the previous season's team, but after ten games, Bradley outfitted the players in new gray uniforms and the team's nickname was changed to "Johnny Rebs."[22] No report has surfaced to indicate the reaction of Buckeyes Leever and Elberfield upon being referred to as "Johnny Rebs."

In a retrospective of Leever's career, *The Sporting News* reported that "Leever's first game was a shutout…. The steadiness and cleverness which has always characterized his work was even then in evidence and he was considered the most reliable pitcher on the team, the others being Jack Chesbro, Henry Schmidt, Otis Stockdale, and Stimmel, all well known names in the world of baseball."[23]

Leever's first game in the Atlantic League came against Lancaster in the third game of the season on April 28, 1897. In his 4–0 three-hitter against the eventual league champions, he struck out seven, a nice number considering the rules of the day. The following morning's edition of the *Richmond Dispatch* opened its report of the game with the ditty:

> Who was it shut Lancaster out?
> 'Twas Leever: Sam Leever.
> Who was it put them up the spout?
> 'Twas Leever; Sam Leever.
> Sam played the game for all was in it.
> He struck a man out every minute.
> Sam is a honey; he's worth much money.
> Is Leever; Sam Leever.[24]

"Leever pitched with more skill and greater speed than has any pitcher who has appeared in this city this year, and he bids fair to take the place once occupied by Tannehill," noted a local reporter. "He is easily the star pitcher of the Richmond team and had the Lancaster lads guessing from the beginning of the first to the ending of the ninth inning. He had as much speed behind the ball as it was possible to put, and his kinks and curves were of an indescribable nature, such as make a batsman feel sick all over in spots."[25]

The closest Lancaster came to scoring was in the sixth inning. With a runner on third, Ralph Seybold hit a hot grounder to third baseman Elberfield, who tossed the ball to first baseman Jake Wells, who got the out, then quickly threw home when he spotted Piggy Ward attempting to score from third. The throw to the catcher was in plenty of time to record the out, but the baserunner argued violently with Umpire McNamara and had to be forcibly ejected from the grounds by police officers.

On May 14 Richmond played Ed Barrow's Paterson, New Jersey, nine at the Boulevard Field and Leever again drew raves from the local press: "Leever, the Professor whose scientific illustrations of how to describe a semi-circle with the sphere have proven so interesting to Richmond folks and so perplexing to the uninitiated batsmen, was in to twirl for Richmond, and he mixed hyperboles and straight shoots together with such skill as to puzzle the Weavers in a most distressing manner."[26]

Toward the end of the game the Weavers began to connect with Leever's pitches and compiled a total of 12 hits. But by that time it was too late because Richmond had built up a big lead and won, 13 to 4. One of the hits off Leever came off the bat of the Paterson's third baseman and clean-up hitter named Wagner. Honus Wagner would bat .379 in 76 games for Patterson before he was signed that July by President Harry Pulliam of the National League's Louisville Colonels. The bow-legged Atlantic League third baseman would go on to become one of the National League's greatest players.

On July 14, Leever took the mound in Philadelphia for the second game of a double header against a team known as the Athletics. These "Athletics" had nothing to do with the Philadelphia Athletics of an earlier time or Connie Mack's aggregation in the 1900s. The 1897 minor league team was owned by William Sharsig and played its games at the city's National League Park when the Phillies were on the road. These Athletics did not last past the 1897 season in the Atlantic League, as they were relocated a year later.

As a sidelight to the Johnnies' games in Philadelphia that day, ex-boxing champion James J. Corbett had been widely advertised as playing first base for the locals, and the Athletics drew more than 6,000 people, many of them women, for the bill. Corbett appeared at the start of the second game and "his march around the ball field was enough to make the bleacherites ring with shouts and handclapping."

The first game, rescheduled from the previous day because of rain, was concluded with the score 6 to 6 in the 11th inning in order for Corbett to perform in the nightcap. With two out in the first inning Leever gave up a single and Corbett was "allowed" to reach first, then third, because of poor fielding on the part of the visitors. Leever seemed to get stronger as the game went along, registering five of his nine strikeouts in the ninth, tenth and 11th innings. However, a local amateur pitcher named Albert Conn also pitched a strong game. The Johnnies did not score until the eighth inning and, with the game knotted at 1–1, Umpire Snyder called the game after the 11th although there was still enough light to play. Manager Wells and his players protested amid the crowd's yells of "play ball!" but the demands were ignored.[27]

On September 3 Leever pitched a 6–0 shutout against the Hartford

Nutmeg Makers and "the Professor was absolutely invulnerable," reported the *Richmond Dispatch*. "The Connecticut lads were unable to touch him for anything and during the entire nine innings that he confronted them they made but one hit, and that was made by old Cy Bowen, their country pitcher, who played in left-field."[28] Leever did walk four and struck out nine.

At Broad Street Park a week later, Leever pitched a five-inning, rain-shortened, three-hit, 8–0 shutout against the Athletics. In his next outing, he beat Paterson on September 14 despite permitting 11 hits and five runs. The following day, Richmond sold Leever's contract to the Pittsburgh franchise of the National League. In its report of the deal, the *Washington Post* wrote "Professor Leever" was "perhaps the most speedy pitcher in the Atlantic League."[29]

Leever pitched his final game for Richmond on September 17 at Newark and lost, 9 to 3, despite permitting only one earned run. Newark tied the game in the third inning when pitcher Bill Carrick struck out on one of Sam's inshoots, but the pitch evaded the catcher. While the Johnnies were attempting to retrieve the ball from beneath the grandstand, Carrick circled the bases for an unusual four-base wild pitch. The following inning, the game was decided when Newark scored six times, abetted by five Richmond errors, three of them by shortstop Elberfield. In the sixth inning Leever retired to right field for the remainder of the contest, then played the entirety of a second game that afternoon in the right field garden.[30]

Leever won 20 games for the fourth-place Johnny Rebs in 1896 and led the Atlantic League in strikeouts. Elberfeld batted .335 and stole 45 bases while with Richmond, leading to his purchase by the Philadelphia National League club in September.

The Pittsburgh Professional Base Ball Club was a charter member of the American Association, organized in 1882 to compete with the older National League. The Pittsburgh club joined the National League in 1887 after Kansas City dropped out. The Pittsburghs seldom competed for a championship in the 1800s and finished above fifth place only once, a distant second in 1893.

The club acquired the nickname "Pirates" in 1891 when they signed a player from the defunct Players' League who was also claimed by the Philadelphia Athletics of the American Association. Philadelphia's players claimed that the action of the Pittsburgh club in signing second baseman Bierbauer was "piratical." The term "pirates" clicked with sportswriters and from then on it was used in the newspapers and eventually became the team's official moniker.

The Pittsburgh entry in the short-lived Players' League built a grandstand on Exposition Grounds. The Pirates moved in for the 1891 season and played their games there until 1909. Exposition Park was predominately a wood structure located on the North Shore of the Allegheny River and close to its confluence with the Ohio and the Monongahela. The ball yard was across from the industrial center and Smoky Point where the steel factories belched black soot that hovered above the city. The "Queen Anne" towers on the grandstand were the Park's most distinguishing features. Unfortunately, the Pittsburgh Nationals' park was prone to frequent flooding whenever the river overflowed its banks.

Left field at Exposition Park was bordered by the B&O Railroad tracks in what was then known as Allegheny City until it became part of the city of Pittsburgh in 1907. The park's outfield was immense, 400 feet down each foul line and 450 feet to dead center. Outfielders played shallow against most batters to cut off bloopers, so when balls did get past them the batters were able to run for awhile. Triples were common and home runs at Exposition, as in most major league parks at that time, were of the inside-the-park variety. In 1902, the Pirates' 5'6" third baseman, Tommy Leach, led the National League with six home runs (his only two home runs that went over the fence came at South End Grounds in Boston on August 14). Wee Tommy finished second a year later with seven homers, of which none made it over the fence on the fly.

A month before the Pirates' 1898 home opener, their home park fell victim to the almost annual spring flooding. "One more flood came down the old Monongahela," reported *Sporting Life*. "The yellow stuff only registered 20 feet, but as the sewers in the park were open the water backed up to the pitcher's slab. The ground keeper had another fit of disgust."[31]

The local ballpark also was a haven for the city's gamblers. That June the club attempted to rid the element from Exposition Park by detailing officers to restrict betting activities in the grandstand. However, six weeks later *Sporting Life* noted, "Cheap gamblers again infest the Pittsburgh grandstand. Manager Watkins should act in this matter."[32]

The *Chicago Daily Tribune* chimed in that September, "Pittsburgh is the most objectionable town in the circuit with the nastiest chorus of rooters. In the right section of the grandstand a lot of professional gamblers openly canvass for bets all through the game. One day the management made a move and threw two bettors out of the stand, but permitted the professionals to ply their trade unmolested."[33]

When the special train carrying 25 Pittsburgh Pirates and recruits arrived at the club's spring training site at Little Rock, Arkansas, the morning of March 7, 1898, Samuel Leever was not among them. The Pirates had paid a "neat sum" for Leever, partly based on the recommendation of pitcher Jesse

Tannehill,[34] and were annoyed when the crafty Goshen "Professor" held out for more money than the Pirates offered. Eventually he signed for an undisclosed amount.[35] Leever was not that impressive when he first arrived in the Arkansas, but as training progressed the school teacher's teammates took notice when he mixed a drop ball and a sharp curve with his speedy pitch.[36]

The star player on the Pirates at that time was right fielder Patsy Donovan, a native Irishman who was beginning his ninth season in the major leagues, his seventh in Pittsburgh. Though left-hander Frank Killen had led the pitching corps since he won 34 games for the Pirates in 1893, another southpaw, Jesse Tannehill, would soon assume the mantle of ace. The former Richmond Bluebird hurler would post a 25–14 record with the '98 Pirates and also would chip in as a pinch-hitter and occasional outfield replacement.

Before the team headed north, Manager Watkins intimated that "Professor" Leever would be kept. The Pirates unveiled their new right-hander in an exhibition game in Kansas City on April 2. Sam replaced Tannehill after the sixth inning with the Pirates up, 7–0. "Professor went on the slab Saturday, and gave a display of wild tossing which would beat a trolley car run away on a big hill," noted *Sporting Life*. "When Sam eased up to get 'em over the Cowboys laid against the ball, counting seven hits in three rounds."[37] The cool weather was not conducive to the Schoolmaster, so he said, and swore he would not be in the best condition until warm weather "sets in to stay."[38]

Pittsburgh opened the season in Louisville on April 15 and lost to the Colonels, 10 to 3. The press commented that "the double-umpire system gave entire satisfaction to the 10,000 spectators."[39] Pittsburgh won the next three games in Kentucky before departing for Cincinnati. On April 29 Leever experienced his first of 13 consecutive opening days before the Pittsburgh home fans. The day began with the customary parade.

"Alleghenians were given more of a treat of music, dazzling uniforms and handsome athletes," wrote Alfred R. Cratty of the *Pittsburgh Chronicle-Telegraph*. "The parade left the Monongahela house at 1 P.M. and was at the Park something after 2:30. This gave the players a chance to practice, while the band blared away at airs and medleys which caused the patriotic blood to thrill with excitement. As the spectators arrived nearly all gave vent to an exclamation of delight at the admirable arrangement of the grounds, etc. The new gates, entrances, etc., were Watty's designing, while the ground keeper imported from Buffalo did the rest. The field is artistically prepared. Paths lead to the much used position, and there should be no need of keep off the grass warnings."[40]

Unfortunately, the opening day crowd was held down to 4,200 due to the threat of rain and the Pirates lost the game to drop their season's record to 6–5. Leever did not get the chance to appear in his first major league game until May 26, 1898, in a game at Exposition Park against Washington.

After the Senators pounded the Pirates' starting pitcher, Jim Gardner, for five runs, Manager Bill Watkins brought in Tannehill to finish the frame. Leever was sent to the pitcher's plate in the second inning. A contemporary account said that the rookie "did good work until the seventh inning, when six hits brought in four runs."[41] Some 1,200 Pittsburghers saw the debut of one of the franchise's greatest pitchers, but that was the last time for awhile that the locals would see Sam on the mound for the Pirates. Watkins had an overcrowded staff of pitchers so it was decided to return Leever to Richmond in order to get him some work. Too much work, as it turned out.[42]

Having pitched in only one National League game, Leever was sent to Richmond on June 2. Two days later, he pitched a five-hitter in his first game back in the Virginia capitol, but he lost to Suffolk, 3 to 0. Leever struggled in his next outing, a 10–6 win over Lancaster, but did make four of his team's 12 hits. The *Richmond Dispatch* reported that he "did not have his old time speed, nor his multitudinous curves and he did not fool the Lancasters a little bit."

After pitching in relief on June 11, Leever missed the club's road trip to Pennsylvania to give his sore right arm some rest. A contemporary report noted, "Leever will put in a few days at the Virginia Hot Springs."[43]

Leever returned to the mound in Norfolk on July 9 and his pitching over the remainder of the season was reminiscent of his work the previous year. Three of his wins were shutouts, the first a 1 to 0 decision over Lancaster's Irvin Wilhelm on July 13. Two weeks later, he pitched a three-hit, 8 to 0 shutout against Allentown and threw yet another three-hit shutout, this one against Paterson, on August 20. His success in Virginia would earn him a recall to Pittsburgh near the end of the season. While in Richmond, he averaged only a walk per game and he continued that great control while in the big leagues.

The Atlantic League season ended on September 10 with Richmond the pennant winner. Lancaster won more games that the Johnnies, but Richmond won on percentage points, .636 to .621, over the previous season's champion.

After sweeping a doubleheader from Reading on the final day of the season to clinch the championship, Manager Wells and his players, several members of the Reading team, and a few leading rooters accepted the invitation of Louis Gisselbrecht to a banquet that night. "The spread was immense and the 'German' fairly outdid himself. Happy speeches and presentations took place. Of course Manager Wells was remembered by his club, and favorite players got little keepsakes they will prize highly."[44]

Despite missing the first third of the season, Leever's league-leading .833 winning percentage, with his 15–3 record, bested the 20–5 (.800) record of Lancaster's Irving Wilhelm. Richmond's Tully Sparks was fifth at 19–11 (.630) and Jack Chesbro's 23–15 (.605) was seventh. Leever also posted good numbers at the plate, a .279 batting mark in 61 at bats.

When Leever and another late-season acquisition, John Cronin, joined the Pittsburgh club in New York, the Pirates were in eighth place, hovering around the .500 mark. On September 15, 1898, Leever pitched in both games of a doubleheader at New York's Polo Grounds. Only about 400 customers were there to watch the double bill, "including a dozen of Teddy Roosevelt's Rough Riders who let out a war whoop after every good play." Pirates starting pitcher Bill Hart gave up five runs in the sixth inning on three walks followed by five hits before he was relieved by Leever, who struck out four and held the Giants scoreless through the seventh and eighth innings. His work was so good in the first contest, Manager Watkins sent him out to start the second game. Though the New Yorkers suddenly found his curves easy to hit in the nightcap, they scored only one run before Tannehill came on to pitch for Pittsburgh in the third inning.[45] Leever's exit from the nightcap was precipitated by a strain in his salary wing throwing a pitch in the first inning. Though the injury was not considered serious at the time, he would miss almost a month.[46]

Leever's next and perhaps best-pitched game for the 1898 Pirates came October 9 at Louisville. After the Pirates scored a run in the bottom of the ninth to tie the game at 2–2, neither Leever nor the Colonels' Bill Magee allowed a baserunner over the next two innings. The contest was ruled a draw by Umpire Robert Emslie after the 11th because the Pirates had to catch a train home for the final three games of the season. Leever allowed but five hits and walked only one.[47]

Leever's first major league win came against the Cleveland Spiders on October 12, 1898. His mound opponent that day was the National League's premier pitcher, Denton True Young. Known as "Cy," Young already had 25 victories under his belt for the season. Young used an underhand delivery that enabled him to spin the ball up to the plate "in bewildering convolutions." However, on that autumn day Leever's curve ball was working well while Young did not have good fortune.

Not a Cleveland batter reached second base until the eighth inning, when Fred Frank opened with a drive over the head of Leever's left fielder that fell for a three-bagger. Moments later the Spider scored on a double by McKean to cut the home team's margin to 3 to 1. However, the Pirates lambasted Young for six runs in their half of the eighth to settle the affair. Pittsburgh's rookie pitcher allowed only three hits in his 9–1 victory.[48] Leever would return to the Pirates for the 1899 season.

In his first couple of years with the Pirates, Leever honed his craft by learning from a pair of veterans, Bill Hart and Billy Rhines. However, the star of the Pirates' pitching staff was Jesse Tannehill, who hailed from Dayton, Kentucky, just across the Ohio River from Cincinnati and only a few miles from Goshen. Though he already had two full National League seasons under his belt, Tannehill was two and a half years younger than Leever. Tannehill featured an outstanding fastball and he eventually would develop a "change up spitter."

Several outstanding pitchers made their first appearance in the National League during Leever's first full season in the major leagues. Making their debuts in 1899 were Joe McGinnity, who won 28 games for John McGraw's Baltimore Orioles, Cincinnati's Frank "Noodles" Hahn, one of the few Southerners in the league, and the quiet Louisville hurler of no-hit fame, Charles Phillippe. The Pirates' pitching staff came to resemble a Richmond alumni club when Jack Chesbro and Tully Sparks joined Leever and Jesse Tannehill in Pittsburgh.

On April 17, 1899, at League Park in Cincinnati, Pirates pitcher Bill Hoffer was injured in a collision with a Cincinnati baserunner in the first inning and had to depart in favor of Leever. Cincinnati won, 8 to 7, with three runs off the school teacher in the eighth. Leever was far more successful in his next outing.

After Leever and the Reds' Ted Breitenstein battled to a 12-inning 3–3 tie two days later, a local reporter wrote, "The twirler from Goshen, O., is a full-fledged wonder and, barring accident, he will be the Pittsburghs' mainstay on the rubber this season. The Reds could do nothing with his delivery, but they were fortunate to get two of their hits at the right time."[49]

Leever did confirm that he wasn't a cold weather hurler after he lost in St Louis, 5–2, on April 23 when rain halted the game after six innings. A week later at Exposition Park, the St. Louis Perfectos scored seven runs off Leever in the first two innings that were played in a pelting rain. In the early going, he could not get his customary tantalizing curve balls and shoots to work in the windy and slippery conditions. By the third inning the rain had stopped and he gave up only two hits and no runs over the final seven frames. He still lost, 7 to 5, to Cy Young.[50]

Twice during the 1899 season, Leever faced off against Louisville's Phillippe, winning on both occasions, 7–5 in Pittsburgh on May 5, and 5–4 again at Exposition Park on June 10. In the first of the two games between the future stars of the Pirates, Leever prevailed mainly because he had a better day at the bat than Phillippe. Both pitchers were shaky at the start and Louisville led 2 to 1 after one inning. Things settled down after that and the score did not change until the sixth, when Pittsburgh landed runners on second and third with two out. Leever singled both runners home to put the home team up, 3–2. Leever developed a Charley horse running out the base hit and Manager Watkins instructed Harley Payne to warm up. However, Leever stayed in the game and the Pirates added another tally an inning later when Phillippe's fielding error and third baseman Wagner's wild throw cost the Colonels a run.

Phillippe got into the scoring act in the bottom half when he sent a short fly to center field that fell in front of the onrushing Tom McCreedy. Charles later scored and Louisville added a second run to tie the score. The Pirates won the game in the eighth when Clingman's fumble of Leever's two-out grounder set up the winning knock. Patsy Donovan followed with a home run to the depths of left-center field that won the game and netted the Pirates' star outfielder a ten dollar gold piece.[51]

On May 11 at Exposition Park, Leever lost to another star rookie, Cincinnati's Noodles Hahn, 1 to 0 on catcher Heinie Peitz's sixth-inning triple to the Lillian Russell sign in center field and a long fly by Hahn. Cincinnati's other three hits were harmless singles. Willie Clark raised the home town's hopes in the bottom of the ninth with a triple, but the next batter, Jimmy Williams, flew out to disappoint the Pirates and their fans.

Leever used his bat to pick up a victory in a game against Washington on Decoration Day, May 30. Opposing Leever was the Nationals' best pitcher, Bill Dinneen, and Leever nursed a tenuous lead until he tired in the eighth, when Washington scored twice to tie the game at 5–5. Leever was first up in the home ninth and slapped a Dinneen pitch that landed fair near the right field foul line, then rolled among the fans standing in front of the bleachers. Leever had pulled up at second base, but Umpire Swartwood awarded him third. The Washington manager argued that the three-base ground rule did not apply to the fringe of people in front of the stands but only to the crowd behind the ropes in right field. The umpire disagreed and Patsy Donovan drove the very next pitch for a single to right. Leever trotted home with the winning run.[52]

Sam Leever was not the only promising new ballplayer to join the Pirates in the spring of 1899. Only one year removed from semipro ball, 22-year-old Clarence "Ginger" Beaumont began his major league career primarily as a pinch-hitter and spare outfielder for the Pirates. After right fielder Patsy Donovan replaced William Watkins as manager only 24 games into the season, Beaumont began to get more playing time, and by the end of June the rookie had forced himself into the center field job. On July 22, Beaumont made six infield hits in six at-bats and scored six runs against Philadelphia. Beaumont batted .352, sixth best in the National League, but that was not even the best mark on the Pittsburgh team. That distinction went to the Pirates' rookie third baseman, Jimmy Williams.

In 1899 Williams led the National League with 27 triples and was dubbed "Home Run" for his nine round-trippers. Jimmy batted .355 for the season, fifth in the National League behind four future Hall of Famers. That year Williams also set the Pittsburgh franchise record for consecutive games with at least one hit. Jimmy had one hitting streak of 27 consecutive games and another of 26. Both streaks were stopped by yet another rookie, Deacon Phillippe of Louisville.

As the season progressed, the school teacher/pitcher began to get rave notices. Unfortunately, Leever's right arm began to bother him, and the Schoolmaster ceased throwing for two days. On July 8, he pitched a 4–0 shutout against the Chicago Orphans. It was a cold day in Pittsburgh and the two teams had to endure delays because of rain in the fourth inning and again in the seventh. Leever allowed only four hits, but five errors by the Pirates kept their pitcher in trouble throughout the contest.

"Mr. Leever is a peculiar looking person, being bald of head and extremely angular," wrote a "Windy City" witness, "but he pitched wonderful ball, and before him Burns' bronco busters were helpless and never a run could they make during the struggle.... The cold and rain seemed not to affect Leever, who, with terrific speed and wonderful curves, slammed the ball across the plate and mowed down the Cowboys almost as fast as they faced him."[53]

"The quiet, easy-going fellow twirled with that cool, calculating way which marked Clarkson when he was in the heyday of his career," noted *Sporting Life*. "He acted as if he knew that he had strong points in the art of deception, and if he applied them properly success would come. The Chicago men fell down without a semblance of a base hit for seven innings. A bunch fanned the breezes, DeMontreville falling twice before Leever's speed, both times when a safety meant disaster. It was a splendid display of strategic serving."[54]

Despite his dominate performance against the Orphans, Leever's pitching wing remained a concern. As William H. Locke[55] reported in *The Sporting News*, "It is to be hoped that the injury is not of a permanent character, but, candidly, I am afraid the big schoolmaster is going to pay the penalty for a willingness to pitch every day, also for not having taken good care of his right fin."[56]

Richmond manager Jake Wells had warned the Pirates about Leever's practice of pitching balls from the outfield during practice and the hurler's propensity for throwing an hour or two each day. However, Leever was not one to accept suggestions gracefully so he continued his long-distance throwing practices and volunteered to pitch out of turn. There were plenty of opportunities because, by mid-season, Leever and Jesse Tannehill were the only effective pitchers on the staff. Fortunately, President Kerr heeded the recommendations to acquire another pitcher from Wells' Richmond club and Jack Chesbro debuted on the mound for the Pirates on July 12, 1899.

Chesbro had been drafted by the Baltimore Orioles following the 1898 season, but after the club's owners transferred their manager and best players to the Brooklyn club, the pitcher was left in limbo. He went back to Richmond in the spring of 1899 and put up a record of 17 wins and 4 losses by July 7 when he was sold to Pittsburgh for $1,500. He only managed six wins and nine losses in 17 starts with the Pirates, but showed enough promise with his curve and a decent fastball for Pittsburgh to keep him when the club was reconstituted in the off-season.

Wells' prediction about Leever's pitching wing came to fruition, for Sam experienced a slump following his shutout of the Orphans. Four days after he was thumped by Brooklyn, 9 to 2, Leever gave up three first-inning runs to the strong Philadelphia lineup before the Pirates even came to bat. However, the school teacher recovered to shut out the Quakers over the next seven innings while his teammates built a 6 to 3 lead. By the ninth inning, Leever was seriously laboring and the Philly team scored five runs to take the lead, 8 to 6. The 5,200 locals on hand did not even have an opportunity to find the exits before the first two Pirates to bat in the bottom of the ninth reached base. Jimmy Williams was up next and lashed a long fly ball that landed in fair territory and rolled into the spacious expanses of Exposition Park. Williams chased the other Pirates runners around the bases, and when he crossed home for a three-run, game-winning home run, he was showered with money from his elated fans.

Leever lost his next three starts, against Boston, Baltimore and St. Louis. In the game with the Perfectos, he didn't last past the second inning as the visitors from Missouri built up a 7–0 lead and eventually won at Expo, 11 to 5. Against Philadelphia on August 7, he took a 4 to 1 into the eighth inning, then was removed after allowing a single and a walk. It would be a different story four days later at Exposition Park.

Much to the delight of a Friday crowd of over 4,000, Leever allowed the Quaker City team seven hits and walked but one of the fence-bangers while handcuffing a batting order featuring future Hall of Famers Elmer Flick and Ed Delahanty. The great Napoleon Lajoie, however, did not play that day. Leever had marvelous support from his fielders and only one opposing baserunner advanced as far as third base. The Pirates built up a 5–0 lead by the fourth inning, but the Quakers' biggest threat came in the ninth when singles by Delahanty and Lauder put two runners on base. With two out, third baseman Williams made a "fine stop" of Douglass' hit close to the third base bag and forced Delahanty to end the game. Leever's shutout was the first no-run game pitched against the Phillies in 1899.[57]

A few days later a pundit wrote in the *Washington Post*, "Twirler Leever of the Pirates has a foxy faculty of insinuating a sluggish teaser, one of those floating slow ones, into his mixture."[58] At the height of his success, Leever explained the nature of his curve ball: "Most spectators at a baseball game have an exaggerated idea of the curve ball in pitching. They think the man in the box can send in all kinds of twisters and thus fool the opposing batsmen. Of course, mastery of the curve ball is part of the pitcher's stock in trade, but control — emphasize the word — and knowledge of the batsmen's weaknesses are more important, and no pitcher with curves can be successful unless he also has control. The throwing of a curve ball is partly mechanical, and to accomplish the result all pitchers use the same motion. The difference is in the degree of efficiency and the control in placing it where the curve will count the most."[59]

Leever did experience a mid–September swoon, likely due to overwork. On September 2 he whitewashed the New York Giants on four hits. After a victory over Chicago on September 6, he would not win another game until the 22nd.

During one four-day span in mid–September, Donovan used Leever in three games, once in relief, and the Pirates lost all three games. In the third of those outings, he pitched well for the first time in two weeks, but lost, 4–3, in 11 innings to Boston after Frank Dillon's wild throw allowed Boston to tie the score in the ninth and force the game into extras. After Leever's loss to Boston on September 19 he came back after three days off and had an easy win over the Giants, 11–2, collecting two doubles and a single himself. Still, his poor pitching performance on the final road trip of the season led him to declare, "I'll be ashamed to go back to Pittsburgh."[60]

On the 26th Leever threw his fourth shutout of the season on a bitterly cold day at Chicago's West Side Grounds in a "funeral exercise" before only 400 chattering bugs. Only two days later, Leever won his own game with the bat in the Pirates' comeback victory over Cincinnati. Leever and the Pirates were losing 4–3, when they came to bat in the eighth inning. Bones Ely led off with a grounder to shortstop, but Tommy Corcoran threw wildly and the Pirates shortstop made it to second. A single followed by a walk loaded the bases. Amid cries from the Pittsburgh crowd to "win your own game," Leever stepped into the box against right-hander Emil Frisk. He laced a beautiful line drive to center field for an apparent single. The Reds rookie center fielder, Sam Crawford, rushed in for the play, but the ball took a bad bounce and eluded his grasp. By the time the ball was retrieved all three baserunners had scored and Leever rested on second base. He moved over to third on a Frisk wild pitch and scored on a sacrifice fly by Beaumont.

Leever would need all the runs he could get due to sloppy defense by Pittsburgh in the bottom of the ninth. To start the frame, first baseman Dillon dropped Leever's throw to allow one runner to reach base. Then Leever fielded Beckley's ground ball and threw it into center field on an ill-fated attempt at the force play at second. Despite the bad start to the inning, Leever regrouped, allowed only one runner to score, and Pittsburgh won, 7 to 5.[61]

A strange ending to a game gave Leever his 21st victory of the season on October 13 against Louisville's Patsy Flaherty. Leever did not give up a hit to the visiting Colonels until the seventh inning, when a double and a single into a rapidly descending haze resulted in a run. Honus Wagner foolishly attempted to steal another run while Leever was fondling the ball on the mound. He came close to getting away with in, but Leever quickly reacted with a throw to catcher Bowerman, who fell over the Dutchman in making the tag. Wagner angrily protested the decision, but eventually went to the bench.

By the end of the eighth inning the playing field at Exposition Park had become engulfed by a fog of smoke from the nearby steel mills. Although the sun was shining, the 1,200 or so spectators could hardly see the outfielders and it was obvious the latter could not track the flight of batted balls. With Pittsburgh holding a 5 to 2 lead, the Colonels complained to umpire Ed Swartwood about the playing conditions and seemed willing to stop the game then and there. However, the umpire ignored their appeals. In the visitors' ninth, a brace of extra-base hits on balls that could have been easy outs under normal conditions led to four scores, and Louisville suddenly had a 6 to 5 lead. At that point Swartwood decided to stop play because he could not see the fielders from home plate. The score automatically reverted to the previous inning, making Pittsburgh a 5 to 2 winner. The declaration led to an instantaneous assault from the Louisville bench. The besieged arbiter was followed to the club office by the fist-shaking Colonels.[62]

Leever finished the season with a record of 21–23 for a seventh-place club (in a 12-team league), and he led the league in games pitched (51) and innings thrown (379). The large number of appearances came as a result of his use 12 times in relief. Leever won two, lost five and held the lead in three games as a substitute hurler.

Long-time Pittsburgh sports writer Ralph Davis later wrote that Leever's arm was so sore following the 1899 season that he became discouraged and asked the Pirates for his release. "He was honest in confessing to his employer at that time that he thought he was all in, but, fortunately for the Pittsburgh club and for Leever, the manager of the Pirates decided to hold him for at least one more year in the hope that he would come around all right. A winter's rest did wonders for the curve-ball artist, and ever since then he has been a great winner."[63]

Though Leever suffered a sore right arm intermittently throughout his career, he never had another losing season, and never again would he allow as many as three earned runs per nine innings pitched for the Pirates.

Following the final game of the 1899 National League season, Leever left immediately for his home in Goshen. Despite his indecision about his future with the Pirates, he would soon join Tannehill and a team of touring major league players managed by Frank Bancroft. The barnstormers were planning to play a few games in Cuba, but the tour through southern states proved so unsuccessful, a visit to the island was dropped.

Sporting Life pointed out that during the trip Leever once pitched for both teams in a game. "He was told to stay on the rubber by Banny (Bancroft) after three hands were out. He did so. Few twirlers would have done so. There is a report that the Pittsburgh management offered Leever an increase of $500 over last season, but he declined it declaring that from the work he presented he should be given much more. The position taken by the club owners is that the past season was the first that Leever had shown anything like good, reliable form, in addition, he is given credit for pitching many games which he did not finish, being relieved because of a fear that retention on the slab would result in disaster."[64]

The National League's contraction in 1900 was the best thing that could happen to Sam Leever, Jack Chesbro, Clarence Beaumont, and the city of Pittsburgh. New team president Barney Dreyfuss sold the Pirates' older stars, Jack McCarthy to Chicago for $2,000 and player/manager Patsy Donovan to St. Louis for $1,000. One of the last players to go was Leever's catcher of two years, Frank Bowerman, who was sold to the New York Giants just before spring training. Bowerman would later be an important character in the Pirates-Giants rivalry.

♦ THREE ♦

A New Era in Pittsburgh

Greater Pittsburgh was the nation's 11th largest city at the dawn of the twentieth century. The population of Allegheny County had risen to 750,000 by the time of the 1900 federal census, and the city of Pittsburgh had more than 350,000 citizens, an increase of almost 50 percent in one decade.

Located where the Allegheny and the Monongahela Rivers meet to form the Ohio, Pittsburgh's nickname of the "Smoky City" was well deserved. Barges and trains moved tons of coal into the area's steel factories where furnaces belched black smoke so dense that the sunlight was often blocked out in the sky. The steel mills needed cheap labor so during the 1890s, Italians, Poles, and Eastern Europeans poured into the city to work in the factories. The German, Irish and English immigrants who had arrived decades earlier gradually moved to the suburbs and utilized streetcars to take them into the city for work each day.

The 1900 baseball season would be Pittsburgh's most successful yet. With a team transformed by the addition of players like Honus Wagner, Fred Clarke and Charles Phillippe from the defunct Louisville club, the Pirates were expected to contend for the pennant.

"So much has been said of Barney Dreyfuss as a wise owner, a smart trader and a man who understands every angle of the baseball business that few know of him as a fan," recalled Honus Wagner. "If you ever sat next to him in a grandstand in the old days, though, and you didn't know him by sight you'd never think the rooter next to you was the owner of the Pittsburgh club. Mr. Dreyfuss would travel with the team, mix up with the players and engage in any of their games, their amusements. He would mix up in practical jokes and give and take. But above all things, he was crazy to see his ball club win."[1]

Barney Dreyfuss named the former Louisville boy manager, Fred Clarke, pilot of the combined Pirates/Colonels team. Major league clubs did not

Business district along Wood Street, Pittsburgh, just after the turn of the twentieth century (Library of Congress Prints and Photographs Division).

employ non-playing coaches until late in the decade so the team captain or a designated veteran took over in the event of the manager's absence. Reserve players and idle pitchers were pressed into service with other duties, performed in later years by coaches. Sam Leever and Charles Phillippe often served as base coaches, hit fungos during fielding practice, and pitched batting practice between starting assignments. Leever was noted for his role in pre-game practice because he forced the fielders to chase down the balls he sent to the outfield. "When Sam is hitting them," noted the *Pittsburgh Press*, "the men work harder than in a game."²

New club president Barney Dreyfuss was taken aback that February when he received a letter from Leever, one of only two unsigned players on the Pirates' roster. Within the long letter, Leever expressed a desire to discuss several points with the owner before signing his 1900 contract. The exasperated owner observed, "For the life of me I cannot understand what Sam is driving at. He does not say that he will not sign for the salary offered — does not even hint that the terms of the contract are unsatisfactory. I don't know what he wants to argue, but I do know that he will not argue any points with me. He has been tendered a contract. If he does not like it, he can let it alone. It is up to him."³

The press speculated that Leever wanted to be traded to Cincinnati, but just before the Pirates were to leave for spring training, he relented on his demands and put his signature to a new contract. Jack Chesbro was still a holdout, but he finally acquiesced and was told he would have to pay his own way to training camp.

The Pittsburgh club spent two weeks in spring training at Thomasville, Georgia, where the Colonels had trained the previous season. When they arrived in Georgia, the team found that the hotel at which accommodations had been secured was crowded, so an adjoining Baptist church was converted into a dorm for the players. The baptismal in the church was used by the ballplayers for bathing.⁴

Spring training was uneventful and the only casualty was Charles Phillippe, who "got his hands mixed up with poison ivy" at the golf course and was unable to practice. On the trip north to Pittsburgh, the Pirates played exhibitions in several cities and spent a few days training in Louisville. The Pirates promised to play a game every day at the old National League Park while in Kentucky, but the split-squad games and a contest with the Rochester club were poorly attended by the locals, who exhibited their disdain for Dreyfuss' abandonment of the city.

On April 3 the new Pirates were divided into two teams for an exhibition game in front of many of the players' former fans. "Pittsburgh" was made up of the starters and the opposition, "Louisville" filled its lineup from among Pirates rookies, substitutes and extra pitchers. Leever started for the "Pittsburgh" team against the former Colonel, Phillippe. Three pitchers played the field for the Louisvilles, Chesbro in right field, Walter Woods at second base and Patsy Flaherty in left field. When Woods replaced Phillippe on the mound, Chesbro moved to second base and Phillippe took over in right field. The regulars throttled the Louisvilles.

Only an average of about 50 persons, mostly friends of the players, attended the games at National League Park. Wrote a local correspondent, "The Pittsburgh management considers they have extended the Louisville people a favor by inviting them to the exhibition games to allow them to contribute a small mite towards the expenses of the Pirates' spring training. However the people have had enough of Dreyfuss and the big league, and have treated the Pittsburgh club with utter indifference."[5]

Due to the abandonment of four of the 12 National League clubs, the 1900 regular season schedule was reduced from 154 to 140 games (the 154-game schedule would be restored for the 1904 season). Single games were scheduled to begin at 3:00 P.M. so that working men could come to the ballpark directly from their jobs.

In a cost-cutting move, the league's magnates scrapped the two-umpire experiment and returned to a single arbiter for its games. The sole umpire would stand behind the catcher until a runner reached base, then would move out behind the pitcher to call balls and strikes. Players often took advantage of the one-umpire system and bent the rules whenever they felt the ump was not looking in their direction.

There were no dugouts on the Pirates' home field until 1909 and players sat on an enclosed bench between the grandstand and the foul line. Participants did not wear numbers, so an announcer with a megaphone would announce the name of the player who was about to bat. A hand-operated scoreboard tracked the runs each inning and the total, but did not indicate balls, strikes, hits and errors as in later times. Umpires did not signal balls and strikes in those days so it was difficult for spectators to figure out what the count was on a batter.

When major league teams went on the road around the turn of the century, they usually took a squad of only about 14 or 15 players, including five pitchers. Ballparks rarely had locker rooms for the visiting teams, so players dressed at their hotel and rode to the park in open, horse-drawn carriages called "tally-hos." Sometime, the visitors' procession served as fodder for overzealous home team supporters.

The Pirates opened the 1900 season in St. Louis on Thursday, April 19. Dreyfuss and Secretary Pulliam dressed the Pittsburgh players in new blue-gray uniforms with navy blue sweaters, stockings and collars.

The "new" Pirates' opening day lineup featured a batting order of Ginger Beaumont in center field, left fielder Fred Clarke, third baseman Jimmy Williams, right fielder Honus Wagner, shortstop Bones Ely, second baseman Claude Ritchey, first baseman Frank "Pop" Dillon, catcher Charles "Chief" Zimmer, and pitcher Sam Leever.

Leever's assignment was to oppose the most famous pitcher in the game, Cy Young. However, Leever pitched to only six batters. In the top of the second inning, St. Louis shortstop Bobby Wallace hit a sizzler right back at the pitcher and the ball struck his right thumb. The fallen hurler recovered the ball and, while sitting, made an accurate throw to Dillon to retire Wallace. Upon examination of the patient at the hospital, his injury was a serious one — a laceration and dislocation of the thumb on his pitching hand. Waddell took over on the mound for the Pirates, and Rube faltered only in one inning. That was the fourth when the Cardinals scored three runs. Pittsburgh's batters were no match for Young's "jump" ball as he struck out nine in his 3 to 0 shutout.

Professional ballplayers in the period before and just after the turn of the century nearly always were tagged with unique nicknames. On the Pirates, Honus Wagner was "Hans" or "The Flying Dutchman," George Edward Waddell was "Rube," Claude Ritchey was "Little All Right," Beaumont was "Ginger" or "Red," Texan Dick Cooley was "Duff" or "Sir Richard" because of his aristocratic manner, shortstop Frederick Ely was "Bones," Jimmy Williams was "Buttons" and "Home Run," Tommy Leach was "Wee," and of course Leever was called "Schoolmaster" and sometimes "Professor."

By 1900, Charles Phillippe was routinely called "Deacon," the nickname bestowed on players of dignified manner who did not use profanity, drink or gamble, vices prevalent among ballplayers. The press often promoted the image associated with the nickname with twaddle like a piece that appeared in the *Pittsburgh Chronicle*: "Phillippe, the Pittsburgh pitcher, has about as unique a position as any toiler in the game. He leads a church choir during the winter months and says he is good at it."[6]

It has often been written that Phillippe, like the Giants' Christy Mathewson, chose not to pitch on Sundays. The fact is Phillippe did pitch on Sunday, though not in Pittsburgh, where it was against the law. His very first appearance in a major league game back in 1899 came on a Sunday, and he often took the ball on the Sabbath. Although he started only one Sunday game in 1901, September 22 in Chicago, he took the mound eight times on the "day of rest" the following season.[7] Phillippe came to dislike pitching on the Sabbath, not because of religious convictions, but because he had notoriously bad luck when he started on Sunday.

Existing "blue laws" in Pittsburgh prohibited the playing of professional baseball on the Sabbath for the entirety of Phillippe's career with the Pirates. The only National League cities that permitted Sunday baseball during that time were Chicago, St. Louis and Cincinnati. Often, The Pirates would play the Friday and Saturday games of a series at Exposition Park, then travel by rail to Chicago or Cincinnati to take advantage of a large Sunday gate.

Phillippe avoided a loss in his first start of the 1900 season in a game against St. Louis on April 22 when Pittsburgh rallied for three runs to tie the game in the ninth inning. He left after the fourth, trailing 3-1, and was replaced by former Louisville teammate, Patsy Flaherty. With the game tied at five when the Cardinals came to bat in the bottom of the ninth, Rube Waddell gave up the game-winning single to Big Dan McGann, his fourth hit of the afternoon. The Sunday crowd of more than 20,000 was the largest to see a game in St. Louis up to that time.

After a 3-3 start, the Pirates returned to Pittsburgh for their home opener at Exposition Park on April 26. Jimmy Williams was in street clothes because of an injury, Pop Dillon was on crutches, and Sam Leever was back in Goshen nursing his sprained thumb. An outstanding crowd of about 11,000 turned out to cheer the city's new team, but they were treated to a dismal performance by the Pirates' pitching. After being driven from the slab, Waddell complained that an attack of pleurisy led to his ineffectiveness, to which the *Sporting News* noted that Rube's "little plaint only caused a smile in baseball quarters."[8] Pittsburgh lost, 12 to 11, but only a seven-run ninth inning in which Noodles Hahn walked two batters with the bases loaded made the final count close. The Pirates lost three straight games to the Reds.

On April 29 Phillippe staggered to an 8 to 6 victory over Cincinnati despite 15 opposition hits, four walks and a hit batsman. The huge Sunday crowd of 16,000 that turned out to the Palace of the Fans overflowed onto the grounds, necessitating the implementation of special ground rules. Back-to-back doubles by the Reds with two out in the ninth inning pushed the game into extras. In the tenth Cincinnati had a single, a double and another single, but failed to score a run because two runners were thrown out at home plate. Pittsburgh won it for Phillippe in the 11th with two runs. The contest took three hours to play, a remarkably long time for a game in those days.

Amazingly, Sam Leever returned to the mound less than two weeks after his thumb injury. On May 2, the Schoolmaster again faced off against the Cardinals Cy Young, this time at Exposition Park. After leadoff batter Patsy Donovan was presented with a large floral arrangement as he stepped into the box, the St. Louis manager reached Leever for a single and eventually scored the game's first run. Pittsburgh jumped on Mr. Young right from the start, plating four runs on five hits in the bottom half of the initial stanza. After that the two hurlers were virtually untouchable for the next five innings. St. Louis began to peck away against Leever with two tallies in the seventh, abetted by a miscommunication between Beaumont and Clarke that allowed Dan McGann's fly ball to hit the turf for a double. To open the eighth, "Crab" Burkett hit a fly ball down the left field line that Clarke couldn't reach. Though everyone from Pittsburgh felt the ball was foul, Umpire Hurst gave the St. Louis batter a double. Moments later the score was tied on a single to center. Another run in the ninth put St Louis ahead, 5 to 4.

Between the first and the ninth innings, Young had allowed the Pirates nothing, but with the verdict down to the final out of the game, Pittsburgh managed to put runners on second and first. Clarke called on the mustachioed William "Pop" Schriver to pinch-hit for the light-hitting Ely. The veteran catcher of 12 years in the National League found a Young delivery to his liking and singled to send Wagner across the plate with the tying run.

After Leever retired the Perfectos in the top half of the tenth, the Pirates went to work on Young in the home half. After Young disposed of Leever, Beaumont singled and went to second on an out. The count had gone to two balls and two strikes on McCreery when the switch-hitting right fielder crushed a pitch that normally would have gone for a triple, but he needed only to pass first base for Beaumont had already crossed home plate with the winning run. Leever was the winning pitcher despite three home team errors and ten St. Louis hits.[9]

Early on, the pranksters from the defunct Louisville Colonels learned that Sam Leever's no-nonsense demeanor and tightfistedness made good fodder for their jokes. Outfielder Tom McCreery recalled an instance where Fred Clarke and Tommy Leach played a practical joke on the Schoolmaster. "Leever knew how to save his money," McCreery told a reporter years later. "One time, over in New York, Barney Dreyfuss was so well pleased with us that he bought us each a Panama hat. This was rather early in the year. Leever had been wearing around an old derby hat. His new Panama was put in its package on a hotel rack. Clarke and Leach got hold of the package when Leever was out. They took out the Panama, and sliced it so that the brim came entirely off, then replaced it in the wrappings.

"Leever carried that thing around the whole circuit with him, never knowing the difference, but along came July he decided to wear the hat and there was hell to pay."[10]

Though Philadelphia was the early pace-setter in the National League race, the Pirates knew the 1900 pennant would have to be wrestled away from Brooklyn, a team further strengthened by the addition of several stars from the defunct Baltimore team. Pittsburgh met the Superbas for the first time that season in a three-game set at Exposition Park starting on May 21. Leever lost the first game, 7–5, when he gave up 13 hits to the visitors and the Pirates chipped in with six errors, three by third baseman Williams. The clubs split the next two games. It was a raucous, hard-fought series and each team accused the other of rowdyism. Ned Hanlon said Fred Clarke intentionally attempted to injure the Brooklyn players, and the Superbas declared they would get even the next time Pittsburgh visited Brooklyn.[11]

Phillippe did not play in the Brooklyn series and next pitched in the afternoon game of a Decoration Day double-bill before a huge assemblage of 15,000 at New York's Polo Grounds. The Pirates were uncharacteristically bad in a 9 to 1 loss to a Giants team the *New York Tribune* had called amateurish after their effort in the morning game against Waddell. In Phillippe's losing effort, the Pirates had the same number of errors as hits, five.[12]

Receiving Phillippe's pitches for the first time that afternoon was veteran catcher Jack O'Connor, obtained in a cash transaction with St. Louis a week earlier. The deal was necessitated because injuries had left the Pirates only one healthy catcher. Even when fit, 39-year-old Zimmer was not a full-time catcher anymore, so the deal was worked out for the 13-year veteran O'Connor, who not only had a bad throwing arm but had worn out his welcome in St. Louis.

At the time Leever and Phillippe pitched in the National League, the catcher was positioned about where they are today, though the receiver did not squat behind the batter as they would at a later time. In the first decade of the century, the catcher stood in a slight crouch from which his mitt provided the pitcher a target high in the strike zone. Catchers wore a wire-basket, cage-style mask and a rubber-ribbed chest protector, and used a round pillow mitt with a pocket in the middle. Shin guards were not used until the second half of the decade.

Manager Fred Clarke was forced to leave the team on June 1 because of a kidney ailment, and reserve outfielder Duff Cooley filled in as field boss until Clarke's return. The club played poorly without their disciplinarian manager and an additional problem arose when Rube Waddell did not show up for a scheduled start in Brooklyn on June 9. He reappeared two days later as if nothing had happened. The Pirates had lost seven in a row by the time Clarke returned on June 17, but he suffered a relapse and had to take another ten days away from the team.

The second week in June, the Pirates went to Brooklyn for the first time. Deacon Phillippe "had the champions at his mercy" for most of the first game of the series and took a 7–1 lead into the last inning. It had been easy for Pittsburgh until that ninth frame when a base on balls, four hits, and Ritchey's fumble gave the Superbas three runs, and the potential winning run stood in the batter's box. With the bases loaded, the game was secured for Pittsburgh when Joe Kelley lifted a high foul ball that was corralled by O'Connor for the final out. After an off-day, Joe McGinnity beat the Pirates and, after another off-day, Phillippe took the mound against Brooklyn again on the 11th. He lasted only three innings before he was pulled out of the game, trailing 4–2. Waddell replaced him and was hit even harder in the 8 to 7 loss. Though there were no fisticuffs, the New York papers accused the visitors of rowdyism for their numerous arguments with Umpire Swartwood.[13]

After Phillippe's victory in the first game of the recently completed series in Brooklyn, the Pirates lost seven in a row, including three straight in Boston and the first two of seven consecutive games against Chicago. Pop Dillon was the first Pirates player to play the price for the club's poor performance when he was sent packing after making only two base hits in the five games he played at first base. Another reason for the slump of the Pirates' offense was a decline in the performance of Jimmy Williams. He suffered a severely sprained ankle that put him out of action for a month and struggled thereafter, batting only .264 for the season. After losing the third base job he had filled with the Colonels in 1899, Tommy Leach played behind Williams and hit only .213 in 51 games as a fill-in.

On June 18, Deacon Phillippe broke the Pirates' losing habit with a 4 to 1 win in Chicago. It was a tough day in the Windy City for the fielders because of the breeze and a tough sun field in left. The first run of the contest came in the third when Jimmy Williams hit a long drive off Nixey Callahan that "floated in the wind" and fell into the right field bleachers. A key play in the contest occurred in the sixth inning when Pittsburgh had runners on second and third with two out. Instead of walking the Pirates' catcher and pitching to Phillippe with the bases loaded, Chicago decided to pitch to Jack O'Connor, even after Callahan's first three tosses went wide. O'Connor made contact on the 3-and-1 pitch. Third baseman Barry McCormick scooped up the bounder behind the bag and threw to first base in plenty of time to get O'Connor but Ganzel could not handle a nasty hop. The ball bounced away to allow two runners to score.[14]

Phillippe only lost a shutout because Ginger Beaumont misplayed Mertes' fly ball in the bottom of the sixth, then loafed after it while the runner went to second base. A second double in the inning gave Chicago their run, but that was it for the day. Phillippe allowed only six hits and struck out eight.

A day later, Rube Waddell pitched 13 innings of shutout ball against Chicago before losing in the 14th. The Pirates' record of 24–27 left them eight and a half games behind Brooklyn in the standings.

The antics of the undisciplined Waddell weighed heavily on manager Clarke. The lefty hurler stayed out late and routinely violated club rules. Rube even moonlighted with a local amateur ball team composed of businessmen. When he injured a finger serving as catcher for the amateurs, Clarke suspended him. Ineligible to play for any other National League club, Rube fled to Punxsutawney, Pennsylvania, and hooked up with another amateur outfit. The Pirates temporarily solved their problem by loaning Waddell to Milwaukee of the American League (a minor league in 1900). He would be recalled to Pittsburgh for the final month of the season.

On the field, the Pirates began to play winning baseball amid the controversy surrounding Waddell and Clarke. Between June 20 and a series against the Superbas that began at Exposition Park on July 10, Pittsburgh won 11 of 14 games. Leever's thumb injury had healed and Phillippe survived some early-season inconsistency to join Tannehill on the list of the National League's leading pitchers.

After an absence from the mound because of the death of his sister Maggie, Leever took the ball for a contest against the heavy-hitting Philadelphia Phillies at Exposition Park June 28. He not only shut out the fence-breakers from Philadelphia, 3 to 0, on only two hits, in each of the first eight innings he faced only three batters. Two of the three opposing baserunners were erased on double plays, and a third was thrown out by Chief Zimmer attempting to steal. Besides pitching a sterling game, Leever made the play of the day in the sixth inning. With two out, his opposing number on the mound, Chick Fraser, hit a line drive that appeared bound for center field. Leever got in front of the smash, knocked the ball down and threw the runner out. The 2,600 locals in attendance gave Leever a rousing ovation.

In the ninth, Leever hit Fraser with a pitch after two were out. The Phillies pitcher trotted to first, but moments later Ely gobbled up a batted ball as it bounced over the second base bag and tossed the ball to Ritchey for the force out to conclude the affair. Big Ed Delahanty could not reach base against Leever all afternoon and Leever didn't have to face the Phillies' other big bopper, Napoleon Lajoie, who missed the game because of a sore hand.[15]

Four days later at Expo, Sam threw a one-hitter against Boston, that sole hit being labeled a "fluke." In the second inning, Chick Stahl hit an easy bounder toward the second baseman, but the ball struck a pebble that sent it over Ritchey's head. Stahl made it safely to second base when shortstop Leach muffed Zimmer's accurate throw and Stahl came home on Freeman's out. The Beaneaters' Bill Dinneen allowed only three hits but lost, 2 to 1.

Just when things were going great for Leever on the field, he experienced one of the worst beatings of his career less than two weeks later in a game against the Phillies. Leever gave up five runs in the first inning and Jack Chesbro relieved him, only to allow 15 hits and 15 runs himself in a 23–8 loss. Honus Wagner even pitched the final three innings, allowing three runs, before the game was called after eight innings so the teams could catch their respective trains.

Phillippe pitched his best game of the season on July 11 when he shut out Brooklyn, 4 to 0, on four hits to run his record to 13 victories and 6 losses. That win over the defending champions pushed the Pirates past the Phillies in the National League standings, but they still trailed Brooklyn by seven and a half games.

Back in 1894, the Martinsville, Ohio, town team won a baseball game with the visiting Higginsport, Ohio, nine by a score of 4 to 3. The winning pitcher in that game was Samuel Leever, the school teacher at nearby Goshen. The losing pitcher for Higginsport was 20-year-old John W. Taylor, known familiarly as "Jack." The Martinsville victory set off a celebration among the residents, and the celebrants adjourned to the Lynchburg distillery. At the next meeting of the Goshen school directors, Sam Leever was voted an increase in his teacher salary and his catcher was made road supervisor.[16]

Both hurlers from that game in Stroup's pasture went on to pitch in the National League. It would take six years, but Jack Taylor would get a chance for revenge. This time, Taylor would pitch against Leever in a game at the West Side Grounds in Chicago on July 15, 1900. The game was played in a gale yet some 10,000 Chicagoans attended.

A pair of Chicago errors led to two runs for Pittsburgh in the top of the first inning. The *Chicago Daily Tribune* blamed "the high wind, which was blowing clouds of dust across the diamond" for Clingman's throwing error on Wagner's grounder that led to the two runs on the second error one batter later. "At that time it seemed as if the tragedy of Stroup's pasture was to be reacted."[17]

However, Pittsburgh shortstop Bones Ely made a wild throw in the bottom of the first with runners on second and third, and the score was suddenly tied. After that, Taylor was the master of the Pirates and the Orphans came away with a 5 to 3 victory to avenge his defeat in that Martinsville game some six years earlier.

Leever pitched well, allowed only five hits, but he couldn't pitch around Ely's two errors that allowed three runners to score. Another run came home in the fifth inning when "a heavy" wind blew Ely out of the path of Bradley's run-producing single.[18]

During the first part of his career in the National League, Taylor developed the reputation as "Pirate killer" and he would face off multiple times against Leever and Phillippe over the ensuing seasons. There were other pitchers that had the Pirates' number. Of course there was Christy Mathewson, for a time the best pitcher in all of baseball. Cincinnati's Bob Ewing and Patsy Flaherty of the lowly Boston Doves also experienced short runs of success against the Pirates. Taylor was a very good pitcher who experienced considerable success when matched against the Pirates' top pitchers, Leever and Phillippe, in the early part of the decade. And it wasn't just Leever and Phillippe who struggled in games against Taylor.

Ed Reulbach, Taylor's teammate in Chicago, recalled that Jack owned Honus Wagner. "Had Wagner been obliged to bat against Old Jack Taylor all through a season his average would have shrunk to .150," said Reulbach. "No other pitcher had Wagner's number as Taylor did. He would make Wagner so sore that the Dutchman frequently shifted and tried to hit left-handed. Honus simply could not guess Taylor right and he knew it."[19]

On August 13, 1900, Pittsburgh let a game against the Giants get away with Deacon Phillippe on the mound. The Deacon took a 4 to 1 lead into the visitors' half of the eight, but first baseman Tom O'Brien's wild throw set the New Yorkers up with runners on second and third. They scored on a single, and Piano Legs Hickman's inside-the-park home run gave New York the lead. Another four-bagger, this one by the Giants' Kip Selbach in the ninth inning, made the final score 7 to 4, New York.

Three days later, the Pirates opened a crucial series against Brooklyn at Exposition Park. Pittsburgh still trailed the Superbas by seven and a half games

Exposition Park with the Smoky City in the background (National Baseball Hall of Fame Library, Cooperstown, New York).

and counted on Phillippe to win the first of the three-game set. However, wild throws by Williams and O'Brien in the visitors' half of the first inning led to three runs and took the fight out of the Pirates. Phillippe departed the game after six innings and Pittsburgh lost, 8 to 0.

Pittsburgh recovered nicely the next afternoon behind Leever to even the series. The Pirates scored four runs in the first inning off Frank Kitson and Leever's breakers were a puzzle to the Superbas' hitters until the sixth inning. A wild pitch figured prominently in the first Brooklyn run, but Leever made up for it in the home half of the sixth when his two-out single send Ely home when the Superbas' second baseman muffed the return throw from the outfield. Leever weathered a late Brooklyn rally to gain the 5–3 victory.

After Jack Chesbro beat McGinnity in the series finale, 8 to 4, *The Sporting News* wrote, "Fully 8,000 people paid to see the contest, and 7,999 of them went away hoarse and fully satisfied. The other fellow had bet $2,000 against Pittsburgh and he was sad. The story of the bet was highly publicized."[20]

Despite ending the Brooklyn series on a high note, the Pirates seemed to lose any hope of catching the defending champions when they lost five of seven at the end of August. An especially disheartening loss occurred in Cincinnati on August 26. After breaking a three-game losing streak against the Reds at Exposition Park on Saturday, the two clubs took the train to Cincinnati in order to take advantage of the lucrative Sunday gate. The players arrived without any problem but the teams found themselves without an umpire for the contest. Sam Leever and Arlie Latham were pressed into service as emergency arbiters.

Phillippe pitched an outstanding game, but a walk to Cincinnati's leadoff batter in the first inning did him in. Following a sacrifice, Jake Beckley's single drove in what would be the only run of the game. Phillippe allowed only two singles the remainder of the contest, but the Reds' Noodles Hahn pitched around six Pittsburgh hits and his fielders pitched in with errorless support. The loss further reinforced the impression that Phillippe just couldn't win when he pitched on the Sabbath.

The Pittsburgh newspapers were unforgiving when it came time to critique the emergency umpires who had been thrust into a difficult situation. One local paper editorialized, "Had there been a regular umpire on hand there might possibly have been a different story to tell for both Leever and Latham made numerous blunders which possibly affected the score."[21]

On September 11, Leever shut out Philadelphia for the second time in 1900, permitting only three singles in his 2–0 win. "Sam made the Spalding do everything but talk," wrote Ralph Davis in the *Pittsburg Press*. "He had a great curve and all kinds of speed and with the assistance of Jack O'Connor mixed up the two styles in a manner that was distressing to the sluggers. His remarkable control was shown when Lajoie, in the seventh, fouled off eight good pitches before he knocked a fly to Williams."[22]

Leever also won his next three starts before his winning streak ended with an 8 to 3 loss in St. Louis on October 9. The day before, Phillippe had won his 20th game of the season in a strange game between the Pirates and Cardinals. He was matched up against Cy Young for the second time in three weeks, Phillippe having come out on top, 7–3, in the earlier contest on September 21.

The Pittsburgh hurler faltered only in the second inning when St. Louis scored twice to tie the game, 2–2. After the first inning, Cy Young held the Pirates hitless until the visitors won it in the seventh on Jimmy Williams' two-out double off the right field fence and O'Connor's single.

Upon the completion of the seventh inning, umpire Bob Emslie suddenly called the game because of darkness even though the sun was shining brightly. It appeared light enough for one more inning, maybe two, and many of the 3,000 angry St. Louis fans made a rush for the umpire, who was only saved from injury by the police and his adeptness at dodging thrown objects.

The Pirates completed September with 18 victories against only nine losses (winning five of their last seven), but the team's bad start was too much to overcome and catch the Superbas. Though the Pirates drew to within two games of the front-runners in September, Brooklyn's early lead in the race held up. Pittsburgh's outstanding finish left them 4½ games back, a solid second.

Jesse Tannehill, at 20–5, had the best record on a very deep Pirates pitching staff. Leever posted a won lost mark of 15–13 and Phillippe was 20–13. Only the stingy Cy Young allowed fewer walks per nine innings than Phillippe. Deacon gave up only 1.35 walks per nine innings on a pitching staff that gave up the fewest bases on balls and had the most strikeouts in the league.

Before the conclusion of the National League season, the *Pittsburgh Chronicle-Telegraph* proposed a best of five games post-season series to be played between the Pirates and Superbas at Exposition Park. Both teams accepted and the proceeds would be split among the players. Additionally, the winning club would receive a $500 trophy cup.

The regular season did not end until Saturday, October 13, so the post-season affair could not begin until the following Monday. Pittsburgh had won the season series against Brooklyn 11 to 8 with one tie, so Ned Hanlon and his Superbas were committed to win the series in three straight games to confirm their status as the best team in professional baseball. The Brooklyn players made no secret of the fact that they had commissioners in the grandstand for the express purpose of wagering large amounts of money on the games at Exposition Park.

Concerning the first game of the series, *Sporting News* correspondent A. L. Gheny reported that some of the Brooklyn players worked a "clever game" that added "no small amount of cash to their string."

"It was no common thing to hear one of their fellows offering to bet that the next ball pitched will result in a foul," noted Gheny. "Evidently the Brooklyn players knew of this, for on the opening day of the series two or three parties in the grandstand wagered their money regularly. As the story goes these sure thing gentlemen had arranged a code of signals with some of the batsmen, who are experts in the art of fouling balls."[23]

Brooklyn's submarine pitcher, Joe McGinnity, dominated the Pirates in the first game. He held a 5 to 0 lead after eight innings and had allowed only three hits. In the bottom of the eighth (Brooklyn was the home team for the opener) Pirates pitcher Rube Waddell attempted to run the base-runner, McGinnity, down between third and home. When Waddell slapped the tag on the Brooklyn pitcher, his knee struck McGinnity square on the temple. McGinnity was knocked out for three or four minutes, but recovered and returned to the mound for the ninth. Previously, he had been invincible, but he struggled through the final inning, allowing two runs on a hit batsman, two walks and two hits before he finally registered the final out.

Sam Leever drew the starting assignment for the second game a day later, but, as a report indicated, "Pittsburgh put up a miserable exhibition of ball playing." Cold weather held attendance down to 1,800, a decided drop from the 4,000 or so at game one. A walk by Leever, followed by his own wild throw, led to Brooklyn's first run in the second inning. Pittsburgh managed to tie the game, but lost it when the Buccaneers' defense fell apart in the sixth inning. Williams' wild throw and O'Connor's drop of Ely's throw to the plate that cost Pittsburgh an out, led to three runs. The final score was 4 to 2.

Although the weather was ideal for baseball, the two losses demoralized the Pirates' supporters and only 1,800 of the most faithful turned out for game three. McGinnity was the last pitcher to warm up before the game, but when it was announced Handsome Harry Howell would pitch for Brooklyn, the gambling odds shifted in favor of the Pirates. The Superbas' gambling associates who had already laid their money on Brooklyn lobbied for Hanlon to use McGinnity again and continued their pleas even after the game started.

At the close of the first inning, Joe Kelley and Hughie Jennings moved over to McGinnity and Kelly was heard to plead, "Now, Joe, go in there and win." But the Iron Man just shook his head and replied, "Not on your life.

With Phillippe pitching the way he is, you fellows can't overcome that lead of three runs."[24]

Phillippe continued his success against the champions by throwing a 10–0, six-hit shutout in which the Superbas did not make more than one hit in any inning. Lave Cross, who tripled in the second inning, was the only Brooklyn batter to reach third base, and he was out at home on first baseman O'Brien's outstanding play on Dahlen's bunt. In the seventh, Phillippe struck out Daly, Dahlen and Howell. It was the only game the Pirates won, and they lost the series three games to one.

Leever came back to start game four after only one day off and was ineffective, leaving after Pittsburgh fell behind Iron Man McGinnity, 6 to 1. Waddell replaced the Schoolmaster and got into a shouting match with Brooklyn third base coach Jimmy Sheckard, who had been heckling the Pirates' pitcher. Rube displayed his middle finger and the two antagonists charged toward one another. Umpire Tim Hurst stepped in between the two as other Pirates rushed to assist their teammate. Sheckard was ejected and the ruckus had no effect on the outcome of the contest that ended with the score still 6–1 in favor of Brooklyn.

In appreciation of his outstanding work during the season and in the series, the Brooklyn players unanimously decided to give the trophy cup to McGinnity. Each participant in the series received a $121 share of the gate and the Brooklyn club management gave McGinnity an additional $100 for his good work.[25]

Fred Clarke offered no excuses for the loss. "We lost the cup series on its merits and have no explanations to make. It is a great satisfaction to know that we rank as the second team in the official standings at the close of the race. That is something for a one-year team to be proud of."[26]

There was surprise that Jesse Tannehill did not pitch in the post-season series. Tannehill said simply he was not asked to pitch. It was no secret that the easily agitated Fred Clarke had problems with both Waddell and Tannehill and had told acquaintances that he particularly wanted to get rid of Tannehill.[27]

Although they lost the post-season *Chronicle-Telegraph* Cup games to Brooklyn, the Pirates were on the verge of an era of greatness. The club made just short of $70,000 in 1900, more money than any other National League club, and now could afford to hold on to their core players in the face of the American League intrusions. The Pirates could even make improvements at key positions.

Just when the Pirates completed the most successful season in their short history, a rift between the Pittsburgh club's owners and a serious challenge from a new major league cast a pale over the franchise. Earlier in the year,

National League owners made a huge miscalculation by refusing to listen to a proposal from American League president Ban Johnson for a new major league. An angry Johnson declared open warfare on the National League, recruited accomplished baseball men and began to raid the older league's teams of their star players by offering higher salaries. Helping to facilitate Johnson's efforts was the National League's unpopular $2,500 salary limit, out of which the players had to purchase their own uniforms.

The Players' Protective Association, in the persons of president Chief Zimmer, vice president Clark Griffith and secretary Hugh Jennings, along with their legal adviser, Judge Harry Taylor of Buffalo, sought an audience at the National League's fall meeting at the Fifth Avenue Hotel in New York. Among their demands were an increase of the minimum salary to $3,000 and free uniforms. The National Leaguers declared that their meeting was closed and tabled the Players' request. The union had already polled the players during the regular season and they unanimously agreed not to sign contracts for the upcoming season until notified by Secretary Jennings.[28]

As result of the National League's refusal to negotiate with the American League or the Player's Protective Association, Johnson's newly anointed major league signed more than a hundred National Leaguers, including such accomplished stars as Cy Young, Napoleon Lajoie, Wee Willie Keeler, Jimmy Collins, and John McGraw.

McGraw had been captain of the Baltimore Orioles, National League champions from 1894 through 1896. He and his Orioles teammates turned the game of baseball into a science, perfecting such plays as the Baltimore chop and the hit-and-run. On the other hand, the Orioles bullied other teams, brawled with opposing players and fans, and baited umpires. This style of behavior, win at any cost, became known as "rowdyism." Pirates manager Fred Clarke employed many of the same tactics in his early years as manager of the Colonels and Pirates.

When the National League contracted to eight clubs for 1900, Baltimore was dropped and McGraw was transferred to St. Louis by means of a trade. He did not want to play there because of his financial interests back in Baltimore. He reported to the Cardinals three weeks after the season started and, after he was injured, McGraw went to the racetrack instead of the ballpark.

John McGraw was ripe for the picking when he met with Ban Johnson in Chicago. McGraw continued to play for St. Louis during the 1900 season, but secretly acted as an American League recruiter. That November, Johnson gave McGraw the rights for an American League franchise in Baltimore, and he was allowed to stock it with players he recruited. He signed his own St. Louis teammate, Turkey Mike Donlin, Brooklyn's star hurler Joe McGinnity, and catcher Roger Bresnahan of Chicago. Ban Johnson sought to sign Honus Wagner, but the Pirates' star player liked Dreyfuss and playing near home enough to sign with the Pirates for about $4,000, less money than the Americans offered.[29]

Wagner practiced all winter for a clay bird shooting championship in his hometown of Carnegie. Then he made the mistake of inviting some of his teammates to the event at his brother's new shooting gallery. Wagner not only finished behind the expert marksman Sam Leever, but also placed behind center fielder Ginger Beaumont.[30] Beaumont was Leever's best friend from the old Pirates, and the Schoolmaster would become fast friends with his roommate Wagner, who like Leever was an avid quail hunter.

Baseball was Leever's first love, but his passion was shooting and he became an expert at the traps. Trapshooting derived its name from the device that hurls the clay targets into the air. Trap simulates the flight of a game bird flushed ahead of the shooter and, in fact, in the original version of the sport, live birds were released from holes in the ground covered with silk top-hats. By the turn of the twentieth century, trap shooting was especially popular among baseball players who participated in the sport during the off-season much as modern athletes play golf for recreation. Shooting would figure prominently in Leever's life.

"He is partial to the 'pump' gun," reported the *Pittsburgh Press*. "He says that when armed with such a blunderbuss he never shoots to hit the game at the first shot, but plugs a few charges in behind the animal first to get it going, and then plugs it for fair when it is at full speed."[31]

Leever's pride and joy was his pointer, "Pat." He swore that Pat was the most intelligent dog he ever saw, and Rube Waddell once offered him $130 for the animal. Leever wasn't about to part with the bird dog for any amount of money, but just before the start of quail season in the fall of 1903 Pat died, a victim of poison. The broken-hearted Leever offered a $100 reward for the identity of the person who poisoned his dog, but the culprit was not discovered."[32]

♦ FOUR ♦

A Pennant Comes to Pittsburgh

The baseball season of 1901 is generally conceded to be the first of the modern era. A major change on the field was a new foul strike rule that was instituted in the National League that season. Previously, any pitch fouled off by a batter was not counted as a strike. Thereafter, in the National League, a foul ball would be counted as a strike until the batter had a two-strike count. This rule change was designed to aid pitchers and shortened the length of games. Additional rules were added to force the catcher to remain behind home plate at all times, and a pentagon-shaped home plate replaced the old-style diamond design.

Like the foul strike rule, the change in dimensions of the plate was a distinct benefit to the pitchers. The old diamond-shaped plate had only been 12 inches wide, but the new five-sided design was 17 inches across. The cumulative National League batting average fell from .279 in 1900 to .259 a year later, and the pitchers' cumulative earned run average dropped from 3.69 to 3.32. The figures declined further in 1902, probably due to the defection of many of the league's top hitters to the American League. Though the latest changes brought the game to the basic rules that still exist today, the owners decided to retain only one umpire for a game, an unimaginable situation today.

Despite the optimism about the Pirates' prospects for the 1901 National League season, relations within the club's front office were strained, to say the least. William W. Kerr was dissatisfied with a subordinate role and jealous of the credit Barney Dreyfuss was receiving as club president. When there was an attempt to depose Dreyfuss and Pulliam at the stockholders' meeting in January of 1901, Barney used a technicality in New Jersey law (the Pittsburgh ball club and been incorporated in that state) to thwart the effort. As teller of the stockholders' meeting, Kerr was automatically disqualified by New Jersey law from becoming an officer or even a director of the club. The Kerr faction filed suit in New Jersey, but the affair was settled on February 18 when Dreyfuss and Pulliam purchased the stock of Mosara, Kerr, Auten and Tener for $35,000. A new stockholders' meeting was held at which Dreyfuss was re-affirmed as president and Pulliam was elected secretary and treasurer.[1] The immigrant who spoke only broken English gained controlling interest in one of baseball's best franchises at the age of 35.

Pirates officials were working to keep star players from jumping to the rival American League when it was learned that the team's first baseman had died from the effects of typhoid and pneumonia. Following the regular 1900 season, Tom O'Brien accompanied the New York Giants and Brooklyn Superbas to Cuba for a series of exhibition games. During the trip by ship to the island, the 27-year-old player fell ill. One of his teammates was said to have told O'Brien to drink sea water as a cure for sea sickness, and he consumed approximately three quarts. O'Brien was unable to play with the team in Havana because he was too ill and on his return the United States, a physician advised him to go to a dry climate in Arizona for his health. O'Brien died in Phoenix on February 3. *The Pittsburgh Dispatch* reported that the player died of consumption.[2]

Charles Phillippe was not highly regarded among the Pirates' top five pitchers the previous spring, and newspaper reports out of the Dakotas said that he had contracted smallpox during the epidemic of the recent winter. As of the second week in March, Phillippe was the only remaining starter from the 1900 club not under contract.

"Phillippe is in the wilds of South Dakota and has not been heard from for weeks," wrote the Pittsburgh correspondent for *The Sporting News* on March 12, "but Dreyfuss and Pulliam are willing to bet hats that he will join the Pirates at Hot Springs on April 1. The Deacon stands high with the management because he is always so willing to do his share of the work and never springs any of the stereotypical excuses so often used by star twirlers."[3]

Another week went by with no word from Phillippe, but when the team assembled to leave for spring training, he was on board. Despite the stories of his illness, Deacon reported to camp healthy and 15 pounds heavier than his playing weight of the previous season. As the players assembled, the Pirates were obviously affected the least of any National League team by raids by American League agents and prepared to go into training with the lineup of the previous season intact except for first base.

After coming close to a pennant in 1900, the Pirates were quite optimistic when they arrived by train for training in Hot Springs, Arkansas. The arrival of the 16 Pittsburgh players, led by Harry Pulliam, created quite a bit of excitement in the Arkansas city. The only absentees were Jimmy Williams,

Claude Ritchey, who had the measles, and catcher Jack O'Connor, who remained behind in St. Louis ostensibly for a mayoral election.

In Denver, Colorado, Jimmy Williams boarded the train to Hot Springs with a ticket provided by the Pirates. He never arrived because, en route, the player was shanghaied by American League agents who convinced him to jump to John McGraw's new Baltimore club. Jimmy's bride of three months, Pittsburgh native Nannie Williams, was astounded when she received a telegram announcing her husband was in Baltimore. His friend, shortstop Fred Ely, suggested that Williams backstabbed Dreyfuss after Williams was paid his entire 1900 salary despite the ankle injury and some Mt. Clemens rehab time.[4]

"I not only lose Williams, but I pay his fare east for McGraw to steal him from me!" grumbled Dreyfuss.[5]

Nestled in the foothills of the Ozark Mountains, Hot Springs was a popular resort because of its therapeutic mineral baths. It was also known for the casinos, horse racing tracks and bookmaking establishments, though the gambling houses were closed during the Pirates' first spring there. Hot Springs would be the Pirates' spring training site for each subsequent season Sam Leever and Deacon Phillippe remained with the club.

The Pirates' practice field was nestled between mountains and a small lake that added to the picturesque setting. A streetcar track ran between the baseball park and a deer park and ostrich farm on the opposite side of the track.[6]

During time off from the daily regime of calisthenics, running and practicing baseball, Sam Leever, Honus Wagner and Rube Waddell put on a trap shooting exhibition for the natives. Once, when Clarke sent the players out for a three-mile run, Waddell got lost. Since he had taken a gun along with him on the marathon, he went duck hunting and returned to camp with several trophies.[7]

"Eagle Eye" Jake Beckley had often boasted that he was the "boss trap shooter" among baseball players, and Leever's teammates urged him to challenge the old Reds mustachioed first baseman to a shooting match. This type of competition would require some type of wager and the frugal Leever was not about to risk his own money even if confident of victory. He indicated to his teammates that he might agree to a challenge match if they would guarantee the purse. The Pirates knew Sam was a good shot but were concerned about the rapid fire required in a regular trap shoot. The match never came off.[8]

Players back then participated in activities today's management would find incomprehensible. On April 5, the Pirates played an intra-squad game of football. In this game of "two-hand" touch, the team's star player, Honus Wagner, suffered a fractured nose and pitcher Rube Waddell sustained a sprained hip.[9]

Fine weather at Hot Springs lasted until the close of the training season. The rain that started up in the Ozarks followed the Pirates as they played their way north to Little Rock, then to Memphis, Dayton and Indianapolis, completely upsetting manager Clarke's training regimen.

When the Pirates arrived in Cincinnati for the season opener, the game was put on hold for two days because of rain, wind and cold. Not one to allow his team to sit idle, Fred Clarke secured the use of practice facilities at Fort Thomas, an army base across the river in Kentucky about five miles from the team's hotel. The Pittsburghers were provided with an armory with an earthen floor of 100 x 200 feet and they were able to put in three hours of practice.[10]

The first contest of the 140-game season was finally played in Cincinnati on April 20. The thermometer was down to freezing and the usual opening day street parade was cancelled. In an effort to dry the field, Cincinnati club officials set bonfires at each corner of the diamond and a large steam roller traversed the dirt portion of the field for much of the morning. The sun was shining by game time, but there were few women in attendance because of the cold and those that did attend were heavily coated and muffled. After a band played a few airs, Cincinnati Mayor Julius Fleischmann didn't waste much time with his speech to the 3,000 shivering "bugs" before he threw out the first pitch.[11]

Phillippe was expected to be Clarke's starting pitcher but it was cold-weather-challenged Sam Leever who drew the opening day assignment. Leever had something to prove after his poor performance at the end of 1900, defeats in his final two regular season starts and a pair of bad losses against Brooklyn in the post-season series. The Reds jumped on the uncomfortable Pirates hurler right from the start. The first four batters he faced hit safely, but Cincinnati got only one run. With no one out and runners on first and second Beckley whacked a double, but the runner that tried to score from first was nailed at home by Clarke's throw. Moments later Beckley was run down between third and home when he thought better about trying to score.

After his fielders bailed him out in the first inning, Leever's limb warmed up and he suffered only one lapse over the remainder of the contest, when opposing pitcher Noodles Hahn tripled in the fifth inning and scored on a sacrifice fly.

The Reds were up, 2–0, in the sixth inning when triples by Clarke, Wagner and William "Kitty" Bransfield, along with a couple of errors, netted the

Pirates four runs and the eventual victory. The Pirates' new first baseman, 26-year-old rookie Bransfield, banged out two hits, including one of the three-baggers.

The son of a Civil War veteran who lost a leg at the Battle of Gettysburg, Bransfield grew up working in a metal factory in Worcester, Massachusetts. He got his nickname as a child when his friends thought he looked like Billy the Kid after they saw the outlaw's picture in *Police Gazette*. They began calling Bransfield "the kid," which eventually became "Kitty" because of the way a German woman at the local candy store corrupted the sobriquet.[12] Another version of the story said that a reporter with impaired hearing thought he heard "Kitty" when someone said "Kid" Bransfield.

After only one game in Cincinnati, the Pirates moved on to St. Louis where the Cardinals defeated Rube Waddell, 10–4, in the season's second game. Phillippe finally got his chance against the Redbirds in the finale of the three-game set at Robison Field. When the visitors came to bat in the top of the ninth inning, Phillippe and the Pirates trailed, 4 to 3. Cowboy Jones retired the first two Pirates in the frame and Clarke was Pittsburgh's last chance. Fred did his bit by taking a fastball in the ribs. As Clarke went to first base, Ginger Beaumont assumed a position in the batters' box. Just minutes earlier Beaumont had robbed Dan McGann of a home run and now he held the fate of the game in his hands. Beaumont's bat was primed for the first pitch and his mighty swing sent the ball on a long ride.

"Like a shell from a 13-inch gun the sphere shot on a line to deep center and the hearts of the St. Louis rooters ceased to beat," recorded the *Pittsburgh Leader*. "On and out it sped, seeming to gain speed as it traveled. Heidrick ran like a fiend and made a frantic attempt to reach the ball as it whizzed over his head, but all in vain. With the whack that filled every heart with despair the leather struck the club house and by the time it was returned to the infield Beau had crossed the plate behind Clarke and defeat was turned into victory."[13]

Phillippe was pinch-hit for in the deciding inning so it was left to Jesse Tannehill to save the game. Two men reached base to start the ninth, but Art Nichols ran into his batted ball for one out and the Pirates completed a speedy double play to end the affair. The two clubs left St. Louis that evening by train to resume their hostilities at Exposition Park.

Heavy rains in Pittsburgh caused the cancellation of two straight games as the swollen Allegheny overran its banks and the Exposition Park playing field was submerged in as much as four feet of water. The left field bleachers even broke loose and floated aimlessly in the outfield. When Harry Pulliam arrived from St. Louis on Thursday there was so much water in the park the club secretary had to borrow a skiff to make his inspection tour. Pittsburgh College offered the use of its grounds to the opposing teams for practice until Expo was in shape.

A year earlier, long-time National League catcher Tim Donahue had predicted Pittsburgh would win the pennant because of the decided advantage of their ball park that was "situated in a river bottom and by the first of July that diamond is like an asphalt street. Second base is six feet lower than the home plate, and first and third each three feet lower. The lines to first and third are banked up like the cushions on a billiard table.... When that diamond banks hard those fellows will beat dozens of infield hits, for every man can bunt, and most of them can chop the ball, and they will be taking two bases on singles where their opponents will be stopped at first on many a two-bagger by the speed of the outfield."[14]

When the Pirates finally played their home opener against St. Louis on Saturday, April 27, portions of the outfield still under water were roped off and a ground rule of two bases was adopted for any batted ball that landed in one of the ponds. Despite having only eight hours' notice that the opening game at Exposition Park would be played, enthusiasm for the 1901 Pirates was evident from the standing room only crowd of 10,017 paid. Still, right and center fields were swamps and could not be used to accommodate any overflow from the packed bleachers.

After the Sunday off-day, Leever coasted into the top of the ninth inning with a 14 to 4 lead over St. Louis. Before the inning was over, the Pirates had "almost" suffered one the worst collapses in the history of the club. The trouble with Leever may not have been mental, but a result of the beating he had taken during the course of the game. In the second inning the Cards' Bobby Wallace hit a fierce line drive flush into Leever's ribs, and later in the contest the Schoolmaster was running the bases when he took a tumble that resulted in a black eye and scratches on his face.[15]

Leever's ninth-inning trouble began when he walked the opposing pitcher, "Wee" Willie Sudhoff. Crab Burkett beat out a bunt after which Heidrick flied out to center for the first out. Then came a succession of four singles followed by Otto Krueger's double that left the score at 14 to 9 with only one out and runners on second and third. Then the Pirates' defense did its part to abet the Redbirds' comeback. Ex-Pirate Pop Schriver grounded to shortstop Ely, who threw wild to first, and another runner counted. Art Nichols, the pinch-runner for Schriver, tried for second and was called safe when Ritchey botched O'Connor's throw. Another run scored on the play to make it 14–11. Leever struck out Sudhoff for the second out, but Burkett made his second single of the inning to plate yet another run. With the potential tying runner at bat and the Pittsburgh crowd in excess of 4,000 squirming in their seats, the game ended meekly when Heidrick hit one back to Leever. The relieved Schoolmaster tossed the ball to his first baseman to finish a hair-raising 14 to 12 victory.[16]

After defeating St. Louis in his first game of the season, Phillippe lost successive starts to the Cardinals and Orphans. However, the club was much more concerned about Rube Waddell, who had performed badly in games against St. Louis and Chicago.

Southpaw Waddell was the closest thing to a power pitcher on the Pirates' staff. Though he threw the fewest innings of the five Pirates starting pitchers in 1900, he led the National League in strikeouts with 130 (strikeout totals would substantially increase a year later when the foul strike rule went into effect). However, manager Clarke could barely tolerate the irascible Waddell even when he was winning games. After Waddell lost his first two outings of the 1901 season, allowing nine earned runs in only eight innings, Clarke could not bear the incorrigible left-hander any longer. The Pittsburgh players also were fed up with Waddell's antics, and things had gotten so bad that catcher Jack O'Connor wouldn't work behind the plate when Waddell pitched.[17]

Even the press called for Waddell's release. Criticism in the *Pittsburgh Chronicle Telegraph* was typical of the city's newspapers: "The Pirate officials should lose no more time fooling with Rube Waddell, but should put a tag on him and ship him back to Butler County. It is a certainty that the players have no confidence back of him and cannot play their game when he is in the box. This is natural, as there is no telling what Rube is liable to do. The least thing sends him up into the air, and games which should be victories are turned into defeats."[18]

On his first day back with the Pirates after he took an unauthorized visit to his parents' home in late April, Waddell took the mound at Exposition Park and was drubbed by the visiting Chicago Orphans, 8–3. Waddell did not get out of the first inning. With his father watching from the stands, Waddell retired the first batter of the game on an infield bounder, but there followed two singles, a wild pitch, and another base hit that plated two runs. Amid cries from the grandstand of "Take him out!" Waddell walked four of the next five batters. When a second runner was forced across home plate, Fred Clarke ran in from his outfield position, took the ball from Waddell and summoned Chesbro to pitch.[19] Following this fiasco, Clarke reportedly told owner Barney Dreyfuss, "Sell him; release him; drop him off the Monongahela Bridge; do anything with him you like, so long as you get him off my ball team!"[20]

That evening, Barney Dreyfuss sold the troublesome left-hander to the

Chicago club. The deal was kept a secret for two days so Rube could be escorted to the railway station to leave town with the Orphans.[21] Dumping the unmanageable pitcher wasn't as difficult a decision because of a National League rule that required clubs to reduce their roster to 16 players by May 1.

On a cold day at Chicago's West Side Grounds in early May, Sam Leever labored through eight innings and the Pirates went into their final at bat trailing, 7–5. After the first two batters went out, Wagner doubled down the third base line, and two singles and a double later, Pittsburgh was suddenly ahead, 8–7. Leever went back to the mound in the bottom half and was touched for two singles with one out. When Chicago's Barry McCormick drove a Leever pitch on a line into left field, the Orphans runner on second, Jack Doyle, thought the ball would fall safely and made a dash for home. Jesse Tannehill, playing the field between starts, gathered the liner in and threw to second base to double up Doyle and secure the victory for Pittsburgh.

In the stands that afternoon was Rube Waddell, the Orphans' new pitching acquisition. During the course of the game, Waddell frequently brandished a Smith and Wesson revolver he had just purchased. According to the *Chicago Daily Tribune*, "Some of the Pirates were alarmed, for 'Rube' had threatened to 'get even' with more than one man before leaving Pittsburgh."[22] Two days later, Waddell started against the Pirates and lost a 4 to 2 decision to a rookie hurler named Lewis Wiltse. It would be the only game Wiltse would win for the Pirates before he was sold to the Phillies that July.

Though he wasn't particularly effective in the early part of the season, Leever didn't lose a game until May 12 in Cincinnati. He did drive in the Pirates' only run of his 6–1 loss with a ninth-inning double. On May 30 Leever was wild and ineffective against Brooklyn before he was relieved by Jack Chesbro in the seventh inning. Pittsburgh rallied to win anyway, 4 to 3.

While the water-logged Pirates slogged along, the New York Giants were the early pace-setters with a sensational young pitcher named Christy Mathewson leading the way. Mathewson mostly relied on a drop curve, complemented by a good fast ball, but when he got into a jam he would go to his "slowball" that would seemingly suspend in the air then plummet down and away from the batter. The pitch would become known as Matty's "fadeaway" and in later years as a screwball.

However, there were problems in the Giants' clubhouse. Mathewson, a college man from Bucknell University, was unpopular with his teammates. Most players in those days had only rudimentary educations, and some of the Giants perceived the handsome collegian as conceited and aloof.

Pittsburgh ran into Mathewson and his "fadeaway" on May 21 at the Polo Grounds. The two-game series was marred by the conduct of the Giants' owner, Andrew Freedman, a notorious Tammany Hall politician. When the assigned umpire, Billy Nash, arrived at the Polo Grounds, the former Boston and Philadelphia third baseman found himself barred from the field on orders from Freedman. After an intense squabble, the two clubs agreed to use two reserve catchers, New York's John Warner and the Pirates' Chief Zimmer, as umpires. Pittsburgh had every right to protest the game, but the Pirates did not want to lose their share of a significant gate from the approximately 6,000 fans on hand.[23]

New York scored an early run when Tannehill dropped a fly ball in shallow right field with a runner on third. Mathewson went on to beat Deacon Phillippe, 2–1, for his seventh straight victory, but the outcome was in doubt until the final batter. Phillippe walked and stole a base off Mathewson in the seventh, but he died there when Leach made the third out. With one out in the Pirates' ninth, Honus Wagner tripled and scored on a wild pitch. The next two Pirates reached base, but Mathewson fanned Tannehill and Ely to settle the affair. However, Wagner's ninth-inning run snapped Mathewson's consecutive scoreless innings streak at 39.

On Pittsburgh's first eastern trip, they dropped seven out of 13 games and fell to fourth place. Up to June, Leever kept the Pirates close to the Giants with the best record on the staff at 11 wins and only 3 losses. On June 2, he beat his old teammate Rube Waddell at Chicago's West Side Grounds to launch Pittsburgh on a four-game winning streak.

In the victory over Waddell, Leever and the Pirates led Chicago 1–0 in the fourth inning when the Orphans put two runners on base with one out. When Cozy Dolan went out swinging at a Leever bender, Danny Green, the runner on second, took off for third base. Catcher Jack O'Connor's throw to Leach had the runner beat by five feet, but the ball bounced off Tommy's hands and rolled into left field. Clarke raced in and fired the ball to home plate. Green never stopped running and scored easily, but just as he reached the plate, on-deck batter Pete Childs got too close to the play and Clarke's throw glanced off his bat. Umpire Dwyer promptly called Green out for interference. The decision caused a stampede from the Chicago bench toward the umpire. The other baserunner, Charlie Dexter, started in from third but Leach kicked him and the pair mixed it up until their teammates pulled them apart. Though the local players and the crowd howled for blood, a riot was averted and Pittsburgh finished off an easy 6–1 victory. Leever gave up only five hits and lost his shutout on a cheap run scored by the Orphans in the ninth inning.

The first-place Giants came to Pittsburgh for a three-game series beginning June 10. Clarke had Phillippe, Leever and Chesbro penciled in to start the three games, while the Giants would pitch Luther Taylor, Christy Mathewson and Bill Phyle, the latter having five straight wins. In the opener, Phillippe took a 3–0 lead into the ninth inning, having allowed only three opposition hits to that point. Suddenly, he became hittable and a Van Haltren triple, followed by a single, put the Pirates' lead in jeopardy with only one out. A round-tripper by "Home Run" Hickman would tie the game, and he came close with a line drive that appeared bound for the left field corner. Third baseman Leach leaped into the air and got his glove on the smash but he couldn't cover it up with his free hand. The ball bounced over to shortstop Ely, who held Hickman at first and Selbach at third. The rally died as suddenly as it began when manager George Davis hit a pitch right to second baseman Ritchey, who started the game-ending double play.[24]

It didn't appear there would be a game the next day when a light rain fell throughout the morning, but the clouds parted around noon and a nice crowd of about 6,000 arrived to watch the contest. Two of the first three New York batters reached Leever for hits but they died on base when he enticed the next two batsmen to ground out. The Pirates quickly got to Christy Mathewson on Clarke's single and a one-out triple by Leach to right field. Leach then scored on Bransfield's single. Pittsburgh added two more runs in the second inning, and after Sammy Strang's single with one out in the first, Leever retired the next 14 batters.

When threatening storm clouds emerged in the west, "the race with the elements was one of the most exciting features of the contest," noted the *Pittsburgh Press*. It began to drizzle when the Pirates came to bat in the fourth inning, so they wasted little time in making three outs. The home town team raced for their positions so the fifth could quickly commence. As the Giants' first batter walked to the plate, it began to rain harder. New York manager Davis rushed up to Umpire O'Day and demanded that time be called. The umpire pointed to the crowded outfield bleachers and declared the game would proceed as long as people remained out in the open. Leever retired the Giants in order and as soon as the third out was registered the savvy fans, en masse, vacated the stands. O'Day promptly called time, and half an hour later awarded the game to Pittsburgh.[25]

Though he struck out only one batter, Leever's stuff had been so dominant that the Pirates' outfielders did not record a single putout. The rain-shortened shutout gave Leever a rare win over Mathewson and victories against the Giants' ace would be few and far between for Leever, Phillippe, and the rest of the Pirates' pitchers. A day later, Chesbro made it three straight over the Giants.

The Pirates experienced a mini-slump during a long eastern road trip toward the end of June. During three straight losses Pittsburgh hurlers allowed

33 runs. Two of the setbacks came in Brooklyn to allow the defending National League champions to pull within one and a half games of the first-place Pirates.

Deacon Phillippe took the mound at Washington Park in the finale of the three-game set on June 28 and not only pitched, but also batted his team to victory. In the fourth inning he came to bat with the bases loaded and two out. He promptly smacked a Jimmy Hughes pitch into center field and two runs scored to give Pittsburgh a 3 to 0 lead. In the bottom of the frame Fred Clarke made a "brilliant" running catch of Wee Willie Keeler's liner with a runner on base to prevent at least one Brooklyn run. Phillippe drove in two more runs in the sixth when he made another timely hit with Pirates on third and second.

Up to the eighth inning, Phillippe had allowed but four hits and appeared to have the game in hand with a 5 to 0 lead. However, the immense heat of that day began to take its toll. Tommy Leach had to retire after the seventh and Wagner moved from short to third. Ely had to come into the game at shortstop despite the fact that he began the day on the bench with a hurt finger.

The Superbas' comeback began in the eighth inning when the opposing pitcher beat out an infield hit with one out. Zimmer muffed a foul ball off the bat of Joe Kelley and the star first baseman used the reprieve to drive out a single. One run scored and Kelley took second on the throw to home plate. With none out, runners on second and third, and Keeler, Sheckard and Daly due to bat, the Brooklyn fans took heart. All three grounded to Ely, and though the two runners scored, Phillippe escaped the inning with a 5 to 3 lead. In the home half of the ninth, three quick outs brought the game to a sudden end. The defending champion Superbas did not seriously challenge the Pirates for first place over the remainder of the season.[26]

The Pirates won 11 of 14 from eastern clubs and sustained their lead in the pennant race for the rest of the season except for a half-day on July 4. While the Pirates were on the road in Boston, a vicious wind storm struck western Pennsylvania. A section of the grandstand at Exposition Park was blown away and Barney Dreyfuss rushed back to Pittsburgh to have a new stand erected before the big July 4 doubleheader against the Giants.

The Pirates lost the first game of the morning-afternoon Independence Day twin bill before an Exposition Park crowd of 12,466. Mathewson outlasted Tannehill and Chesbro in a 12-inning, 5–3 Giants win that put New York in first place by percentage points.

A rainstorm that began just after the conclusion of the morning's extra-inning battle did not completely run its course until after three o'clock. By game time for the afternoon contest, the Exposition Park field was a muddy bog. However, thousands of excited fans gathered outside the gates insisting on being allowed into the park despite the steady drizzle. Hoping to avoid a riot and damage to his ballpark, Dreyfuss ordered the gates opened and tickets were sold. There were even a few hundred patrons who wandered over from the nearby site of the Ringling Brothers Circus after its matinee performance was cancelled due to the rain. Copious amounts of sawdust and cinders were spread on the base lines and a crowd of 7,500 scrambled for the rain-soaked bleachers and grandstand seats to root their Pirates back into first place.[27]

The Giants were not enthusiastic about playing in the mud and their performance showed it. The Pirates sent nine batters to bat in the first inning and tallied four runs, the key play being Dummy Taylor's slip in the mud fielding Lefty Davis' bunt that allowed the Pirates to load the bases with no one out. Pittsburgh added three more runs in the second and Leever coasted in the Pirates' 12 to 0 romp.

"These Smokeville chaps have a shade the best of us in the mud," said the Giants' Charley Hickman. "They're used to it. In the spring of the year when the river rises they play games with a foot of water in the outfield. Fred Clarke told me that Hans Wagner can wade as fast as Chief Zimmer can run."[28]

Deacon Phillippe beat the Giants the next afternoon, but the game was marred by controversy in the very first inning. As in Leever's game less than 24 hours earlier, the Pirates started fast against George Phyle. With runners on first and second with one out, Hickman's grounder to shortstop appeared to set up an easy double play, but Lew Carr's hasty throw to first was dropped by Bransfield. However, the game's sole umpire called Hickman out at first, sending the Giants into a rage.[29]

"Two teams and their substitutes and 4,000 spectators saw him do it, but umpire Colgan who turned towards the plate as soon as the ball reached the first baseman's glove called the runner out," admitted a Pittsburgh scribe. Giants manager George Davis argued so vehemently he was ejected.

The Pirates scored three runs in the first inning and Philippe got into the act in the second when his long fly allowed a teammate to tag up from third base and score to make it 4 to 0. Pittsburgh won easily, 7 to 2.

After the game, the New York manager said his team would not take the field for the Saturday game if Harry Colgan was the umpire. National League President Nick Young, who was in the pocket of the New York ownership, notified Colgan not to appear on the Pittsburgh grounds for the final game of the series. Barney Dreyfuss had not heard from Young so he threatened Davis with forfeiture of the game if the Giants did not play. However, when

Four ♦ A Pennant Comes to Pittsburgh

Colgan was a no-show at the ballpark, the Pirates became more concerned about losing a large Saturday gate than the identity of the umpire. President Dreyfuss agreed that Pirates catcher Jack O'Connor and a Giants reserve infielder named Charlie Buelow could serve as umpires for the day's game. The game was played without controversy and the Giants lost again, this time to Chesbro, 6 to 2.[30]

Though things were going great for his team, Sam Leever had a rough second half of the season. On June 19, he had to leave a game at the Polo Grounds in the third inning after being hit on the arm by a Mathewson delivery. He initially claimed Mathewson hit him on purpose because the Schoolmaster had shut the Giants out two weeks earlier in Pittsburgh.[31]

Thereafter, the Pirates' leading winner to that point in the season was plagued with soreness in the right arm and shoulder. Though the Mathewson pitch contributed to his problem, Leever later admitted the long-term effect was due to a relief stint in Philadelphia on June 29 when he came into a game without time to warm up sufficiently. After a valiant effort in a 14 inning 4 to 2 home loss to Philadelphia on July 12, he went on the shelf for nearly two months.

"Christy Mathewson helped to lose yesterday's game," opined the *Pittsburgh Press*. "Sam Leever, who pitched it, is still suffering from a sore arm. Matty put his wing out of commission early last month by soaking him with a speedy inshoot and Sam was nearly all in when yesterday's game ended. He did not have speed at any time during the afternoon and saved his arm by using a cross fire, which proved effective. It might have been a wise move to relieve him after the ninth inning, but Clarke kept him on the rubber because he was successful without speed."[32]

Though unable to pitch, Leever still managed to contribute to the team as a base coach. The job of the coach was to make the baserunner aware of the game situation, the location of the ball, and strategy. Unlike other base coaches, Leever yelled encouragement to the hitters, pressing them to make the most of their at-bat. Leever also had the peculiar habit of trailing a baserunner around the circuit after a safe hit. "He gets behind a runner and follows him all around the bases — a pace-pusher, as it were," explained the *Cincinnati Post*.

During a game against Cincinnati on July 25, 1901, Umpire Hank O'Day warned Leever several times about pacing the base runner. After the sixth ultimatum from the umpire to stay off the diamond, Leever was ordered off the field for the remainder of the game.[33]

Instead of forcing Leever to work after his arm was injured, the Pirates went out and secured another capable hurler to fill the void while he recuperated.

That June, the Pirates traded reserve infielder Elmer Smith to the New York Giants for veteran left-handed pitcher Ed Doheny. According to Ralph Davis, the Giants gave up Doheny so cheaply because "he allowed the social pleasures to steal his vitality and he was labeled 'all in' by Freedman."[34]

Barney Dreyfuss preferred pitchers that used a sidearm motion, and the southpaw Doheny had that type of delivery out of which "the ball came up wickedly" with a "nasty shoot" that drove many a batter away from the plate.[35] He won six games and lost only two for Pittsburgh over the second half of the season. Because of the National League's 16-player limit, Doheny pitched for Pittsburgh without a contract until reserve shortstop Lewis Carr was released to make room for the Pirates' new hurler.

After Leever sat down due to injury, Phillippe increasingly became the number one pitcher on the staff, winning 14 of his first 18 decisions. "Good old Deacon Phillippe, with his strong right arm, pulled the team out of at least two dangerous holes on the Eastern trip," wrote the *Pittsburg Chronicle-Telegraph*. "The Deacon is a great favorite with the fans, and his popularity is the result of good hard, honest work."[36]

During the 1901 season Honus Wagner became a shortstop. That spring, Tommy Leach was moved from the outfield to third base to fill the spot vacated by the defection of Jimmy Williams. In June, Clarke convinced Wagner to move from right field and replace an ailing Leach at third.

On July 25, Barney Dreyfuss unceremoniously released Bones Ely, the Pirates' regular shortstop since 1896. The infielder's output at the plate had declined, but he still was a fine defensive player even at age 38. Ely condemned the owner for his decision, but later it was revealed that the player was released because he had agreed to jump to the American League and offered to persuade teammates to join him.

Dreyfuss later revealed that he had received a tip that American League agents had infiltrated his team and planned to recruit as many Pirates as would agree to jump leagues. The club president immediately put contracts before the Pittsburgh players, who were given the option to sign a contract through the 1902 season or leave the team. Every one of the Pirates signed a new contract. The two players fingered as agents dealing with the American League were Ely and catcher Jack O'Connor. Ely was released, but O'Connor was retained despite his questionable loyalties.[37] More importantly, the dismissal of Ely precipitated the move of Honus Wagner to the shortstop position.

The move of Wagner to the infield opened up the right field spot for Alfonzo "Lefty" Davis. Davis was batting only .209 for the Brooklyn Superbas when he was released that June. Deacon Phillippe, who played with Davis when the two were with Minneapolis, urged Fred Clarke to give Davis a trial.

Clarke then asked Dreyfuss to sign Davis as an extra outfielder so Wagner could devote all of his time to playing the infield. Phillippe's confidence proved out when Davis batted .313 and displayed a strong throwing arm as he became the Pirates' regular right fielder the remainder of the 1901 season.[38]

The National League assigned two umpires to officiate the series between first-place Pittsburgh and second-place St. Louis that began on July 26 at Robison Field. In game one Phillippe was given a six-run cushion before the Cardinals even came to bat, but after that it was downhill for him and the Pirates. The Cardinals' four-run rally in the third inning was abetted when the home team's players prevented catcher O'Connor from retrieving Ritchey's overthrow when it rolled under their bench. While O'Connor and the Cardinals were in a shoving match, Bransfield ran over to recover the ball, but two runners scored and the batter made it to third. O'Connor argued vehemently with Umpire O'Day, who he felt should have called interference on the opposition. Patsy Donovan attempted to push the irate catcher away from the umpire and the two players began to grapple with one another. Cardinals pitcher Ed Murphy reached over Donovan's shoulder and sucker-punched the Pittsburgh catcher in the jaw, knocking him out cold. When O'Connor shortly came to, he went after Murphy and players had to restrain him until the police arrived. Murphy was the only player ejected and was fined $5 for his actions.[39] With Pittsburgh clinging to a 6 to 5 lead, Chesbro came out instead of Phillippe for the fourth inning. St. Louis ultimately prevailed, 12 to 7.

Pittsburgh evened the St. Louis series behind Tannehill a day later, and Honus Wagner played his first game as the Pirates' shortstop. He handled ten chances flawlessly and participated in two double plays. The *Pittsburgh Press* noted that Wagner "acted as though he had played the position for years."

Phillippe came back to start the Sunday game in St. Louis with only one day's rest. A crowd of 21,372, many of them armed with horns, cow bells or megaphones, was the largest to witness a game at the Mound City's National League grounds. A weakened Phillippe was again ineffective in the loss by a score of 5 to 3. The Pirates were particularly incensed because they felt the Cardinals' Crab Burkett went out of his way to spike catcher Chief Zimmer when he scored one of the St. Louis runs.

St. Louis owner Frank DeHaas Robison promised his players a cash bonus if they beat the Pirates in three of the four games, but Chesbro salvaged the finale for Pittsburgh on Monday with an 8 to 0 shutout. Pittsburgh left town with the same three-game lead over St. Louis as when they arrived on Friday.

Following a Pirates victory over the Reds in a Sunday game at Cincinnati's League Park that August, the opposing players were timed while running from home plate to first base. The fastest time for the 90-foot sprint was three seconds flat, logged by Ginger Beaumont, the Pirates' leadoff hitter. Beaumont's chunky build (5'8", 190 pounds) belied the blazing speed that made him so adept at beating out infield hits. Beaumont would lead the National League with a .357 batting average in 1902, and scored 100 or more runs each season from 1900 to 1903, with a league-high 137 in 1903. When he first broke in with Pittsburgh, opposing ballplayers teased him because of his given name—"Clarence, Clarence, don't dirty the seat of your pants." Clarence became "Ginger," the nickname given him by Barney Dreyfuss because of his aggressive style of play.

Beaumont was probably Leever's closest friend on the Pirates before and after the merger with the Louisville Colonels. A. R. Cratty wrote that the pair were "firm friends," and Patsy Donovan, their manager in 1899, recalled that Leever and Beaumont often "sat in their room at night and while Sam played *Arkansas Traveler* on the fiddle, Beau smashed jokes to the heart's content."[40]

Before the Pirates left Cincinnati, Leever paid a visit to Secretary Harry Pulliam. The Schoolmaster shocked the Pirates executive by asking to be laid off without pay while nursing his ailing arm. Pulliam would not discuss such an arrangement and told Leever he would get his full 1901 salary whether he pitched another game or not.[41]

During the time Phillippe was given to rest his arm, the Philadelphia Phillies made a strong rush and moved to within one game of the Pirates' league lead. After Ed Doheny beat the Cubs' Rube Waddell, 5–1, on Sunday, August 11, the Pirates received a welcome break. The schedule gave the players six days of pleasure and relaxation at Atlantic City to get their minds off the pennant race. President Dreyfuss personally conducted the 20 players (except Ginger Beaumont who was given permission to go home instead) to the resort city. To keep the players sharp, the Pirates played three games against a local independent team. The third game in the resort city drew an estimated 5,000 spectators.

On Sunday, August 18, Leever attempted to pitch in Cincinnati, but in warming up he found that he could not curve the ball without wrenching his right arm, so he had to give up the effort. When the Pirates moved on to St. Louis, Leever remained in Cincinnati, "having his arm rubbed daily by a specialist."[42]

On August 22, it was reported that the "surgeons ... have been unable to bring the (Leever's) wing around." A discouraged Leever told reporters, "I think my pitching days are over. My arm is lame and weak, and if I had my way about it I would go home and stay there. But the club wants me to stay and is willing to pay my salary, even if I don't pitch another game this season."[43]

The day of the bad news about Leever, Phillippe pitched his first regulation game in almost three weeks. He did not allow St. Louis a hit in the first six innings, and only in the seventh did the Cardinals break through with a pair of runs on three singles. The bottom of the ninth started out badly for Phillippe when consecutive singles put runners on first and third. With none out and the tying runners on base, a large cheer went up from the crowd when the Cards' Dick Padden sent a shot right over second base that appeared to be a sure safety.

"While the crowd looked on, amazed, Wagner fairly hurled his burly form in the path of the ball back of second base, scooped it up before any one realized what had happened, touched second base and with a quick, true throw to Bransfield, completed a double play."[44]

The runner on third scored, but Phillippe retired McGann on a routine fly ball to preserve Pittsburgh's 4 to 3 victory. Harry Pulliam called Wagner's game-saving play "one of the greatest stops and double plays ever made." Phillippe's victory made it three of four over St. Louis and dropped the Cardinals to five and a half games out of first. They were not a factor in the pennant chase after that series.

The pairing of Wagner with second baseman Claude Ritchey would give the Pirates a solid combination at the keystone sack for the next five seasons. Wagner's good friend Ritchey was best known for his fielding prowess. He was first among all National League second basemen in fielding percentage five times between 1902 and 1907, as well as the league leader in double plays twice for the Pirates. Ritchey also gained somewhat of a reputation as a clutch hitter, and Honus Wagner once commented, "Claude was never a great hitter except in a pinch. But then is when you could bet on him. That is why the fans gave him the name of Little All Right."[45]

In the final week of August, the Pirates received a report from Cincinnati that Sam Leever had been killed in a railway accident. In short order Harry Pulliam received a letter from Leever, stating, "There is absolutely no truth in the rumor."[46]

Leever would finally start a game again for Pittsburgh on September 6. From September 4–6, the Pirates played three doubleheaders on consecutive days against the Giants in New York, sweeping all six games. The Pirates destroyed the Giants by scores of 12–6, 10–3, 15–1, 15–7, 15–2 and 13–4 in games pitched by Tannehill, Chesbro, Doheny, Ed Poole, Leever, and George Merritt. Wagner collected 15 hits in the series and started a triple play in the nightcap on September 5 after a diving stab of a line drive. In his first game since July 12, Leever pitched a complete game in the Pirates' 15–2 win on September 6, but he was obviously not up to his previous form.

The victories in New York extended the Pirates' win streak to ten games, but the Phillies were on a nine-game winning streak of their own. Philadelphia was four and a half games behind Pittsburgh when the Pirates came to the Quaker City for a three-game set to begin the day after the Giants series. The Phillies gained another game on the leaders when their ace, Al Orth, defeated Phillippe in the series opener on September 7. However, the Pirates unlimbered their bats and Tannehill and Leever were recipients of all that offense in 11–5 and 8–5 victories the next two days. Philadelphia never got closer than five games thereafter, and the Pirates finished them off for good with three straight wins at Exposition Park a week later. Phillippe got his revenge in the opener, beating Orth, 5 to 1.

Behind Deacon Phillippe, Pittsburgh defeated the Brooklyn Superbas on September 27 at Exposition Park to clinch their first-ever National League pennant. It wasn't an easy win as the Pirates entered the bottom of the eighth inning trailing 4 to 2. Brooklyn had scored two runs to take the lead in the seventh largely due to an error by Wagner in his haste to make a quick play. When the Pirates came to bat in the eighth, Brooklyn's Frank Kitson had been untouchable since the third inning. Lefty Davis was up first and he brought the crowd to its feet with a liner to deep left-center field that rolled all the way to the fence. It could have been an easy home run had Davis not fallen after passing second base, and he had to settle for a triple. Kitson worked carefully to Fred Clarke and the Pirates' field boss drew a walk. The dangerous Ginger Beaumont tapped a pitch back toward the mound that took one bounce right to the Brooklyn pitcher. Kitson dropped the ball but recovered in time to catch Davis in a run-down between third and home. Davis darted back and forth, dodging several Superbas, until he was finally tagged out. However, his actions allowed Clarke and Beaumont to move up to third and second. Next up was Wagner, carrying a huge club nicknamed the "Dutchman." The mighty shortstop was determined to atone for his error that had allowed Brooklyn to take a lead in the contest. Kitson straightened and sent a fast pitch toward the plate.

"There was a crash that startled the patrons of the Exposition," reported the *Leader*. "The ball sped like lightening, shot past Kitson and over second base into the outfield; and while the frenzied fans shouted like mad Clarke and Beaumont crossed the plate with the runs that tied the score."[47]

The Superbas center fielder fumbled the ball and by the time he returned it to the infield, Wagner had taken second base. Next up was Bransfield. He too made solid contact with a Kitson pitch and singled to left field, sending Wagner racing toward home plate. The *Leader* was led to proclaim, "A cannon shot single from the bat of first baseman 'Kitty' Bransfield battered down the last barrier between Pittsburgh and the baseball championship and drove in the all-important tally that gave the Smoky City her first pennant."[48]

However, the game wasn't over. Pittsburgh only held a 5-4 lead and Deacon Phillippe still had to retire the Superbas in the top of the ninth. When the first Brooklyn batter reached on an error and the next man singled, the 4,000 fans in the stands held their collective breath. Kitson tried to sacrifice the runners, but his bunt in front of the plate bounded into the hands of Chief Zimmer, who made a snap throw to third base for the force out. Wee Willie Keeler tried to punch a pitch over the infield, but Wagner backed up and corralled the little fly. The final obstacle to the championship flag was Jimmy Sheckard, but he could only manage a grounder to Ritchey, who tossed to Wagner for the force at second.

"Cheer after cheer rent the air," a correspondent said of that moment, "and, as the victorious Pirates made a rush for the clubhouse, a loud ovation was accorded each and every one for his part in landing the coveted flag."[49]

The crowd that attended the game spread the good word, and newspapers posted announcements on their bulletin boards that the pennant had been won. All the local morning editions had front page spreads about the champion Pirates. A large crowd was expected to honor the champions at Saturday's contest with Brooklyn, but the game was rained out.[50]

A much larger crowd than attended the pennant-clinching game honored the players at the final home game of the season on October 2. It was "Railroad Day" at the park and neither the threatening weather nor drizzling rain restrained the enthusiasm of the railroaders, who turned out in force. A long procession of carriages and tally-hos delivered rooters to Exposition Park. Preceding the game, the Railroad Club presented the champions with a handsome silver trophy cup as an expression of appreciation. The Pirates and the visiting Boston Triumvirs went through the motions of playing a game. Leever pitched for the home team, which came out on top, 8 to 4.

The Pirates, with the National League's best pitching (southpaw Tannehill and Phillippe finished first and second in earned run average, while Leever and Chesbro were one-two in winning percentage), captured their first pennant by a comfortable 7½ games over the Philadelphia Phillies. Leever went 14 and 5, but was limited to only 20 starts. Phillippe led the club in wins with 22 and completed 30 of the 32 games he started. He gave up only 38 bases on balls in 296 innings pitched, and over his last seven games allowed a total of only four walks with no walks in three successive games.[51]

"The success of the Pittsburgh club in 1901 was mainly due to the pluck, energy and unwonted liberality of financial expenditure in securing a winning team for his club which marked the work of its enterprising and persevering

1901 National League Champions. Top row: Chesbro, Zimmer, Merritt, Phillippe, Poole, Wagner, Yeager. Middle row: Burke, Doheny, Clarke, O'Connor, Bransfield. Bottom Row: Davis, Leach, Tannehill, Beaumont, Ritchey (National Baseball Hall of Fame Library, Cooperstown, New York).

president, Mr. Dreyfuss," wrote Henry Chadwick, editor of the 1901 *Spalding's Guide*. "Moreover, it was more harmonious as a team than its adversaries and did less kicking, the latter being a weakness that characterized every team in the league in 1901 to a more or less extent."[52]

There would be no Chronicle Cup series for the 1901 pennant winners, nor would there be any other type of post-season championship games for the newly crowned champions. On October 4 a crowd of nearly 6,000 (5,000 paid) entered Exposition Park to honor their new champions in the Pirates' "second annual field day." There was a parade, several athletic events with the players as participants, a greased pig chase, and a farcical pick-up baseball game between two teams made up of Pirates. Wagner, Davis and Beaumont finished at the top of most of the throwing and running contests, but there also was a shooting contest in which Leever, Phillippe, Beaumont and Wagner all tied, breaking eight targets each.[53]

Following the regular season, the entire Pirates team went on a two-week barnstorming trip through Pennsylvania, a sort of victory tour. The Pirates played local amateur teams in Homestead, Charleroi, Johnstown, Altoona, DuBois, Jamestown, Warren and Greenville. Leever, Phillippe, Chesbro, Tannehill and Doheny pitched in every exhibition game and Wagner even took a turn on the mound in the game at DuBois. The tour and field day netted an additional $1,400 that was divided among the Pirates players. The barnstormers returned to Pittsburgh on October 15 to attend a dinner given by Barney Dreyfuss at the exclusive Hotel Schenley.[54]

Phillippe's annual trips to his sheep ranch[55] in South Dakota diminished in length as the years went by. Unlike many of his teammates, he tolerated the smoke-filled air of the city and preferred to spend his winters in the Pittsburgh area. At the start of the baseball season, he took quarters at the Brunswick Hotel in Allegheny, only five minutes from the ballpark. However, that fall Phillippe relocated to the fashionable neighborhood of Oakland.

Phillippe was a raw-boned, green, country boy when he first came to Minneapolis wearing a derby hat so large it covered his ears. It was once written that the first time he had a soda at a local drug store he tried to blow off the foam. Within a couple of years though, the up-and-coming star player was fully initiated in city life. One story held that after he moved to the Smoky City, he fully underwent a transformation and "he became used to appearing on the public highways in flaming red neckties, clean shirts and slender canes."[56]

At 29 Phillippe was still a bachelor, though rumors persisted he had a lady friend in Oakland. He grew weary of the gossip about his romantic prospects and when a rumor made the rounds that he had married, he said nothing to refute it.

Phillippe's best friend on the Pirates was the affable Dutchman, Honus Wagner. Both loved hunting and began to spend considerable time together during off-seasons indulging in shooting matches, hunting for game, and other pursuits. The pair was also included in a tight-knit group on the Pirates that played pinochle during the baseball season's down times.

Another close friend for all the years Phillippe remained in Pittsburgh was manager Fred Clarke. Clarke's disciplinarian ways grated on many players, especially nonconformist types like Rube Waddell and Jesse Tannehill, but the laid-back Phillippe stayed in shape and always wanted the ball when the club needed him.

After baseball was done for 1901, Clarke, Wagner and Phillippe were inseparable, meeting at their headquarters in the Smith Building to discuss the day's events, dreaming of hunting, or planning trips to Carnegie to face the traps. When a live shoot of birds was cancelled because of bad weather,

Clarke and Phillippe spent the day ice skating at the Duquesne Garden in preparation for Clarke's plunge into the sport of ice hockey.

Phillippe had learned to play ice hockey in his youth in South Dakota and was an accomplished skater. He and Clarke regularly reported to the rink, and Clarke quickly became a good skater and stick man. The activity was also of great benefit to Phillippe as the fast pace of the game built up his endurance and mental acumen. He would report to the next spring training in perhaps the best condition of his career.[57]

In mid–February Clarke made his debut as a hockey player with the Bankers' team of the Western Pennsylvania League against the Quaker City team of Philadelphia. Reports indicated Clarke handled himself creditably.

Phillippe kept moving about between watching Clarke and Wagner rehearse and perform. On Saturday, February 8, he was among a crowd of 2,000 in Carnegie watching Honus play basketball for a local team in a game with the unbeaten five from Steubenville, Ohio.[58]

When it came time to report for spring training at Hot Springs, the trio was fit and ready. And the result would be the most one-sided championship season in the history of major league baseball.

♦ Five ♦

The Best Pitching in Baseball

A winter storm in late January 1902 left downtown Pittsburgh in a blanket of white, and the girls from the high school on Fifth Avenue anxiously streamed outside at the end of the morning session to frolic in the freshly fallen snow. Their play quickly evolved into a game of snowball tossing. Momentarily, a tall, distinguished gentleman happened to walk by. He smiled at one of the "prettiest girls nearest to him" and she responded with the shout, "Give it to that big fellow, girls!" The young women's attention was directed at the man, who found himself caught in a crossfire of projectiles from the snowball-wielding females. The well-dressed gentleman took a few hits, but little did the girls know they had picked for their target perhaps the hardest-throwing pitcher on the Pittsburgh Pirates baseball team — Charles "Deacon" Phillippe.

After Phillippe arrived at the Smith Building and dusted the snow off his overcoat, he had a story to tell. "Dodging (snowballs) was like trying to stop a hitting streak when the boys have their eye in. The only way, as they say out West, was to dive in and do the Roman act. I did so. You see my arm has had a long rest and I sent home a couple of warm ones. Of course I didn't want to hurt the recipients, but lest they forget, as that English poet says, I sprinkled a little speed on the ones delivered to the most active girls."[1]

The forecast for the 1902 National League season was a bright one for Phillippe and the Pittsburgh Pirates. During the recent winter, National League clubs again lost many players to the American League raiders. That is, every club except Pittsburgh. The Pirates, en masse, remained in the fold, largely because Barney Dreyfuss had "persuaded" them to sign contracts for the 1902 season midway through the summer of 1901.

"I have no fear that any members of the Pittsburgh club will desert," Dreyfuss said early in the season. "The men have two-year contracts, calling for nice figures. They have been well treated and I see no reason why they should desire a change."[2]

Nor would the so-called union, the Players' Protective Association, be a thorn in the owners' sides. The opportunity for players to jump to the new league for larger contracts not only hurt the National League, but the better paid stars soon lost interest in a union. Even the former president of the organization, Chief Zimmer, and one of its most prominent members, Fred Clarke, had given up on the Association by 1902.

Just before the new season opened, Dreyfuss noted, "Not a member of the Pittsburgh team, unless it be Tannehill, has belonged to the Players' Protective Association since last spring. The union is defunct in the League."

The Pittsburgh club even secured a couple of players from the American League. Catcher Harry Smith came from the Philadelphia Athletics, and a promising shortstop named "Wid" Conroy signed with the Pirates after spending 1901 with the Milwaukee Brewers of Ban Johnson's league.

William Conroy acquired the nickname "Widow" as one of the older boys on his sandlot team and was known as "Wid" throughout his professional career. In 1900 Connie Mack invited Conroy to try out for his Milwaukee team in the Western Association and took Wid to Philadelphia when the American League became a major circuit a year later. The addition of Conroy to the Pirates was also said to be responsible for Ginger Beaumont's off-season training regimen that led him to lose 15 pounds because he was afraid he was going to be benched so Wagner could return to the outfield.[3]

The 1902 Pirates did have a problem in right field and fielded a less than distinguished catching corps. Over the course of the season, a talented Pirates pitching staff had to work with four different receivers; England native Harry Smith was able to catch in only 50 games because of a sore arm; 35-year-old Jack O'Connor was behind the plate in 42 games; 41-year-old Charles "Chief" Zimmer caught 41 games; and rookie Ed Phelps became the number one backstop after joining the club in September. O'Connor and Zimmer were veterans who knew every batsman in the league and could usually call the most effective pitch to use against them. Through the use of banter throughout an at-bat, the old-timers had a knack of rattling an opposing player into swinging at a bad pitch.[4]

The Pirates opened the regular season on April 17 by edging the Cardinals, 1 to 0, before 10,000 wildly enthusiastic St. Louis fans. Deacon Phillippe, on the way to his fourth 20-victory season in a row, drew the starting assignment for the defending champions.

John Farrell led off the home team's first with a single and was sacrificed to second base. The big crowd was expectant of an early score and generated a great noise from horns and cheers. "Phillippe grinned one of those sardonic grins which used to rile the Cardinals," noted the *Pittsburgh Leader*, "and the three corkscrew benders he served up to Hartman no living man could handle. Hartman laid down his bat with disgust written plainly all over his face."[5]

The next batter managed to get wood on one of Phillippe's benders but only managed a weak grounder to Ritchey, who threw to first for the third out. The contest evolved into a pitching duel between Phillippe and Cardinals right-hander Stan Yerkes. Neither team managed any semblance of a scoring threat through the fifth inning and it became evident that it would take a break for either to score. That happened for Pittsburgh in the sixth. Tommy Leach reached base on a one-out single to bring to bat Jack O'Connor, who topped a roller to shortstop. Otto Krueger easily played the ball, but in his haste to start a double play the sphere escaped his grasp and rolled into shallow center field. Before it was recovered, Leach was on third and O'Connor was safely at first. Phillippe was up next and the scoring opportunity was apparently lost when he hit a potential double play grounder right at second baseman Farrell. Farrell attempted to tag the oncoming O'Connor, but the catcher abruptly stopped and backed up a few feet. The move confused Farrell, who threw to first to retire Phillippe, but O'Connor had sufficient time to reach second base and Leach scored the only run of the game.[6] Phillippe appeared to get stronger as the game progressed and got errorless support from his fielders while scattering seven hits and walking none.

Much to the distress of Cardinals owner Frank DeHaas Robison, the Pirates swept the three-game series in St. Louis, then returned to Pittsburgh where Sam Leever would pitch the 1902 home opener at Exposition Park on April 22. Leever had reported to Hot Springs in fine shape after having spent part of the winter as manager and star pitcher of a baseball team in Pensacola, Florida.[7] Actually, Leever had already made one regular season start, but it didn't count. The day after Phillippe won the season opener, Leever took the mound in St. Louis before about 5,000 attendees. Time was called in the second inning because of a short rain shower, and in the third a dust storm blew in. Rookie Umpire Joe Cantillon called the scoreless contest because of darkness. The sun re-emerged within a few minutes but the Pirates were already in their coach on the way to the hotel.

A parade through the streets of Pittsburgh and Allegheny City preceded the opening game festivities at the ballpark where the announced throng of 13,750 crowded on all sides of the playing field after the stands and bleachers were filled. Both the Pirates and Reds lined up at home plate and, preceded by a brass band, marched to deep center field where the steel flag pole had been erected. After a brief ceremony, the Pirates raised the 1901 pennant to the top of the staff, while the band played "The Star Spangled Banner." As the large American flag was unfurled, the large crowd broke forth into a chorus of "cheers, tooting of horns, and ringing of bells, making altogether a racket seldom heard, even on a ball field."[8]

A local firm distributed several thousand megaphones to the crowd "and they worked double time" during the game. Cincinnati built up a 3 to 0 lead against Leever by the sixth inning. It could have been worse had not Clarke's good throw to Chief Zimmer nailed the Reds' Bill Bergen when he tried to score all the way from first on a double.

Pittsburgh pecked away at Cincinnati's lead with two runs in the sixth inning and one in the seventh to tie the game at 3–3. The Pirates won it in the bottom of the eighth when Leach singled, went all the way to third on Zimmer's sacrifice, and scored on a single by Lefty Davis.

After celebrating his key hit, Leach made things tough for Leever in the ninth when he made a neat pickup of Dutch Beck's grounder but made a low throw to first that Bransfield couldn't handle. Two outs later the tying run rested on second and the Reds' good-hitting catcher, Heinie Peitz, pinch-hit for the pitcher. Peitz hit a hard grounder at Leach, but this time he didn't have to throw. He stopped the missile and put a tag on the base runner heading toward third base. Despite permitting 13 hits, Leever won the game, 4 to 3.[9]

Phillippe's win the next day was much easier, as the big right-hander was in total control except in the fourth inning when the Reds scored two runs. Cincinnati got another run in the ninth on Wagner's bad throw attempting to complete a doubleplay, but the game was never in doubt as the Pirates piled up 11 runs off Bob Ewing. Phillippe was right in the middle of the offensive outburst. He singled and scored a run in the sixth inning and came to bat an inning later with the bases loaded. He responded with a hit to deep right-center that cleared the bases and made a nice slide into third to beat Dummy Hoy's throw. Moments later he raced home on Davis' fly out, the pitcher's third run scored of the day. Pittsburgh won 11 to 3.[10]

The Cubs of Chicago arrived in town on April 24 trailing Pittsburgh by one game and won the first two games of the series, 5–3 and 4–2. The next day, the Pirates went about remedying their second-place standing.

Leever had a much stronger outing than his previous performance as he shut out the Chicago club, 7 to 0. The game was played in a heavy wind that was so strong that part of the right field fence at Exposition Park blew down just before the start of play. Scores of boys assembled at the break in order to get a free peek at the action, and a couple of policemen attempted to chase them away. During the course of the game the towboat *Monterey* blew over in the Allegheny River, but no hands were lost.

Leever was at his best despite the weather conditions. He allowed just three hits and one of that number, Charlie Dexter's line drive that went for a double, was juggled, then dropped by Ginger Beaumont. No Cub reached third base until the ninth inning, when Mike Lynch drew a base on balls and advanced to third on a high throw. The Cubs' Bunk Congalton hit a vicious line drive to center field that Beaumont snared about a foot off the ground. Lynch tagged up and started home because Beaumont was off-balance and would be unable to make a throw all the way to the plate. However, Beaumont pitched the ball to Wagner near second base, and he relayed a strike to Zimmer. The Pirates catcher put the tag on the runner for a double play that guaranteed the shutout.[11] That win started the Pirates on a ten-game winning streak.

The evening of Leever's shutout, the two clubs took the train to Chicago in order to take advantage of a large Sunday gate. Deacon Phillippe was opposed by the Cubs new southpaw, James St. Vrain, before a huge crowd of 17,000 at West Side Grounds. The onlookers filled the grandstand, bleachers and adjacent roofs. Eventually the throng overflowed onto the field six rows deep against the outfield wall. The contest between the veteran Pirates hurler and the 18-year-old rookie appeared to be a mismatch, but St. Vrain shut out the visitors for seven innings. When the Pirates came to bat in the top of the eighth, the score was knotted at 0–0.

The young side-wheeler quickly got into trouble by hitting the opposing pitcher to start the inning. Lefty Davis bunted, but the poised young pitcher pounced on it and threw to second before Phillippe reached the bag. Phillippe was dead to rights, but shortstop Joe Tinker dropped the ball. After making a good play and seeing his fielders let him down, a rattled St. Vrain hit the next batter, Fred Clarke, to load the bases. Ginger Beaumont brought home two runs with a sharp single to right field.

A 2–0 lead for Phillippe going to the bottom of the ninth would normally be money in the bank. Over eight innings, he had allowed but one safety, and that single was the only ball hit out of the infield. But things got interesting when Tinker and Frank Chance, the latter pinch-hitting for the pitcher, both singled. A sacrifice put the runners on second and third with one out. Next up was left fielder Dakin Miller, whose catch diving into the left field crowd had saved the Cubs in the fifth. Phillippe "took an extra grip on the ball and accentuated the drop curve," before which the Cubs had been helpless all afternoon. An overmatched Miller struck out. It was Phillippe's eighth and most important strikeout of the game. He could be a strikeout pitcher when he needed to.

As the crowd urged Chicago third baseman Charlie Dexter to get a two-out hit, he could only manage a sharp ground ball right back at the pitcher's box that bounded off Phillippe's shin and rolled toward the third base line.

Phillippe scrambled after the ball and fired a strike to first base just in time to retire his former Louisville teammate.[12]

As the season progressed, the Pirates pushed all opposition aside with ease. They won 15 of their first 17 games and by the end of May were in first place with a record of 30 wins and only 6 losses. Phillippe won his first five decisions in 1902 before losing to Brooklyn on May 8. He rebounded nicely with wins over Chicago and New York, the latter a two-hit shutout on May 22.

In those days clubs often had several pitchers warm up just prior to the start of a contest to confuse the gamblers as well as the opposition. It was no different that May afternoon at Exposition Park when Doheny, Leever, Chesbro and the eventual starter, Phillippe, all warmed up for the game with New York. Pittsburgh exploded against the Giants' Roy Evans in the third inning for five runs while Phillippe retired the first 12 New York batters he faced, four on strikes. The first opposition hit was catcher Bowerman's scratch single between Phillippe and Jimmy Burke to lead off the fifth. Phillippe plunked the opposing pitcher to lead off the sixth and Evans was forced at second on George Van Haltren's roller. Van Haltren then attempted a steal of second base.

"A crack as of a bone breaking was distinctly heard in the stand," reported the *New York Evening Sun*. "As Van stretched out on his back, Umpire Bob Emslie shouted, 'He broke his leg, sure.'" The veteran outfielder was carried off the field and a doctor on hand confirmed that Van's right leg was broken just above the ankle."[13]

The Giants' pinch runner made it to third, but was stranded there. The Giants' only other hit of the contest came in the seventh when third baseman Tommy Leach made an ill-advised throw on Lauder's grounder. However, the Giants runner got greedy and was thrown out trying to make it all the way to the third station. Phillippe retired the final seven batters he faced, four, including the final two of the game, on strikes. He had nine strikeouts, right fielder Sheriff Jones being victimized three times.

A week later Chesbro saved a game for Doheny after Doheny nearly blew a six-run lead in the morning half of a Decoration Day twin bill against Chicago at Exposition Park. That win put the league-leading Pirates eight and a half games up on second-place Chicago when the two teams took the field for the afternoon act of the twin bill. Phillippe found himself locked in a pitching duel with the Cubs veteran journeyman Jack Menefee who once compiled a 13–25 won-lost mark splitting the season between Louisville and Pittsburgh.

A crowd of about 12,000, including a large number of women, filled the stands and hundreds stood on the field in front of the outfield fence. Twice, Chicago's right fielder, Art Williams, had to back up almost to the standees to corral long fly balls.

Phillippe matched zeros with Menefee until the sixth inning, when the Cubs scored four runs. The Pirates' sloppy play had more to do with the rally than Phillippe's hurling. Charlie Dexter followed Davy Jones' double with a grounder to shortstop, but Wagner feinted a throw to freeze the baserunner at second, then threw late in his attempt to beat the speedy runner to first. The Pirates were indignant at the call and surrounded Umpire Thomas Brown. A batter later, Frank Chance was down two strikes when he managed to get plunked with a Phillippe pitch to force home the game's first run. Catcher O'Connor was so mad about the turn of events that he threw the ball at Umpire Brown who managed to dodge the sphere at his position near second base. After all this there were still no outs, but the next batter, Hal O'Hagan, hit a ball right back to the pitcher. Phillippe threw home to force Dexter, but a steamed O'Connor fired the ball over the first baseman's head in an attempt to complete a double play. Two runners scored and O'Hagan came home moments later on a single.[14] The Buccaneers eventually lost, 4 to 0, the first time they were shut out in 1902.

Sam Leever was used sparingly in the first half of the season due to a sore arm. After blanking Chicago on April 26, he made only four starts in May. On May 12, he went to the box against Boston, but had to retire after only one inning. He tried it again on May 20, but had to give it up after allowing four runs through six innings because his arm just "played out." He was replaced by Chesbro, who got the victory on a ninth-inning run. Leever would not pitch again in a National League game until June 21. Though he wasn't sharp against St. Louis, allowing 11 hits and three walks, he managed a complete-game, 4–3 victory. In his next start, eight days later, he proved he was back to form with a 6–0 shutout in Cincinnati. Despite the time he missed, the Schoolmaster still compiled a 15–7 won-lost record for the 1902 season.

Despite Clarke's increasingly difficult task of completing a daily lineup, the Pirates continued to decimate their opponents, even as player after player went down with injury. Honus Wagner started the 1902 season at shortstop, but played only 44 games at that position because he was being moved around to replace incapacitated teammates. All three Pirates outfielders missed significant periods of time due to injury, forcing the versatile Wagner to shuffle between outfield positions. Wid Conroy became Pittsburgh's regular shortstop before being suspended for a month by the National League for fighting with Chicago's rookie shortstop Joe Tinker. When Kitty Bransfield suffered a knee injury in mid–August, Wagner moved to first base and played 32 games there.

Pitcher Jesse Tannehill, a switch-hitter, was pressed into outfield duty for 16 games.

Despite the instability of the Pirates' everyday lineup, the pitching staff was reliable and efficient. The big five, Phillippe, Leever, Tannehill, Doheny and Chesbro, started 134 games between them and completed an amazing 125 of those games. Phillippe finished 29 of his 30 starting assignments. Leever was left behind because of a sore arm when the club left on an Eastern road trip on June 6, but the staff was so deep, the Pirates won five of eight games without him, though one of the victories came by forfeit.

For the Pirates' first visit to the New York Giants' home park that June, Barney Dreyfuss adorned each of his players with eye-catching panama hats. About 5,000 patrons at the Polo Grounds were treated to the fashionable parade of champions that included Dreyfuss and Pulliam. While the disabled outfielder, Van Haltren, watched from the Giants' clubhouse with his cast-encased leg propped up on pillows, the two teams played to a 4–4 tie that was called after 11 innings because of impending darkness.[15]

Next day, the *New York Evening World* noted, "A crowd of Pittsburghers, Panama-hatted, arrived during their practice and in songs told of the awful fate of the Giants. The incident was one which recalled scenes at a big football battle between the teams of Yale and Harvard. Another thing to help the Pirates along was the presence of Phillippi in the box."[16]

The Buccaneers had the game well in hand before the more than 9,000 local fans had a chance to settle in their seats. Davis led off the game with a triple to center, Clarke singled him home, and the Pirates' boss scored on a sacrifice fly after the Giants walked Wagner to pitch to Bransfield. Philippe shut out the Giants on only four hits and, during his final at-bat, drove a Roy Evans pitch into the right field bleachers for a rare out-of-the-park home run.

When the Pirates rolled into Chicago with their "jipijapa" decorated headgear, Charles Dryden commented in the *Chicago American*, "B. Dreyfuss is responsible for the Panjura epidemic. He paid $18 each for 18 hats and lavished them upon his young men at a total cost of $324. All the Pirates look very nice except Tommy Leach. Owing to the smallness of his stature and the immensity of his hat, Tommy resembles a short-stemmed toadstool after a refreshing rain on a hot summer night."[17]

The Pirates were awarded a forfeit win in the final game of the road trip in Boston on June 16. The Pirates took a 3–0 lead behind Tannehill into the top of the fifth inning. The weather had threatened all afternoon, and Clarke and his men were anxious to complete the inning so it would become an official game. Beaumont and Wagner quickly struck out as the rain drops intensified. Bransfield hit a grounder to shortstop and Herman Long made a rainbow throw to first that Bransfield easily beat. He was allowed to take second base unchallenged, then third. By this time it had begun to pour and Umpire Joe Cantillon awarded the game to Pittsburgh. The umpire claimed he had warned Captain Long several times that if he did not play properly, the game would be forfeited to the Pirates. Ironically, the rain lasted only about five minutes and the game could have been resumed, but the forfeit stood.

The Pirates had two days off following the forfeit game in Boston and played a couple of exhibition games on Tuesday and Wednesday before returning to regulation play in Chicago. Though attendance in National League games had declined because of the lopsided pennant race, the Pirates could still earn hefty paydays with exhibition games in non-major league cities. On June 17 the Pirates lost a game in Kitty Bransfield's home town of Worcester before 5,100 locals. Manager Clarke chose to play the game using the old foul strike rule, but got beat at his own game as a lanky, towering right-hander named Fred Falkenberg held the champions to two runs and shut out Honus Wagner in four at-bats.

The next day, Phillippe pitched a complete-game victory, 7 to 3, against the Wilmington Athletic Club. The attendance figures for three non-league contests, 6,400 in Newark, 6,500 in Wilmington, and 5,100 in Worcester, more than doubled the average gate in the games played against National League clubs in Philadelphia, New York and Boston during their Eastern tour.[18]

A day after Leever made his first start since May 20, Jack Taylor and Deacon Phillippe engaged in one of the most extraordinary games in National League history on June 22, 1902. During the course of 19 innings, Taylor held Honus Wagner hitless in eight at-bats while beating Phillippe, 3–2, at West Side Grounds in Chicago.

Phillippe would have been the hurler who walked off the field victorious if not for a ninth-inning error by his shortstop and a dropped ball by his catcher. Pittsburgh was up 2 to 1 when Joe Tinker grounded to shortstop and was safe at first when Conroy threw low to Bransfield. Bobby Lowe reached base when his sharp grounder glanced off Bransfield's shin, but while Umpire O'Day was watching the play at first, Conroy intentionally blocked Tinker's path to third base and Joe had to return to second. Schaefer grounded to Conroy, who forced Lowe, then threw to first in an attempt to complete the double play. Meanwhile, Tinker rounded third with his head down and headed homeward, do-or-die. The throw to first was too late to retire the runner there, but Bransfield shot the ball to catcher Harry Smith in plenty of time to get the on-charging Cub at the plate. In his haste to make the play, Smith dropped the ball and by the time he picked it up, Tinker had touched home plate to tie the score.

The Pirates had a chance to win it in the tenth with one out, the great Wagner at bat, and runners on second and third. When Taylor struck out the famous Dutchman, the crowd of almost 10,000 went into a tizzy. It still took a nice play by Lowe on Bransfield's grounder to get out of the inning.

After that, the two pitchers rattled off scoreless innings one after the other. Taylor allowed 14 hits over the course of the contest but he walked only one batter compared to the three passes that Phillippe allowed, all to center fielder Davy Jones. When the Cubs prepared to bat in the bottom of the 19th, it was apparent that it would be the final inning whether the home team scored or not.

Canadian Bunk Congalton led off the home 19th by driving a Phillippe pitch to right center. It looked like at least a triple, but, amid the roar from the crowd, Beaumont and Wagner closed on the flying sphere. Beaumont grasped it just as Wagner collided with him. Both men tumbled head over heels, but a prostrate Beaumont held up his glove hand with the ball in it, to turn the home crowd's cheers into silence.[19]

The loyalists were revitalized when Johnny Kling beat out a scratch hit just out of the reach of Tommy Leach. With Tinker at bat, the Chicago catcher dashed for second and slid in safely under a high throw by Harry Smith. Tinker grounded out to shortstop Conroy and with twilight fading, it was up to Chicago's veteran second baseman, Pittsburgh native Bobby Lowe, to settle the verdict.

Lowe went after Phillippe's first pitch and bounced a perfectly placed single between Leach and Conroy. Kling ran home to settle the second-longest game to that point in the history of the National League, short by one inning of Chicago and Cincinnati's 20-inning, 7–7 tie game in 1892.[20] The marathon took only three hours and seven minutes.

"The battle on the west side was perhaps the most remarkable that ever was played on a National League field," wrote Hugh Fullerton. "Taylor was on his mettle. Half a dozen times he pitched himself out of desperate situations.... When the nineteenth inning came the crowd was on the verge of lunacy and, when Lowe's sharp drive sent Kling home with the winning run the crowd was crazy."[21]

In a postscript to the affair, several overzealous Cubs fans gathered about the Pirates following the game and sought to exact retribution from Wid Conroy for blocking the base paths to Chicago runners on at least two occasions. During the verbal exchange between the mob and players, a handful of the more enraged fans pelted the Pirates with projectiles. Fortunately their aim was as misguided as their intentions.[22]

The historic extra-inning loss was only a minor setback for the Pirates.

At the end of the long day, their record stood at 37–12, still nine games ahead of second-place Chicago. The next day, the Pirates righted their ship with a 7 to 2 victory behind Ed Doheny, but the excitement of the day came in the fourth inning when the clubs' shortstops, Tinker and Conroy, went at it at second base. Tinker was on first base when Lowe beat out a slow grounder to the first baseman. As Tinker approached second base, the Chicagoan pushed Conroy away from the bag. Conroy rushed at Tinker, who "pushed his open hand over the greater part of Conroy's face in the manner so irritating to belligerents."[23] The two players scuffled until the combatants were pulled away by their teammates.

All this led the *Chicago Daily Tribune* to editorialize, "The trouble took place in the fourth inning and came as a natural result of Sunday's contest in which Conroy spiked Schafer and once deliberately tried to block Tinker.... The Pittsburghers never have earned bouquets for their gentlemanly demeanor on the field, and as a matter of fact are the most unpopular champions that ever won a National League pennant." [24]

Of course the Pirates' version of the affair was that Conroy had a right to his share of the bag and Tinker could have gotten over his displeasure without a fight. At that point, Conroy only defended himself.[25] The evening of the fisticuffs, John T. Brush, chairman of the National League's executive committee, announced an indefinite suspension of both players involved in the fight pending an investigation.

With regular left fielder Davis away from the team because of an eye ailment, Harry Pulliam immediately telegraphed him to join the club as soon as possible since Wagner would have to move from the outfield to shortstop during Conroy's suspension. However, the Pirates' juggernaut did not miss a beat, reeling off eight straight victories before they were temporarily derailed by Brooklyn's Wild Bill Donovan, who out-pitched Leever at Exposition Park, 2 to 0. The loss marked Leever's first setback in the 1902 season.

Phillippe was rewarded with a well-earned rest after his famous 19-inning effort in Chicago. Upon returning home on Thursday, he was given a long weekend off. Of course, he could not stay away from Pirates headquarters, where he was besieged by sportswriters seeking his account of the marathon against the Cubs. He told them he was pretty tired after the game, but after getting a bath he felt like a lighting cock. He added that "he tried his best to win the combat, but it wasn't in the wood." [26]

Phillippe didn't pitch again until Tuesday, July 1. Of much more historical importance than the Pirates' 4 to 3 win over Cincinnati was a meeting that day in New York between John McGraw, manager of the Baltimore American League club, and Giants owner Andrew Freedman.

McGraw was annoyed that Ban Johnson supported the league's umpires in McGraw's numerous run-ins with them. He had also learned that Baltimore might be dumped following the current season in order for the American League to put a club in New York. Freedman seized the opportunity and signed McGraw to become the Giants' player-manager for four years at $11,000 a year, the highest salary for a player or manager in the league's history.

Freedman and McGraw then plotted a strategy designed to deal a crippling blow to the American League. Once back in Baltimore, McGraw called a meeting of the team's directors. He demanded reimbursement of the $7,000 he paid out of his own pocket for players' salaries and other expenses. When the payment was not forthcoming, McGraw demanded his release, which was tendered on July 8. Acting behind the scenes, McGraw then engineered a deal by which Freedman purchased a majority of Baltimore Orioles stock. As principle owner, the new boss released the Orioles' best players. The Giants signed four of the "ex"–Orioles, including Joe McGinnity and Roger Bresnahan. Two others, Joe Kelley and Cy Seymour (who would break Honus Wagner's hold on the batting championship in 1905) went to Cincinnati, whose owner John Brush had secretly agreed to purchase the New York club from Freedman.[27]

Barney Dreyfuss publicly commented that he was glad to have McGraw back in the League, but the two would soon become bitter rivals and enemies. Pitchers, especially Deacon Phillippe, weren't especially happy to have an accomplished hitter like Seymour back in the National League. In 1899, when Seymour played with the Giants, he hit a pitched ball back at Phillippe that broke the third finger on the hurler's left hand. After joining the Reds for the second half of the 1902 season, Seymour duplicated his '99 act by driving a hot one at Phillippe, the ball striking the same finger.[28]

On July 4, Pittsburgh planned the largest Independence Day celebration in its history, and about 600,000 people turned out to welcome President Theodore Roosevelt as he toured the city. At Exposition Park, temporary seating was installed to increase the capacity to 10,000 for a morning-afternoon doubleheader with Brooklyn.

Tannehill threw a two-hitter in the morning game, winning 3–0 before a crowd of 10,500. Unfortunately, rains in the morning caused the river to back up through the sewers and onto the playing field. By afternoon game time, the water was more than knee-deep in center and right field. Barney Dreyfuss wasn't about to give up the large gate from the crowd of 10,290. A ground rule was adopted, allowing only one base for a ball hit into the outfield lake. The umpire handed the pitcher a dried ball after nearly every other pitch. The Pirates won again as Chesbro polished off the Superbas in the afterpiece, 4 to 0.

On July 6, 1902, Phillippe got another shot against Jack Taylor before a large Sunday crowd in Chicago. Neither was as sharp as in their earlier affair, but Taylor was at his best when the visitors threatened to score. Pittsburgh lost a raggedly played affair, 8 to 3. Nevertheless, when the first-place Pirates returned home the next day, they were greeted at the station by 2,000 admirers.

On July 11, Lefty Davis broke his ankle in a game against the Giants in which Phillippe prevailed over Leever's old Richmond teammate, Tully Sparks, 6 to 3. In the fifth inning, Davis led off with a single and took off as Clarke swung and missed for a third strike. Davis made it safely to second for his team-high 19th swipe. However, his spikes stuck in the ground during his slide and he suffered a serious injury to his leg. While Davis was being hauled off to the hospital, Tannehill came into the game as a pinch-runner, then replaced Davis in left field the next inning.[29]

"Alfonso Davis will be missed on the trip," opined Alfred R. Cratty of the *Chronicle-Telegraph*. "The Nashville lad is the life of a party. He is ever singing, dancing or chattering. Lefty is rather clever as a vocalist, ala Dick Cooley, who could earn a living on the stage by black face work. Davis has one stock song which he hums day and night, and the gang cannot choke him off. 'Melancholy Mose' is the title. The boys say that they have heard it oftener than 'Play Ball.'"[30]

Dreyfuss wired Wid Conroy, who still had two games to serve on the 20-game suspension for his fight with Tinker, and ordered him to rejoin the club for the games in Cincinnati. Two days later, Tannehill's finger was knocked out of joint in the sixth inning of a game in Cincinnati and he had to be replaced by Leever, who completed Pittsburgh's 3–1 victory.

Before 5,700 fans at Exposition Park on July 12, Jack Chesbro struck out 11 Giants and outpitched Christy Mathewson in a 4–0 Pirates victory, one of eight shutouts "Happy Jack" threw that year. On his way to a 28–6 record for the season, at one point Chesbro threw 48 consecutive scoreless innings. Then, after allowing a run, he began another streak of 26 straight innings without an opposition score. It has often been written that Chesbro's dramatic improvement in 1902 was due to his use of the spitball, but the evidence, and Jack's own recollection, is that he did not use the wet one on a regular basis until 1904.[31]

Pittsburgh sports writer Alfred Cratty wrote of Chesbro, "Speed is Algy's forte. There have been days when catchers behind him vow the ball comes in so fast that it is pretty hard to clutch. It was a good day for the Pittsburgh management when it held on to the man. About two years ago Boston wanted him. For some time talk as to a deal held sway."[32]

On July 22, the Pirates began a highly volatile series with St. Louis at Robison Field. After losing to the Cardinals, 10–4, on the 23rd, Sam Leever came back against the same club three days later. The Schoolmaster held the Cardinals to only one hit, by George Barclay, but that base hit cost him a run in Pittsburgh's 5 to 1 victory that wasn't assured until the Pirates scored three times in the ninth inning. Based on a pitching line that included two wild pitches and two passed balls, Leever did not get sterling support from his catcher, Jack O'Connor. The St. Louis–based *Sporting News* noted, "Had not O'Connor got miffed and refused to run after a passed ball the locals would not have put a man across the plate." [33]

The two clubs split the first four games and St. Louis officials expected a large Sunday crowd for the finale. The Cardinals were assisted by the fact that both Honus Wagner and Tommy Leach were not in the line-up, the Dutchman because of a suspension for abusing umpire Brown in the first game and "Wee Tommy" due to a muscle strain.

That Sunday Doheny was ineffective for Pittsburgh, being tagged for seven runs and 11 hits before he was removed for a pinch-hitter in the eighth inning and replaced by Phillippe. The Pirates were held scoreless for the first five innings and the spectators jeered them unmercifully. The crowd was especially indignant toward Clarke, whom they saw as a villain for his spiking of first baseman Art Nichols the previous Wednesday. The Pirates rallied in the late innings for six runs but fell one short of victory.

At the conclusion of the game a mob formed at the visiting team's exit. The Pirates were insulted and jeered as they exited the field. Three players, Ritchey, Beaumont and Conroy, were jostled by the mob before they reached their bus, and the crowd's anger reached a fever pitch when they spotted Fred Clarke. A man named Jacob Fisher rushed toward Clarke and, after screaming an obscenity, struck the Pirates' manager twice in the face. Jimmy Burke, a Pittsburgh substitute who happened to hail from St. Louis, grabbed a bat and threatened to fight back, but his teammates restrained him. Even after the players reached their bus, the mob threw "bricks, stones and pistol shots and missiles of all kinds" at the open coach, causing minor injuries among the players and bystanders. Had the Pirates not submitted to the taunts and insults with passive restraint, they would have been mobbed. A platoon of police finally arrived, arrested Fisher and two other men, and the Pirates were allowed to depart after a 15-minute struggle between the officers and the horde. The next day, a St. Louis newspaper wrote that Cardinals owner Robison sent word to the police judge that he would pay the fines of all parties involved in the riot.[34]

The Pirates met the McGraw-led Giants for the first time when they visited the Polo Grounds for a four-game series beginning on August 2. Clarke's men had little trouble with the Giants on this occasion, leaving town with a four-game sweep. Jesse Tannehill bested Christy Mathewson, 3–0, in the third game, and Chesbro duplicated the feat the next day with a five-inning shutout.

"A clean sweep of four games at New York was most pleasing," wrote the Pittsburgh columnist in *Sporting Life*. "Col. Barney evidently enjoyed this result, for he could thus picture the anguish on the face of his former friend, Andrew Freedman. New Yorkers could not understand the easy twirling manner of Tannehill. All the players will agree that it is fine control, marvelous change of pace, a good head and coolness."[35]

Leever had a bad outing against Brooklyn the day before the Giants series when he was tagged for 13 hits. Still, it took a wild throw by Bransfield and a passed ball by Smith to allow Brooklyn three sixth-inning runs that cost Pittsburgh the game in regulation. The contest ended in a 6–6 tie when it became too to dark to play after the tenth inning. So it wasn't a surprise after Pittsburgh fans read the newspaper reports of Leever's second successive "failure" a week later in Philadelphia that he came in for a round of criticism.

Against the Phillies, Leever blew a 2 to 0 lead with two outs and no one on base when a walk, three singles, "some dubious work by Sam Leever and then a doubtful base hit which Wid Conroy did not secure" led to the three runs that gave Philadelphia a victory.

"Coming as it did," reported *Sporting Life*, "the upset attracted more than usual attention and, by the way, here fans seemed to blame all on 'Prof. Sam.' Some were real mean in their denunciation of the Ohio lad for letting that game get away. They accused him of being weak-hearted and all sorts of things. Men who had often wagered big sums on games that Sammy pitched could not rap him strong enough for this one slip up."[36]

Leever's collapse was one of only two Pittsburgh losses to the Phillies for the entire 1902 season. Philadelphia had been Pittsburgh's main rival in the 1901 pennant race, but during the off-season the club was decimated by American League raids that took their biggest star, Ed Delahanty, and two 20-game-winning pitchers. The Pirates would feast on the Phillies in 1902, winning 18 of 20 games while going 10–0 vs. Philadelphia at Exposition Park.

The Pirates' long road trip that began on July 20 in Chicago ended with the club's return to Exposition Park on August 16. The Bucs left town with a 56–16 record and returned home with a 69–23 ledger.

In August, the American League's war on the Nationals finally caught up with the Pirates. On August 20 President Dreyfuss announced the suspension of Jack O'Connor who, while under contract to the Pirates, acted as an American League agent to lure Pittsburgh players to that rival organization.

It was reported that the catcher was not only suspended but was barred from the Pittsburgh ballpark. It was also indicated that steps would be taken at once to have O'Connor blacklisted, so that in the future he would not be able to play in the National League or any organization affiliated with that league.

O'Connor was accused of arranging meetings between select Pirates players and American League President Ban Johnson and Cleveland owner Charles Somers in the Allegheny Hotel room of Jesse Tannehill. That evening, O'Connor recruited six teammates to listen to the American League's offer.

In the days following the disclosure of the American League's plot, there were rumors about Pittsburgh players jumping to the rival league. Fred Clarke was quoted as saying that every one of his men had been approached by American League agents. *Sporting Life* added that "Tannehill was offered $5,000 for next season by an American League club, and Chesbro $5,500, while Wagner cannot show better than a $4,800 offer. Clarke is said to be concealing an offer of $20,000 for three years; Davis, too, has been offered $3,000 for next season."[37]

"I will not stand for any treachery or disloyalty from anybody while in my employ," Barney Dreyfuss emphatically stated. "No player can be a stool pigeon for the American League and draw salary from the Pittsburgh club at the same time."[38]

Almost three months after the "treachery," the story made the newspapers about how Dreyfuss caught wind of the American League plot in advance. According to the piece in the *Cincinnati Enquirer*, it happened when the Pirates took a break in Atlantic City following a series in Boston.

Fred Clarke had injured his leg sliding into second base on Wednesday, August 13, in Boston so Dreyfuss sat on the bench during Tannehill's 6 to 1 victory in the finale of the series the next day. On Friday the Pirates beat a team of amateurs in Atlantic City, 18 to 1. Later that day, Tannehill and Burke got into a scuffle wherein Tannehill's arms were pinned behind his back, causing his left shoulder to pop out of joint. The pitcher had suffered previous dislocations and was taken to a hospital where he was given ether before the shoulder could be forced back into place. Burke was too distressed to observe the procedure, so Dreyfuss and the doctor were left in the room with the groggy southpaw. To the astonishment of Dreyfuss, Tannehill began to babble about a plot by the American League to raid the Pittsburgh club of its players.[39]

That evening National League umpire Tim Hurst told the Pirates owner that he had seen Jack O'Connor in conference with Ban Johnson at the Gilsey House. Another story that implicated O'Connor was information Dreyfuss received from John McGraw that O'Connor had betrayed the Pittsburgh club at Hot Springs in 1901 when he assisted the former Baltimore manager in getting Jimmy Williams to jump the Pirates and join the Orioles.[40] Based on these revelations, Dreyfuss dispatched his assistant secretary, Walter Smith, to track O'Connor's movements. Smith tailed the catcher to Pennsylvania Station where O'Connor met Ban Johnson and Charles Somers, vice-president of the American League. Smith was able to discern the group was going to the Lincoln Hotel and immediately notified his boss. Dreyfuss and Harry Pulliam went to the hotel where they saw O'Connor, Tannehill, Leach, Chesbro, Harry Smith, Davis and Conroy arrive at the room of the American League executives.[41]

Jesse Tannehill, Pittsburgh Pirates, 1900 (National Baseball Hall of Fame Library, Cooperstown, New York).

The next day, August 20, was an off-day, but Dreyfuss called a team meeting anyway. When the plotting players did not show up, he sent Clarke to Tannehill's hotel room where a meeting was being held between players and Ban Johnson. When the volatile manager showed up, Johnson hid in the lavatory. Dreyfuss chuckled that Clarke knew the American League president was hiding there and "made himself at home for the next five hours, keeping Johnson in his hiding spot, afraid to come out."[42]

Once Dreyfuss confirmed O'Connor's clandestine meeting with Johnson and Somers, he ordered the immediate release of the treacherous catcher. Right fielder Lefty Davis, still out of the lineup with a broken leg, would be dismissed late that September for being an American League agent. Philippe had vouched for Davis when he was first signed by Pittsburgh, and Davis' play in 1901 had been stellar. Davis was the roommate of his promoter, Phillippe, in his first season with the Pirates, but a year later began rooming with Tannehill.[43]

"This year Mr. Davis fell into bad hands," wrote Alfred Cratty. "He picked for a roommate one of the vets on the team who has ever been noted for convivial habits. They took quarters in Allegheny and from that time on

Lefty began to fall away in his play.... Mr. Davis might have had a chance to stay had he not been caught red handed at his tricks. The night that Mr. Johnson and Somers were prowling about here Cols. Harry and Barney had occasion to be out late. They chanced on a side street when who should come along, not alone by the bye, but the man they least expected."[44] Davis' days with the Pirates would soon be over.

When Dreyfuss learned that Ban Johnson was headed to Massachusetts with a proposition for Kitty Bransfield, at home recuperating from an injury, he instructed Harry Pulliam to contact the first baseman before the American Leaguer reached Worcester. Johnson registered under the name of "R. B. McRoy" at a Worcester hotel, then sent for Bransfield. After his meeting with "McRoy," Bransfield agreed to the two-year Pirates contract proposed by Pulliam and received an additional $1,500 as reward for his loyalty.[45] "Ban Johnson made a strenuous effort to secure Bransfield," announced Pulliam. "But I telegraphed Kitty, and the American League president got a very cold reception in Massachusetts."[46]

On the ball field, the Pirates didn't miss a beat. Clarke's men continued their mastery of the Giants when McGraw and his players came to Exposition Park in late August. In the first game of a doubleheader on August 21, Honus Wagner moved over to first base, where O'Connor had been playing for the injured Bransfield. Leever held the Giants to only three scattered hits and pitched the Pirates to a 2–0 victory over Christy Mathewson. He also reached the Giants' ace pitcher for a double. That win was the Bucs' seventh straight over the Giants since McGraw took the helm, but the winning streak was snapped in the nightcap when Phillippe was drubbed, 8 to 1. McGraw played shortstop for the Giants in both games and went 0-for-6, although he drew a walk off each of the Pirates' pitchers.

Secretary Pulliam announced on August 22 that Phillippe, Leever, Doheny, Merritt, Bransfield, Ritchey, Wagner, Beaumont, Clarke and Sebring had signed contracts for 1903, and that Smith and Zimmer had accepted terms. The remaining players were given until September 1 to re-sign with a newly installed affidavit from the signatory affirming that he had read the contract, understood the same, accepted the terms and swore to carry out its provisions.[47]

After new team secretary Will Locke met the team in Boston on August 26, he wired Dreyfuss that he was certain Chesbro, Tannehill, Conroy, and Burke were going to the rival league. Leach, he said, was liable to stay with the Pirates because he realized that he owed it to President Dreyfuss.[48] A remorseful Leach, who had always been a favorite of the owner, returned an uncashed $1,000 American League check and asked Dreyfuss to forgive him.

In addressing his players' treachery, President Dreyfuss paid tribute to the integrity of Deacon Phillippe: "If they were all like Phil," said he, "a base ball man's life would be one round of pleasure. You never need to watch that big fellow. He is a man."[49]

When Harry Smith sprained a knee only one day after O'Connor's dismissal, 41-year-old Chief Zimmer had to catch every game, including doubleheaders, for over a week. Harry Pulliam was instructed to recruit another backstop as soon as possible. The St. Louis Cardinals were pursuing an outstanding young catcher on the Rochester Eastern League club named Ed Phelps, but the Pirates swept in and acquired him, much to the dismay of Stanley Robison. Pulliam said it did not matter that the Cardinals were not given the chance to make a counter-offer as Pittsburgh was "prepared to get him (Phelps) at any cost."[50]

One club that plagued Sam Leever all season was Brooklyn. After two losses and the 6–6 tie against the Superbas, Leever squared off against the Brooklynites in the second game of the Labor Day doubleheader on September 1. The Pirates' triumph in the opener meant a victory by Leever would clinch a share of the National League pennant.

It wasn't easy as Leever's fielders put him in a hole right from the start. Second baseman Burke fumbled Willie Keeler's grounder for an error, and Keeler went to third on a single. Dahlen hit an easy bounder to Leach, but he threw it well over Wagner's head at first base. The Dutchman dived in the stands in an attempt to recover the sphere, but the Brooklyn fans made sure they kept the ball well away from the big Pirate. The only thing Wagner could get his hand on was a pop bottle that he tossed to catcher Harry Smith. Leever and the Pirates now trailed, 3 to 0.

Down 7 to 4 in the eighth inning, Pittsburgh managed to tie the score. Frank Kitson was knocked out of the pitcher's box by the time Leever's single off Roy Evans sent Burke scurrying home with the tying run. The Pirates took a lead in the ninth on Wagner's single, a stolen base and Burke's fourth hit of the game.

Still, the game was not decided until the final out. Keeler brought the Washington Park crowd to its feet when he led off the ninth with a triple to right. Cozy Dolan smacked a wicked grounder to third, but Leach made a "phenomenal stop," held the runner and threw the Dolan out at first. Neither Dahlen nor McCreery could drive Keeler home and Leever escaped with a narrow verdict the *Brooklyn Eagle* described as "lucky" as he "was saved repeatedly from utter annihilation by wonderful catches on the part of Clarke and Beaumont."[51]

Ed Phelps made his debut for the Pirates behind home plate in the first game of a doubleheader at Brooklyn on September 2. With the rookie behind the plate, Phillippe picked up the 5 to 3 victory in the game that guaranteed the pennant. The clinching game received little notice for it had been a foregone conclusion since May that the Pirates would take the pennant. Within two weeks, Dreyfuss would call Phelps "the best catcher the Pittsburgh club ever had."[52]

The Pirates suffered a temporary poor stretch right after clinching first place. On September 4, Pittsburgh did not score a run in a doubleheader at Boston, but lost only once. The Beaneaters scored their only run in the second inning of the first game on an error by Tommy Leach, and Jack Chesbro went down to defeat, 1 to 0. The second game was delayed by a rain shower and despite a generous application of sawdust, the slow track undoubtedly hurt the speedy Pittsburgh offense.

In the afterpiece, Leever allowed only three hits and only one Boston runner got as far as second base. A journeyman named John Malarkey pitched for Boston and his fielders bailed him out of jam after jam. With the score still 0–0, the contest was called because of darkness after Fred Clarke made a "brilliant running-in catch" for the final out in the ninth inning.

The Pirates experienced a rare series loss in the 1902 season when they dropped two out of three games at the Polo Grounds in early September. The Pirates beat Mathewson in the first game on Saturday, but after the customary Sunday off, the Giants beat Chesbro and Leever for a doubleheader sweep on Monday. The day was significant in that Jimmy Sebring debuted in Pittsburgh's unstable right-field slot. 20-year-old Sebring came from the same Worcester team that had provided first baseman Bransfield. The youngster made the best of his opportunity in the big leagues, batting .325 in 19 games. However, Frank Dwyer, manager of the Detroit Americans, chimed in that a month earlier he had signed Sebring to a contract to play for the Tigers in 1903. Jimmy confirmed that he had received $100 in advance money from Dwyer, but he had never signed the Tigers contract as Dwyer claimed.[53]

Even before Pittsburgh's pennant was a foregone conclusion, attendance had waned in National League ballparks. On September 11, the Pirates played a doubleheader in Philadelphia before an announced crowd of 402. The next day, only 582 came out to see Leever beat the Phillies, 5 to 2. The American League benefited from Barney Dreyfuss having locked up his players through the 1902 season because it left the Pirates a great deal stronger than the other National League clubs that lost players to the rival league during the off-season. Attendance figures of 243,826 for the Pirates' 1902 championship season were the club's lowest in the decade.[54]

After Jesse Tannehill signed an American League contract for 1903, the

Pirates decided that the traitorous pitcher would play the outfield or pitch every day for the unstated reason that the club wanted to punish the disloyal player. But after right fielder Tannehill made a bad throw in the second game of a doubleheader in Brooklyn on September 2, Clarke benched the disgruntled player. Jimmy Burke assumed the vacated right field job for a few days until rookie Jimmy Sebring took over the position for good. Following a public argument between Tannehill and Clarke in New York on September 6, it was widely reported that the pair had several run-ins during their three seasons together on the team. According to Pat Egan, a correspondent for the *Pittsburgh Times* and friend of both players, Clarke first chastised Tannehill the spring following the Louisville-Pittsburgh merger with the remark, "Barney understands that you are lazy. Get a hustle on you." Tannehill responded, "That's right. You go and play left field and I'll pitch the game."[55] Tannehill pitched his last game for Pittsburgh on September 18, 1902, defeating St. Louis in ten innings, 7–6, for his 20th victory of the season.

The Pirates won their 100th game in a doubleheader at Chicago on Sunday, September 21, 1902. Phillippe captured the first game 4–1, and Leever followed with a victory in the second act by the identical score. A time limit for the twin bill was set for 5 P.M., and the pitchers obliged by finishing the games in times of 1:40 and 1:35.

Deacon Phillippe's 20th victory of the 1902 season came in one of the strangest games in National League history. When Barney Dreyfuss demanded that the final game of the season go forward despite the rain-soaked condition of Exposition Park's field, Cincinnati played most of their men out of their normal positions in protest. Reds first baseman Jake Beckley started on the pitcher's mound for the only time in his career, pitched four innings and allowed eight runs, four of them earned. Outfielders Cy Seymour and Turkey Mike Donlin also pitched for the visitors. Reds rookie pitcher Rube Vickers handled the catching duties and set a modern major-league record with six passed balls, mainly because he made no effort to corral wide pitches. Joe Kelley and Seymour openly smoked cigarettes during the game to show their contempt for having to play ball when the grounds were in such bad condition. Dreyfuss was so displeased with the two players' behavior, he threatened to make examples of them at the league meeting. Though the local fans saw an 11–2 Pirates victory, Dreyfuss refunded the ticket price to any customers that wanted their money back, and the Reds returned their share of the gate to prevent a riot by unhappy fans.

In addition to penning a protest to the league about the Reds' lackadaisical play Dreyfuss also announced the outright release of pitcher Tannehill, which meant the club had decided to forgo any legal proceedings against the player. A member of the Pirates since 1897, Tannehill expressed no regrets about leaving Pittsburgh. "Barney Dreyfuss is all right, but his manager is a bad 'un," he said.[56]

That June, Barney Dreyfuss had proposed a post-season series between his Pirates and the champion American League team or a handpicked team of stars. In his statement to the press, Dreyfuss declared, "I am willing to back my team (through a wager) to the extent of $5,000 for a series of five games with the team which wins the American League pennant. I am willing that the opposing team may take on any player in the American League, to strengthen up with. I think the Pittsburgh team is the best ball team in the country, and though I do not care to be personally interested in a post-season series, I am willing to put up the money for my men and let the winners of the series also take the entire gate receipts."[57]

The Pirates cruised to their second straight National League pennant with a 103–36 record. They held first place except for one day, April 24, and finished 27½ games ahead of second-place Brooklyn, still a major league record as the most lopsided pennant race. One Pirate or another led the league in nearly every offensive category: Ginger Beaumont in hits and batting average,

1902 Pittsburgh Pirates National League Champions (this photograph must have been taken late in or just after the 1902 season as three dismissed Pirates, O'Connor, Davis and Tannehill, are not shown, but Chesbro is still with the team (far left, second row). Phillippe is third from the left, back row, and Leever is standing second from the right (courtesy Pittsburgh Pirates).

Tommy Leach in home runs (with six), and Honus Wagner in slugging, runs batted in, runs scored, doubles, and stolen bases. The top five National League pitchers in winning percentage were Pirates.

By the end of the 1902 season, tensions between the two major leagues had thawed enough that a post-season match-up of the league champions could be a distinct possibility. Over in the American League, Connie Mack's Philadelphia A's rose from fourth in 1901 to a first-place finish due in great part to the pitching of Rube Waddell, who won 25 games.

Though Barney Dreyfuss had earlier challenged the American League champion to an exhibition series following the regular season, the raids on his club that August caused him to rethink the idea. Instead, Dreyfuss agreed to have the Pirates face a contingent of all-stars from the opposing circuit in a best-of-five series beginning in Pittsburgh on October 7. There was no big purse at stake or a trophy to win. Dubbed the "All Americans," the American Leaguers assembled a squad that included four future members of baseball's Hall of Fame.

The "All Americans" organized by Umpire Joe Cantillon included first baseman Harry Davis, shortstop Monte Cross, and outfielder Topsy Hartsel of the champion Philadelphia A's; "Mister Shortstop" Bobby Wallace of the St. Louis Browns; outfielder Fielder Jones (.321) and catcher Billy Sullivan of the Chicago White Sox; third baseman Bill Bradley (.341) of the Cleveland Broncos; first baseman George "Scoops" Carey of the Washington Senators; and outfielder Dick Harley from Detroit.

The pitching staff was also stellar: Cy Young (32–11 with Boston and well on his way to 511 wins lifetime); Cleveland's Bill Bernhard; Win Mercer of Detroit; and Addie Joss, a 17-game winner as a rookie for Cleveland. The A's Rube Waddell was not available, his right wrist injured by a line drive during an exhibition game in Wilmington on September 25.

Also a member of the All Americans' squad was the premier second baseman in the game, Nap Lajoie of Cleveland, who finished the 1902 season with a .366 batting average. Lajoie began his career in the National League with Philadelphia, then jumped to the rival Athletic's in 1901 and batted a league record .426 (accomplished against a lot of minor league–quality pitchers in a league that had not yet adopted the current foul strike rule). Lajoie moved to the Cleveland American League Club for the 1902 season, but played in just 87 games because the National League obtained an injunction against him playing in Pennsylvania. He risked arrest if he took the field in a Pennsylvania city.

The absence of Lajoie from the All Americans' lineup for the games in Pittsburgh was an obvious handicap for the visitors. In the second game, first basemen Carey and Davis had to cover second base for Lajoie and Carey's error cost the American League Stars a run.

The Pirates were also shorthanded for the series. 20-game winner Jesse Tannehill had been released and Ed Doheny was unavailable because of a late-season sprained ankle he sustained while playing with his son in their New York hotel room. It was also evident that 28-game winner Jack Chesbro had signed with the American League for the 1903 season, so Fred Clarke had only Sam Leever and Deacon Phillippe to handle all the Pirates' pitching chores.

On the day the Pirates were to play their first game against the All Americans, Dreyfuss met with Chesbro at the club's offices. Although nothing was revealed about the particulars of the meeting, it was surmised, based on the demeanor of the participants, that Chesbro might return to the Pirates in 1903. That decision would soon be taken out of the hands of the particulars and the issue would be decided by a commission set up to settle player contract disputes. The meeting between the owner and player was amicable, and Dreyfuss wished Chesbro "good luck" as he parted.

Tuesday, October 7, 1902, was a dreary, rainy day at Exposition Park and only 2,200 fans came out to see a game with historic implications. The American League did not adopt the new foul strike rule until 1903 and since National League rules were used in the first game, Hank O'Day called balls and strikes with Silk O'Loughlin of the American League in charge of the bases.

The National League champions started like gangbusters in the first inning with two runs off Cy Young. Beaumont tripled and trotted home on Clarke's double. Clarke scored on an infield out to make the score 2–0. It began to rain in the third inning and Young seemed to lose focus as he slipped and slid in the muck. The Pirates added two more runs to take a 4–0 lead.

By the final inning, the All Americans had done nothing against Sam Leever after Hartsel and Jones had opened the fifth with successive singles. When he stepped into the pitcher's box to start the ninth, Leever had retired 12 consecutive batters.

The trouble began when Harley dribbled a little roller perfectly positioned between the pitcher and the first baseman. Ritchey charged in and made a desperate throw that pulled Bransfield off the bag. Next up was Monte Cross, and the A's shortstop drove a clean single to right. Though there were two on and none out, Leever still had a four-run lead. This all changed moments later when Sullivan tripled to the flagpole in center field to plate the two baserunners. Sullivan scored on Young's long fly ball to center field and the Pirates' comfortable lead was down to one run. Hartsel also got good wood on a Leever pitch and hit it hard to center field but Beaumont was able to haul it in. Jones grounded to Wagner, who threw to first in time to preserve the Pirates 4 to 3 victory.[58]

In a meeting of the Pittsburgh players on Wednesday, they decided to invite Chesbro to pitch in the series. Chesbro promised to do so, but he failed to appear in uniform for the second game. The next morning, the Pirates held another meeting and, by unanimous vote, elected not to allow Chesbro a player's share for the series.[59]

In "one of the fastest games ever," just 85 minutes, the Pirates prevailed in the second contest between the rival leagues. About twice as many spectators came out to Exposition Park and Phillippe didn't let them down as he held the American League stars to just three hits in a 2 to 0 shutout. Addie Joss pitched almost as well but suffered a tough loss due to errors by the Americans. The All Americans were further hampered when third baseman Bradley was called home because of his brother's illness. Bobby Wallace moved to third and Carey, normally a first baseman, played the first eight innings at second base.

The first run of the contest was scored in the fifth inning. Wagner led off with a grounder to the second baseman and made it to second when Carey threw wild to first. He advanced to the third station on Bransfield's out and scored on the Pirates' first hit off Joss. Ritchey's smash caromed off Monte Cross and bounded into center as Wagner cantered across the plate.

It appeared Pittsburgh would break the game open in the eighth. With a run in and Pirates on second and third with one out, Bransfield hit a line drive right to second baseman Harry Davis, who stepped on second to double off Wagner.

Phillippe was touched for only the Americans' third hit when Mercer, pinch-hitting for Joss, led off the ninth inning with a single. Hartsel struck out and Fielder Jones also went out to leave it up to a former Pirate, Harry Davis. Davis hit a ground ball to Bransfield at first for what should have been the third out. Bransfield fielded it cleanly and made a good toss to the pitcher covering the first bag, but Phillippe dropped the throw. As the ball rolled away Mercer scampered to third base and probably could have scored but didn't risk it as the Americans needed two runs to tie. However, it didn't happen as Wallace grounded into a force out at second to end the game. As was his custom, there was no post-game celebration by Phillippe and he solemnly walked to the clubhouse.[60]

In 1911, Addie Joss said of Phillippe, "I regard him as one of the headiest pitchers in the game today, this from studying him at a distance. His biggest asset is an abundance of knowledge about the game, and control also has served him well all these years. However, I only pitched one game against Phillippe in my life, and that was in Pittsburgh in 1902. The impression I gained then has been a lasting one."[61]

The series moved to Cleveland's League Park for the third game on October 10. The announced attendance was 3,300, but *The Sporting News* reported it was more like 2,400. The National League's foul strike rule was in effect for the odd-numbered games, so the American League crowd was unfamiliar with the rule. Every time a foul hit was called a strike they hollered "robber" at the umpire. According to one reporter, this was a distinct handicap to the Americans in game three, when the Pirates' Leever, not known as a strikeout pitcher, fanned eight.

Leever and Cleveland's Bernhard went the distance for their respective teams in an effort that led Henry P. Edwards of the *Cleveland Plain Dealer* to write, "Better ball was never pitched by Sam Leever and Bill Bernhard." Each pitcher allowed only four hits. The *Pittsburgh Chronicle Telegraph* stated Leever "pitched his best game of the season against the All-Americans."[62]

Leever retired the first nine men he faced. Hartsel led off the fourth inning with a single but was doubled up on Jones' attempted sacrifice. The Americans did not advance a runner as far as third base until the ninth inning. Jones led off by grounding to third and was safe on Leach's low throw. Davis sacrificed the runner to second and up to bat came the dangerous Lajoie. With his home-town fans pleading for a hit, he could only manage a ground ball to Wagner. Davis went to third while Wagner was throwing Lajoie out at first. Wallace already had two hits off Leever so Leever gave him four wide ones to send him to first base. The inning ended when Harley could not locate any of Leever's benders and struck out.

The contest was eventually called after 11 scoreless innings, completed in only 90 minutes. In light of the no-decision, the teams agreed to play only one more game.

The Americans finally got a victory in the fourth and final game of the series. The interest rose above the previous contest as 4,765 paid to watch an anticipated duel between Cy Young and Deacon Phillippe. Except for a Tommy Leach error on a ball hit by Lajoie in the seventh inning, the game could well have been another double goose-egg affair. After Leach "booted Lajoie's tap half way across the diamond," Lajoie moved to third on a single by Bobby Wallace and scored the winning run on a double by Dick Harley.

The Pirates had their best chance to score in the fourth inning with Clarke on third base with one out. When Wagner drove a fly ball to shallow right field, Clarke tagged up and took off for home the instant the ball landed in the hands of Topsy Hartsel. Hartsel quickly made an accurate throw to home plate and as Clarke neared his goal, he saw the throw reach catcher Sullivan. Clarke attempted an evasive slide, but Sullivan did not have to move to apply the tag. As Hartsel walked to the bench the American League crowd gave him a resounding cheer until he disappeared from view.[63]

Pittsburgh had other opportunities to dent the scoring plate, but the fates were against them. With Phillippe on second base and Clarke on first with no one out a couple of innings later, Ginger Beaumont attempted to punch a hit through the left side of the infield. Because of the length of the grass plus the soggy condition of the field, Bobby Wallace got to the ball near second base too late to get Clarke. However, Phillippe tripped going to third and Monte Cross beat him to the bag in time to take Wallace's throw for a force out on the embarrassed pitcher. Instead of having the bases loaded with none out and Leach and Wagner due to bat, the bad break allowed Young to wriggle out of the jam.[64]

In another instance, with Beaumont at bat and Clarke on first, the Pirates attempted the hit-and-run play. Beaumont hit a low liner toward center field, but unfortunately for the Pirates second baseman Lajoie was running over to cover the bag after Clarke broke from first. The ball took one bounce to Lajoie, who touched the base, then threw to first to retire Beaumont for the double play. Young escaped with a 1 to 0 victory, but Phillippe deserved a better result than a loss. With the final out the mighty Pirates' offensive machine completed their 20th consecutive inning without scoring a run. On the other hand, the All Americans made a grand total of four runs and scored in only two of the 38 innings pitched by Leever and Phillippe.

The duel between Honus Wagner and Nap Lajoie went to the Dutchman, who collected five hits in 15 at bats during the series. The American League batting champion was 0-for-7 in two games against Leever and Phillippe.

Sporting Life headlined the series as an "Inter-League Clash" with the subtitle, "Four Great Games between Pittsburgh and All-Americans." However, the games received little notice in the nation's newspapers. *The Boston Globe* put the report of one of the inter-league games as filler at the bottom of a column listing the boxing results at the Lenox Athletic Club.

The Monday following the inter-league games, the Pirates commenced to fulfill an obligation to play exhibition games against area amateur teams. The first stop was Sharon, Pennsylvania, for a game that saw most of the Pirates playing out of position. Merritt pitched; Phillippe was his shortstop, and Leever patrolled right field. The barnstorming major leaguers won, 9 to 4.[65]

Leever had decided not to pursue the vocation of teacher during the off-season and accompanied two other avid sportsmen, Phillippe and Wagner, on a four-day hunting trip to Washington County immediately following the barnstorming trip. Following the hunt, Phillippe departed for South Dakota to check on his holdings and visit his widowed father.

Phillippe was supposed to remain at his Midwest farm for a couple of months but returned to the Smoky City in mid-November. He told the *Pittsburgh Press*, "I found the ranch in good shape. The fall season out there was mild but before I started east I drove the herd to shelter and saw to it that it would be well protected this winter. Crops were heavy and the cattle show it."[66]

Before he left the city back in October, Phillippe convinced Barney Dreyfuss to put up the $1,500 to pay off the note on his South Dakota wheat farm. A few months later the owner and employee purchased an adjoining farm. When the partners received a lucrative offer for the land they agreed to sell. According to Dreyfuss, his share came to $7,000, a very generous return on his original investment. Phillippe used his money from the sale to purchase another farm that would be entirely his own.[67]

Despite the successes of the past season, the Pirates were dismayed by the defection of almost half of their players to the American League. Seven of the 1902 Pirates — Jack Chesbro, Jesse Tannehill, Tommy Leach, Jack O'Connor, Harry Smith, Wid Conroy, and Lefty Davis — appeared set to join a new American League club in New York for 1903.

Barney Dreyfuss went to the National League's annual meeting in December, 1902, with a mission. Tired of the continual warfare with the American League, Dreyfuss pushed for an agreement to make peace with the rival circuit. Harry Pulliam, secretary of the Pittsburgh club, was elected to the National League's presidency and a commission was appointed to arrange a peace conference with the Americans.

In January, 1903, an American League delegation led by Ban Johnson met with the National League in Cincinnati to discuss an end to the warfare between the two circuits. An interested observer at the conference was Sam Leever, who said he was there out of curiosity and a desire to see "a settlement that would put an end to the contract-jumping and other evils, which a base ball war breeds."[68]

The delegates agreed that the leagues would respect each other's player contracts, thus ending a player's option to jump to the opposite league. The National Leaguers promised not to oppose the Americans' plan to put a team in New York provided Ban Johnson agreed not to place a club in Pittsburgh.

A major sticking point in the negotiations was how to distribute players whose contracts were in dispute between the two leagues. When the meeting deteriorated into heated exchanges, the magnates adjoined for the day. After talks resumed, the Cincinnati club agreed to withdraw its claim to outfielder Sam Crawford as a gesture of peace. Barney Dreyfuss chimed in by offering to give up the Pirates' 20-year-old outfielder, Jimmy Sebring, who was also claimed by the Detroit Tigers.

Ban Johnson accepted the olive branch and reciprocated by renouncing any American League claim to Sebring. The owners amicably went about bargaining for the disputed players. The Americans agreed to give up their claim to Tommy Leach, but only if Pittsburgh awarded Wid Conroy to their new New York club, which was now without a third baseman. Reserve catcher Harry Smith also was returned to the Pirates, but Dreyfuss did not retain the star pitcher, Jack Chesbro.

To administer the newly installed structure of Organized Baseball, a National Commission was established, composed of the two league presidents and a chairman chosen by the presidents. The Commission was to see that the terms of the National Agreement were followed and would rule on disputes among the signature clubs. There were no concessions to the players in the deal nor was there any modification of the reserve clause as employee rights reverted to the pre-war status. In other words, the players had no rights.

On January 12, 1903, Cincinnati owner August "Garry" Herrmann, spokesman for the National League delegation and president of the new National Commission, announced the completion of an agreement to end the warfare between the leagues and bring "rock-ribbed stability" to the game.

♦ Six ♦

Three in a Row

The city of Pittsburgh was atop the baseball world as attention turned to a new season in the spring of 1903. During a June trip to western Pennsylvania, a *New York Evening World* correspondent penned an idealized description of the city's station preceding a game between the Pirates and the New York Giants. "Magnificent weather, hundreds of pretty women in Paris gowns, automobile and coaching parties, and $50,000 in betting money greeted the Giants this afternoon when they played their second game here with the champion Pirates. It was a crowd worthy of what has now come to be known even abroad as the sportiest city in America. From the forges of Carnegie, the coke mountains of Frick and the garish bars along Fifth Avenue and Smithfield Street there emerged a swarm of humanity, bitterly eager to see New York humiliated."[1]

When the Pirates gathered in March, 1903, for the trip from Pittsburgh to spring training at Hot Springs, Arkansas, their most pressing need was obvious. The club had to revamp a pitching staff decimated by the loss of Chesbro and Tannehill. Phillippe and Leever would not have to carry the load alone. Also returning was Ed Doheny, whose 16–4 record in 1902 was the second-best winning percentage in the National League.

Harry Pulliam, the new National League president, was replaced in the capacity of Pirates secretary by William H. Locke, who was described by one Eastern columnist as "a pleasant gentleman, courteous, accommodating and thoroughly alive to the rights and privileges of the second party to any contract with him. There is nothing small nor mean about anyone connected with Dreyfuss, as he is known to be one of the squarest men ever connected with baseball, and Mr. Locke is one of his kind."[2]

The team's trip to Arkansas was a major production. Some 300 Pirates fans gathered at the railway station to see the team off on the evening of March 17, and the local newspapers covered the trip in detail. The club had arranged for the players to have a sleeping car all to themselves. The train arrived in Hot Springs early the morning of the 20th and the Pirates were greeted there by a band and crowd estimated at 3,000, most of whom accompanied the team to the hotel.

There were several candidates to fill out the rest of the pitching staff anchored by Phillippe, Leever and Doheny: Brickyard Kennedy, an 11-year veteran who had been released by the Giants; 6-foot-5 Fred Falkenberg, a raw University of Illinois alum; University of Bucknell product Bucky Veil; and Irvin Wilhelm, who had attracted Barney Dreyfuss' attention when he pitched back-to-back one-hitters for Birmingham of the Southern League the previous season. Fred Clarke liked to keep his starters fresh by utilizing a five-pitcher rotation, but it was obvious none of the newcomers could be counted on in a tight pennant race. During the spring, Deacon Phillippe recognized deficiencies in Fred Falkenberg's delivery and tried to help the rookie.

"When Falkenberg was with the Worcester team," Deacon later recalled, "he pitched two games against the Pirates, and fooled the best batters on the team. For some reason or another Falkenberg could not get going right last spring and could do nothing. I know what ailed the big fellow, and told him but to save his life he could not get back into his stride, though he worked ever so hard to do so."[3] Falkenberg started six games for the Pirates in 1903, losing four of them. He became a starter for Washington during the 1905 season and spent eight years pitching in the American League. By 1913 he was known as "Cy" and had developed a nasty pitch known as the emery ball. That season, *Baseball Magazine* named him along with Walter Johnson as a member of their "All-American" team from the junior circuit.

During the spring, the Pirates played several exhibition games against minor league teams and won only one. The *Pittsburgh Dispatch* was not impressed with the Pirates' chances for a repeat. "The prospects for bringing the pennant again to Pittsburgh are dim."

In what was almost an annual event, Exposition Park was again ravaged by spring storms. After rain and wind of several days duration, the grandstand was missing part of its roof, a section of the surrounding fence was lying in the street, and right field was under water. Dreyfuss and club Vice-President O. S. Hershmann went about the arrangement of contracts for immediate repairs to Exposition Park.

Among improvements added to the project were a new home team clubhouse with a larger plunge bath and lockers for all members of the team. The old clubhouse was prone to flooding, but the new one would be set on high piers to elevate it above the flood line. A new bleacher that could accommodate 2,500 to 3,000 persons was added to the right wing of the grandstand and extended to the right field fence at the foul line. A new double right field fence three feet thick was constructed to prevent "deadheads" from watching the games from outside the park.[4]

Pittsburgh began the quest for a third consecutive pennant on April 16 against Cincinnati, one of the favorites to challenge for the 1903 pennant. The Pirates unveiled new uniforms for the season opener at the Palace of the Fans — dark bluish-black caps with the letter "P" in front, royal blue collars on off-white wool jerseys, and blue- and gold-striped socks.

The weather that day was anything but fair, and the wildness of Cincinnati pitcher Jack Harper (he gave up eight walks and 11 hits) kept the local patrons sitting in the cold for almost two hours. Deacon Phillippe added to the discomfort of the 12,000 chilly fans as "his speed made the Reds' eyes sore."[5] Phillippe allowed only two Cincy hits in his 7 to 1 victory and only a wild throw in the ninth inning cost him a shutout. Pittsburgh completed a four-game sweep of the Reds as Doheny, Wilhelm and Veil turned in creditable pitching performances.

The Pirates returned to Exposition Park for their home opener on April 21. About 3,000 of the record crowd stood along the foul lines and in the outfield, forming a large human horseshoe. A band preceded the entrance of the baseball teams, riding in horse-drawn carriages. The official song of the National League, "In the Good Old Summer Time," was played, after which Harry Pulliam made a speech and conducted the ceremony of hauling down the previous year's pennant and hoisting a new one "amid deafening noises of all kinds and loud cheerings from the 18,010 persons present."[6]

Once play began, Phillippe was uncharacteristically ineffective as he gave up nine runs on 13 hits in six innings and the Pirates lost to St. Louis, 9–8. Phillippe left in the sixth inning, down 9 to 4, and was replaced by Falkenberg.

Sam Leever made his first start of the 1903 season at Exposition Park two days later and gave up 11 hits, but had enough offensive support to get the victory. Right fielder Jimmy Sebring hit two home runs to the deepest environs of center field, and the Buccaneers defeated the Cardinals, 8 to 4. Leever had one of the Pirates' 12 hits and scored a run.

Leever's next start, on April 29, was much better. He recorded the first of his league-high seven shutouts as Pittsburgh defeated St. Louis, 4–0, at Robison field. The Schoolmaster, "whose arm some fans thought gone," the *Pittsburgh Press* reported, "shut out Patsy Donovan's husky team of Cardinals on but three hits.... He had the team completely at his mercy during the whole nine innings and at no time did they have a ghost of a show to score."[7]

The next day, the Pirates defeated the Cardinals and Mordecai Brown, 13 to 4. Phillippe gave up eight hits and struck out six to even his record at 2 and 2. Tommy Leach's bases-loaded inside-the-park home run highlighted a five-run sixth inning for the Pirates, and Phillippe contributed to the offense himself with three hits.

Phillippe prided himself in his hitting. During the Pirates' three-year championship run he batted .230, .221 and .210, not that bad for a pitcher. "The reason pitchers are not harder hitters is because of the lack of practice," he once said. "I know that if I had the opportunity as the other batters on the team, I think I would have just as good a batting average at the close of the season as the majority of the players. The regular players who are in the game every day get their eye on the ball, and by constant training can manage to keep their batting eye, while it is different with the pitcher who only works on an average of twice a week, and during the layoff will lose his stride in the batting line."[8]

While the team was on the road, Phillippe was a member of the club's "Pinochle Club"

An uncomfortable looking Samuel Leever in an awkward pose in an undated photograph. From the looks of the uniform and the tattered undershirt, perhaps he couldn't afford a glove (courtesy Pittsburgh Pirates).

which included newly acquired utility infielder Otto Krueger, Claude Ritchey and Honus Wagner. During down time on trains or in hotels, the quartet was inseparable until the group was broken up with the trade of Krueger before the 1905 season.

Five wins in six games had pushed Pittsburgh into first place when, on May 6, 1903, Phillippe experienced possibly the worst collapse of his major league career in a game against the Cubs at Exposition Park. After allowing two hits in each of the first two innings, he pitched six consecutive innings without allowing a safety. It appeared the Bucs finally had Chicago's Jack Taylor's number with a 4 to 2 lead going into the ninth. With Phillippe on the mound, a victory seemed to be a foregone conclusion.

The trouble for the Pirates began when Dick Harley led off the visitors' ninth with a single. Later in the inning, Doc Casey drilled a bases-loaded single to make the score 6–4 in favor of the Cubs, and Johnny Evers followed with a two-run triple. Three more runs tallied to make the final score 11 to 4. Phillippe had completely lost it; The Chicago safeties were all hard-hit and all nine runs in the inning were earned. Jack Taylor was the winner, the third time in 11 days he had beaten the Pirates.

The Pirates lost to Cincinnati the next day, although the big news was Honus Wagner's ejection by Umpire James "Bug" Holliday. The trouble occurred in the fifth inning when Wagner grounded to the Reds' shortstop. Fred Clarke, who had been on second, attempted to advance to third base and was thrown out. Third baseman "Topsy" Magoon complained about the Pirates manager's hard slide and the two exchanged insults. When play resumed, Wagner attempted to steal second, sliding aggressively into the base, whereupon Cincinnati second baseman Jack Morrissey claimed Wagner intentionally tried to spike him. The Reds players surrounded Wagner and the belligerents would have come to blows had not umpire Holliday intervened. In his report to President Pulliam, Holliday wrote that Wagner abused him and was therefore ejected from the field. Upon reading the umpire's account, Pulliam made his good friend Honus Wagner the first player he disciplined as league president.

Wagner had been playing right field since Jimmy Sebring was sidelined that April due to illness, so when the Dutchman began his three-day suspension on May 8, right field was manned by George Merritt, who had won three games as a pitcher for the Pirates in 1901. Wagner's suspension prompted Fred Clarke to announce that the Pirates would no longer resort to rowdyism, and for the most part they played clean baseball for the remainder of the season.

In his first start since the breakdown against the Cubs, Phillippe pitched his second shutout of the season on May 10 as the Pirates edged the Reds, 1–0, before an unusually large crowd of 20,000 at the Palace of the Fans. On the Sunday excursion to Cincinnati, Phillippe gave up five hits and did not allow a walk. That was enough to trump the four-hit pitching of Noodles Hahn. The Wagner-less Pirates scored the game's only run in the first inning when Tommy Leach tripled into the standing room crowd with two outs and scored when center fielder Joe Kelley dropped Merritt's fly ball after he made a long run to get to it. Wagner's pal Otto Krueger played an outstanding game at shortstop, and in the fourth inning he knocked down two batted balls headed for the outfield and threw his prey out at first base each time.[9]

Four days later, Phillippe gave up six hits and struck out six batters as the Pirates defeated host Philadelphia, 5–1. The Phillies only hit the ball past the infield seven times, and left fielder Clarke had the only outfield chances. Not only did Phillippe have an outstanding pitching performance, he was a major factor offensively with a double, two singles, two runs scored and a run batted in.

The Pirates moved to the Polo Grounds the following Saturday for their first visit to the home of the league-leading New York Giants. Christy Mathewson defeated the Pirates in the first game of the four-game series on May 16, but the next day Ed Doheny outpitched Joe McGinnity in the Pirates' 3–2 win. Doheny also earned a suspension when, after hitting a pop-up in front of the plate, he threw his bat at Frank Bowerman while the big catcher was attempting to catch the fly.

Though the umpire had already called Doheny out on the infield fly rule, the fans thought the Pirates pitcher intentionally tried to hit Bowerman. As the crowd booed, Doheny turned toward the stands, which further incited them. After the game, a mob followed him to the clubhouse and pelted the Pirates with rocks. For his actions, the National League president suspended Doheny for three days without pay.

The Giants regained first place from the Cubs in the third game of the series with a 4 to 3 victory. Phillippe was the losing pitcher though his seven strikeouts suggest he had good stuff. After getting the victory in relief, Mathewson came back the next day and blanked the Pirates, 2–0.

That loss to Mathewson on May 20 was the first time the Pirates were shut out on the season, but they did have their chance against him. The Giants' ace suddenly became hittable in the sixth inning, but Pittsburgh couldn't cash in a run. He got careless with the opposing pitcher, Leever, who drove a pitch almost to the right field fence, where George Browne retreated and gathered in the long fly. Still, the Pirates were able to load the bases with two out. Unfortunately, Kitty Bransfield struck out to end the scoring threat. Leever had himself to blame for the loss. His wild pitch allowed the Giants to score in the first inning and a hit batsman contributed to the Giants' other run. Mathewson was the winning pitcher in all three New York victories in the four-game set.

The Pirates had a little better luck across the bridge in Brooklyn, splitting a four-game series with the Superbas. Worse than the mediocre showing of the club on the field was the number of players on the sick list. Fred Clarke had to leave the team because of lumbago or kidney trouble, depending on which doctor was to be believed. Second baseman Claude Ritchey was out with a strained arm, Bill Kennedy couldn't pitch because of an injury, and catcher Harry Smith was out of the lineup with a split finger, leaving all the work behind the plate to Ed Phelps. Furthermore, Tommy Leach had to return to Allegheny because his young son was seriously ill with pneumonia.

Possibly the stress due to the illness of his son contributed to Leach's decline as a third baseman in 1903. He made 65 errors in 127 games (an .879 fielding percentage) at the hot corner after committing 39 miscues in seven more games a year earlier.

Phillippe lost a game by one run in Brooklyn on May 23 when the Superbas tagged him for three runs in the ninth inning. Because of Clarke's illness and the absence of Leach, Krueger had filled in at third and George Merritt took over in left.

Late in the Pirates' contest in Boston on May 26, Merritt broke his ankle sliding into second base, leaving the club with only two able bodied outfielders. Having only joined the club a day earlier, pitcher "Kaiser" Wilhelm was the team's emergency outfielder, but he was scheduled to pitch the game against the Beaneaters on the 27th. Phillippe agreed to take up the position in left field for his regular season only appearance as a position player during his 12-year tenure with the Pirates. He batted seventh, collected one hit and accepted three chances in the field, erring once. However, the Pirates were drubbed, 7 to 1, Bransfield's home run the Buccaneers' only run. The *Pittsburgh Gazette* noted that Phillippe's error was a "hair raising muff" of a fly ball that permitted a runner to score. The loss dropped the third-place Pirates to four and a half games behind the first-place Giants. Phillippe got the next day off as an obscure substitute named Reddy Grey made his only major league appearance in left field on May 28.

When the Pirates returned home for a morning-afternoon doubleheader on May 30, they were a severely crippled team. Krueger covered third base when Leach missed the morning game with Cincinnati because of his son's illness. Wilhelm was put in Clarke's left field spot, batting ninth behind Phillippe, who was the starting hurler. A Decoration Day crowd of 7,076 saw Phillippe win the opener when Jimmy Sebring scored the ninth-inning run that sent former Pirate Eddie Poole down to a 3 to 2 loss.

Tommy Leach arrived at the park in time to play in the afternoon contest. However, a man was stationed at the telephone in the club office and a cab was waiting at the park entrance ready to convey Leach home in case there was any change in the little boy's condition. Krueger moved into the troublesome left field spot.

In the afterpiece, Leever and Cincinnati's Noodles Hahn battled to a 3–3 tie after eight innings, and Sebring drove in the winning run with his ninth-inning hit. Surprisingly, it was the substitute, Krueger, who may have saved the game for the Pirates with a catch that Ralph Davis wrote was "one of the prettiest double plays ever seen on the home grounds." Steinfeldt was on second base when Jake Beckley hit a long fly ball that appeared to be hopelessly out of Krueger's reach. "But," wrote Davis, "the little fellow went after it and captured it. He then quickly sent the ball spinning toward the plate and Steinfeldt tried to score on the out. The ball got there just ahead of him on a beautiful throw, and the Red-Leg was out, much to his disgust and the satisfaction of the crowd."[10]

Neither Leach nor Clarke accompanied the team to Reville for an exhibition game on Sunday, but Tommy was in the lineup on Monday when McGraw's Giants came to Exposition Park for a three-game series. It was no surprise that Christy Mathewson took the mound for the visitors in the first game. The "Pirate Killer" won easily, 10 to 2, over Doheny. Four of Mathewson's ten victories to that point in 1903 were over the Pirates. Worse, the Pirates fell six games behind New York in the loss column.

With Honus Wagner filling in as manager for the ailing Fred Clarke, who was still suffering severe back pain, the Pirates beat the Giants, 7–0, on June 2. Deacon Phillippe allowed only one runner to advance as far as third base and he struck out eight batters, including the side in the fifth inning. During Phillippe's shutout, Giants catcher Frank Bowerman was thrown out of the game for arguing balls and strikes, then sat in the stands from where he criticized the Giants' back-up catcher, John Warner.

According to the New York papers, Pirates manager Clarke learned of Bowerman's comments and he sought out Warner, a former teammate of Clarke in Louisville. Clarke quoted Bowerman as saying, "If I was catching Pittsburgh would not make so many hits." He further intimated that Bowerman had a low opinion of his replacement's ability, which made Warner so furious he would not speak to Bowerman the rest of the road trip.[11]

When Bowerman found out what Clarke had said, he became determined to get even and bided his time until he got a chance to confront the Pirates' manager. He would get his opportunity when the Pirates visited New York later that month.

The day after Phillippe's shutout of New York, Leever bested Joe McGinnity, 5–0, before a mid-week crowd of 5,000. Claude Ritchey made four hits and scored Pittsburgh's first run on the back end of a double steal. Ginger Beaumont hit a home run to deep center field in the fifth, the same inning the normally placid Christy Mathewson was thrown out of the game for kicking dirt on the umpire while he was coaching at third base.

Irvin "Kaiser" Wilhelm made a rare start for the Pirates on June 4 and shut out the Boston Beaneaters in the opening contest of a three-game series at Exposition Park. A day later Doheny coasted to a 9–0 victory as the Pirates racked up 17 hits against Boston's Togie Pittinger. Pittsburgh's fourth shutout in a row set a new major-league record. Clarke went 5-for-5 and Ginger Beaumont went 4-for-5, including his second homer in a week.

Dedicated to keeping the scoreless streak intact, Phillippe took the mound against Boston on June 6 in a light rain. He turned in one scoreless inning after another while Pittsburgh built up a four-run lead as the rain gradually intensified. In those days the rules stipulated that play was to continue until the spectators vacated the open stands to seek shelter. When Boston's at-bat concluded in the fifth inning and the game became official, the Pittsburgh bleacherites "arose as one man and filed out to seek shelter from the rain, and at the same time yelled for the umpire to call the game." Though the "water and mud were knee deep," Umpire Hank O'Day, a former major league pitcher, stubbornly refused to suspend play. After Wagner led off the bottom of the sixth with a triple, Beaneaters manager Al Buckenberger asked that the game be stopped to protect his players from injury. O'Day relented and the Pittsburgh pitching staff had its fifth consecutive shutout.

After the Sunday off-day, the Phillies, now managed by former Pirates catcher Chief Zimmer, arrived in town to face the red-hot Pirates pitchers. Leever shut out the Phillies, 2–0, to continue the team's scoreless streak. However, the home crowd was on the edge of their seats as the lowly Phillies mounted a rally in the top of the ninth. Trailing by only two runs, Philadelphia put runners on second and third with two out. Klondike Douglass pinch-hit for the Phillies' pitcher with the streak and the game on the line. With a count of one ball, Douglass lined a Leever pitch toward left-center field. Playing deep at shortstop because two were out, Wagner took two steps toward second base and "sprang into the air like an enraged beast." The star shortstop speared the ball in his glove and nearly turned a flip as he hit the ground with the ball, the game, and the streak secure in his grasp. Wrote Frank McQuisten in *The Pittsburgh Dispatch*, "Little children in the coming years may forget the year Columbus discovered America ... but they will never — no, never — forget the day that Hans Wagner made that catch!"[12]

The following afternoon, Philadelphia reached Wilhelm for a run in the fourth inning to end the Pirates pitchers' consecutive scoreless inning streak at 56, still a major league record. The Pirates won the game anyway for their seventh straight victory.

A day after Phillippe served as a substitute umpire in Doheny's 7–4 triumph over the Phillies, he got the Pirates back on the shutout track in a game with Brooklyn at Exposition Park. With a steady drizzle falling throughout the game, he threw his third straight scoreless game. In the third inning, play was stopped with Brooklyn's Dutch Jordan at bat. A "delegation of Pittsburghers gathered around, and after some speech making, blowing of horns, and ringing of bells, presented the player with a diamond stud."[13] After the Pittsburgh native's admirers departed the field, he singled to left. The interruption didn't seem to bother Phillippe as he easily disposed of the next three batters to strand Jordan. He did not allow another opposition base runner until the eighth and completed a three-hit, 9–0 shutout. Phillippe's battery mate, Ed Phelps, went 3-for-3 with a stolen base, leading Chief Zimmer to call Phelps "the best catcher in the game" and "a coming star."

Following two rainouts and the Sunday off-day, the Pirates notched another shutout on June 15 when Leever whitewashed the Cubs at Exposition Park, 3–0. Chicago's Jack Menefee also pitched well enough to win, but his defense let him down in the second inning. With two out and runners on second and third, Leever punched a short fly to right field. First baseman Chance, second baseman Evers and right fielder Hartley all went after the ball. According to reports, Hartley could have caught the fly, but stopped a few feet away for fear of colliding with Chance. The ball dropped in safely and the two Pittsburgh runners scored. The Pirates scored a third run when Bransfield tripled and scored on a short sacrifice fly.

In his third consecutive shutout, the Schoolmaster allowed only one hit (a single by the opposing pitcher, Menefee), walked two, hit one batter and struck out three. Leever had not allowed a run since May 30 when the Reds scored two runs in the eighth inning of Pittsburgh's 4 to 3 victory.

Leever's win moved the Pirates into second place in the National League. The triumph was the tenth consecutive win for the Pirates, and their eighth shutout in ten games.

The winning streak continued on June 16, but it didn't come easy. The Chicago Cubs took a 3–0 lead against Phillippe in the second inning, largely due to a pair of errors by first baseman Bransfield. Not only were they down by three runs, Jack Taylor was the opposing pitcher. Pittsburgh needed a break and they got one in the fifth inning when the Cubs messed up another pop fly.

Claude Ritchey lifted a fly ball to short center field with Tommy Leach on first base. Evers, Tinker and center fielder Davy Jones each thought the other would catch the ball and it hit the ground for a hit. Phelps beat out a bunt to fill the bases. The infield moved in as the pitcher came to bat, but Phillippe singled over second base to plate two runs and Phelps raced to third. The catcher came home with the tying run when the next batter, Ginger Beaumont, flied out to Jones.

Honus Wagner scored the lead run in the sixth after he reached on Evers' error and worked his way around the bases on a passed ball, an infield out, and Ritchey's double. Phillippe pitched scoreless ball after the first inning and Pittsburgh won, 6–3. The win for Phillippe was especially sweet after his ninth-inning meltdown against Chicago six weeks earlier; 7,100 happy Pittsburgh bugs finally saw the Pirates beat Jack Taylor.

Leever's 12 to 2 victory in Boston on June 19 was the team's 13th straight and vaulted the Pirates into first place to stay. Boston didn't score until the eighth inning, which ended Leever's scoreless streak at 36 innings. However, the Buccaneers' rampage did not end until they had racked up 15 straight victories.

The Pirates rolled into New York the evening of June 25 in first place, two and a half games ahead of the Giants. The next day, Deacon Phillippe, Fred Clarke, Honus Wagner and Secretary Will Locke took a streetcar from their hotel to the Polo Grounds for the first game of the series. The Polo Grounds was one of the few major league parks to provide dressing facilities for the visiting team, so the three players were in civilian clothes. Once inside the clubhouse, Clarke encountered an apparently friendly Frank Bowerman, who suggested that Clarke accompany him to a ticket office for a discussion of a private nature. According to a report in *The Evening World*, Giants secretary Fred Knowles was at his desk when the pair entered. Phillippe and Wagner went on to the visitors' clubhouse, while Locke remained in the corridor.

Once inside the isolated Polo Grounds office, Bowerman's demeanor turned to anger and he accused Clarke of degrading him to the press. The irate Giants catcher caught Clarke unawares with a solid fist to the jaw, knocking the manager to the floor. The much heavier Bowerman landed on Clarke and continued to pummel the fallen man with his fists. An accomplice of Bowerman, said to have been Roger Bresnahan, stood outside the room to prevent anyone from interfering with Bowerman's ambush. After a few minutes, policemen on hand to provide security for the game showed up and pulled the belligerents apart. The Pi-

Pirates Manager Fred Clarke (George Grantham Bain collection, Library of Congress Prints and Photographs Division).

rates' players were astonished when Clarke walked into the dressing room with disheveled clothing, his face covered with bruises, and one eye seriously swollen. [14]

To show that it would take more than a beating from one of the Giants' bullies to keep him out of that day's lineup, Clarke assumed his normal position in the third spot of his batting order. When he came to bat with two out in the first inning, "A loud laugh went up as he showed a discolored eye."[15]

Bowerman took a position on the Giants' bench, his only injuries from the fight being scratches and cuts on his knuckles from pounding Clarke's head and face. Of course, John McGraw had Christy Mathewson ready to pitch the opener, and the Giants' ace extended his personal winning streak against Pittsburgh to five, defeating the Pirates, 8–2. Sam Leever took the loss when the Giants' four-run fifth inning sent him packing. At the end of the day, both clubs had nineteen losses, but Pittsburgh still held first by virtue of three more victories than New York. An outraged Barney Dreyfuss sought redress against Bowerman from the league office, but President Pulliam demurred. Clarke, on the other hand, just wanted the matter dropped.

A record Polo Grounds crowd of 32,240 showed up for the game on Saturday afternoon. The grandstands and bleachers were filled so part of the crowd overflowed onto the field and stood, packed against the stands, almost to the base lines. Some of those who couldn't get in swarmed the 155th Street Bridge, and Coogan's Bluff was black with spectators.

The Pirates threatened in each of the first four innings, but got only one run for Phillippe. New York took the lead in the last of the fourth inning when third baseman Leach's error with two outs prolonged the frame and permitted the Giants to score two runs.

Pittsburgh tied it in the seventh when the Giants' right-fielder misplayed Wagner's single into two bases and Hans scored on Bransfield's single. After the sixth inning, Philippe did not permit an opposition hit and in the bottom of the seventh, he retired the side on three pitches.

Beaumont led off the 11th inning with a double to right, but moments later he was run down between second and third on Clarke's tap to the pitcher. Clarke made it to second during the run-down, after which McGinnity awarded Wagner first base with four wide pitches. The runners moved up one station on Krueger's grounder, then Leach sent them both scurrying home on his two-bagger.

Phillippe finished off the New Yorkers in the bottom of the 11th to snap the Pirates' two-game losing skid with the exciting 4 to 2 victory. The Pirates made fifteen hits, including four by Honus Wagner, but also stranded 15 baserunners.

His win at the Polo Grounds was Phillippe's seventh victory in a row, not having lost since May 23 in Brooklyn. Three of the seven wins were shutouts, including a three-hitter and a five-hitter. During the streak he beat Eddie Poole, the Giants' Dummy Taylor, Vic Willis, Roy Evans of Brooklyn, Jack Taylor, Boston's Wiley Piatt, and Joe McGinnity. He finally lost, 5–4, to Brooklyn on July 1 when the Superbas scored all of their runs in the final three innings. He then reeled off four more consecutive victories.

On July 4, the Pirates swept a doubleheader from last-place Philadelphia, 7–0 and 7–1, at Expo. The morning crowd numbered 12,070, but the afternoon affair drew only 7,050 because of the rain that began to fall an hour before the second game was to start.

The grandstands and bleachers were packed for the morning affair with the Phillies, and the crowd was ushered onto the outfield, lined four and five deep along the lines. Ralph Davis noted, "The cheering at times was deafening, while hundreds of revolvers were brought into play to help along the noise."[16]

Sam Leever threw an eight-hit shutout in beating Fred Clarke's brother-in-law, Chick Fraser, and, after a delay because of the rainstorm, Deacon Phillippe won the afterpiece. He might have gotten another shutout had not catcher Phelps been injured running the bases in the morning game. The only Philadelphia run of the day scored just after Phelps' replacement, Art Weaver, dropped a foul fly that should have been "the easiest kind of picking."[17]

Ginger Beaumont went 3-for-3, including two doubles, and scored three times in support of Phillippe's hurling that pushed the Pirates' record to 46–20, five games ahead of second-place New York. Unfortunately, Fred Clarke strained ligaments in his right shoulder while making a diving catch of a fly ball during Phillippe's game. The manager would be out of the lineup for almost a month.

Though it didn't seem serious at the time, Phillippe strained his back pitching in the mud on Independence Day. Clarke wanted him to take a break from the team right then, but Phillippe insisted that the club needed him and promised to take a few days off when the team was in better shape.[18]

The Giants arrived in Pittsburgh for a key four-game series beginning on July 15. Extra policemen were put on duty to prevent violence between the participants and fans. The home crowd reserved most of their taunts for Bowerman, who had been fined $100 for his assault on Fred Clarke, but during the day there was no violence perpetrated by fans or players.

As usual, Mathewson pitched the first game and once again won, although it took 14 innings. Leever took on McGinnity the next day and the Giants' submariner didn't make it out of the fifth inning. Center fielder Ginger Beaumont took batting honors in the Pirates' 16–4 win by going 4-for-5, including two inside-the-park home runs, a triple, and five runs scored. Leever, who had two hits himself, gave up ten hits, all singles, and raised his record to 13–4. Pittsburgh beat the Giants in the third game of the series and Phillippe was given the task of making it three straight over New York on July 18.

John McGraw announced that Mathewson would pitch against Phillippe on Saturday and the words "Mathewson will pitch tomorrow," in letters a yard long, were written in chalk on the path leading to the visitors' bench. Mathewson saw the announcement and rubbed it out with his feet. Matty declared his 14 innings three days earlier was enough pitching for the week and he would not go in the final game of the series. Bowerman, annoyed by the roasting given him by the Pirates' fans, said he would not play either. The 10,000 in attendance, most of whom were expecting Mathewson to pitch, were surprised when Umpire Emslie announced that Roscoe Miller would pitch for New York.

Going into the bottom of the ninth inning, Phillippe had allowed two runs, but Miller also had surrendered only two tallies. The Pittsburgh crowd sighed when Claude Ritchey was thrown out at home plate trying to score on a fly ball to left field, temporarily saving the game for New York. Then the red-hot Ginger Beaumont came through with a drive off the right field fence and Art Weaver dashed home with the winning run.

Following the big series with the Giants, the Pittsburgh club went into a mini-slump, dropping three straight games in Chicago. In the middle game, Leever gave up three runs in the third inning, but blanked the Cubs the rest of the game. Leever brought the Pirates to within a run in the seventh inning with his two-run triple, but that was all the Pirates would get. Honus Wagner made the final out in the ninth with two runners on base.

On July 24, the Pirates snapped their longest losing streak in two years with a 7–4 victory against the St. Louis Cardinals at Exposition Park. Tommy Leach hit a three-run home run in the first inning, left fielder Otto Krueger went 4-for-4, including two triples, and pitcher Deacon Phillippe was 3-for-3 with a base on balls and scored three times. Phillippe gave up nine hits and was able to overcome five Pirates errors, three by Leach, to raise his mound record to 15–6.

Late that July, Ed Doheny abruptly left the team and went home to Andover, Massachusetts. Doheny had exhibited erratic behavior for some time, but it had noticeably worsened in recent days. Late one night during the summer, pitcher Bill Kennedy was awakened in his room at the Monongahela House by a pounding at the door. Bill found his roommate Doheny standing in the hall wearing his robe. The confused pitcher claimed that he had been give an electric shock through the wall and said, "I'll wager that they're trying to work a panel game on me."[19]

Doheny picked up his 12th victory of the season in the opener of a three-game set in Cincinnati, then went completely off the deep end. He returned from a cobbler's shop screaming that the shoemaker was after him and was trying to kill him. At dinner the next evening, he hurled a plate at an imaginary policeman. The paranoid hurler also believed he was constantly being followed by detectives.

The morning of July 28, Doheny told Clarke he could not stand it any longer and was going to "give the detectives the slip and go home." Clarke argued the point and Doheny agreed that he had been royally treated by the club. After lunch Clarke and Doheny played a game of billiards, after which the pitcher bade his manager and teammates farewell before he left for the train station where he would take the two o'clock "Big Four" for Andover.[20]

A day later, *The Pittsburgh Post* explained Doheny's absence from the club with the headline: "His Mind is Thought to Be Deranged." Doheny consulted a doctor who deemed his affliction "a mild form of nervous prostration." The pitcher would return to his club on the 15th of August and rejoin the starting rotation.

The Pirates' casualty and sick list at the end of July was quite lengthy. Second baseman Claude Ritchey was suffering dizzy spells, Harry Smith had a bad hand and a lame knee, Bucky Veil was sick, Brickyard Kennedy had a gash in his leg from broken glass, Jimmy Sebring had a sore ankle, and Deacon Phillippe made the list because of a "lame back." Fred Clarke returned to the lineup long enough to reinjure his shoulder. Honus Wagner again took over as acting manager when Clarke was ordered to his home in Kansas for a week of rest.

Phillippe missed a start because of the sore back that had been bothering him for weeks, but was still able to help the team in St. Louis on July 31. Down one run to the Cardinals in the ninth inning, Phillippe pinch-hit for Fred Falkenberg and tripled. He then scored the tying run on Beaumont's ground ball when the Cardinals' shortstop threw wildly trying to head Phillippe off at home plate. After two were out, Honus Wagner tripled and scored the winning run on Sebring's sacrifice fly. Left in the game to pitch the ninth, Phillippe gave up two hits but escaped the inning unscored upon to save the game for Falkenberg. Phillippe was advised by a physician to take a break from the game, but Deacon refused to do so as long as the team was in such a dire need of pitching.

With Sam Leever his only healthy pitcher and the club in danger of running short on players, acting manager Wagner sent for Irving Wilhelm, who was recuperating from an illness at his home in Wooster, Ohio. The telegram arrived late at night and was opened by the pitcher's young wife since he was at a fishing camp some 15 miles away. In the face of a bad storm, she started out in a horse and buggy to bring Irving back in time to catch the morning train for Chicago. A few miles out of Wooster, Mrs. Wilhelm was forced to take shelter in a farmhouse due to a storm, but when it slackened she drove on to the fishing camp. The couple drove at breakneck speed to the railway station, but missed the first train to Chicago by two minutes. Wilhelm caught a later train.[21]

Wagner had no choice but to ask the ailing Phillippe to pitch the game of August 4 in Chicago. Phillippe was touched for a run in the first inning, then held the Cubs to only three additional hits and no runs the rest of the way. Unfortunately, the Pirates could not manage a score off Chicago's Jocko Menefee and lost, 1 to 0. That evening, Phillippe left the team and caught a train home to give his back some rest.

The low point of the Pirates' temporary swoon came August 5 when atrocious fielding gave Chicago six unearned runs off Sam Leever in the first inning. Down 9 to 2 after three innings, Leever was happy to give way to Wilhelm. The Pirates committed seven errors during their eight innings in the field, and The *Chicago Daily Tribune* accused the defending champions of quitting. Ironically, the pitcher who was the beneficiary of the Pirates' dismal performance was, of course, Jack Taylor.

Another loss to Taylor on August 9 was the Pirates' fourth setback in five games. Meanwhile, the Giants won seven in a row to pull within five games of first-place Pittsburgh.

On August 18, the Pirates snapped a two-game losing streak with Leever's 3–0 win over Beaneaters in Boston. It also was the Pirates' first shutout since July 8. Fred Clarke's two-run single in the fifth inning and Honus Wagner's run-scoring double in the eighth provided the runs that gave the Schoolmaster his 18th win of the season.

After Sam Leever's shutout of the Beantowners, the *Pittsburgh Press* editorialized, "The Schoolmaster held the Triumvirs down to three hits so puzzling was his delivery. He had superb control, especially of his sharp drop and the manner in which he mixed speed with slow balls was astonishing."[22]

Leever explained the nature of his various curve balls: "The balls which are usually classed under the head of curves are the outcurves, the drop ball, the jump ball, and the so-called inshoot, which is really misnamed, as the inshoot is a ball thrown naturally which breaks in. I grasp the ball the same way to throw these different varieties, a firm hold on the sphere with my thumb, index and middle fingers. The outcurve is then allowed to slide over the top of the index finger with a sweeping side-arm delivery. The curve is rather gradual, but is supposed to take the greater degree of variation from its course as it reaches the plate. The drop ball leaves the hand directly over the top of the index finger with a full-arm motion and a quick snap of the wrist as it leaves the hand. It is probably the hardest ball in the category on a pitcher's arm. It is frequently combined with the outcurve, producing the outdrop."[23]

A postponement of the opening game of the Pirates' crucial series in New York forced the teams to schedule back-to-back doubleheaders at the Polo Grounds on August 20 and 21. Pittsburgh's league lead shrank to four games in the first game on the 20th when the Pirates set a National League mark for inept fielding, committing six errors in the first inning to give the Giants seven runs toward their 13 to 7 win. Mathewson was unusually wild, received relief in the sixth inning, but still got his 23rd win. Ed Doheny was the victim of his teammates' poor support.

Phillippe won the nightcap, 4–1, to restore the Pirates' five-game lead. He would have had a shutout but for Leach's error in the third inning. Leach's wild throw landed Bowerman on second base and he scored on a sacrifice fly. Fred Clarke put Pittsburgh ahead for good when he drove a Luther "Dummy" Taylor pitch over the right field ropes for a home run.

In another doubleheader the next day, the Pirates and Giants again split, with the Buccaneers taking the opener, 3–0, on Leever's five-hitter. Joe McGinnity also allowed only five hits, but Pittsburgh's hits came when it counted. Wagner's double in the fourth drove home a run and he later scored on a sacrifice fly. Two innings later Beaumont doubled and scored the third Pittsburgh run on Leach's single. Christy Mathewson came back for the second straight day and won the nightcap for New York, 9–5, his eighth victory over Pittsburgh in 1903.

Deacon Phillippe earned his 20th victory of the season on August 28, defeating the St. Louis Cardinals, 4–1, at Exposition Park. A heavy rainfall delayed the start of the first of two scheduled games until three o'clock. Once the contest got under way, Phillippe was strong throughout despite the slippery conditions. He gave up eight hits, struck out five, did not allow a walk and also made two hits. The Pirates scored their four runs in the third, and Beaumont's overthrow of third base led to the Cardinals' lone run in the eighth inning to cost Phillippe yet another shutout. The earlier rain delay led to the postponement of the second game.

Another Pittsburgh winning streak in late August/early September erased what suspense there was left in the pennant race. On September 3 the Pirates extended the streak to 11 straight wins with a 6 to 3 victory over the Cincinnati Reds. Ed Doheny was the winning pitcher to raise his record to 16–8. Nobody could know that it would be his last major league game. On September 22, Doheny, overcome with paranoia, was taken home to Massachusetts by his brother.

On September 4, the Pirates won their 12th game in a row with Leever's 3 to 1 victory over Cincinnati at Exposition Park. The Pirates, with 80 victories and only 37 losses, increased their lead in the National League standings to nine and a half games after New York split a doubleheader with Brooklyn.

Two days later, the Pirates made it 14 in a row with a 5 to 1 victory over the Cubs at Chicago's West Side Grounds. Phillippe tossed a three-hitter and only his wild pitch in the second inning cost him the shutout. That win in Chicago was the final road game for the Pirates, who increased their lead over the Giants to ten games.

The Pirates clinched the National League pennant on September 18. Ninth-inning rallies pushed Pittsburgh to a doubleheader sweep of Boston while a New York loss assured the Bucs of their third consecutive title. The first game of the doubleheader would also be the final start of the regular season for Sam Leever.

By the final month of the season, both Leever and Phillippe were suffering sore shoulders due to the toil from the long season. As a reward for their outstanding work, Clarke allowed his two star pitchers to leave the club for a fishing trip.

Called "one of the best in the world today" in *The Sporting News* after the 1903 regular season, Leever compiled a 25–7 won-loss record with a league-leading 2.06 earned run average and led the league with seven shutouts. He completed 30 of the 34 games he started in pitching 284.1 innings.

While he was supposed to be resting in the final days of the regular season, Leever further aggravated his sore shoulder while trapshooting in a tournament in Charleroi, Pennsylvania. He was referred to a Youngstown chiropractor named John "Bonesetter" Reese, who was paid $500 by Barney Dreyfuss to assist club trainer Ed Laforce for the upcoming "World Series." A former steel worker who had no medical training, Reese had the reputation throughout professional baseball as a miracle worker. In this case, though, his techniques of massage and mysticism were not successful.

Leever used a treatment of his own design for over a week when he kept his arm in hot water for hours every day and worked with Trainer Laforce between soakings. A well-respected Pittsburgh physician noted that the attempt to "boil out the pain" further weakened his pitching arm.[24] Leever was an avid and accomplished trapshooter his entire life, but his injury participating in that sport late in the baseball season dearly cost the Pirates in the 1903 World Series.

Deacon Phillippe's regular season record was 25–7 with a 2.43 ERA, the fifth season in a row the Deacon won 20 or more games. He struck out 123 batters and walked only 29 in 289.1 innings pitched. Though the Deacon pitched in his final regular season game on September 23, the first World Series in modern baseball history would bring enduring fame to the Pirates' big right-hander.

♦ Seven ♦

The First World Series

As he had done a year earlier, in August of 1903 Barney Dreyfuss challenged the American League pennant winner to a post-season championship series. He commenced negotiations for the October games with the owner of the Boston Americans, runaway leaders in Ban Johnson's league.

On September 18, the day after Boston clinched the American League pennant and one day before the Pirates locked up the National League title, Dreyfuss and Henry Killilea of Boston signed the agreement to play a post-season series. Though the deal was not officially announced to the public for another ten days, the magnates agreed to a best-of-nine-game series that was to begin at Boston's Huntington Avenue Grounds on Thursday, October 1, 1903. The first three games would be played in Boston, the clubs would move to Pittsburgh for the next four, and return to Boston to complete the series. The owners agreed to split the gate receipts, each would provide and pay for one umpire, and the minimum price of admission would be 50 cents. Killilea announced that the club would keep 50 percent of the series receipts, but that was not acceptable to his players, whose contracts would expire at the end of the regular season as compared to the Pirates who were bound to their club until October 15. The series appeared to be in jeopardy due to the Boston players' threat of what amounted to a strike, until Ban Johnson intervened and the players were promised 60 percent of the club's share.[1]

The September 19 edition of *Sporting Life* reported that there might be no World Series because the Pittsburgh team was so "crippled" it might have to bow out. Of course there were problems with Leever's shoulder, Ritchey's thumb and Doheny's head, third baseman Tommy Leach was doubtful because it was suspected he had blood poisoning in the middle finger of his throwing hand, and their biggest star, Honus Wagner, was still suffering from a ligament strain in his left leg sustained in Chicago on Labor Day.[2]

Just when things couldn't get worse, they did. During the second game of a doubleheader in Brooklyn on September 19, Otto Krueger was hit in the head by a pitch thrown by the Superbas' Bill Reidy. The Pirates' substitute third baseman was unconscious for over an hour before he was revived. Later in the same series, Fred Clarke hit a home run pinch-hitting for Gus Thompson, but the manager aggravated an old knee injury when he slipped between third base and home. The mishap finished Clarke's regular season. Though the Pirates left-fielder was said to be questionable for the Pittsburgh-Boston World Series, the Pirates announced they would play the Americans even without Clarke or any of the other disabled players. In the end, only Krueger and Doheny would not be available for the post-season games, though several other players were not in the best of health.

At 11:30 A.M., September 28, the Pirates, all 15 of them, boarded a train in Pittsburgh, their eventual destination Boston for the first game of the big series. They stopped off in Buffalo for a tune-up game with the Eastern League team there, then took another train the next morning for Boston. Detraining at Back Bay Station, the Pirates took carriages to the Hotel Vendome, which would also host numerous Pittsburgh fans and several gamblers.

Gambling was a prominent part of professional baseball in the first decade of the twentieth century. Fans bet with one another in the stands during games, club owners bet with one another, and players wagered on their own team. *Pittsburgh Dispatch* reporter Frank McQuiston acted as the representative for a syndicate of gamblers and came to Boston with $15,000 to bet on the Pirates.[3] Several Pirates gave two-to-one odds that their team would win, though it's questionable whether the business-savvy Phillippe or the tightfisted Leever indulged in those activities.

A professional gambler named Sport Sullivan made between $4,000 and $8,000 betting on the series. Some 17 years later, Sullivan would be implicated in the conspiracy to fix the 1919 World Series between Chicago and Cincinnati. In 1903, though, no one gave credence to the notion that players could fix a game. The common belief held that the game of baseball was too open for a player to intentionally throw a game.

"Since I first saw or played a game of base ball I have never known a man to take a penny for a shady purpose," postulated Deacon Phillippe. "A ball player could not fake and do it naturally. When the fine points of baseball are pounded into him, he is at the same time inspired with an all-conquering desire and determination to win, if possible, this being stronger in baseball, I believe, than in any other sport. Any departure from this could be easily detected. There is such a thing as making an error or fluke at a critical stage, but in doing such a trick in most cases the guilty man would be so far from his natural manner that his teammates, at least, could detect it. I have never known a man to throw a game and never expect to have the experience. Baseball is totally unlike all other sports, and it will always remain clean and above board."[4]

Game day on October 1 was mild and cloudy. A well-dressed crowd of 16,242 fans from all parts and classes of Boston filled Huntington Avenue Base Ball Grounds for the historic game. With that many ticket holders, the outfield area that would constitute the warning track in the future was roped off for part of the overflow crowd. Boys who peddled scorecards also sold boxes for the standing-room outfield fans to climb on for a better view.

Deacon Phillippe was confident, saying "We will win the series from Boston. We won't have a cinch, but we will win. I am in superb form, and have asked Manager Clarke to allow me to pitch three of the first six games. Sam Leever has made a similar proposition. We believe we can beat Collins' men without difficulty, and that is the reason we made the proposition."[5]

As soon as the Pirates arrived at the Bostons' Grounds they quietly warmed up and took infield practice. As he had on numerous occasions during the regular season, Sam Leever batted balls to the infielders. The precision of the Pirates in fielding and flawlessly whipping the ball around the infield drew applause from the Boston crowd.

After the Bostons completed their 15 minutes of infield practice, umpires Hank O'Day of the National League and Tommy Connolly of the American met at home plate with Fred Clarke and Boston manager Jimmy Collins. They decided that any ball hit into the crowd standing in the outfield would be a ground-rule triple.

Opposing Deacon Phillippe on the mound for the Americans was the legendary Cy Young, a 28-game winner in 1903, who, at 36, was still one of the best hurlers in the game. However, this would not be his day.

The Pirates couldn't have scripted the first inning any better. Young retired the first two batters before Tommy Leach drove one of his underhand deliveries into the crowd in right field for a triple. Wagner brought him home with a single, and the Dutchman stole second base moments later. Bransfield was safe at first on shortstop Parent's fumble and when Lou Criger, the Boston catcher, threw the ball over Parent's head into the outfield on Bransfield's delayed attempt to steal second, Wagner scored and Kitty motored on to third base. Ritchey walked and he too stole second base as Criger threw to third in an effort to catch Bransfield off the bag.

"The Pittsburgh rooters were on their feet on and off at these stages, but when Sebring hit to left for a single, scoring Bransfield and Ritchey, there was bedlam," wrote John H. Gilbert in the *Pittsburgh Post*. "Every mother's son of them was on his feet yelling like mad and sailing his hat in frantic delight

... including Barney Dreyfuss, forgetting the dignity that becomes old age, indulging in the wildest kind of antics, while all around them was dense silence."⁶

When Phelps reached first base on a missed third strike by the Boston catcher, Phillippe became the ninth Pirate to bat in the inning. Although he struck out, Phillippe had a 4 to 0 lead before he made a single pitch. Boston still had plenty of time to get back into the game, but Phillippe served notice right away it would be a tough day for the opposing batters. Lefty batter Patsy Dougherty, a .331 hitter during the regular season, was first up and Phillippe fanned him on three pitches. Third baseman Jimmy Collins, a future Hall of Famer, was next, and he too struck out. The Pirates hurler struck out five of the first seven batters he faced.

Phillippe toiled in apparent ambivalence to the demonstrations of the largest Boston baseball crowd in history. The Boston rooters pressed into service every rattle, horn and other noisemaking conveyance to be found in their effort to unnerve the visitors.

In the top half of the second inning with two out, Fred Clarke was thrown out at second when he jogged on a ball he thought had rolled beyond the ropes for a ground-rule triple. As the manager ran out to left field between innings, Phillippe told him not to worry, "I've got my fast pitch going all right, and I guess we can hold them." Phillippe proceeded to strike out the side and even received applause from the Boston crowd as he walked off the diamond.⁷

In the seventh inning, the Pirates' Jimmy Sebring sent a drive over the right fielder's head. Assuming the ball would go into the crowd behind ropes in the outfield, Boston's Buck Freeman casually pursued the ball. By the time the ball stopped rolling some ten feet from the ropes, the Pirates runner was already turning third. The Boston center fielder ran over and retrieved the ball, but by the time the relay made it to the catcher, Sebring had scored to become known forever as the player who hit the first home run in World Series history.

Phillippe continued to set down the Americans' batters with ease, allowing only two hits, before Boston managed two ground-rule triples that led a pair of runs in the seventh inning. By that time the Pirates had a seven-run lead and Phillippe coasted to a 7–3 victory. He struck out ten and walked none, though he hit one batter.

The Boston Post reported, "To Phillippe mainly belongs the credit for Pittsburgh's victory.... His high drop ball and a wide out curve that swept continually beyond the reach of the longest bat kept Captain Collins's men stretching their necks and shoulders in a vain effort to connect."⁸

During the game, 22 telegraph operators at the park flashed inning-by-inning news of the historic contest to cities throughout the country. The *Pittsburgh Leader* called the first game of the Series "one of the greatest days for baseball enthusiasm which Pittsburgh has ever known. The intense interest shown on all hands in the outcome of the first game in the series for the world's championship was in the same rank as that over the results of presidential elections and international yacht races.... Bulletins were on every hand in greater quantity than for any daylight event of the past, and stores, saloons and private offices scored each inning with the crowd."[9]

When asked about Phillippe's performance, Fred Clarke responded, "Phillippe had a delivery that was most difficult to solve. The way he cuts loose with his benders is a caution." National League President Harry Pulliam could only gush, "Phillippe's pitching was simply wonderful. The pleasure I feel over Pittsburgh's victory cannot be described." He also predicted the Pirates were "certainly the greatest aggregation of tossers in the world and will win the present series in a walk."[10]

In that first game, the Pirates also learned about a group of noisy Boston followers who called themselves "Royal Rooters" and were accompanied by a band. Throughout the Series, Boston's rabid fans tormented the Pirates with a popular song of the day, "Tessie," substituting their own unflattering remarks for the normal lyrics. Eventually, the constant serenade of "that damn song" began to grate on the Pirates' nerves.

Normally, the pitching match-up for the second day would appear to favor the Pirates slightly with Leever on the mound. Unfortunately, the right-hander's limb had not responded to Bonesetter Reese's manipulations. In fact Clarke had no option other than Leever's sore arm for Game Two. Threatening weather held the Boston crowd down to 9,415, though the grandstand was filled well before the 3:00 P.M. game time. A steady rain began around 2 P.M., but the game started on time. When the Bostons took the field to start the first inning, the sky was dark and overcast, a factor that could make the pitchers' deliveries particularly effective.

Leadoff man Patsy Dougherty greeted the "Goshen Schoolmaster" in the bottom of the first with an inside-the-park home run that landed just short of the ropes in right center field. Boston scored another run off Leever to take a 2–0 lead and Bucky Veil came out to replace him when the sides changed positions in the middle of the second.

The *Pittsburgh Press* noted that Leever "had absolutely nothing, neither speed, curves nor control, and Manager Clarke quickly saw that Boston was preparing to slaughter him."[11] Veil, a 22-year-old right-hander, pitched well for the Pirates, but the Americans' Bill Dinneen was virtually untouchable, allowing but three hits and striking out 11 in his 3–0 shutout.

When Fred Clarke asked Phillippe the morning of Game Three how he felt, Phillippe replied, "I am in condition to pitch just the same kind of ball I twirled on Thursday, and if that won't beat Boston, then they are too strong for me."[12]

The second-game victory invigorated the Boston fans. Almost 19,000, more than double the capacity of Huntington Grounds, pushed their way into the park for Saturday's Game Three. The patrons spilled out onto the field and a force of 100 policemen brandishing water hoses attempted to control the mob. Other fans sat perched on the top of fences, and adjoined rooftops were "literally black with people." Behind the catcher, a space of about 30 feet had to be cleared of fans, and men stood ten-deep in front of the stands behind home plate. The playing field was completely surrounded by a ring of humanity. The players were even unable to use their benches and sat in the grass on opposite sides of the catcher,

Hits into the overflow crowd amassed only 150 feet beyond the base paths would be ruled ground-rule doubles. During the course of the game, the crowd standing on the field became ill-tempered when Boston fell behind. The horde behind the outfield ropes opened up for the Boston outfielders, but closed ranks when Clarke, Beaumont or Sebring went back for fly balls.

Working on just one day's rest, Phillippe came right back with a four-hitter to win the third game. Pittsburgh scored a run in the top of the first off "Long Tom" Hughes. In the third inning, the Pirates added a second run and had runners on second and third with no one out when Cy Young was summoned to replace Hughes. Young plunked Wagner with a pitch to load the bases, but it appeared the old war horse would get out of the jam without further damage when he retired two batters on a foul out and a force at home. With two down, Jimmy Sebring grounded to Fred Parent, but the little shortstop fumbled the ball and another run scored.

Boston broke through with a run in the fourth inning, but thereafter Phillippe allowed only a walk until the Americans scored again in the bottom of the eighth on a pair of hits after two were out. The Bostons may have sensed that Phillippe was tiring with that eighth-inning rally, but the Pirates hurler quickly dispelled any hope of a comeback in the ninth. Trailing 4–2, the American Leaguers went down meekly in the final frame. After a pop-out and a ground out to short, Phillippe fanned Hobe Ferris on a pitch his catcher couldn't handle, but Phelps corralled it and threw the runner out at first to end the game.

The Boston newspapers again praised the Pittsburgh right-hander. He was pitching inside of "a great ring of humanity, 40 deep, sitting, standing or lying around the entire field within 200 feet of the bases, yet in nine full innings he allowed only two balls to be hit within the crowd."[13]

"I feel just as good now as I did before the game," Phillippe said afterwards. "My superb physical condition surprises even myself. I never felt better in my life.... If Fred will let me, I'll pitch two more games of the series, and I should win them both. It's easy money. I told him to call on me whenever he needed me or wanted me. I'll be ready."[14]

The Pirates arrived at Union Station in Pittsburgh just before 7 P.M. the evening of their third-game victory, but Phillippe was nowhere to be seen. A cheering and unruly crowd of about 5,000 had assembled at the depot in anticipation of the arrival of the team's train, and word was sent ahead to Fred Clarke that police would not be able to keep the horde from swamping the Deacon. To avoid any possible damage to the Pirates' star pitcher, Phillippe was smuggled off the train at the East Liberty Station and made his way home by streetcar.[15]

Charles Louis "Deacon" Phillippe (courtesy Pittsburgh Pirates).

There was no baseball in Pittsburgh on Sunday, but there was plenty of news. The *Pittsburgh Press* reported that the Pirates had signed a former member of John McGraw's Giants. Roscoe Miller won 23 games with the Detroit Tigers in 1901, but by the end of the 1903 season he appeared to be used up at age 26. Miller won only three of 16 decisions in two seasons with the Giants before McGraw cut him loose. However, the Pirates could point to the case of Doheny, who had little success in New York before becoming one of the best hurlers in the league with Pittsburgh.

However, the big news that day was Fred Clarke's announcement that Sam Leever would not pitch again in the series against Boston. "Leever, I am afraid, will be unable to take part in any of the games," he said. "His arm is in very bad shape and although everything possible has been done for it, it refuses to come right. This is a bad handicap, but it has taken none of the confidence out of the rest of the boys."[16]

An off-day on Sunday followed by a rain-out on Monday allowed the Pirates to come back with Phillippe in Game Four on October 6. Barney Dreyfuss resolved to avoid a repeat of the crowd control problem of the third game in Boston so he negotiated with a local circus owner to have workers install an extra 1,800 seats in front of grandstand for the expected overflow crowd. However, the threat of rain limited the attendance at Exposition Park to 7,600, and the previous day's downpour left the field in poor condition. An application of sawdust to the soggy field did little to improve the playing conditions.

After Phillippe retired the side in order to open the contest, the Pirates scored a run in the bottom of the first inning off Dinneen. Boston broke through with a single run in the fifth inning on a two-out RBI single by catcher Lou Criger. The contest was not tied for long. Beaumont tripled over the center fielder's head in the home half of the fifth and scored when first baseman LaChance slipped in the mud trying to recover Leach's hard smash.

Phillippe helped his own cause with a base hit to lead off the bottom of the seventh. Left fielder Dougherty fumbled the ball and the Pirates' pitcher went on to second base. Beaumont sacrificed Phillippe to third and Ginger made it safely to first when Dinneen failed to cover the bag. Boston played the infield in to cut off the run, but Leach lined a pitch down the right field line that was just fair by inches. Leach's triple scored the two men on base, and he scored on Wagner's single. Phillippe preserved the 5–1 lead through the eighth inning, but by the ninth, he was a tired pitcher.

Much to the delight of the New England "Royal Rooters" contingent, the first three Boston batters in the final frame singled, plating one run. A force out sent another runner home for the visitors. By now, the home crowd that gave Phillippe a loud ovation only minutes earlier had fallen silent while the Boston fans, accompanied by their rented 40-piece band, were worked up to a frenzy. With the bases loaded and only one out, Duke Farrell pinch-hit for Boston's light-hitting catcher and drove a long fly toward the left-center field gap. Racing "with the speed of a greyhound," Fred Clarke made the catch for the second out, but another run tallied to make the score 5–4. Boston's last hope came down to another pinch-hitter, Jack O'Brien, batting for pitcher Bill Dinneen. Mustering everything he had left, Phillippe got two quick strikes, then induced O'Brien to pop out to second baseman Claude Ritchey.

The final out set off an instantaneous celebration among the Pirates faithful. Phillippe was hoisted on the shoulders of adoring fans and was carried from the field. If his arm wasn't already tired enough, Phillippe shook hands with supporters in the clubhouse for half an hour after the game. That evening, players of both clubs were guests of the management at the Avenue Theater. The Pirates were treated to hearty ovations as they were escorted to their private boxes.

Pittsburgh now held a commanding lead of three games to one in the Series, but they would be at a decided disadvantage for Game Five. Phillippe's arm was dead tired and Leever was hurting. Boston manager Collins was prophetic when he told reporters, "We will win two games if it takes an arm. Phillippe can't do all the pitching."

Clarke took a chance on 36-year-old Bill Kennedy to oppose Cy Young, in game five, and Ole "Brickyard" made it a contest for five innings. Then the roof caved in. It wasn't all Kennedy's fault as the Pirates made three errors behind him in the fatal sixth and none of Boston's first six runs were earned. Boston built up an 11–0 lead before the Pirates scored a run. Kennedy would not pitch another game in the major leagues.

Manager Clarke had no choice but to use Leever in the sixth game. He couldn't rely on one of the youngsters so it was Leever or nobody. The day before the game, Leever told Clarke that he was in shape to pitch.[17] Rumor was that Leever bet $200 of his own money that the Pirates would win the sixth game, an unlikely wager considering the way he labored each time he threw.

Despite the cold weather, Leever turned in a credible performance. The Schoolmaster held Boston scoreless for the first two innings, but the Pirates' defense let him down in the third. Three Boston runs that inning were capped by a wild throw by Leach. An overthrow by Wagner on a relay from Beaumont allowed another run to score in the fifth. After Boston scored a run in the seventh on Parent's triple and a double by LaChance, Leever finally hit his stride. However, the Pirates were down 6–0 with only nine outs left and they had done nothing against Bill Dinneen over the first six innings.

In the bottom of the seventh, Pittsburgh finally put together a rally and actually threatened Boston's big lead. Sebring and Phelps opened the frame with singles, but Clarke had to let Leever bat because he didn't trust any of the available arms on the Pirates' bench. Leever grounded out to first as the two runners advanced a base, and Beaumont's single up the middle sent Sebring scurrying home. Clarke kept the rally going with a double over the left fielder's head that plated Phelps and Beaumont. Leach hit a long drive to center field that was caught for the second out, but Wagner and Bransfield worked Dinneen for walks to load the bases. With the tying runner on base, Claude Ritchey came to bat. With the crowd cheering, and at the same time pleading, Ritchey punched a grounder that shortstop Parent gobbled up and forced Bransfield at second base to end the inning.

After permitting ten hits and two walks over the first six and a third innings, Leever retired the final eight batters he faced. However, the Pirates' hitters did not have another big inning left in them. In the eighth, Dinneen retired the side in order. Beaumont gave the Pirates and their fans a glimmer of hope when he led off the bottom of the ninth with a single, his fourth hit of the game. Clarke hit a line drive which for an instant appeared to be heading into center field, but Fred Parent picked it off just before the ball hit the ground and threw to first base to double up Beaumont. After one more batter, Dinneen was being carried off the field on the shoulders of the "Royal Rooters."

"Sam didn't show much evidence of a weak wing," noted the *Pittsburgh Press*, "and he pitched good enough to win had he received the support he deserved, but he didn't get it, and thereby hangs the tale of the Pirates' defeat."[18]

The seventh game was scheduled for 3 P.M. on Friday, but after Fred Clarke visited the ballpark at noon, he hastened back to Pirates headquarters and announced that the day's contest was postponed until the next day.

"The wind over there must be blowing 60 miles an hour," he told the newspapermen. "Talk about breezes in Kansas — they're not to be compared with the one that is raging over at the park. A player would run a great risk in playing in such weather."[19] Boston manager Jimmy Collins responded with indignation. "What's the matter with you people?" he pressed Clarke. The Pirates' boss just replied that it was too windy and the game was off.

The postponement would greatly benefit the Pirates. Not only had the Boston club made arrangements to return home that evening, it appeared Cy Young's speed ball would give the Americans a decided advantage in overcast conditions. The extra day off meant Phillippe could come back and pitch on Tuesday plus Barney Dreyfuss got a Saturday game that meant the mill workers could attend.

With the Series tied three games to three, Young and Phillippe squared off in the final game at Exposition Park. In contrast to the previous day, the weather was ideal, the sun was shining and the wind was not a factor. On game day, a parade of more than 20 carriages followed by 500 Pirates rooters, and accompanied by Guenther's Greater Pittsburgh Band, marched from downtown to Exposition Park. Each rooter wore a large pin adorned with the Pirates' colors, red and navy blue, and gilded with "Loyal Rooters, Pittsburg, 1903." As hundreds joined the procession along the way, the rooters shouted, "Phil, Phil, Phillippe, Phil!— He can win, and you bet he will!" [20] It was obvious Pittsburgh's hopes now rested solely on the right arm of their iron man, Deacon Phillippe.

Fans scrambled for tickets, some paying a premium price outside the stadium. The attendance was over 17,000, the largest crowd at Exposition Park up to that time. During pre-game warm-ups, Pirates captain Fred Clarke was hit on the leg by a bat that slipped out of the hands of Kitty Bransfield. It was an ominous prelude to what was to come, and Clarke hobbled through the final two games as he joined the lame Honus Wagner among the walking wounded.

The gates to Exposition Park were opened at noon and within an hour the grandstand and bleachers had been filled. The ticket holders overflowed onto the field and ropes were stretched across the environs of the outfield, with the fans were compelled to stay behind them. Though the people stood five rows deep there still wasn't enough room, and several of their number made a perilous climb to the top of the outfield fences where they remained perched awaiting the start of the game.

Not only had Phillippe pitched 27 innings since October 1, the Boston batters had adjusted to the break of his pitches. Boston went ahead, 2–0, in the first inning on triples by Jimmy Collins and center fielder Chick Stahl, and the American Leaguers never trailed in the contest. One of the few positive notes for Pittsburgh came in the third inning when Phillippe came to the plate. As players of both teams gathered around the Pirates' ace, an admirer walked up and gave him a diamond horseshoe stickpin, paid for by the fans, as a token of their appreciation. Phillippe "blushed like a coy school girl"[21] and thanked the fans before handing the present to Kitty Bransfield for safe keeping. Phillippe stepped into the batter's box and belted a clean single off of a Cy Young fast ball. News accounts described the ovation as deafening.

The Pirates managed single runs in the fourth, sixth and ninth innings. Clarke did not pinch hit for Phillippe in the bottom of the ninth, and Phil lined Young's first pitch to center field, sending Sebring home with Pittsburgh's final run. The Americans took the Series lead for the first time with their 7–3 win.

Boston had finally beaten Phillippe, who worked his fourth complete game in the Series. He allowed 11 hits, but due to three Pittsburgh errors only five of Boston's seven runs were earned. A .355 hitter during the regular season, a hobbled Honus Wagner went hitless for the third straight game and also made an error.

"We have no fault to find with Phillippe for losing the seventh game of the series," Manager Fred Clarke admitted to the newspapers after Phillippe started for the fourth time in ten days. "It was expecting too much of him to ask him to pitch, but we have no one else to depend on."

"It was the old story of the pitcher going once too often to the well and getting broken," wrote Ralph Davis. "Poor Deacon Phillippe! ... He pitched good ball at that, but Young outdid him, and luck was with the Bostons. Every time they hit a ball it seemed to go right into the crowd. Ground rules were in force and a ball into the throng went for a triple. Boston made five of them on such hits, and nearly every one of them developed into a run."[22]

"He went up against the Bostons once too often," reasoned *The Sporting News*. "It is natural to suppose that after a team has faced a pitcher three times in less than two weeks, that they should have had time to familiarize themselves with that man's style of pitching sufficiently to hit him."[23]

Now the Pirates would have to make the 23-hour train ride back to Boston and win two games at Huntington Avenue Baseball Grounds to capture the World Series championship. The despondent Pirates didn't even bother to change clothes at the ballpark following their disappointing effort in Game Seven. They walked across the Union Bridge to the railway station where they boarded the team's special car before changing from their baseball uniforms. The Pirates' train was held up in Albany, New York, to allow the American Leaguers' special to catch up. The players' cars were now attached to the same locomotive and the opposing players were able to mingle and chat with one another during the trip. Compared to the battles of the National League season, the games of the first World Series were described by Fred Clarke as "free from any sort of friction."[24]

Underscoring the Pirates' pitching problems was the news that greeted the team when it arrived in Boston. Clarke was hoping Ed Doheny might be available to pitch and even brought the troubled pitcher's uniform to Boston with the team. However, the paranoid Doheny became agitated when the Pirates lost three games in a row at Exposition Park. His wife sent for the doctor, but Doheny took a swing at the medicine man and accused him of keeping him away from the team. On October 11, Doheny went berserk at his home and assaulted a male nurse with a stove poker. That evening, the 26-year-old pitcher was committed to Danvers Insane Asylum in Massachusetts. The already disconsolate Pirates were stunned at the news.[25]

Clarke planned to use Leever in the eighth game for as long as he could go, but a torrid downpour on Monday led to the postponement of the game for a day. Now, Clarke asked Phillippe to come back on two days' rest and make his fifth start, this time against a well-rested Bill Dinneen.

Tuesday, October 13, 1903, was a cold, overcast day in Boston. The crowd was the smallest in the series, about 7,500. Though empty seats were seen in the grandstand and bleachers, a small number of fans were allowed to stand behind the outfield ropes in center field, again putting the ground-rule triple in effect.

Before the players took infield practice, the two teams were gathered together for a combined photograph. The expressions on the Pirates' faces appeared serious though somewhat resigned to the inevitable.

Phillippe pitched well, walked none and allowed just three runs on eight hits, but Dinneen was better. He pitched a four-hit shutout as the Americans won, 3–0, to take the Series. The Buccaneers' only serious threat came in the fourth inning when they put runners on first and third with two out. The lead runner, Tommy Leach, was out at home on a delayed double steal attempt to end the inning.

The game was scoreless into the bottom of the fourth. Boston's Buck Freeman led off with a triple and catcher Phelps fumbled Parent's bunt in front of the plate to put opposing runners on first and third. After Parent was sacrificed to second, Ferris singled to center field, scoring both Boston baserunners. The Pirates went quietly as Dinneen retired the last seven batters he faced and struck out the mighty Wagner to end the series. The instant Wagner swung and missed the third strike, the Boston fans exited the grandstand and swarmed their heroes in spontaneous celebration. As the World Series champions were hoisted to the shoulders of their fans, the Pirates gathered their equipment and solemnly departed the field.[26]

Following the final-game loss, Phillippe responded to a question about his team's performance with the comment, "My arm is numb and I am tired."[27] Phillippe established World Series records which still stand: games started in a single series and innings pitched. He captured all three Pirates victories and walked only three batters in 44 innings pitched.

Almost 50 years after the event, Fred Clarke paid tribute to Phillippe's performance in the 1903 World Series: "If he couldn't do it, I do not know who could. That was no decision of mine, depending on Phillippe. Sam Leever had jammed his shoulder practicing with a new shotgun. Ed Doheny had gone off the reservation. When we accepted the challenge from the Red Sox for the first World's Series, it was Phillippe or nobody. Maybe it was too much to ask of any pitcher, but he had to go for me in the seventh game, his fourth start in ten days, and in the eighth game, his fifth start in 13 days, and he lost both."[28]

Both teams attended a performance at the Colonial Theater the evening of the final game of the World Series and the players were wildly cheered. That same night, Barney Dreyfuss threw an impromptu banquet for the Pirates and home town newspaper men at the Hotel Vendome. At the dinner Dreyfuss made a short speech in which he complimented his players for their brave fight under discouraging conditions. He added that his intention was to give the players all of the club's receipts if they won the Series and he had decided put the club's $6,699.56 share of the gate into the players' pool anyway because of their gallant fight. When the owner was encouraged to recover $7,000 of his own gambling losses after betting on the Pirates, he declined. Naturally, the announcement generated great enthusiasm among the diners.[29]

Once he returned to Pittsburgh, an exhausted Deacon Phillippe indicated he was anxious to get back to South Dakota for a hunting trip. But first there was the business of distributing World Series shares to the team. A meeting was held in which the Pirates' share of the gate receipts, totaling $21,060, was divided among 16 players. Each of the 16 shares amounted to $1,316.25, more than the victorious Boston players' $1,182 individual share. A half-share was mailed to Mrs. Doheny, wife of the ill pitcher. Checks for the married players were made out to their wives.

That wasn't all. President Dreyfuss turned to Phillippe and said, "I have something more for you." He then presented the pitcher ten shares of quite valuable stock in the Philadelphia Traction Company, which operated trolley cars in Pittsburgh. "This," said Dreyfuss, "is for your earnest, faithful work in going to the slab whenever called on and trying with might and main to carry the colors of the Pittsburghs to the front."[30]

After the Series, Sam Leever was accused by some writers of cowardice and giving less than his best effort in the second game. Ralph S. Davis, the Pittsburgh correspondent for *The Sporting News*, felt compelled to write a strong article in support of Leever, who was apparently still in considerable pain weeks after the Series ended. "There were many people who believed that the story of Leever's sore arm was a myth, invented for the purpose of covering up his cowardice. It was published in one city that Sam had really gone back on the Pittsburgh team in a pinch, when they needed him badly.

"The charge that Leever 'laid' down is absurd in the extreme" added Davis. "There is not a more honest man in the game than Leever."

Three days after the end of the World Series, Leever went hunting in the vicinity of Midway, Pennsylvania, with a party that also included Honus and Al Wagner. After Leever fired a few shots on the first day out, his right arm became so painful he was forced to give up the hunt.

John Murphy, the groundskeeper at Exposition Park, was along on the hunt and said he never saw anyone suffer more acutely than did Leever. Leever's arm was so sore he quit the party, went to the railway station and took the first train to Mt. Clemens, Michigan, for rehabilitation of his aching limb.

Before he left for Mt. Clemens, Leever said, "I shall stay at the resort until I feel that my arm has fully recovered its strength. I am not going to risk having to report for duty in the spring with a weak wing. I would rather not pitch at all than pitch with a poor arm. If I can't get into condition I would be only a detriment to the team. After I leave Mt. Clemons, I will go right home to Goshen, and spend the winter quietly there."[31]

The 1903 World Series ultimately defined the perception of both Charles Phillippe and Samuel Leever. Any time that Series is discussed the first name mentioned is not Wagner, Dinneen or even Cy Young; it is the "iron man" performance of Phillippe. The Deacon immediately earned almost immortal status in Pittsburgh. Despite his subsequent failures, he was rarely criticized in the city and received positive press throughout his baseball career, even during his days in outlaw ball.

On the other hand, there were some in the city that never forgave Leever for not being fit for the Series. Any time Leever experienced a couple of bad outings or suffered one of his frequent ailments he came in for a round of criticism. It wasn't fair, but he was perceived as the eccentric pitcher who cost Pittsburgh the first World Series championship, and the modest and unassuming Philippe was the one who gave all he had to win without complaint, but it was just too much for one man to achieve.

Years later when Phillippe was manager of Pittsburgh's United States League club, a visitor to his office happened to break out in song, "Tessie, you are the only, only," before Phillippe abruptly stopped the crooner. "That confounded tune," the annoyed ex–Pirates pitcher exclaimed. "It haunts me in my sleep. It will always haunt me. That fool tune and words knocked me out of a world's record and a championship."[32]

♦ Eight ♦

Mugsy McGraw's Giants

The Pittsburgh Pirates' pre-season of 1904 presented the same urgency as the previous spring — rebuilding the pitching staff around Leever and Phillippe. Nevertheless, Phillippe predicted another championship. "I look for the hottest possible kind of race for the next National League flag with Pittsburgh running just a nose ahead of the others. I think the first four teams will be Pittsburgh, New York, Chicago and Cincinnati." He only made one mistake in the order of finish — and that was with Pittsburgh.[1]

The Pittsburgh Dispatch disagreed with Deacon's assessment, "If the pitching department of the Pittsburgh team is as weak as some people seem to think, there will be no pennant floating over the Smoketown grounds next year. The teams of the National League are much stronger this year than they were last."[2]

The club's three veterans, Leever, Wagner and Phillippe, were the most prominent bachelors on the team until Leever took the plunge that winter. However, he didn't bother to tell his teammates he was to be married that off-season.

Leever headed to spring training with a delicate right shoulder and a new bride, having eloped to Newport, Kentucky, to marry the former Margaret Malloy of Goshen on February 27, 1904. The new Mrs. Leever was the sister of James Malloy, who pitched in one exhibition game for the Pirates in 1903 after he was recommended by Leever. "No one ever dreamed that he would steal away and be married without the knowledge of his friends," wrote Ralph Davis.[3]

When Leever boarded the Pirates' railroad car in Indianapolis for the trip to Hot Springs, Deacon Phillippe grasped him by the arm, dragged him into the darkened sleeper and shouted, "Boys, here's Leever. Turn out and congratulate the bashful bridegroom."

There was a parting of each berth's curtains and Pirates players quickly filled the aisle to give Leever a hearty reception. Sam finally escaped and made his way to another car where he ran onto Fred Clarke. When taken to task for denying his marriage, Leever said it was only a joke.

"What!" shouted Clarke. "Marriage a joke? Sam, my boy, you will soon wake up to a realization of the fact that married life is no joke."[4]

Leever maintained that he stayed in shape by chopping wood and ice skating over the winter, but the early news out of spring training on his right arm was not good. From the start, Leever advised Barney Dreyfuss and Fred Clarke that his pitching wing was no better. Both of them tried to convince Leever that with a few days of practice his arm would improve and the club's owner even told Sam he would remain with the club to the close of the season with full pay whether he played or not. The pitcher countered that after the current season, if he could hold out, he would never play baseball again.[5]

For pitching insurance, Dreyfuss purchased left-hander Wyatt Lee from the Washington Senators during spring training. It was reported that Dreyfuss paid Washington $5,000 for the pitcher, a high price at that time especially for a hurler who had won only 13 games over the previous two seasons.

Reports on the status of Leever's arm remained grim until April, when Ralph Davis wrote from Hot Springs. "Sam Leever's arm is also coming around all right and the champion twirler of 1903 will again be one of the Pirates' dependants. There was considerable anxiety felt over the condition of the Goshen boy's whip, but it's beginning to look as if some of those fears were groundless."

"Deacon Phillippe is in the best condition of any of the Pittsburgh slab artists," the Smoky City pundit continued. "Cold weather has no terrors for the South Dakota lad.... He has been in his element during the training, while a number of his teammates were suffering from colds. 'Why, I wish it would remain like this all summer,' said Phil one day when the players were hugging the fire."[6]

Except for their two aces, no pitcher from the 1903 Pirates' staff would win a game for the club in 1904. Fortunately, former Giants right-hander Roscoe Miller would pitch well for the Pirates in the early part of the season. The Pirates also added a young Ohioan, Charlie Case, whose only major league experience had been in three games with Cincinnati in 1901. Another newcomer was submariner Jack Pfiester, who won 19 games and struck out 195 batters with San Francisco of the Pacific Coast League in 1903 before his purchase by the Pirates late in the season. However, the promising southpaw had little success for the Pirates in 1904, going 1–1 with a 7.20 earned run average before he was shipped to the Western League that May. Jack returned to the major leagues two years later and became a mainstay on the great pitching staffs of the Chicago Cubs' four-time National League champions.

On the other hand, John McGraw boasted that his New York Giants had the best pitching in baseball. Returning for the Giants were two 30-game winners from the previous season, Christy Mathewson and "Iron Man" Joe McGinnity, a sensational rookie named George "Hooks" Wiltse, plus Luther "Dummy" Taylor, a deaf-mute who would win 21 games in 1904.

Little attention was paid to the Pirates' "scrubs" that spring and the press devoted most of their attention to Phillippe, now the club's brightest star because of his work in the previous fall's World Series. By this time in his career, Phillippe was at the top of the baseball world. Everyone that followed baseball knew of the "Deacon."

During the off-season both major leagues agreed that each team would play a 154-game regular season schedule, 14 games more than the previous year. The National League also issued an order mandating enforcement of the balk rule that had been loosely interpreted in past years.

The celebrated Deacon Phillippe pitched and won the opening game of the 1904 season in St. Louis, after which the team went into a funk, losing 12 of its next 16 games. There were ominous signs early in the year that Phillippe was not the same pitcher he was in 1903. The *Pittsburgh Leader* reported that his opening day victory "can hardly be attributed to 'Phil's mas-

Defending National League Champions — Spring 1904. Standing: Moran, Leever, Phelps, Diehl, Thompson, R. Miller, Carisch, Scanlan, H. Smith; middle row: Sebring, Veil, Wagner, Phillippe, Bransfield, Leach; bottom row: Warren, Ritchey, Krueger, Beaumont, Camnitz, Clarke (courtesy Pittsburgh Pirates).

terly pitching,' because candor as well as the box score compels the admission that he was hit much harder than 'our own' slugged Taylor."[7]

Four days after the opener, the usually reliable Phillippe was battered around by the Cincinnati Reds and left the game in the fourth inning after allowing six hits and eight runs. Lew Moren made his sole appearance that season for the Pirates and "showed a total disability to handle major leaguers." The Pirates lost, 18 to 4.

Sam Leever had not fully recovered from his shoulder injury when the season began. He did not start a game on the mound until a rainy April 24 and then, with his new wife in the stands, he argued a second-inning balk call so strenuously that he was ejected and suspended indefinitely "for mildly assaulting Umpire Johnstone."

Before the game, Leever and umpire James Johnstone had a conversation about the league's new interpretation of the balk rule. Once the game began, Leever did not object to Johnstone's first balk call, but when a Cincinnati baserunner was awarded home because he slightly raised his left foot, Leever hit the roof. When Johnstone attempted to explain his call, Leever pushed him aside in disgust. The Pirates' pitcher was immediately ordered off the field.[8]

Following his ejection, Leever was succeeded by rookie Jack Pfiester, then Watty Lee. The latter gave up two runs in the ninth inning to make the Reds 6–5 winners. Five days later, National League President Pulliam telegraphed Barney Dreyfuss that Leever's suspension would be for three days. Leever announced that he would refuse his salary if any fine was deducted.

The Pirates' revamped pitching staff would allow an average of seven runs in the team's first 17 games. Compounding their bad start, the Pirates sat idle for five days late in April because of bad weather.

An omen of the team's poor pennant chances occurred on Friday the 13th that May. A brass band, made up of fire fighters from Reading, Pennsylvania, attended the game and struck up the tune "Tessie," prompting an angry reaction from the home fans. In the game itself, Pittsburgh was shut out, 2–0, by Brooklyn's Ed Poole, a former Pirate (1900–02).

True to John McGraw's prediction, New York got off to a strong start. By the time the Giants came to Exposition Park that May for the first time in 1904 the Pirates were mired in seventh place, eight games behind the New Yorkers. The league had restored the two-umpire policy on a partial basis for 1904, though a pair of arbiters was always assigned to games involving the Pirates-Giants rivalry.

On May 16 Sam Leever was the victim of two errors by third baseman Leach in a five-run Giants outburst in the fifth inning. Down 5–0 against

Christy Mathewson seemed to spell doom for the Pirates. Clarke decided to remove Leever from the game when his turn at bat came up in the bottom of the fifth inning with Phelps on base and two out. Leever argued until Clarke let him bat.

There were 6,360 persons in the park and the *Pittsburgh Press* reported that "Men who have watched every game played at Exposition Park in many years declare that they never saw the equal of that demonstration yesterday, nor did they ever witness a greater ovation than was given to Pitcher Sam Leever when he went to bat after the Giants had scored five runs in the fifth inning."[9]

The decision to let Leever bat paid off. After Mathewson balked Phelps to second, Leever singled to give the Pirates their first run. In the top of the sixth, Mathewson reached Leever for a two-out triple to deep center. Leever retired the next man to strand Mathewson, who had expended considerable energy legging out his three-bagger only minutes earlier. In the Pirates half of the sixth, Mathewson's offerings suddenly were hittable and the home team plated five runs to take the lead.

"Then the crowd broke loose afresh," reported the *Press*, "and the stands fairly trembled while thousands of feet stamped with might and main. Women threw their handkerchiefs in the air, men tossed up their hats, some stamped, some clapped their hands and all cheered with all the power of their vocal organs.... It was a wonderful demonstration and it lasted for fully 10 minutes."[10]

Leever kept home plate closed to the Gothamites for the remainder of the contest and Pittsburgh escaped with a 6–5 win that signaled yet another deafening demonstration by the fans. The loss marked the end of Mathewson's eight-game winning streak against the Pirates.

Iron Man McGinnity pitched a two-hit shutout in beating Phillippe, 7–0, in the second game of the series. Employing a hard and sharp breaking pitch out of a side-arm delivery, McGinnity would win 35 games for the Giants and "save" five others in relief. He started a pitch near his shoes, almost scraping his fingers in the dirt of the mound as he went through with the throw. He did not strike out many batters, but the upward movement of his pitches induced numerous ground-outs and pop-ups that allowed him to retire batters on a minimal number of throws.

The Pirates came up with an unexpected savior in the finale. Pitching against his former teammates, Roscoe Miller won a 2–1 duel with Dummy Taylor on May 19. The series victory over their number one nemesis spurred the Pirates to play better. The club reeled off six straight victories to move into fifth place. Phillippe pitched shutouts in consecutive starts against the

Beaneaters and Reds in late May, Roscoe Miller also pitched a shutout against Boston, and Leever had two impressive outings with victories over the same club though he wasn't around at the end of either of them.

On May 20, Leever was hit on the arm by a pitch from Boston's Vic Willis and had to retire after pitching the sixth inning. Pittsburgh had a big lead and Phillippe finished up for him in an 8–2 win at Exhibition Park.

Five days later, Leever left for a pinch-hitter in the bottom of the ninth inning, down 1–0 to Boston. The pinch-hitter, fellow pitcher Watty Lee, drove a long fly over the center fielder's head for a triple. The next batter, Ginger Beaumont, hit Pittinger's first pitch into the right-center field gap. Before the ball could be returned, Lee had scored the tying run, and the fleet Pirates centerfielder had circumnavigated the bases for a game-winning inside-the-park home run.

On the mound, Watty Lee didn't come close to earning the Pirates' investment. Lee pitched in five games, winning only once before he was released by the Pirates following a 9–1 loss to Cincinnati on May 26. President Dreyfuss was convinced the Washington club had traded him damaged goods because he felt the Senators knew the young man had a lame arm before the deal was made.[11]

Following his release by the Chicago White Sox, Patsy Flaherty returned to the Pirates on June 10, 1904, and the new arrival responded with an 8–4 victory over Boston. In 1903 Patsy lost 25 games for the White Sox, but a year later the veteran left-hander perfected a wicked spitball at the right time for the Pirates. He would win his first three starts for the Buccaneers and lead Pittsburgh's pitchers with 19 victories.

Deacon Phillippe's inconsistent season was exemplified by his performance during a fiasco at Exposition Park on Decoration Day, May 30. A morning game between the Pirates and St. Louis Cardinals was rained out and despite skies heavy with low dark clouds nearly 10,000 fans arrived for an anticipated pitching duel between Phillippe and the visitors' Charles McFarland that afternoon.

Though the Cardinals had pretty good pitching with a staff that included Jack Taylor and Kid Nichols, their lineup was made up of unknowns and has-beens. Among the latter was 37-year-old first baseman Jake Beckley, who played for the Pirates from 1888 to 1896. At the start of the second inning it began to a drizzle and developed into a heavy rain, compelling the people in the grandstand to retreat. The rain became harder and harder, but umpire Bob Emslie insisted that play continue. Before the end of the fifth inning, Fred Clarke asked the umpire to stop the game, although the Pirates trailed only 1 to 0. Emslie refused to call it. He cited the rule that stipulated "the umpire shall suspend play only if the rain falls so heavy as to cause the spectators in the open field and open stands to seek shelter."[12] He pointed to the stands behind home plate where many fans had assembled despite the rain.

By now, mud added to the inconvenience of the soaked players, who began to beg the bleacherites to leave. Both managers beseeched the umpire to call the game after the Cardinals added a second run in the sixth inning. Neither the rain-soaked patrons remaining in the stands nor the umpire would yield. The game went the full nine innings and the Cardinals were victorious, 13 to 0. In Phillippe's day pitchers expected to pitch the entire game, and he was not one to ever come out of a contest he was physically able to complete. He remained in for the duration despite trailing 8–0 after the seventh inning. The Cardinals reached him for 20 hits and the Pirates made four errors. Some said that Phillippe was never the same after pitching all those innings in the World Series, and the effect of the rain that Decoration Day further affected his arm.

Phillippe had an outstanding outing against the Giants at the Polo Grounds on June 8. He allowed only two hits but lost, 2–0, to Joe McGinnity when the Pirates could not plate any of their nine baserunners. Errors by Ritchey and Bransfield led to New York's two runs.

Phillippe beat the Phillies, 5–1, on June 16, but a dangerous eye infection put him on the shelf for two months. Ralph Davis condemned the Pirates' abuse of their star pitcher in his column on July 2, 1904. "As I feared and predicted in my letter several weeks ago, 'Deacon' Phillippe was sent to the hospital tent as a result of that farcical game which he was called upon to pitch against the St. Louis Cardinals on Decoration Day in the midst of a heavy downpour. He contracted a severe cold and finally had to go Cambridge Springs to recuperate."[13]

The Pirates won seven games in a row from June 10–17 to pull within six games of first place. Pittsburgh split the first two games of a set with the Cardinals at Exposition Park, then the two teams moved to St. Louis for a Sunday doubleheader. The first game would be an intriguing match-up between Sam Leever and Jack Taylor, now a Cardinal.

Taylor's relationship with Chicago had soured despite win totals of 22 and 21 over the previous two seasons. During the Cubs/White Sox post-season series in the fall of 1903, Cubs president Jim Hart became suspicious of Taylor's work during the three games he pitched. That December, Hart traded Taylor and rookie catcher Larry McLean to the St. Louis Cardinals for pitcher Mordecai "Three Finger" Brown and catcher Jack O'Neill.

When the Cardinals visited Chicago early in the 1904 season, Taylor was chided about losing three games in the City Series of the previous fall and exclaimed within the earshot of several people, "Why should I have won? I got $100 from Hart for winning and I got $500 for losing." Witnesses repeated the remark to Cubs President James A. Hart, who then reported it to President Pulliam and Chairman Herrmann of the National Commission.[14]

The change of scenery did not seem to affect Taylor's performance against the Pirates, though Pittsburgh scored three runs in the first inning against him in the opener of the June 19 doubleheader. After that, Taylor slammed the door on the Pirates while St. Louis chipped away against Leever, eventually prevailing, 4 to 3. Four days later in Pittsburgh, Taylor and Leever squared off again. After allowing two runs on four hits, Leever retired, because his "arm went wrong." Taylor continued his mastery of the Pirates, allowed only one run due to an error, and pitched the Cardinals to a 3–1 victory.

The "wrong" in Leever's arm was a flare-up of rheumatism in his pitching arm and he "wasn't worth a rap" for a week.[15] His arm responded slowly to treatment and he started only twice between June 27 and July 26.

Leever was pressed into service during the second game of an Exposition Park doubleheader with the Cardinals on July 29. During the first inning, the lone umpire, Bob Emslie, was forced to leave the game after his wrist was badly injured by a foul tip. Leever and pitcher O'Neil of St. Louis were designated substitute umpires for the remainder of the contest, eventually won by the Cardinals in the ninth inning on a three-run rally against Mike Lynch.

Since the Pirates lost, the locals were not kind to the novice umpires. "Their work was not satisfactory," declared the *Pittsburgh Press*, "and Case, who pitched for Pittsburgh, complained after the game that O'Neil had gone wrong on at least 25 strikes. Leever missed one decision on base that was detrimental to the locals' chances."[16]

In addition to the disability of both Leever and Phillippe, catcher Eddie Phelps went on the shelf after his thumb nail was torn off by one of Flaherty's nasty benders. On July 15, Fred Clarke injured his back when he turned a complete somersault after a long run for a shallow fly ball.

The day of Clarke's injury, Barney Dreyfuss was said to have remarked, "If we get through this season without having some player killed, I guess we will be fortunate."[17] To give confidence to his team's diminishing prospects for 1904, Dreyfuss did not dispute a story that he made a $100 to $500 bet that Pittsburgh would win the pennant.[18] To boost his sagging pitching staff, Dreyfuss had signed a collegian from Brown University *The Pittsburgh Gazette* touted as "a star of the Mathewson type." The lefty-throwing Mike Lynch made his major league debut in St. Louis on June 21 and would win 15 games for the Pirates over the remainder of the season.

The cold in Deacon Phillippe's eyes worsened as time went by. He resorted to wearing a pair of dark goggles, but on July 9 the discomfort compelled him to consult a physician. The specialist told Phil the trouble was very serious and ordered him to stay away from the ballpark. He was encouraged to enter the hospital for treatment, but refused. He then was placed on a dangerous drug, belladonna, a powder derived from a poisonous Eurasian plant. Within nine days Phillippe was back at Exposition Park and was permitted to practice. Though his eyes continued to give him trouble, the Pirates expressed hope that the pitcher would be back in the lineup in another week.[19]

By July, it was evident that the Pirates were not going to repeat as National League champions in 1904. Already trailing the Giants by 12½ games on July 1, Sam Leever was the first to publicly admit Pittsburgh was not going to finish first.

"New York will win the pennant," the veteran pitcher told Ralph Davis. "I cannot see it any other way. Look at the record they have made and the hold they at present have on first place.... If the Giants should win even half their games in the West that would settle it."[20]

The Pirates won six straight games from June 27 to July 4, but the Giants ran off 18 consecutive victories to effectively end any chance anybody had of overtaking them. The Pirates did not fall below fourth place after June 14, but injury and misfortune continued to plague them over the second half of their season. In addition to Phillippe's eye problems, Clarke's back injury and a severe leg infection sidelined the manager for all but 72 games, the great Honus Wagner missed 24 games, and a serious beaning knocked catcher Ed Phelps out of the lineup.

There were other problems, too. While Clarke was at home in Pittsburgh hobbling around on crutches, Honus Wagner, as team captain, took the helm as acting manager. During Clarke's absence, Wagner and right fielder Jimmy Sebring exchanged words about by the young outfielder's lethargic play. *Sporting Life* reported that since the spring there had been a Sebring faction and a Leach faction on the team after pitcher Bucky Veil beat up "Wee Tommy" in a fight at a St. Louis hotel. When his friend Veil was released, Sebring became surly and uncooperative. The report also noted that Sebring attempted to assault Wagner when the Dutchman censured the young outfielder for a bad throw.

Sebring was unable to play after he suffered a badly sprained ankle in a game with Cincinnati on July 31. Two days later, he showed up at Union Station where he was expected to accompany the team on their Eastern trip. When he was handed his sleeper car upper berth ticket by President Dreyfuss, the injured outfielder told his boss he didn't think there was any need for him to travel to New York. Dreyfuss became upset with the player's attitude and informed Sebring he "could quit the team." Instead of boarding the team's train, Sebring went home.[21] The player was suspended and a local amateur named Ernie Diehl who had been recommended by Sam Leever accompanied the team on the Eastern road trip that opened in Brooklyn on August 3. On August 11, Jimmy Sebring was traded to the Cincinnati Reds for outfielder Harry "Moose" McCormick. McCormick had just been obtained by the Reds in a trade with the New York Giants. Giants owner Brush became irate when he heard that Cincinnati's Garry Herrmann aided Pittsburgh by trading the player the Giants had just sent to the Reds.[22]

Sebring rebounded in 1905 and was hitting .286 after his first 58 games for Cincinnati when, in August, he left the Reds to join his hometown Williamsport, Pennsylvania, minor league team in the "outlaw" Tri-State League. Normally a player abandoning his club to play for an "outlaw" team would be blacklisted by the league office, but Sebring's wife was seriously ill and needed him to care for her on a daily basis.

When he wasn't tending to his wife, Sebring earned a living playing independent ball until he was reinstated in 1909. Unfortunately, Sebring's return was a failure as he managed only eight hits in 81 at-bats as Brooklyn's center fielder. It became obvious in the autumn that Sebring's decline in major league skills was more than just rust. His kidneys were failing and he was diagnosed with Bright's Disease. Just six years after he became a hero by hitting a home run in the first World Series' game as a 21-year-old rookie, Jimmy Sebring collapsed in convulsions and died on December 22, 1909.

Problems with the troublesome Sebring and Phillippe's vision were not the last of the Pirates' woes. Following Sam Leever's 4 to 1 victory over Brooklyn on August 4, the Pirates, with Tommy Leach acting as manager, proceeded to Philadelphia late the following evening for a series with the Phillies. After losing on Saturday, most of the Pirates used their Sunday off-day for a trip to Atlantic City.

On Monday, the players loaded into their horse-drawn omnibus for the ride to the Phillies' ballpark. The vehicle was handled by a driver the Pirates had used for nearly 20 years. It was said that it was "Hayes' delight in the old Pittsburgh days to give the boys a close call to a collision."[23] A short distance from the hotel, the rear wheel of the team's bus collapsed while it was negotiating a turn at the corner of Chestnut and 19th Streets. The spooked horses bolted, dragging the overturned carriage and its unfortunate occupants along the road for a short distance. While the jostled players went about extricating themselves from the wreck, two street cars collided not ten feet away resulting in an injury to one of the motormen.[24]

Barney Dreyfuss recalled that Sam Leever was found gasping for breath with a huge bat bag lying across his throat. "'Take it off!' was Sam's yell. He was pinioned solid; could not budge."[25] Amazingly, there were only two serious injuries. First baseman Kitty Bransfield hurt his foot and pitcher Roscoe Miller sprained his wrist. Miller was given a leave of absence to recuperate, but the injury would end the hurler's career.

Not surprisingly, the Pirates appeared to be in shock during their contest with the Phillies. Despite cuts on his face and ear, catcher Fred Carisch assumed the first base position for the disabled Bransfield. Rarely used substitutes Ernie Diehl and Harry Cassady started in the outfield and Otto Krueger played third base. The first Philadelphia batter Mike Lynch faced hit a line drive at the hurler's head. Lynch ducked, but he didn't recover his composure until the Phillies had three runs. Lynch was left on the mound to absorb a 15 to 5 thrashing.

The Pirates came back to take the next two games from the Phillies. Sam Leever made his regular start on Wednesday and won, 6–3. The Pirates won three of four in Boston, but lost catcher Harry Smith due to a torn ligament in his shoulder.

When the club rolled into New York on August 16, John Harris, a local scorecard man, greeted Barney Dreyfuss with the question, "Well, anyone killed to-day?" "Yes," responded Dreyfuss, after which the little owner recounted the wreck of his players' bus in Philadelphia.

After being absent from the mound for more than seven weeks, Deacon Phillippe assured Fred Clarke on Saturday, August 6, that he was "rounding into shape." Phillippe told the *Pittsburgh Leader* he expected to leave the following Wednesday night and join the team in Boston.[26]

Phillippe made his return to the mound in Boston on August 15. The first pitch delivered by Sam Leever to the game's first batter, Phil Geier, was hit back to the pitcher's box. The hot shot was stopped by Leever with his pitching hand and he was able to throw the runner out at first. However, Leever was forced to retire with a badly split hand. Phillippe came in to pitch and performed remarkably after the long layoff. "The clever strategic pitching of Phillippe was too much for them," noted the *Chronicle Telegraph*.[27]

It was well that he did because Boston's small right-hander Ed McNichol allowed the Pirates only two runs. In the second inning Phillippe struck out Pat Carney and Pat Moran with runners on second and third. Boston managed to score a run in the fourth inning on a single, a stolen base and another hit. After that no Boston man reached first until after two were out.

In the ninth inning with two down, Carney smacked a hot one at Leach that he knocked down, picked up and threw wildly to first, allowing the batter to take second base. A pitcher named Tom Fisher pinch-hit for McNichol, but Phillippe easily disposed of him by strikeout to preserve a 2–1 victory.

Three days later, Phillippe did not pitch that badly against the Giants at the Polo Grounds but lost to Joe McGinnity, 6 to 0. Phillippe allowed only six hits, but Pirates errors in each inning in which the Giants scored cost him any chance to match McGinnity's effort. He would get his revenge when he beat McGinnity 5 to 3 before an overflow crowd at Exposition Park on August 23. After the first inning, when his wildness allowed New York to score two runs, he kept the Giants frustrated the remainder of the afternoon to earn his tenth victory of the season.

In his next outing, Phillippe was ineffective, departing after having allowed six runs and 11 hits in five innings to the last-place Phillies. "I have the sorest arm I have ever had," he told the newspapers. "It was in sore shape before the game and I could tell when I was warming up that I was going to have trouble with it. Every fast ball I pitched brought pain that I could scarcely stand, and between innings my arm felt as if it was being torn apart."[28]

Phillippe attributed the recent arm woes to his previous start against the Giants when he wore only a short-sleeved blouse. But before the game ended the temperature dropped and the pitcher became chilled. "I think I must have caught cold in it," he surmised of his arm.

Five days after his abbreviated start against the Phillies, Deacon gave up six runs in a loss to Boston though two of the Beaneaters' tallies were erased when the contest was called because of darkness before the Pirates could bat in the bottom of the seventh inning. After another poor performance in his third consecutive loss — seven runs on fifteen hits against Cincinnati on September 6 — Phillippe was left behind in Pittsburgh when the team departed for a road trip that evening.[29]

Given a leave of absence for the remainder of the season, Phillippe did give his salary limb a tryout during a September game he pitched and won for Fairmont against a team from Frostberg, Maryland. He didn't exert himself, gave up ten hits though he struck out 11 batters, and made two hits himself.

Sam Leever gained some measure of revenge for all those losses to Jack Taylor on September 2 in a 10 to 1 blow-out win over his Ohio nemesis and the Cardinals. The Pirates also managed a one-run win over Taylor in October to run their winning streak against him to three games.

After the season, National Commission President Herrmann made the accusation that an acquaintance of Taylor's, a gambler named McCormick, won a large sum of money on the game Taylor lost in Pittsburgh on July 30, 1904. It wasn't one of Pittsburgh's big guns, Leever or Phillippe, that beat Taylor, it was his own wildness and the journeyman Roscoe Miller who came through with a good game.

After reviewing affidavits from the umpire of the suspect game, Taylor's catcher that day, and the Cardinals manager, all stating that Jack pitched to win the game, the National League directors (Pulliam, Herrmann and Soden) unanimously acquitted him of the charge of dishonesty. However, the directors found Taylor guilty of a charge of "misbehavior" and fined him $300. Eventually, Taylor was also cleared of any wrong doing in the 1903 Chicago City Series despite his statement about being paid $500 to lose. But following these acquittals, the Pirates had his number.

Though the Pirates were hopelessly out of the 1904 pennant race by the first of September, there were still some fireworks the final month of the season. According to the custom of the time, straw hats were to be worn only during the spring and summer, so it was not fashionable to wear them after Labor Day. Practical jokers on ball teams regularly sought out victims in hotels or trains in order to smash straw lids displayed after their expiration date. Following a doubleheader at Exposition Park against the Cubs on Saturday, September 10, the Pirates and Cubs boarded the train bound for Chicago to continue their series where Sunday baseball was legal. Also aboard the Lake Shore sleeper were the players from the White Sox and Naps, who were making the same trip because baseball on the Sabbath was also illegal in Cleveland. Once the train got under way, the restless players went about the coaches, crushing any straw lids they could find.

The players knew Sam Leever wore his straw hat from the ball park to the train and some of them conspired to find the Schoolteacher's dicer and smash it. The Pirates held back, because they knew better than to mess with Mr. Leever. When the assassins approached his sleeper berth the marksman pitcher elevated his ever-present gun and fired a shot through the roof of the car. The startled vandals immediately abandoned their plans and scattered.[30]

In Chicago the next day, Leever further punished his tormentors by pitching the Pirates to a 5 to 1 victory, his 16th of the season. The first eight innings were played in a constant drizzle and there were frequent delays to dry the baseball each time it came in contact with the wet turf.

The Pirates finished fourth in 1904, 19 games behind the first-place Giants. It would be the lowest Pittsburgh finish in the 11 years the duo of Leever and Phillippe pitched for the club. Due to the eye infection and a sore arm, the Deacon was limited to only 21 starts and he won 15 fewer games than in 1903. Leever rebounded from the early-season shoulder soreness and finished with a record of 18–11, though he did not pitch a single shutout.

Though Dreyfuss always said he wasn't sad to see them go, he must have been depressed when he looked at the American League's statistics and saw that Jesse Tannehill won 21 games for Boston and Jack Chesbro used a devastating spitball to accumulate a 41–12 record with the New York club.

John McGraw and the New York Giants snubbed the Boston American League champions by refusing to participate in a World Series following the 1904 regular season. The Giants' club president told the press, "There is nothing in the constitution or playing rules of the National League which requires its victorious club to submit its championship honors to a contest with a victorious club in a minor league."[31]

An exasperated Barney Dreyfuss, who had committed to play a postseason series against an American League team at the end of the season, arranged a best-of-five series against Pittsburgh's fourth-place counterpart in the American League. Only one day after the regular season finale in Chicago, the Pirates were in Cleveland playing a game that ended in a rain-shortened 2–2 tie.

Sam Leever got the Pirates' only victory in game two of their post-season series. The first five innings were scoreless, but both starting pitchers struggled thereafter. Leever staggered to a 7–4 victory despite allowing 13 hits. The Naps won the poorly attended series, two games to one, with two other contests ending in ties. Deacon Phillippe did not appear in the post-season affair.

That October, Phillippe announced he would travel to Redfield and Brookings, South Dakota, to visit his folks for the first time in two years. When he told Barney Dreyfuss of his plans, the club president went to his private office and returned with a piece of paper. "Just reminds me," said Dreyfuss. "I have a letter from a man out in South Dakota who inquires if you are still living." Phillippe smiled and replied, "Good joke; I have been close to being a dead one this year."[32]

The Pirates' "Pinochle Club" was broken up before the 1905 season when utility player Otto Krueger was traded to Philadelphia along with Kitty Bransfield and reserve outfielder Harry McCormick for infielder Del Howard. In addition to losing a member of his pinochle foursome, Deacon Phillippe also lost his catcher of the previous two seasons as Ed Phelps was dealt to the Cincinnati Reds for veteran backstop Heinie Peitz, who was noted for his work with young pitchers.

The trade of Bransfield was not a surprise. He was unhappy in Pittsburgh and grew tired of the constant roasting he received from the local fans. After an outstanding first season with the Pirates in 1901, his production declined each succeeding season. "Kitty" batted .223 with only 26 extra-base hits in 139 games during the 1904 season.

"Bransfield is glad to shake the dust of the Smoky City from his feet," wrote Ralph Davis. "Bransfield, though one of the most conscientious players in the business, has never been a favorite with the fans, and this opposition to him has sometimes affected his playing for the worse."[33]

Additions to the Pirates' 1905 roster included a fleet-footed outfielder named Otis Clymer, who stole 56 bases for Buffalo a year earlier, and a big first baseman named Bill Clancy, from Montreal in the same circuit. Del Howard, the player obtained in the Bransfield deal, was a 27-year-old rookie who had given up a promising baseball career in 1900 due to the wishes of his wife. He returned to baseball in 1904, and the left-handed first baseman led Omaha of the Western League in batting.

The Pirates would go into the 1905 season with the same pitching staff that completed the previous campaign. The club would have a healthy Deacon Phillippe ready to go along with holdovers Leever, Flaherty, Lynch, Case and Chick Robitaille. Dreyfuss would bring in competent additions in the second half of the season when the Pirates' younger pitchers faltered under the weight of a tight pennant race.

Despite Leever's 18 victories in 1904 there was some criticism of the pitcher because it was considered a decline from his work in 1903. That spring Clarke ordered Leever to work with the rest of the pitching staff instead of playing the outfield for the substitutes, Leever's accustomed arrangement in preseason practices.

Toward the end of training, *Sporting Life* printed the surprising remark, "It is whispered in Pittsburgh that unless Leever can show better form than last year he will go."[34]

Bad weather plagued the Pirates during their time at Hot Springs. While many of the players filled their down time at the horse track, Leever found a surprising attraction to the roulette wheels in the city's casinos. After the repeal of Hot Springs' anti-gambling laws in 1903, it became Leever's annual routine each spring to stroll down the streets of the city and pick one of the gambling houses for an evening game of chance. He would buy a dollar's worth of the checks, 20 for a dollar, and he would risk one check per turn of the wheel. This would give him at least 20 turns plus any additional spins if he won. He often won, but would never stay in a casino more than an hour. Sometimes, teammates might drop in to watch him play his 20 chances while habitual gamblers all around him were losing thousands of dollars.[35]

Leever was known to bet on baseball games, too. However, he didn't believe in risking more than 50 cents at a time.[36] When it was rumored that Leever was involved with the organization of the new bank in Goshen, a friend noted that he couldn't see Leever loaning money to anybody. Another time Leever became upset when he lost a dollar on a race horse named Lady Jocelyn. Nearly the whole team lost money on the tip about a sure thing at the New Orleans race track. "Don't howl, Sam," a friend told him. "Remember you won $16 on a two-dollar bet which Perk Kennedy tipped off. You are still $15 ahead."[37]

At the conclusion of the team's practice of March 15, Phillippe and several of his teammates began the walk back to their Hot Springs hotel. They had gone only a short distance when a streetcar, "one of the little, rocking, bobtail affairs," on the Hot Springs street railway rolled past. Upon spotting Fred Clarke in the car, Phillippe attempted to jump on board without signaling the motorman to stop. He grasped the handrail on the front platform as he attempted to step on the lower rung. The pitcher's foot slipped and he was thrown beneath the front of the car. The motorman failed to notice the man clinging to the handrail, his legs dragging on either side of the rail. Only when the startled passengers began to yell was the car brought to a stop, after Phillippe had been dragged some 50 feet over the sharp stones in the roadbed. Had he not been able to hang on to the handrail with one hand, he may well have been cut in two by the car's wheels.[38]

As it was, two fingers on Phil's left hand were lacerated and both legs from the knees down were bruised and scraped. His uniform and stockings were tattered and his shoes had been cut to pieces. The injured ball player was placed in the streetcar and was taken to the Eastman Hotel, where he was attended by a physician. Though his wounds were painful, there would be no long-term affects. He had escaped a potential career-ending injury and, reported H. V. Arkle of the *Sunday Press* less than ten days later, "Phillippe is in exceptionally good form and has done the most effective work in practice games."[39]

Just before the 1905 season began, the National Commission issued an edict that all betting must be stopped at major league ball parks, whether the municipal officials took a hand in its suppression or not. Barney Dreyfuss declared that he was wholly on board with the policy and said that it would not be necessary to make any arrests after warnings were given.[40]

Deacon Phillippe returned to form in 1905, winning 20 games to match Leever's 20 victories. That spring Phillippe worked on a spitball that would break downward out of the strike zone and inward toward the batter. He maintained the pitch would be a "winner" once he got control of it.[41]

Patsy Flaherty drew the starting assignment for the Pirates' first game of the season and responded with a 9–4 victory in Cincinnati. The next day, Deacon Phillippe didn't pitch well and lost to the Reds, 7 to 0. He was replaced in the sixth inning by Charlie Case, then was thrown out of the game in the eighth by umpire Bill Klem. He drew the wrath of Klem after he supported Clarke when the latter squawked after being thrown out trying to steal third base.

After the Pirates took three of four games in Cincinnati to start the 1905 season, a crowd of just under 13,000 braved strong winds and cold temperature for the Pirates' first home game. Leever cruised to an 8 to 4 victory over the

Cardinals after which one local scribe was led to pen, "Leever never had more speed in his life and his curves never had a better break."[42] Two Pittsburgh errors led to a first-inning run and the other three St. Louis tallies came in the ninth after the verdict was decided.

Phillippe took the mound for the second time on April 23 in Chicago, opposed by the Cubs' Mordecai "Three Finger" Brown. Only one run was scored in the contest. With two outs in the home half of the eighth inning, Brown swung at what should have been the third strike. The wild pitch got past Pittsburgh catcher Peitz and the Chicago pitcher made it all the way to second base. With 21,000 West Side fans urging him on, Doc Casey hit a Phillippe pitch for a double that scored Brown and gave Chicago a 1–0 lead. After the Pirates went down in the ninth, Deacon became a loser, despite pitching a five-hitter. Nine Pittsburgh baserunners were left on base during their scoreless effort. In the two games Phillippe had pitched thus far in 1905, the Pirates had scored no runs.

After Phillippe pitched a 3 to 2 victory against the Cubs on April 29, Ralph Davis wrote for the *Press,* "The Deacon used the spit-ball frequently and pretended he was using it many more times. Phil is like all other pitchers that are using the deceptive delivery — he hasn't always got perfect control of it. He is charged in yesterday's game with two wild pitches, and both of them are due to the salivated sphere."[43]

Deacon started a game against Cincinnati on May 8 that would develop into a near riot before more than 5,000 bugs at Exposition Park. Otis Clymer was the first Pirate to bat against Orval Overall in the home half of the first inning and grounded out. Reds first baseman Cliff Blankenship felt he was spiked intentionally by Clymer and ran up behind him as the Pirate walked toward the bench. The angry Blankenship struck Clymer twice about the head before the umpire jumped between the players. Rather than retaliate at the time, the rookie Pirates right fielder invited Blankenship to the clubhouse where the pair could finish their dispute. Umpire George Bausewine immediately suspended both players. On his way off the field, Blankenship was pelted with bottles and even a knife throw by the local fanatics.

After the belligerents exited the field, the game resumed and Deacon Phillippe allowed only five hits and pitched around three errors to gain the Pirates a 2 to 1 decision. The Reds scored their only run in the fourth on a single by Fritz Odwell, two outs, and a steal of home by the Reds outfielder. An inning later the Pirates got their runs on a rally that began with Phillippe's single.

Fred Clarke maintained the incident at first base that day was the culmination of a conspiracy on the part of the Cincinnati players in an earlier series to knock the Pirates' best players out of the game.[44] The Pirates said

Clymer's actions were related to an incident in which Blankenship bumped Honus Wagner while the star shortstop was running the bases. However, in the same series, Wagner poured a foul-tasting chemical on the game ball so the Reds' star spitballer, Bob Ewing, would be discouraged from licking his fingers before delivering a pitch.[45] Regardless of the provocation, Barney Dreyfuss said he would pay any fines the National League levied on Clymer, a stance he later reversed.

Pittsburgh played their first series against John McGraw's New York Giants in mid–May. Phillippe was unavailable to pitch because of an elbow injury sustained when he was hit by a pitched ball from the Phillies' Charles Pittinger on May 12. So it was up to Sam Leever to get the Pirates off to a good start in game one of the series at the Polo Grounds.

Leever was opposed by Christy Mathewson, who was expected to extend the Giants' unbeaten streak to nine games. Leever's former Maysville teammate, Dan McGann, put the Pirates in an early hole with a two-out home run to left field. However, Pittsburgh managed to take the lead with two runs in the fourth inning on a Del Howard double, Wagner's well-placed hit to right field, and Mathewson's wild throw on Clancy's tap in front of the plate.

Pittsburgh took a 3 to 1 lead into the ninth inning, then broke the game open with a four-run outburst. McGann hit his second home run in the bottom of the ninth, but other than the two four-base hits, Leever was the master of the Giants on that day. "The Pittsburgher has rarely ever pitched in better form," recorded *The New York Times*, "being steady at all times, and completing the nine innings with one battery error to his credit."[46]

"Sam Leever proved my theory regarding the New Yorks," beamed Barney Dreyfuss. "Give them a low curve ball with a fast one now and then you will not find them dangerous in the scoring line. In Leever's game he used nothing else than a fine low curve, which he made break over the corners, and now and then followed up with a high fast pitch. Mertes and others went after them a mile away. Now and then some of the men almost broke their backs in the swings."[47]

McGraw's actions during the third game of the series overshadowed anything that happened on the field during the Pirates' stay in New York. As Pirates pitcher Mike Lynch was leaving the field after he allowed two second-inning runs, McGraw began to berate the hurler and called him several vile names. "You're a dirty, big quitter!" was the only remark suitable for the tabloids to print. Manager Clarke, coming in from left field, overheard the slurs and confronted the Giants' manager. Umpire Jim Johnstone intervened before blows were struck. Considering McGraw the instigator, the umpire banished him for the remainder of the game. For good measure, the arbiter also ejected Mathewson from the coaching lines for what Ralph Davis called "urging the hoodlum element (among the Giants) to seeds of disorder and unsportsmanship." McGraw left his team's bench and relocated to a small closet next to the dugout. Clarke protested, but Johnstone replied, "He's off the grounds as far as I'm concerned."[48]

The next day, Pirates owner Barney Dreyfuss was standing near the Polo Grounds press gate when McGraw appeared and began to taunt him, "Hey, Barney!" Hey Barney!"

Dreyfuss ignored the taunts, but McGraw continued, "Hey, Barney! Wanna bet?" McGraw defied Dreyfuss to bet $10,000 on the day's game and insinuated that the Pittsburgh owner hadn't picked up some markers he had given.

John J. McGraw, Manager, New York Giants (National Baseball Hall of Fame Library, Cooperstown, New York).

A livid Dreyfuss wrote a blistering letter to his former protégé and now league president, Harry Pulliam, describing McGraw's behavior. McGraw responded to the complaint by telling Pulliam he was hand-picked by Dreyfuss to become president because of his role as the Pirates' secretary. The league's directors dismissed Dreyfuss allegations, but dictated a $150 fine and 15 days' suspension for McGraw's comments to President Pulliam. However, the Giants' attorneys secured a Superior Court injunction blocking the suspension.

The whole affair escalated the feud between the Pirates and Giants. When he visited rival National League cities thereafter, fans and players greeted the Pirates' owner with cries of "Hey Barney!" Oh, how he hated those Giants.

Following Leever's first-game victory in the hotly contested series, the Pirates lost the next three and departed New York six and a half games behind the Giants. Pittsburgh's losing streak reached four games on Tuesday when Phillippe lost a 1–0 pitching duel against Irving ("Not Cy") Young in Boston. The Bucs stopped the bleeding a day later with an 11 to 1 victory behind Leever at the South End Grounds.

During a game in Cincinnati on May 28, both Phillippe and Leever suffered uncharacteristic meltdowns. Phillippe took the mound and lasted only one and one third of an inning, allowing four hits, two walks and a hit batsman. He was relieved by Leever, and he too was ineffective. After giving up two runs in the fifth, Sam was thrown out of the game for arguing with umpire Bob Emslie. Down 7–0 and having brought along only two pitchers for the Sunday excursion to Cincinnati, Fred Clarke sent out a reserve outfielder, Del Howard, to finish the game. Howard actually pitched creditably except for the seventh inning, when the Reds added five more runs.

Emslie wasn't in a particularly good mood that day and added two more ejections to his résumé, one to Reds second baseman Miller Huggins for arguing and another to Honus Wagner for using foul language. As he departed the field, Wagner taunted the umpire even further by "scornfully grasping his nose with his thumb and index finger." Much to the delight of the 8,972 customers at the Palace of the Fans, Emslie summoned two policemen who escorted Wagner from the ball park. National League President Pulliam mandated a three-day suspension for the shortstop's actions that afternoon.[49] President Pulliam also assessed fines of $30 for Wagner and $10 plus a one-day suspension for Leever.

On June 7, the Giants came to Exposition Park for the first time in 1905. The two clubs split the four games, which came off without incident, except that Barney Dreyfuss refused to shake the hand of New York owner John Brush.

In game three of the series, the Giants scored five runs in their first at-bat against Leever. Clarke wanted to pull him during the Giants' onslaught, but the Schoolmaster insisted on completing the inning. In the bottom of the first, Joe McGinnity could not retire a single batter before McGraw rushed first-game winner Mathewson into the contest with three runs in and two Pirates on base. After Pittsburgh added three more runs to take the lead after one inning, Phillippe was sent in to quiet the Giants' offense. He struck out the side in the second and allowed the Gotham club only one more run. The Pirates jumped on the Giants' ace for three more runs in the second and upon extending their lead to 12–5, Mathewson appeared to ease up, perhaps in frustration over his team's six errors. This led to cries of "quitter" from all parts of the field.[50]

On June 28, Pirates first baseman Bill Clancy suffered a broken finger from a pitched ball thrown by the Cardinals' Jack Taylor. Clancy was batting only .229 at the time so he was released and another rookie, Del Howard, previously a utility player, assumed the duty as full-time first baseman.

On July 2, Deacon Phillippe took the mound against the Reds with a burly young Canadian named George Gibson behind the plate. In Gibson's first game in the major leagues, the first Cincinnati batter to reach base took off for second. "I rocked back on my heels and threw a bullet, knee high, right over the plate," Gibson recalled. However, second baseman Ritchey and shortstop Wagner, used to the rainbow lobs from the other Pirates catchers, were slow in covering the bag and the ball sailed into center field. After the inning ended, Wagner assured the young backstop it would not happen again.[51]

The Pirates lost that July 2 game when errors led to three Reds runs in the fifth inning, but the team realized they had something special behind the plate in Gibson. Gibson would be the regular catcher for both Leever and Phillippe for the remainder of their major league careers.

In the nightcap of a July 4 doubleheader sweep at Exposition Park, Leever beat the Reds, 8–1, and Honus Wagner electrified the holiday crowd with a daring steal of home. Two days later, Phillippe picked up the Pirates' fifth straight victory in his 5–2 win against the Cubs' outstanding rookie hurler, Ed Reulbach, in Chicago. The Pirates' winning streak ended with a loss at West Side Grounds the next morning, but Leever came back in the afternoon half of the Saturday double dip and beat "Buttons" Briggs, 5–1.

Despite the Pirates' winning ways, they couldn't gain any ground on the first-place Giants, who matched them victory for victory. On July 15, the second-place Pirates opened a four-game series in New York, seven games behind in the standings.

In the opener, the Giants staked Joe McGinnity to an early 6–0 lead against Sam Leever. At the end of five innings Leever was out of the game and it appeared the Giants would coast to an easy victory. However, the Bucs scored two runs in the sixth and five in the seventh inning to take the lead and drive McGinnity from the game. Christy Mathewson shut out Pittsburgh over the last two and two-thirds innings to keep the score 7–6. In the bottom of the ninth, George Browne hit a two-run homer off Mike Lynch to give New York the 8 to 7 victory. Browne was carried off the field by ecstatic Giants fans.

After the Sunday off-day, Pittsburgh came back to win the game on Monday, 3 to 0. During Phillippe's four-hit shutout "with the thermometer almost bursting," no Giants batter advanced past second base and Honus Wagner broke open a 1–0 ballgame in the eighth inning with a mammoth two-run homer onto the elevated railroad tracks behind left field.

"Every effort was made to unnerve Phillippe," recorded *The New York Times*, "but the Pittsburgher handled himself like a veteran and had the New York batsmen at his mercy."[52]

The next day, the Pirates edged the Giants, 2–1, on George Gibson's home run off Christy Mathewson. While covering first base during the contest, Mathewson was bowled over by Fred Clarke. Matty dropped the ball but Clarke was called out for interference. The game was halted for several minutes while Mathewson's injured hand was being attended.

Down 2–0, the Giants mounted a rally in the seventh inning. Sammy Strang, pinch-hitting for Mathewson, lined a hit to right field. As Otis Clymer went to field Strang's hit, a spectator in the bleachers threw a bottle at the Pirates' right fielder. The missile missed its target, but umpire James Johnstone stopped the game until order was restored. In a game during which six Giants were tossed out of the coaching box, Pirates pitcher Charlie Case remained calm in the face of the hostile crowd and finished the inning without further damage. Pittsburgh went on to win by one run.

The Pirates beat the Giants again on Wednesday, but the game was even nastier than the day before. Pittsburgh's Patsy Flaherty was driven from the mound when the Giants scored three runs in the second frame, and Sam Leever took the mound for the third inning. He staggered at first, getting out of a two-on, no one out jam, but New York added two runs to their total an inning later. Down 5–2 in the fifth inning, Pittsburgh began their comeback and eventually took the lead. The rally was marred by disreputable conduct from the crowd and Giants players.

After Clymer and Clarke reached to open the fifth, Leach beat out a bunt to load the bases. Giants first baseman Dan McGann and pitcher Luther Taylor argued with umpire Klem at the decision. Taylor was eventually pacified by Frank Bowerman and returned to the mound. However, McGann grabbed the umpire's coat and had to be pulled away by a teammate before the assault worsened. McGann was immediately ordered off the field. Wagner drove in two runs on his long drive off the left-field fence and Leach scored moments later to tie the score on Howard's sacrifice fly. Wagner then stole third and scored on Dave Brain's grounder to Bill Dahlen, giving Pittsburgh the lead, 6 to 5. On his way in to the bench, center fielder "Turkey" Mike Donlin complained that Wagner should have been called out at third, and he too was sent to the clubhouse. The ejection of a second Giant was followed by a fusillade of beer glasses from the right field stands. One missile hit Klem in the back and several more landed nearby, but "the appearance of a big cop put a stop to the Western habit."[53]

The activities of the top of the inning apparently rejuvenated Leever and he quickly retired the Giants in the home half of the fifth. He allowed only two baserunners over the next three innings, a bunt hit by Browne in the sixth and a single by Strang after two were out in the seventh. Leever gave up eight hits, walked one and hit a batter during his seven innings of work, but his defense played errorless ball and Pittsburgh pulled off an 8 to 5 victory. At the game's conclusion, umpires Klem and Johnstone were escorted from the field by police officers."[54]

The Pirates left New York five games out of first place and moved on to Philadelphia where they continued to pile up victories. Phillippe beat the Phillies on July 20, blanked Boston on the 25th and threw another shut out, this one against the Brooklyn Superbas, on July 29. Over a period of 12 days, Phillippe won four games, three of them shutouts. Despite all their success, the Pirates actually lost ground to the Giants, who won 12 straight games.

Leever pitched an outstanding game at South End Grounds in Boston on July 27. The ex-schoolteacher allowed only two hits (a double by Ed Abbaticchio and a single by Cozy Dolan), issued no free bases, and retired the last 16 batters he faced. Wagner's error in the third inning cost Leever the shutout, and Boston clung to its tenuous one-run lead until the eighth inning. The Beaneaters Irv Young was tagged for nine hits, but a base on balls in the eighth and left fielder Delahanty's error in the ninth were responsible for Pittsburgh's 2–1 victory.

On August 2, the Giants invaded Pittsburgh for another volatile series. By this time, the antics of McGraw and his players had not only made the Giants the most hated team in Pittsburgh, but in all of baseball. New York won the opener as Christy Mathewson prevailed in a duel with Phillippe, 3–1. Honus Wagner was thrown out at first in the fourth inning on a close play, then displayed his displeasure by firing a ball near umpire George Bausewine during warm-ups between innings. Bausewine ejected Wagner from the game.

Leever bested Joe McGinnity, 10–4, in the second game, and the Pirates also won the third game on Friday. The largest crowd in Exposition Park history, 18,383 screaming fans, was on hand for the finale that Saturday.

The Pirates scored three runs early off Christy Mathewson and carried a 5–1 lead into the seventh inning when the Giants tallied four times to tie the score. Phillippe relieved the Pirates' starter, Charlie Case, in the eighth and held New York scoreless through the top of the ninth.

Much to the delight of the Pittsburgh faithful, Claude Ritchey led off the home half of the ninth with a ground-rule double into the overflow crowd standing in center field. The cheers of the fans had barely subsided when George Gibson attempted to sacrifice Ritchey to third. Mathewson pounced on the bunted ball and fired to third baseman Art Devlin, who bobbled the low throw just as Ritchey slid into the bag. Umpire Bausewine seemed hesitant to make a call. Confusion reigned and Ritchey remained on the base. Mathewson slammed his glove to the turf and stomped off the field amid jeers from the frenzied fans. The Giants tried to get the base umpire, Bob Emslie, to make the call, but he had not seen the play and correctly declared the call was Bausewine's. Devlin made some disparaging remarks and the angry umpire punched the Giants' third-sacker in the face. Devin staggered away and, according to a Pittsburgh newspaper, hid behind big Dan McGann.[55]

McGraw ranted and raved at the lack of an out call and, after several minutes, Bausewine gave the Giants' manager three minutes to have his players return to their positions and continue the game. When McGraw ignored the deadline, the game was forfeited to the Pirates.

By this time, much of the capacity crowd had poured onto the field and surrounded the Giants, who retreated to their bench in fear for their safety. With the assistance of Clarke and the Pirates' players, policemen escorted the visiting players from the field to the waiting carriages. All along their route down General Robinson Street to the Allegheny River Bridge, the mob pelted the players and their horses with stones. Amazingly, the Giants came out of the affair with only minor bumps and bruises. Meanwhile, the Pirates celebrated having shaved another game off New York's league lead.[56]

In a post-script to the story, *The Washington Post* reported that about $50,000 wagered on the New York–Pittsburgh game of August 11 was held up until the league president upheld the forfeit.[57]

After the Giants left town, National League president Pulliam announced that the Pirates' best player, Honus Wagner, was suspended for three games and fined $40 for his actions in the first game of the Giants' series. Without their star, the Pirates dropped three of five home games against lowly Boston.

Despite his team's slump, Phillippe continued to pitch sterling baseball for the Pirates. He beat the Boston Beaneaters, 3–2, on August 7, but two days later he experienced a rare ejection during a loss in the second game of a twin bill at Exposition Park. It occurred in the last inning with the Pirates in the field. Sam Leever had been on the mound since the fifth inning, having relieved Homer Hillebrand, who went to center field to replace the ailing Ginger Beaumont. While Leever was pitching to Abbaticchio someone on the Pittsburgh bench yelled "Dan McGann" at umpire Bill Klem on any pitch called a "ball." The umpire warned the Pirates that if it was repeated he would punish the entire bench. A moment later, the name was yelled again, and

Klem, "turning with a majestic wave of his hand he swept the whole bench of its occupants and stood with folded arms as he saw the men move out." First went Robitaille, Lynch and Case, followed by Phillippe and Gibson. Klem then pointed his finger to the last three men on the bench and said "get out." Peitz and Harry Smith started toward the gate, but Flaherty hesitated, only to be told to hurry up. The ejected Pirates and the team mascot all drew automatic $10 fines from the league office.[58]

When the game ended with the 3 to 2 score in favor of the Bostons, the local mob of gamblers was in a sore mood because the betting odds had been 10 to 3 in favor of the Pirates. When the gamblers caught sight of Klem departing the scene, the umpire was seriously threatened.

"Klem was forced to secrete himself in the women's waiting room in the grand stand while many angry 'and light pocketed individuals went looking for him,'" reported *Sporting Life*. "About three hundred tough looking fellows hung around until forced out of the gates by the police." Klem hung around the park for about a half-hour, then slipped from the grounds by a side gate.[59]

Two days following his ejection in Boston, Phillippe won a 1–0, 12-inning pitching duel with Tully Sparks of the Phillies. Only 1,490 Pittsburghers came out on a Friday afternoon to see the masterfully pitched contest. Pittsburgh finally won it in the bottom of the 12th after two were out. Wagner reached base on an error by the Phillies' third baseman, stole second, and scored on a Del Howard single, only the Pirates' third hit off Sparks. Phillippe allowed six singles and two walks in his 12 innings of work.

Phillippe won his next start, against the Superbas, and was scheduled to start the opener in the big series at the Polo Grounds on August 21. Leever was also pitching well, not having lost since the July 15 debacle against the Giants.

Phillippe squared off against Mathewson in the opener, but the Deacon's supporting cast played poorly throughout. The Pirates made four errors, two by catcher Pietz, and Fred Clarke badly misjudged a fly ball. A four-run fourth inning by the Giants gave them a five-run lead and erased any doubt as to the final verdict.

"There has hardly been a time in his baseball career when he (Phillippe) gave such a weak exhibition in the box," commented a reporter. "He was not hit freely, but in watching the bases he was careless and ineffective and toward the latter part of the game the local men ran bases on him with impunity."

In the sixth inning, McGraw, who was coaching at third, signaled Devlin to steal third, which he accomplished easily, and then Devlin stole home, "the feat being greeted with the greatest enthusiasm of the day."[60]

The opening game of the series was played without incident other than

McGraw's ejection in the seventh inning by umpire Johnstone for disputing a decision. Though each team garnered eight hits, the Pirates lost 10–2.

Mike Lynch got the Pirates' only win in the series the next day, and Leever lost the finale to McGinnity. Pittsburgh went to the bottom of the fifth inning with a 2–1 lead, but Leever was driven from the game after he was tagged for four runs. McGraw wasn't around to see the rally because of his ejection for improper language while arguing a strike call the previous inning. His men took two of the three games to push their league lead to nine games.

As the pennant race moved into September, all of the Pirates' outfielders were hurting. Clymer was out with a broken finger, replaced by an emergency acquisition from Des Moines, Bob Ganley. Once one of the fastest men in the league, Ginger Beaumont's knees were so bad he was only able to play 97 games in the outfield. Left fielder Fred Clarke ruptured a blood vessel in his foot, forcing the ailing Beaumont back into the lineup only one day after the former batting champion returned from rehabilitation at Mt. Clemens. However, between Leever's loss to the Giants on August 23 and the second game of a double-header in St. Louis on September 12, the Pirates won 19 of 21 games to pull within five games of the first-place Giants. Sam Leever was the club's hottest pitcher during the stretch, winning all four starts, two of them by shutout.

One of those two losses during the Pirates' hot stretch was Deacon Phillippe's 1–0 defeat in the first game of a doubleheader on a cold and drizzly day at Chicago's West Side Park. Phillippe pitched hitless ball for the first five frames and continued his shutout through ten innings. However, Chicago's Bob Wicker did not allow a safety after the fourth inning and the contest was still scoreless when the home team came to bat in the bottom of the 11th. Up to that time, Phillippe had allowed only two singles, though his defense made four errors he was able to pitch around. With one out, Doc Casey lined a Phillippe pitch into the right field corner. By the time Bob Ganley returned the ball to the infield, the Cubs runner stood on third base. Pittsburgh's infield moved in close for a play at the plate as Artie Hofman came to bat. The batter poked an easy grounder to the first baseman, but Howard threw badly to the plate and Casey scored the winning run. In the nightcap of the doubleheader, the Pirates' new-side wheeler, lefty Al Leifield, made his major league debut with a 1–0 win over the Cubs in a game called after six innings.

While the Pirates were playing their best ball of the season, Deacon Phillippe could not buy a break. In his next start after the hard-luck loss in Chicago, the Reds thumped him for five runs before he was replaced by Flaherty to start the fifth inning. He suffered another tough-luck loss in the second game of a Saturday doubleheader on September 12 in St. Louis. He and Cardinals pitcher Jack Taylor battled pitch for pitch and the score was tied at 1–1 when St. Louis came to bat in the bottom of the ninth.

Light-hitting Cardinals second baseman Harry Arndt led off the home half of the ninth with a line drive that seemed destined for left field. Honus Wagner raced over and leaped into the air in an attempt to snare the sphere. The Bucs' star shortstop got the ball in his glove, but he couldn't hold it. Phillippe tried to pick Arndt off first, but Howard lost the ball and the Cardinals baserunner made it to third base with the potential winning run. The next two batters went out easily to bring to bat the opposing pitcher. Though Jack Taylor was a nemesis to the Pirates on the mound, he wasn't much of a hitter. Arndt knew Phillippe had a deliberate windup when delivering a pitch and decided to take the chance.

Phillippe whipped a quick strike across to Taylor, but on the next pitch Arndt made his move with a daring dash for home plate. The pitch was low but across the plate. Gibson trapped the ball in the dirt with his glove, but before he could pick it up and apply a tag, Arndt scored the winning run.[61]

Due to several rain-outs, Phillippe did not pitch again until September 21 and he fared poorly, departing after only five innings, down 7–1 to the Phillies. Fresh off three losses in Chicago, the Giants came to Pittsburgh on September 25 for their final series of the season with the Pirates. The second-place Pirates trailed New York by five and a half games.

Despite a personal four-game losing streak, Phillippe took the mound for the first game against Mathewson with Pittsburgh's slim pennant hopes squarely on his shoulders. In a remarkably uncharacteristic performance by the best control pitcher of the twentieth century, Phillippe hit three Giants batters — all in the first inning.

His first pitch of the game plunked Roger Bresnahan on the left shoulder. A sacrifice and a single by Donlin plated the game's first run. Phillippe then hit McGann on the shoulder, and Mertes was also hit by a pitch, loading the bases with one out.

"Those New York batsmen," wrote Alfred Cratty of the *Chronicle-Telegraph*, "Bresnahan, McGann and others, have a habit of running up on the pitch while at the bat thus worrying the twirler. Such a reliable man as Phillippe hit three men in one round because of these tactics."[62]

A double play could still get the Pirates out of the inning down only by one run, and Phillippe almost got it when Dahlen rapped a routine grounder to Wagner at shortstop. Wagner fumbled it and then threw wildly over the first baseman's head, allowing all three Giants to score. New York added another run in the inning, but for all practical purposes with Mathewson pitching for the opposition, the verdict was decided as soon as Wagner's throw sailed past Hillebrand. Wagner had to retire because of his bad wrist after he batted in the bottom of the first inning.

The Pirates raised the home fans' hopes with a pair of runs in the third inning and pulled to within 5 to 3 with a single run in the sixth. Phillippe managed to hold the Giants at bay until the top of the eighth inning when McGann walloped his first pitch to the bleachers in right and Mertes followed with another terrific drive against the left field fence for another triple. Dahlen's single sent Mertes home and a third run scored following third baseman Brain's error on a bunt and Mathewson's single. Phillippe pitched a complete game for the Pirates, a 10 to 4 loss.

A disconsolate Ralph Davis wrote of the day's loss, "The defeat administrated to 'good old Deacon' Phillippe was a most humiliating one.... Clarke and Phillippe have been associated together long enough for the former to know that when Phillippe is so wild that he hits three successive batsmen with pitched balls he is far from right and not fit to continue in the game. No one will think of accusing Phillippe of not doing his best, for the true old veteran has proved many times in the past that as an earnest, conscientious worker he has no peer."[63]

Joe Vila, the chief muckraker in New York's sports tabloids, could not resist taunting the Pirates in his column: "Alas, poor Barney! Alas, poor Pirates! You will have no trouble in seeing your finish this year. How those pennant aspirations went a glimmering.... Never mind Barney, if you don't win the pennant next year, or the next or the next or the next to that or still the next one after that do not get discouraged; there may yet come a time when you will be an also-ran."[64]

The loss took the heart out of the local club and the Pirates dropped the remaining two games of the Giants series. Phillippe got one more chance in 1905. The Pirates beat Brooklyn, 10–4, the day after the Giants series, but Phillippe wasn't around long enough to get the win, leaving with one out in the third after the Superbas scored three runs.

The Pirates lost their last five games of the season but still finished in second place with 96 victories. Leever led the major leagues in won-lost percentage with his 20–5 record, and despite his September slump, Phillippe won 20 games in a season for the seventh and final time. Phillippe registered his career high in strikeouts, but he also issued more walks than any season other than his rookie year. His experiment with the spitball may well have been the reason for the increase in both statistics.

Following the regular season, Sam Leever and teammate Charlie Case decided to engage in a pitching duel, backed by amateur players, for the championship of Clermont County, Ohio.⁶⁵ The game's results did not make the wire services, but Leever wrote a letter to the Pittsburgh newspapers detailing their match-up at New Boston, Ohio, on October 18. According to the Schoolmaster, his team won and there were a total of 25 strikeouts in the game. Leever admitted that Chase struck him out once, but he turned the tables on his younger mound mate by fanning him three times.⁶⁶

That fall, Leever was occupied by learning the ins and outs of his brand new automobile. Ralph Davis reported that Leever's "one trying experience was when he tried to speed in front of the home of Governor-elect Pattison, of Ohio, and was humiliated by the bursting of a tire." ⁶⁷

A. R. Cratty of *Sporting Life* wrote that Leever ran a close second to Fred Clarke as a financier among ball players. "The announcement is just made that Samuel is the boss of the telephone ranch at Goshen, O. Every message sent over the wires in that section yields the old man a revenue. The exchange is in his house. He gets a percentage on messages. Then again the veteran earns a little wad of cash selling gun powder made from the formula — which he bought about two years ago from a man in South Dakota. Leever has the Ohio territory."⁶⁸

After his 1905 commitment to the Pirates was satisfied, Deacon Phillippe delayed his annual trip to settle his affairs in South Dakota to go with Honus Wagner on his annual fall hunting trip. Wagner was accompanied by his famous bird dog he had named "Tessie" from the tune that became immortal in the 1903 World Series.

Sporting Life reported that "On their first trip they stopped in a hunting lodge far out in the tall timber and slept in tiers a la the hunkies who build railroads. The man who had the top bunk got all of the smoke. One morning he arose looking so black that his pals did not know him."⁶⁹ Phillippe's letter describing his experiences on the Wagner expedition was reprinted in the newspaper: "Hans Wagner and I were members of a party who have been hunting in the Northern part of the State. We found game rather scarce and all we had to show for our 19 days' outing is a bunch of 56 pheasants and a few rabbits. Considering that there were six in the party the haul is rather light."

Phillippe recounted a story in which Wagner, attempting to cross a swollen creek, fell into the water and it took considerable effort for the others to extract him. "Strange to say," he wrote, "the dunking did not seem to affect the Carnegie German in the least — he did not even contract a cold."⁷⁰

Phillippe added that he planned to leave immediately for a hunting trip in Indiana, which led Ralph Davis to write, "Deacon Phillippe, who usually spends his winters here, although his home is in the cold Dakota, has gone out to Indiana to spend time with some relatives, and to attempt to decrease the supply of game in the Hoosier State. Phil will be back this way about the first of the year. Pittsburgh smoke does not disagree with the big fellow."[71]

Before he left for his trip, Phillippe speculated on the upcoming baseball season, "It looks to me as if we are going to be in the next race. President Dreyfuss is going the limit in getting players and Manager Clarke is hustling harder this winter than ever before. It is a certainty that every man under contract to the Pittsburgh Club at the close of the last race believes that we have a fine chance for the 1906 flag."[72]

Honus Wagner had something to say about his friend following Phillippe's decline in the final month of the season. "I expect to see Deacon Phillippe pitch the game of his life next season. Phil has gained fifteen pounds in weight and this will be a good thing for him in his pitching. Phil now goes 185 pounds, which is just about right for a man of his height. He can put more speed behind a ball than he could at 170 pounds, at which he pitched last season."[73]

♦ NINE ♦

Transition

When the Pirates pitchers assembled at Hot Springs, Arkansas, in March, 1906, there was a prominent addition to the previous season's 20-game winners, Sam Leever and Deacon Phillippe. After he lost a record 29 games for the seventh-place Boston Nationals in 1905, veteran sinkerball pitcher Vic Willis was acquired by the Pirates on December 15 in exchange for three journeymen. Although the tall, lanky right-hander would turn 30 a week before the season began, he already had eight major league campaigns and four 20-win seasons under his belt.

"With a team like the Pirates behind me," announced Willis upon his arrival at Hot Springs, "I believe that I will win the big percentage of my games. At least, I will do my best. Those notices sent out from Boston about my being all in were started by someone jealous of my good fortune in getting away from the Hub." [1]

The addition of Willis meant that someone on the Pirates' pitching staff had to go. The odd man out became Pat Flaherty, who was shipped to Columbus as result of his poor 1905 performance.

While the Pirates were celebrating the acquisition of Willis, Sam Leever wrote a letter during the winter to several individuals, including Barney Dreyfuss and Pittsburgh sportswriters, saying that he was considering retirement. He had always said he wanted to quit baseball before he was "all in."

"Leever is a veteran, but he is far from being all in and he will probably be with the Pirates for several seasons yet," reported *The Sporting News*, "unless he does make his bluff good by retiring suddenly from the game.... According to the official figures, he was the leading pitcher of the National League last season, although, according to the popular idea, Mathewson of New York was the greatest ever." [2]

Leever finally acquiesced the second week in March and returned his signed contract to the Pirates. "Sam says that he has wintered well and believes that he will be able to start right in at the beginning and pitch good ball all season," wrote Ralph Davis. "He says that his arm feels better this spring than it has for years at this time and he is confident that he will have another successful season."[3]

The Pirates opened the season with both their center fielder, Ginger Beaumont, and third baseman Tommy Leach disabled. Leach was diagnosed with appendicitis and for a while it was thought he would need an operation, but his condition improved and he eventually returned to the field. Beaumont's ailing knee was so bad he did not play in the outfield until June. The Pirates still won their first two games of the season in St. Louis before returning to Pittsburgh.

An overflow crowd of 17,036 squeezed into newly renovated Exposition Park for the Pirates' home opener on April 17. The field had been elevated three feet to reduce the effect of flooding, and new center field bleachers increased the seating capacity by more than 2,500. Nevertheless, thousands in attendance for the opener stood behind ropes that encircled the playing field.

It was a beautiful day as Deacon Phillippe and Cincinnati's "Tornado Jack" Weimer engaged in a sparkling pitching duel. Phillippe was uncharacteristically wild, allowing two walks and throwing two wild pitches, but he managed to keep the Pirates even in the scoring column. Phillippe did have a good day at the plate, helping to make up for the absence of Beaumont and Leach with three hits, and he scored the Pirates' first run. The score was tied at 2–2 in the visitors' half of the tenth inning when Reds first baseman Charlie Carr delivered a two-out single and moved to second base on a wild pitch. Cy Seymour smacked a hit to center field and Carr turned third and headed toward home. Bob Ganley got to the ball quickly, but it appeared he had little chance to retire the runner at home. His throw was slightly up the third base line and when catcher Fred Carisch moved in that direction to catch the ball, Carr tried to run around the catcher and come up on the other side. This maneuver drew chuckles from the crowd as Carisch easily tagged him out. The Pirates finally won it for Phillippe in the bottom of the 12th inning after Honus Wagner doubled into the overflow crowd in left field. The next batter, rookie first baseman Joe Nealon, sent a drive over the center fielder's head to score Wagner with the winning run. Once Wagner crossed the plate, hundreds of fans surrounded Nealon in an effort to shake his hand and pat him on the back. The rookie finally escaped the throng and made it into the clubhouse.[4]

Less than 24 hours after his great moment at Exposition Park, Nealon learned of the huge earthquake that struck his father's home in San Francisco early the morning of April 18. The quake and resulting fire killed hundreds and left 520 city blocks of destruction before the blaze was finally contained three days later. For two days, Nealon did not know the fate of his family until he received a telegram that his father and sister were fine and they did not have to leave their home on Nob Hill.[5] Third baseman Tommy Sheehan's wife and child were also in San Francisco and until he learned they were safe his play was so affected that Tommy Leach had to return to the lineup prematurely.

Sam Leever didn't fare well in his first start on April 18. The Schoolmaster departed the pitching slab after he gave up three runs to the Reds in the fourth inning. The Pittsburgh defense fell apart behind rookie Ed Karger in the seventh when Cincinnati scored three more runs without benefit of a hit, and the Pirates lost, 7–4.

McGraw's Giants were again the early pace-setters in the pennant race. Deacon Phillippe pitched Pittsburgh into second place on April 30 with a shutout of Cincinnati at the Palace of the Fans, but the Giants and Pirates would have a new competitor for the pennant in 1906. Frank Chance had taken over as manager in Chicago during the 1905 season and his intensity and demanding style invigorated the Cubs.

On May 4, the Pirates returned to Exposition Park to begin a five-game series with Chance's Cubs. Chicago routed Pittsburgh in the first four games of the series before Sam Leever salvaged the finale by beating the Cubs' ace, Mordecai "Three Finger" Brown, 3 to 2.

Leever would achieve his last 20-win season in 1906, but none of those 22 victories were more challenging than the one at Exposition Park on May 8. The Pirates' brass even debated on whether to play the game because of the rainy conditions. A cold rain fell almost continuously through the first two innings, and the bottom of the first had to be delayed because of a downpour.

The Pirates took a quick 2 to 0 lead after Brown walked Nealon and Frank Chance couldn't field Sheehan's slippery bunt. After failing to get a bunt down, Fred Clarke drove a pitch into right field that bounded past Schulte for a triple. Chicago tied it with a run off Leever in the third inning and another in the fifth. In the latter instance Schulte's long drive scored a runner from first and the Cubs' right fielder tried for an inside-the-park home run. Center fielder Leach and shortstop Wagner made an accurate relay to Gibson, who blocked the plate and tagged Schulte for the third out.

Brown fell down in the muck during the fourth inning when he tried to field a bunt and by the sixth inning his back had tightened. Bob Wicker replaced Brown in the seventh inning. Bob Ganley led off the Pirates' eighth with a single, was sacrificed to second and went to third on Wagner's out.

Nine ♦ Transition

While Wicker was pitching to Nealon, Ganley made a dash for the plate and scored easily when the Cubs' hurler threw the ball past catcher Kling.

It was raining hard when the Cubs came to bat in the ninth, but umpire James Johnstone would not call the game until Leever registered the final out. Leever's victory in Chicago started him on a 26 inning scoreless streak.

After losing four out of five games to the Cubs, the Pirates lost a pair of games to the Phillies, then reeled off ten victories in 11 games. Three of the wins came against second-place New York. The visiting Giants took the field at Exposition Park in the opener of a series on May 16 clad in all-black uniforms. The new garb didn't help as Vic Willis shut out the New Yorkers, 11–0. A day later, Leever faced just 27 Giants batters, allowed only three singles, walked none, and beat Joe McGinnity, 2 to 0. Two of the three Giants' baserunners were erased in double plays, and the third was caught stealing. Only one New York batter received as many as three balls from Leever.

The Pirates got the only run they needed in the opening frame, though it was surrounded with controversy. With two out, Tommy Leach singled, stole second and took third on Roger Bresnahan's errant throw. Center fielder Sammy Strang fumbled the wild throw and the Pirates suddenly led 1–0 when Leach was awarded home on interference by third baseman Devlin. The Giants protested bitterly to plate umpire Johnstone, but to no avail. Wagner then singled and after he stole second, Billy Gilbert was ejected for swearing at base umpire Emslie that the Dutchman was out. The Pirates added a second run in the eighth, abetted by an error by Gilbert's replacement at second.

If things weren't going bad enough after John McGraw garbed his men in black, the Giants' manager was arrested the day of game three. McGraw and his players were riding in a bus from the ball field after Leever's shutout when several boys began jeering and throwing pebbles at the New Yorkers. McGraw struck at the boys with a whip and hit 13-year-old Neil Brady in the eye.

The following morning, McGraw was taking a bath at his team's hotel when the constable arrived with a warrant. The lawman had to cool his heels for three hours in the hall waiting on the manager to appear. The charge was "striking a small boy with a buggy whip while riding in from the grounds" the previous day. However, the magistrate could find no scratches on the boy, whose father happened to be an ardent supporter of the Pirates. A doctor reported the boy's injury was not serious, whereupon the youngster's father agreed to settle the case. McGraw paid the court $25 and was said to have "slipped a generous amount of money into the hand of Mr. Brady."[6]

Christy Mathewson, in only his second start of the season, was still weak from a bout with diphtheria when he took the mound for the game that afternoon. McGraw's ace was pounded for 14 hits and lost to the Pirates, 7–6.

Honus Wagner tripled, singled twice and picked Bill Dahlen off second base in the ninth inning with the hidden ball trick. Dahlen, intently watching the Pirates' Al Leifield on the mound, forgot about Wagner until the shortstop gently tagged him with the ball. McGraw was so furious with Dahlen he slapped him with a $100 fine, which he later rescinded. Dummy Taylor beat Phillippe, 5–1, in the final game of the set before a Saturday crowd of 16,290, the largest at Exposition Park since opening day.

In early May, 1906, the Cincinnati Reds asked the other National League clubs to waive claim on former Pirates catcher Ed Phelps and two other players. Phelps went to Reds President Garry Herrmann and was given his ten days' notice of unconditional release on May 9. The catcher went home to Albany, New York, and wrote to Barney Dreyfuss about the possibility of employment in Pittsburgh. The Pirates were in need of help behind the plate following the release of Harry Smith because of physical problems and the lack of offense from young George Gibson.[7]

A deal with Phelps was worked out and he resumed his old position with the Pirates on May 21. Then, on June 17, 1906, National Commission President Garry Herrmann awarded Phelps to Boston of the American League. According to Herrmann, President Pulliam had, on May 13, advised the Cincinnati club that all National League clubs had waived claim to Phelps, and five days later the Reds sold the player to the Red Sox for $1,500.[8]

When Phelps learned that Harry Pulliam had ordered him to report to Boston, the catcher became furious at the decision and said he would retire rather than report to the American League. Dreyfuss threatened to seek an injunction to keep Herrmann from weakening the Pittsburgh team because the Reds' president had bet money against the Pirates. Dreyfuss maintained that during a Reds road trip to New York the National Commission president, who also owned the Reds, bet $6,000 against $2,000 that Pittsburgh would not win the pennant in 1906. *The Sporting News* reported that a New York bookmaker named Leo Meyer and George Considine, proprietor of the Metropole Hotel, took the short end of the bet.[9]

Though indignant, Herrmann relented within two days and persuaded the American League to return Phelps' contract to Cincinnati, which Garry said cost him $1,500. The Reds then released Phelps to Pittsburgh — unconditionally.[10] However, that wasn't the end of the story.

Though Herrmann expressed regret about making the bet against Pittsburgh winning the pennant, a few days later he further strengthened the Giants by selling the defending National League batting champion, Cy Seymour, to McGraw and Brush for $10,000. Herrmann insisted the deal was made because Cincinnati needed the money, but Pirates supporters and the Pittsburgh press howled that the deal smelled like he was hedging another bet he had made that Chicago would not win the pennant.[11] For the 72 games he played with the Giants, Seymour led the team in batting average and home runs, and drove in 42 runs, but it still wasn't enough to bring a third straight pennant to New York.

In 1905 and 1906 Barney Dreyfuss made attempts to rid Exposition Park of the notorious gambling element. However, his efforts could only affect what went on inside the ballpark. *The Sporting News* reported that since their expulsion from Exposition Park, the gamblers would meet at a downtown Pittsburgh hotel before each day's game. "They make their wagers there and large sums are bet daily," wrote Ralph Davis. "Then they attend the game in a body and sit always in the same section of the grandstand. They do not bet during the game — but they express opinions according to the way their money is placed."[12]

Following their early May series with the Giants, Pirates pitchers Willis, Leever and Leifield pitched consecutive shutouts against the Boston Nationals. Pittsburgh remained hot, but couldn't get closer than two games behind the Cubs, who were winning at a record pace.

"Let me say that in the spring trip," noted Barney Dreyfuss. "Leever had about as much speed as any I have looked at in years. It was simply marvelous the way Samuel shot them over the plate."[13]

Leever pitched two scoreless innings in relief to get credit for a 7 to 6 win in Philadelphia on May 14, shut out New York on May 16, and gave a coat of whitewash to Boston five days later. His scoreless inning streak ended at 26 in the third inning of a game in Brooklyn on May 26. Leever lost to Elmer Strickett, apostle of the spitball, 4 to 2, in a game played in a constant drizzle.

After having a won-lost record of 12–12 on May 14, the Pirates went into a twin bill at Robison Field on July 1 with a record of 42–20, two games behind Chicago. That day, Sam Leever and Jack Taylor would face each other for the final time in the first game of the doubleheader.

Leever was touched for 12 hits, walked one, hit a batter, and another reached on Wagner's error, but he still won, 6 to 1. St. Louis left 13 runners on base and scored only once, while Pittsburgh provided Leever with six runs. That game was the last time Taylor pitched for the Cardinals because that very afternoon he was traded back to the Cubs for a pair of rarely used substitutes and some cash. The day turned sour for the Pirates when Phillippe lost, 3–1, in the nightcap.

The trade of Taylor by St. Louis was no surprise. The previous fall, he was accused of throwing games during the 1905 City Series between the Cardinals and St. Louis Browns, won by the Americans, five games to two. However, the league took no action against the pitcher on those charges and he returned to the Cardinals the following spring. The next incident involving the volatile pitcher occurred in Chicago on Decoration Day, 1906, when Taylor flew into a rage against Cardinals Manager John McCloskey following an argument in Chicago.[14]

The Pirates went on to lose the final game of the St. Louis series on July 2, then faced off against the Cubs in a crucial six-game stretch, five at Exposition Park and the finale in Chicago on Sunday. A record crowd in excess of 20,000 jammed into Exposition Park for the start of the doubleheader with the Cubs on Independence Day. The huge crowd was disappointed as the Pirates lost both games, the first, 1–0, despite a one-hitter by Lefty Leifield. The Buccaneers' bats were again silent in the nightcap, as Vic Willis also lost, 1 to 0. Leever lost to the Cubs, 6–3, on July 5, and it was up to Phillippe to salvage the fourth game of the set against Jack Taylor.

Phillippe found himself in a hole in the first inning after Frank Chance smacked a home run over Beaumont's head in center field with a runner on base. Down 2–0, Phillippe shut out the Cubs the remainder of the contest. The Cubs blew a chance to extend their lead in the top of the fourth. With Chicago runners on first and third with no one out, Phillippe got a break when catcher Heinie Peitz threw out Harry Steinfeldt at second when the Cubs third baseman tried to advance on a short passed ball. The runner at third, Frank Chance, returned to the bag. With one out, Tinker attempted to push a bunt between the pitcher and first baseman Nealon, but Phillippe pounced on it and looked Chance back to third. When Phillippe threw to first base, Chance broke for the plate. Nealon was alert and fired home in time to get the Cubs manager, who protested vigorously that he was safe. Pittsburgh tied the score in the home half of the fourth when Phillippe's single sent Nealon home with the tying run. After that the two veterans matched one scoreless inning after another until the tenth.

In the bottom of the final frame, Taylor experienced a streak of wildness, issued two walks and hit a batter to load the bases with one out. Fred Clarke inserted himself as a pinch-runner for Phillippe, who had walked and made his way around to third base. Tommy Leach punched a single through the drawn-in infield to make Pittsburgh a 3–2 winner.

After losing four of six games against Chicago, the Pirates remained within striking distance of the Cubs, but never got closer than four games. The Giants came to Exposition Park on July 21 with a half-game lead over the Pirates for second place. Pittsburgh pushed past McGraw's rowdies in the standings by taking the first three games of the series. Only Christy Mathewson's 3–0 win over Phillippe in the fourth game prevented a sweep.

The most excitement in the Giants series occurred in Leever's 4–3 win in game three on July 24. Pittsburgh's reserve catcher, Heinie Peitz, who was coaching at third base, verbally disparaged Joe McGinnity until the Giants' pitcher complained to umpire O'Day. Peitz protested that he had said nothing out of the way. When the fourth inning ended, McGinnity got into an argument with the erstwhile coach on his way to the bench. The angry Giants pitcher took a swing at Peitz, who retaliated by knocking McGinnity down and then jumped on the fallen New Yorker. The two wrestled around on the ground until they were pulled apart. The players and umpires thought the affair was over, but they did not consider Mayor Charles Kirschler of Allegheny, who was sitting in a box with his superintendent of police. The mayor ordered McGinnity's arrest, a patrol wagon was backed up to the players' gate, and the pitcher was hauled off to the police station still dressed in his Giants uniform. Secretary Knowles of the Giants followed the coppers and put up a $50 forfeit for McGinnity's appearance in court the next day. McGinnity left for New York that night.[15]

The National League fined Peitz $30 and gave him a five-day suspension for his part in the row, but McGinnity drew a more severe penalty, ten days off without pay and a $100 fine, for what President Pulliam described as "an attempt to make a slaughter house out of a National League park."[16]

McGraw got some measure of revenge three weeks later by sweeping Pittsburgh out of second place with five straight wins over the Pirates at the Polo Grounds. Especially frustrating was the game on August 10, when Leever lost 1–0 on an eighth-inning, two-out hit by Spike Shannon. Not only were the Pirates held to one hit by Luther Taylor and Hooks Wiltse, who pitched the ninth, that single hit was made by pitcher Leever. The loss also snapped Leever's personal six-game winning streak that began with a 9–0 whitewashing of the Superbas on July 9. Following the loss to Dummy Taylor, Leever embarked on another winning streak, this one of five games that included shutouts of Boston and St. Louis.

The Pirates' record of 14 wins and 16 losses in August doomed them to also-ran status and ultimately a third-place finish, 23½ games behind Chicago, which won a record 116 games.

On September 11, 1906, Cincinnati and Pittsburgh played a remarkable game at Exposition Park in which the two teams battled 15 scoreless innings in only two hours and 45 minutes. Phillippe pitched the first ten innings and allowed seven hits, including a triple to right fielder Frank Jude, who was one of two Reds stranded on third at the end of an inning.

In the bottom of the tenth inning, manager Clarke sent Beaumont out to pinch-hit for Phillippe, and Willis finished the game for Pittsburgh. Bob

Ewing went the distance for Cincinnati in the longest major league game ever played in Pittsburgh up to that time.

Though they couldn't overtake New York for second place, the Pirates did get some measure of satisfaction against the hated Giants in September. On September 19 Sam Leever won the game at the Polo Grounds that officially eliminated McGraw's team from the pennant chase. Leever gave up some long hits, two home runs to Seymour and Burke's triple, but persevered to win, 5–4, in a game shortened to eight innings because of darkness. In the second game of a doubleheader at the Polo Grounds a day later, the Pirates touched Christy Mathewson for seven hits and Deacon Phillippe held on for the 3–2 win.

In the Phillippe victory, Mathewson was tagged for three runs in the third inning and Phil took a 3–1 lead into the bottom of the fifth, which would be the final inning due to the first game's late start and impending darkness. It started out harmlessly enough when Spike Shannon bounced to Wagner, who threw wildly to first allowing the Giants' leadoff batter to take second. Cy Seymour's single scored Shannon to narrow the Pirates' lead to one, and Bresnahan drew a disputed walk later in the frame to put Phillippe's victory in jeopardy. With two outs and runners on second and third, Dan McGann hit a scorcher to center field, but the ball stayed in the air long enough for Bill Hallman to catch it for the final out.

Four days later in Boston, Phillippe benefited from another shortened game because of the Pirates' scheduled boat train to New York. After Pittsburgh took the first game of a doubleheader, they jumped out to a three-run lead early in the nightcap. In the home half of the second, Boston loaded the bases on two singles and a fumble by Ritchey. Although Phillippe was not a strikeout pitcher by this point in his career, he bore down and struck out the next two batters to retire the side. Pittsburgh won, 6–0, but Phillippe's luck ran out when he lost to Philadelphia, 9–3, on September 27 in his final start of the 1906 season.

The Pirates won 93 games in 1906, which wasn't bad considering the decline in the once mighty Pittsburgh offense. Center fielder Ginger Beaumont was an invalid the first half of the season, got into only 80 games, and batted just .265 with one stolen base. Right fielder Otis Clymer broke his left leg just above the ankle sliding into second base, and after only 11 games he was done for the season. Tommy Leach had to sub in center field for Beaumont, which left a hole at third base that was never satisfactorily filled.

The 1906 season was a disappointment for Deacon Phillippe. He went 15–10, but he started only 24 times, the first time in his career (except for 1904 when he missed much of the season due to an eye infection) that he started less than 30 games. At times, Phillippe displayed the form from the early years of the decade, but he was not consistent. His pitches still had the speed, but his curves and drops did not have the break of old. Although he walked only 26 batters in 219 innings pitched, the lack of control within the strike zone made his breaking pitches hittable.[17]

On the other hand, 34-year-old Sam Leever achieved his last 20 win season. He won 22 games, lost only 7, and threw six of the club's 27 shutouts.

Wrote A. R. Cratty, "Ever since 1903 when Leever was 'not there' when the world's championship games were played it has not been hard to find patrons having slim confidence in the school teacher's work. Still they could not make any predictions about Samuel being 'all in,' or even guess that he was going to lose this or that game. Leever had fooled them so many times that about all a critic secured for his prophecy was a ghastly smile from listeners."[18]

There was a rumor printed in the newspapers following the Cubs-White Sox World Series that a trade was proposed in which the Pirates would send Deacon Phillippe, Tommy Leach and outfielder Bob Ganley to Philadelphia for third baseman Ernie Courtney, left fielder Paul Sentelle, right fielder John Titus and a couple of pitchers.[19] Barney Dreyfuss dismissed the report out of hand and the first contract he handed out in 1907 went to Deacon Phillippe, who was said to sometimes affix his name to a Pirates contract without even glancing at the salary figure named therein. Dreyfuss had sworn to Phillippe back in 1899 when the pitcher signed his first contract for $1,200 that he would be taken care of. The owner advised Deacon in investments and by 1907 Deacon was a wealthy pitcher.[20]

Phillippe was offered a job coaching the pitchers for the 1907 Harvard University baseball team, but only if he could remain with the collegians until April 1. Manager Fred Clarke torpedoed the offer when he insisted that Phillippe go to spring training with the rest of the team on March 1.[21]

Among the talk at Hot Springs that spring was speculation about the financial worth of some of the Pirates' veterans. Fred Clarke owned a large amount of land in Kansas, Wagner's Carnegie property was worth, according to the valuation of borough tax assessors, $32,000, and Sam Leever had became a moneyed man from his frugal ways.[22] Secretary Locke related an amusing anecdote about Fred Clarke selling his second-hand automobile to Leever, who after using the same for a year disposed of the machine for a sum almost equal to the price he paid for it.[23]

Hardly had the ink dried on the sale of the Boston National League club when Barney Dreyfuss worked out a trade with new owners George and John Dovey, Kentucky friends of the Pirates owner since boyhood. Dreyfuss had drummed up persons of money in Pittsburgh and Kentucky to help the Doveys in the purchase of the New England club, and the new owners were beholden to him.[24]

The Pittsburgh owner had long coveted Boston's popular Italian/American second baseman Ed Abbatichio to attract the Smoky City's burgeoning Italian population to Exposition Park. The deal was a big gamble and Dreyfuss probably overpaid for Abbatichio, who had held out the entire 1906 season because of a salary dispute with the Boston club. The deal was consummated on December 11, 1906, and to get Abbatichio Dreyfuss gave up long-time second baseman Claude Ritchey, pitcher Patsy Flaherty, and an additional player yet to be named. The third player turned out to be the eight-year veteran Ginger Beaumont, who was actually a throw-in as part of the deal because the Pirates decided his lame leg made the long-time center fielder a liability. The trade left only Phillippe, Leever, Wagner, Clarke and Leach from the team that began the Pirates dynasty in 1901.

At the insistence of Clarke, spring training in Hot Springs was preceded by a visit by the team to the mineral springs at West Baden, Indiana. "The idea of bringing the men to West Baden is to clean them out," he said.[25] The players filled their stomachs with large quantities of water at West Baden, and before the spring was over the Pirates got more water than they bargained for. Heavy downpours swamped the team's practice field and even more rainfall played havoc with the team's schedule after the regular season began.

When the Pirates arrived at Hot Springs for training camp, President Dreyfuss was there awaiting them. Another early arrival was 32-year-old catcher Harry Smith, who had missed the previous two seasons due to his injured throwing arm. This spring, though, the news on Smith's lame wing was the best in three years and he appeared ready to rejoin the Pirates' backstop rotation. But what most of his teammates would remember about Smith was his role as the chief practical jokester on the team.

Honus Wagner recalled that Barney Dreyfuss was an accomplished horseman, so Smith and his accomplices tied an unbroken steed to the hitching post of the team's hotel. Dreyfuss boasted that he could ride the horse, but as soon as he swung into the saddle the animal bolted down the driveway. Dreyfuss hung on for dear life as the horse tore madly down the hilly Hot Springs street. At an intersection, the horse's hoofs slipped and as it fell, Dreyfuss flew about 25 feet in the air. A crowd gathered around the bruised Pirates owner, who remarked, "By Jimminy, it's a good thing I jumped."[26]

It was ironic that the happy-go-lucky jokester Harry Smith would be roomed with the stoic Samuel Leever. However, the two hit it off and when Smith was knocked unconscious by a pitch to the head that summer, Leever was distraught. The fallen catcher was carried to the team's hotel for treatment by a doctor and fully recovered after a few days off.

The news out of Arkansas regarding Sam Leever was optimistic, considering the hurler's history of threatening retirement during the spring. "Leever is said to be acting like a young colt and to be leading the boys in the stunts," reported *The Sporting News*, "This too, is encouraging, for the Goshen boy in the past never hankered for much work in the spring."[27]

Harry Smith and Sam Leever, spring training, Hot Springs, Arkansas, 1907 (courtesy Pittsburgh Pirates).

However, the news Barney Dreyfuss received from Pittsburgh the second week in March was very discouraging. The city experienced its "worst flood in 100 years" and Exposition Park suffered considerable damage. Water in the Allegheny River reached a height of more than 36 feet, whereas it only required a gauge of 18 feet to put the overflow into the ballpark.[28]

The Pirates would be hurt by bad spring weather more than any other club. Pittsburgh had six exhibition game cancellations and postponements of 12 championship games.

Phillippe drew the opening day starting assignment for 1907 and lost a one-run decision to Cincinnati on a sloppy field at the Palace of the Fans. Beaumont's replacement in the batting order was a 27-year-old rookie named Edward "Goat" Anderson, who came to the Pirates from South Bend of the Central League. Anderson batted only .206 and committed 11 errors afield for Pittsburgh in his only season in the majors. Beaumont proved the Pirates wrong when he was able to manage one more outstanding season, batting .322 in 150 games for the Boston Doves.

After the season opener, snow and rain caused the postponement of the Pirates' next three games. The club did not play its second game until their home opener at Exposition Park on April 17. Only 8,000 fans braved temperatures in the 30s to watch the home team lose to "Pirate Killer" Jack Taylor and the Cubs.

In mid–May the Pirates played Boston for the first time since several of their 1906 teammates had joined that club. Pittsburgh won the first two games before Leever faced off against ex-Pirate Patsy Flaherty on May 15. Former Pirate Dave Brain scored the first Boston run in the seventh inning when he singled, was bunted to second and scored on a single. Flaherty took a four-hit, 1 to 0 shutout into the ninth inning and retired the first two batters on grounders to Ritchey and Bridwell. The crowd was making its way to the exits when Wagner slammed a Flaherty pitch over the left fielder's head and steamed into third with a triple. Abbaticchio blooped a Texas Leaguer into right field and the game was tied.

Leever retired Boston in the bottom of the inning to send the game into overtime. Pittsburgh went down in order in the tenth and Leever retired the first man he faced in the home half. The next batter, Flaherty, hit a routine grounder to the second baseman, but Abbaticchio fumbled it for an error. After Tenney popped out, Beaumont sent Flaherty scurrying to third on a single to right field. Another former Pirate, Del Howard, was next and hit a scorcher past Alan Storke at third base to deliver the winning run. This would not be the last time Leever and the Pirates would have to deal with Patsy Flaherty during the 1907 season.

When the Giants swaggered into Exposition Park on June 14, the Pittsburgh fanatics greeted Roger Bresnahan with derisive jeers when the New York catcher appeared wearing bulky shin guards. Catchers had worn the face mask and chest protector for some time but shin guards had only been experimented with by using padding beneath the player's leggings. Bresnahan's shin guards were obviously modeled after a cricketer's leg pads, bulky in construction with a knee flap that came up to the thigh.

The Giants' backstop first wore the devices on opening day, but when the Pirates went to the Polo Grounds in early May, Fred Clarke protested the use of the new equipment on the grounds that it could be of danger to opposing base runners. Clarke claimed that during his attempt to score a run he sprained an ankle because of Bresnahan's equipment. On May 21, National League president Pulliam dismissed Pittsburgh's protest of Bresnahan's shin guards.

Before Bresnahan's invention, catcher's legs were vulnerable to foul tips or fast balls in the dirt, but some backstops still refused to adopt the "unmanly" protective devices for years. Despite his manager's earlier protest, Pirates backup catcher Harry Smith began to use the same style of shin guards later that season.[29]

The Pirates took two straight from the Giants in their rain-shortened June series. Despite a 26–18 record on June 15, Pittsburgh was already ten games behind the soaring Cubs, a second consecutive pennant well within their sights. Fred Clarke tried to improve his club's offense with changes in his day-to-day lineup. Anderson's poor batting led to his benching in mid-June, and Tommy Leach moved to center field. Then Leach's replacement at third, Tommy Sheehan, was spiked badly by Cincinnati's Hans Lobert on June 25. Sheehan's wound required 12 stitches and the former Amherst College recruit, Alan Storke, took over at the hot corner and did a creditable job. Pitcher Mike Lynch, who had only been used sparingly, asked for his release, supposedly so the Brown University alum could study law. Instead, Lynch signed a few days later with the New York Giants. His departure left the Pirates with only five pitchers, Phillippe, Leever, Willis, Camnitz and Leifield.

The Pirates lost four games in a row to the sixth-place Reds in late June just prior to a series in Chicago. On June 29, Deacon Phillippe defeated one of the Cubs' aces, Ed Reubach, 2–1, for the Pirates' third win in as many days at West Side Grounds.

Phillippe nursed a tenuous 2 to 1 lead into the bottom of the ninth inning and quickly disposed of the first two Cubs batters. Chicago suddenly gained life when Harry Steinfeldt drove a ball off third baseman Alan Storke's head into the pop box seats in front of the bleachers for a double. Clarke galloped in from left field for a conference with his pitcher. Phillippe then intentionally passed Frank Chance, the hurler's only walk on the day. Johnny Kling lined a single to center field, but Tommy Leach charged in and fired a strike to catcher Gibson. The Pirates' backstop ran up the line and tagged Steinfeldt before he ever got near home plate to conclude the contest.

The Pirates, with Sam Leever on the mound, defeated the Cubs a day later in the first game of a Sunday doubleheader. The win gave Pittsburgh four straight over Chicago in their home park, but after Jack Taylor and Vic Willis battled to a 13-inning, 4–4 draw in the second game, the Pirates still found themselves 11 games behind the defending National League champions.

The Pirates played outstanding baseball in July, winning 21 of 29 games. Leever pitched back-to-back shutouts — against St. Louis in the first game of the Independence Day doubleheader at Exposition Park and against Philadelphia on July 8.

On July 15, Phillippe not only defeated Brooklyn 4 to 1 at Washington Park, he had a key bunt hit in the sixth inning when the Pirates scored all their runs. After Gibson walked, Phillippe attempted to sacrifice the catcher to second. The Superbas pitcher threw to second in an attempt to retire Gibson, but the throw was late and both runners were safe. Following another walk, Tommy Leach lifted a high fly ball that drifted over the left fielder's head and all three Pirates on base scored.

On August 1, the Pirates ran into Patsy Flaherty again. Again Leever was on the mound for Pittsburgh and he had a 1–0 lead with two out in the fifth inning. Boston's manager/first baseman Fred Tenney started a rally with a bunt base hit that surprised third baseman Tommy Sheehan. Dave Brain singled and Beaumont scored both baserunners with a double. In the seventh Brain tripled over Fred Clarke's head in left field to score two more runs. Leever drove in Pittsburgh's second run with a hit in the bottom of the inning, but the scoring ended there. Boston and Flaherty won, 4 to 2.

Leever lost three starts in a row before he threw another shutout, this one against Brooklyn, on August 14. Deacon Phillippe matched his teammate with a whitewash of his own the next day with the identical final score, 8–0.

After their victory against Leever on the first of August, the Boston Doves lost their next 15 games. Then, at the South End Grounds on August 19, Leever took the mound against Flaherty yet again. Fresh off a shutout of Brooklyn four days earlier, Leever was in control for the first six innings, taking a 2–1 lead into the seventh. Three Pirates errors to begin the inning opened the gates for a six-run Boston outburst. A disgruntled Leever left the game, replaced by recent acquisition "Frosty Bill" Duggleby, who gave up three more runs in the eighth.

As the Pirates' highest paid player, Honus Wagner used part of his salary to purchase a "big touring car" in the summer of 1907. He enlisted the help of Sam Leever, who had owned an automobile for over a year. The first drive in the new vehicle was recounted in the *Pittsburgh Gazette* on August 4, 1907: "There are more curves to an automobile than Honus Wagner ever dreamed of and the famous shortstop was struck out in last evening's twilight by the machine which he recently bought and with which he ventured out for the first time on the streets of Carnegie."

Capable of reaching a top speed of 18 miles an hour, the two-cylinder machine became only the third motor car to grace the streets of Carnegie. Wagner solicited Leever to pilot their maiden drive through town. After "spitting on his hands," the veteran hurler twirled the steering wheel and accelerated the vehicle. The automobile lurched forward and banged into a sack of potatoes lying well up on the sidewalk. Over-adjusting, Leever steered the machine across the street onto the sidewalk on the opposite side.

Finally, the former school teacher got the vehicle headed toward Wagner's home, but only two blocks away a pedestrian walked into the path of the ballplayer's motor car. Leever applied the brake to bring the machine to a stop in the middle of the road. Only when Wagner's tailor came along and volunteered to take the wheel did the players complete the trip to their destination.[30]

When the Giants came to Exposition Park in early August for a five-game series, the Pirates managed only one win. Phillippe not only put on an outstanding pitching performance to win game three, his single with the bases full in the second inning gave the Pirates their first two runs. He allowed only four hits in his 5 to 2 victory, and the Giants' runs each scored on errors.

The Giants' four-to-one series win vaulted them over the Pirates into second place. It was reported that Barney Dreyfuss was so frustrated he offered his players an additional $500 each if they beat out "Mugsy" McGraw for second place. A club official officially denied the story, but the Pirates lost three straight games leading up to a big series at the Polo Grounds beginning on August 22. The Pirates opened the set with a 20–5 thrashing of the Giants in a game started by Christy Mathewson.

The day after the rout, the two teams played a doubleheader. Leever allowed only six hits in the first game, but the score was tied at 2–2 after nine innings. Wagner opened the visitor's tenth with a double off McGinnity and the Dutchman took third on an out. Storke grounded to rookie second baseman Larry Doyle who made a bad throw to the plate in an effort to keep Wagner from scoring. The big Pirates shortstop slid in safely and landed atop catcher Bresnahan. While the Giants' catcher lay pinned on the ground, Storke ran all the way around to third base. Moments later, Doyle made a fine catch of Sheehan's liner but threw wildly toward home as Storke scored after tagging up. Leever came away with a 4–2 victory and Pittsburgh also won the second game on a five-inning no-hitter by Howie Camnitz. Former Pirate Mike Lynch was the hard-luck loser for New York.

Though he allowed no hits in his start, Camnitz did walk four and hit two batters. One of his errant fastballs hit Frank Bowerman just above the left temple. The big catcher dropped to the ground, out cold with his fingers twitching uncontrollably. An ambulance rushed the seriously injured and still unconscious player to the hospital. Bowerman checked himself out of the hospital the next day, reported to the ball park and demanded to play despite the huge lump on the side of his head.[31]

The Pirates' double victory on Friday pushed them past the Giants into second place. Mathewson returned to the Polo Grounds mound only two days after the first-game debacle and beat Phillippe, 7–4. The Pirates hit Mathewson hard in the first three innings. Just after a single by Clarke, a Wagner triple and a fielder's choice put the Pirates up 4–3, the game was delayed by a disturbance in the stands. A Pinkerton policeman went up into the left field bleachers after a boy who did not return a game ball. The crowd didn't like the way the rented cop treated the boy and went after him. Punches were exchanged and the Pinkerton became entangled in a melee with several of the bugs. Additional policemen had to rescue their associate from the angry crowd. After the game resumed, Mathewson was untouchable the remainder of the contest.[32]

The Pirates blew the lead in the fifth inning and Phillippe was relieved by Willis after the Giants scored three runs with the benefit of only one hit. The New York rally was abetted by Phillippe's wide throw on an easy force play at second, the third baseman's low throw to the plate in an attempt to get one runner, and catcher Smith's drop of Phillippe's throw home on McGann's easy tap to allow another runner to score.

The roles of Deacon and the Schoolmaster in the Pirates' pitching rotation would gradually decrease as the 1907 season progressed. The success of Nick Maddox as well as the arrival of young pitchers Bill Otey and Charles "Babe" Adams pushed Phillippe and Leever to the end of the bench. Phillippe started only once on the mound after August 31 because the Pirates decided to go with the younger pitchers since the pennant was out of reach.

Twenty-year-old Nick Maddox had two minor league no-hitters with Wheeling of the Central League before he came to the Pirates in September. The young right-hander made his major league debut at Exposition Park on September 13 with a 4–0 shutout of the St. Louis Cardinals. Three days later, he beat the Cardinals again, 4–2, at Robison Field. In just his third major league appearance, Maddox did not allow a hit during his 2–1 victory over Brooklyn.

Leever made his final start in 1907 on September 21, one day after the Maddox no-hitter. Leever came out on top, 1–0, in a duel with Brooklyn's outstanding rookie hurler, Nap Rucker. The closest Brooklyn came to scoring off Leever came in the seventh inning when Harry Lumley singled and made his way around to third base with two out. Leever broke a pitch across the plate for the third strike on Al Burch to end the threat. After allowing only five singles and two walks over nine innings, Leever was removed for a pinch-hitter in the bottom of the ninth frame and Tommy Leach gave him a win with a two-out, bases-loaded hit that scored the only run of the contest.

Though first place had been decided in favor of Chicago, the Giants and Pirates played an interesting series in Pittsburgh late that September. Before the game on Monday, September 23, John McGraw handed umpire Bill Klem the lineup card with Roger Bresnahan's name on it. The two argued about whether the catcher could play because of his ejection the day before in Cincinnati. When Klem turned away from the manager, he was hit in the face with a glass of water. No one admitted to throwing the water, but Klem got his revenge in the sixth inning when he ejected McGraw and Art Devlin for arguing. The Pirates won the game, 2 to 1.

On Tuesday, Christy Mathewson shut out the Pirates, 2–0, but Klem ejected four more Giants, including McGraw, for swearing. Nick Maddox continued his late-season mastery in the final game of the New York series. Pirates captain Honus Wagner stole four bases, including second, third, and home in the second inning. Not to be outdone, manager Fred Clarke also swiped four bases for the only time in his career. Two more Giants were ejected, raising Klem's number of scalps to eight for the three-game series.

Maddox finally proved to be human, losing to the Phillies, 3–2, at Exposition Park on the 30th. He rebounded and won his fifth game out of six starts when the Pirates edged the Reds, 2–1, in Cincinnati on October 4.

Pittsburgh finished in second place, but 17 games behind a superior Chicago club. Leever finished the season with a record of 14–9, completed 17 of 24 starts, and threw 216.2 innings. Phillippe also won 14 games, three of them as a relief pitcher.

Following the 1907 National League season, many of the players went on the customary barnstorming tours in order to supplement their regular Pirates salary. Phillippe withdrew from the trip at the last moment, passing on the $260 share each of the barnstormers would receive. He said he had trouble with his arm, but his teammates would soon discover that was not the real reason for his absence. He was always secretive about his personal life, and his teammates only learned of the long-time bachelor's impending marriage just one day before the event.[33]

On October 28, 1907, Charles Phillippe married a 27-year-old divorcee named Belle Perry. The nuptials had been rumored for over a year and the couple obtained their marriage license from the Allegheny County Orphans' Court a week earlier on the bride-to-be's birthday.[34] Belle's nine-year-old daughter from her first marriage would also assume the surname Phillippe, and Deacon was recognized as Mary Isabelle's father for the remainder of his life.[35]

The newlyweds traveled to Phillippe's ranch in South Dakota for a couple of weeks before returning to their permanent home in the fashionable Bellevue District of Pittsburgh. According to Ralph Davis, "Phillippe has made big money as a ball player, and he has not only saved it, but much of it has been judiciously invested, getting large returns, and placing Phillippe among the wealthiest of ball players."[36]

In October of 1907, catcher Harry Smith and Sam Leever traveled to their team's exhibition games with Honus Wagner in his automobile. Since he was a more experienced motorman, Leever did the lion's share of the driving. Once, the Pirates were playing in a small town northwest of Pittsburgh when the ice cream stand collapsed. Wagner, who was umpiring, "heard the crash and called the game to ascertain if his auto had blown up. When assured his gasoline wagon was safe, the game was resumed."[37]

Sam Leever's wife Margaret used to say about Wagner, "I always knew when spring training was just around the corner because here came Hans." But even Leever wasn't exempt from the pranks of his good friend Wagner. People around Goshen talked about the time he tricked Leever, who had been asleep, into looking out his lower-floor hotel window. Wagner was two floors up in Deacon Phillippe's room, where he had been playing cards, and from where he dropped a bundle of wet towels that hit the sleepy Leever in the back of his head.[38]

Whenever Wagner reminisced about his years in baseball, he always had a few anecdotes about his friend Sam Leever. "Schoolmaster Sam Leever was a great pitcher and about him are many good tales," Wagner wrote in 1915. "One year he was somewhat off form and told President Dreyfuss that he just could not do his best in cold weather. The season ended and the Pirate barnstormers had a very cold and blustery fall. One day they were scheduled to play at Beaver Falls, Pennsylvania.

"Dreyfuss looked out of his office window and saw snowflakes. To his secretary he said: "'What's the next train for Beaver Falls?'

"'Why Beaver Falls?' asked the secretary.

"'I want to see what kind of cold weather pitcher Leever is.'

"Dreyfuss sat huddled up in an overcoat and saw Leever pitch with the snow flying and hold Beaver Falls to one scratch hit and no runs.

After the game, Dreyfuss taunted the former school teacher, "You're a poor cold weather pitcher, aren't you?"

"Well, I hadn't a thing at that," exclaimed Sam, "but that snow helped my speed."[39]

♦ Ten ♦

World Series Champions

When the contract of Sam Leever was returned to the Pittsburgh club's office in February, 1908, the Pirates were not surprised that he threatened to hold out. Shortstop Honus Wagner, the best player in the National League, if not in all of baseball, made $5,000 a year earlier, then became a holdout the following spring. After he received his contract offer for the upcoming season, Leever replied to the club with a lengthy letter. The first page of his correspondence took club officials aback. "I am just in my prime," he wrote. "If I cannot earn my salary now, then there isn't a chance of such a condition coming hereafter. On this basis I therefore think that I am entitled to a stipend of $5,000 a year."[1]

After all, his 1.66 earned run average was fourth-best in the league the previous season. However, his won lost record was just 14–9, and at age 36 he was considered old for a starting pitcher.

The frown on Barney Dreyfuss' face turned to a scowl as he scanned the three-page letter. Then he read the final sentence: "Your contract is satisfactory and I enclose it with my signature." Dreyfuss could only smile in response to the rare practical joke by the usually humorless Schoolmaster. "There is only one Leever," noted Secretary Locke. "Pitchers may come and pitchers may go, but how about Sam going on well, say for a long time."[2]

Ralph Davis of the *Pittsburgh Press* and special correspondent to *The Sporting News* once wrote about Leever's spring training regime, "Leever has not done much work on the slab, devoting the larger part of his time to the training of the youngsters and playing the outfield. The veteran is a valuable man to have around, even if he never plays a game until the middle of the season, for Sam has a knack of making the youngsters like him, and he has a peculiar way of imparting most valuable information to them in a manner that forcibly brings it home."[3]

Reports out of Pittsburgh around the first of the year said that Deacon

Phillippe was well adjusted to his role as a married man. "Deacon Charles Phillippe is dabbling in society," noted *Sporting Life*. "Phil is in a clever set in his new home. With his pretty better half he is planning to enjoy life. Card parties, receptions, etc., are plenty in the Bellevue district. The big twirler and wife will not miss many of them during the season. Charles is a skillful card player. He can also trip to the strains of waltz and two-step melodies."[4]

Before the team returned to the East that spring, the Pirates, including Phillippe and Leever, spent a day at the Kansas ranch of Fred Clarke and played exhibition games in the area when the weather permitted. The trip also gave Phillippe a chance to reunite with his oldest brother Sidney in Oklahoma City, where the Pirates were scheduled to play an exhibition game. The game was rained out, but he was able to visit with his brother, who had a farm in Payne County, Oklahoma. The reunion was the first time in 22 years the Phillippe brothers had seen one another.[5]

"I never ate so much in my life as the time I was among the forty wolves who sat down to the spread in Clarke's barn," admitted club secretary William Locke. "Genuine Kansas grub with an appetite sharpened by four hours' tramp over the ranch, watching Fritz, Cap's banner dog, working on jacks, listening to Homer Hill-

John Peter "Honus" Wagner (George Grantham Bain collection, Library of Congress Prints and Photographs Division).

ebrand, and Deacon Phil telling that Clarke had the best ranch they had ever run across. These and other things made us eat a memorable dinner."[6]

When Clarke, Honus Wagner and Harry Smith motored to Winfield, Kansas, for a game against a local nine, they were attired in cowboy outfits, corduroy trousers, flannel shirts, broad-brimmed hats, and revolvers. They greeted the other Pirates with a regular "Comanche yell," noted the *Press*.[7]

Things were not as amiable as they appeared on the surface. Honus Wagner and catcher George Gibson were holdouts and Tommy Leach declared he would never play third base again because it was ruining his future in baseball. "The Flying Dutchman" insisted that the only reason he joined the Pirates in Kansas was because of a promise he made to Fred Clarke. The day before he returned to Carnegie, Wagner told the newspapermen that he did not intend to play baseball in 1908.

The reports about Phillippe in spring training were glowing. "Deacon Phillippe is in much better shape now than he was a year ago," reported *The Sporting News*. "Indeed, Phil's activity at West Baden surprised the other Pirates, and the 'Deacon' himself believes that he is due for one of the most successful seasons of his long career. At West Baden, he demonstrated that he had control, which was, up to two years ago his strongest point."[8]

The good news did not last for long. During the Pirates' trip from Kansas City to St. Louis for the opening game of the regular season, Phillippe mentioned to a teammate that he had a twinge in his shoulder. The remark seemed odd, for Phillippe seldom was heard to complain. The rheumatic pain spread to both shoulders and put his mound duties on hold.[9]

In 1908 there were a couple of new developments in major league baseball. A dull-gloss, leather-surface ball was introduced and a new rule prohibited pitchers or fielders from soiling the ball with dirt or grass stains to intentionally discolor it. In May, Barney Dreyfuss introduced a tarpaulin, 120 feet square, made from brown paraffin duck cloth to protect the Exposition Park infield from inclement weather. The tarpaulin and its transportation device were designed by the Pittsburgh Waterproof Company. After a game or in the case of threatening weather, the truck would be rolled out and the infield covered with the tarpaulin. The tarp more than made up for Dreyfuss' investment of $2,000 and soon other clubs adopted similar tarpaulin systems.[10]

The Pirates filled the troublesome right field position in 1908 with a speedy Texan named Owen Wilson. Once the club moved into Forbes Field, the lefty-batting Wilson used the park's spacious dimensions to become baseball's premier triples specialist. The first base position had plagued Fred Clarke since the trade of Kitty Bransfield before the 1905 season, and it would be no different in 1908. Harry Swacina would play the most games at first base (50), but he batted only .216. Third baseman Alan Storke moved to the opposite side of the infield for 49 games, and Jim Kane played 40 games at first base in his only major league season. Late in the season, another rookie first baseman, Warren Gill, appeared in 27 games, then disappeared from the major leagues.

Samuel Leever went into the 1908 season with a damaged right ear after the "hide was blown off" in an explosion at his smokeless powder mill near Goshen. Leever was precariously close to the volatile powder when a spark set it off and "blew things around the county in cyclone-like fashion."[11]

On April 17, Leever pitched a 3 to 0 shutout against St. Louis in Pittsburgh's third game of the season. The Pirates' star shortstop and defending National League batting champion was not on the field for the contest. Honus Wagner missed the club's first three games before Barney Dreyfuss finally caved and agreed to pay the Dutchman the unprecedented salary of $10,000—twice his 1907 pay.

Deacon Phillippe pitched only once in the first month of the season and gave up three runs on four hits and a walk in that one-inning relief stint in Pittsburgh's second game. His second appearance came at Exposition Park on May 15 when Vic Willis was driven from a game by the Phillies' six-run outburst in the third inning. Phillippe was left in to complete the 11 to 0 loss and he suffered an injury to his right thumb on a line drive hit by Phillies catcher Red Dooin.[12]

After losing two out of three games with the Phillies, the Pirates dropped three straight at Exposition Park to the lowly Superbas. The third game was especially hard to swallow, a 5 to 0 loss absorbed by Leever. A. R. Cratty wrote, "Possibly not since the Pittsburgh-Louisville merger has the local nine shown so badly as in the closing series of the fourth week in May with the Brooklyns. The pitching staff was all awry, the offense miserably weak, and the club was downed thrice by Donovan's band." Clad in civilian clothes in the grandstand, Deacon Phillippe could hardly stand to watch. "Guess I had better get out of here," the veteran pitcher remarked with a grin.[13]

The Pirates won four of the seven remaining games in the home stand, then left town following a doubleheader at Exposition Park on May 30 for another twin-bill in Chicago the next day. The disabled Deacon Phillippe and Lefty Leifield, who was suffering from a pulled muscle in his pitching arm as well as boils on his feet, were left behind in Pittsburgh. Maddox, Leever, Willis and Camnitz would have to handle the club's pitching load for awhile.

During 1908, Sam Leever would be best against his old rivals, the Giants. On May 11, he bested Iron Man Joe McGinnity, 5–2; on June 10 he won a 1–

0 pitching duel against Hooks Wiltse; and on July 10 at Exposition Park, he was the winning pitcher in relief of Irving Young when Tommy Leach's inside-the-park-home run broke a 6–6 tie.

In his shutout of the Giants on June 10, Leever allowed six scattered hits and walked only one batter while the Polo Grounds crowd of 8,000 watched their favorites whitewashed by a hurler who was deemed past his prime.

The *Pittsburgh Dispatch* noted, "Sam Leever pitched a careful game and never was in danger of being scored on, so cut and dried were the methods the Giants used in attempting to sidestep the coat of whitewash the Pirate pedagogue fitted on their protesting chests."[14]

The key play of the contest occurred in the second inning. Roger Bresnahan walloped a Leever pitch into deep left field. When he passed the initial bag, the Giants catcher made contact with substitute first baseman Jim Kane. The baserunner was so sure interference would be called that he leisurely strolled to second base. Fred Clarke retrieved the ball and his throw reached shortstop Wagner just as Bresnahan approached the bag. When Wagner put the tag on the Giant and umpire Hank O'Day gave the out signal, Bresnahan complained bitterly but the arbiter refused to rule interference on the play. Although umpires Klem and O'Day had been watching the play on the ball in the outfield rather than the runner, John Heydler, secretary of the National League, was at the game and concluded that the contact between Kane and the base runner was incidental and ruled Bresnahan could have reached second had he continued to run instead of complaining about interference.

The Pirates scored the only run of the game off Hooks Wiltse in the fourth inning. When Kane came to bat with two out and a runner on second he was booed heatedly by the crowd. Bresnahan was cursing the rookie from his position behind the plate when the baserunner, Fred Clarke, made a break for third just as Wiltse went into his windup. Kane was able to hit only a slow grounder through the middle of the diamond, but Clarke never slowed down as he turned third. Shortstop Al Bridwell had to make a quick choice whether to throw home to head off Clarke or try to get Kane at first. He decided on first where Kane beat the throw. First baseman Tenney quickly relayed the ball to Bresnahan, but it was too late to get the tag on Clarke before the Pirates manager touched home plate.

The Giants' chances against the Schoolmaster were few and they blew their final opportunity to tie the game in the ninth inning. A Pirates nemesis, Cy Seymour, led off with a single, his third hit of the game. McGraw elected to put on the hit-and-run with Bresnahan at bat. He lifted a long fly to right field that was caught by Owen Wilson. The Texan's strong throw to Kane arrived before Seymour could get back to the bag, to complete a double play.[15]

In a pennant race that finished with only one game separating three teams, Leever's shutout and the Giants' gaffs that afternoon had significant ramifications.

The Pirates got some help for their ailing pitching staff from the Doves of Boston on June 18 when Fred Clarke engineered a deal for the veteran left-hander Irv "Young Cy" Young. Young had been the best pitcher on a very bad club in 1905 and 1906 and wanted to get away from the losing ways of the Doves. Boston finally agreed to Young's wishes because his crossfire was no longer the effective pitch it had earlier been. The Pirates gave Boston pitchers Tom McCarthy and Harley Young, the latter a raw collegian with a wicked fast ball and a devastating break. McCarthy had been picked up on waivers from Cincinnati in late May, but he had been of little value.

Pittsburgh and Chicago set the pace in early April before New York took over first place for a few days. The Phillies and Reds held the top spot for short periods in May before the chase settled down to a three-team race. On June 29, the Pirates dislodged the Cubs from first place for four days, then lost their hold on the top spot due to a July 4 doubleheader loss at Exposition Park. Leever took the mound against Mordecai Brown in the morning game, but pitched only the first inning in which he gave up the game's only two runs and escaped a bases-loaded jam when the third out was recorded. Leifield shut the Cubs out after that, but Pittsburgh had no chance as the "Three Fingered" one was flawless in a two-hit, 2–0 whitewash of the Pirates.

Deacon Phillippe rejoined the ranks of active pitchers in the afternoon half of the twin bill. The Cubs knocked Camnitz out of the game after a five-run first inning and Fred Clarke sent Leever out for mop-up duty. After Sam was pinch-hit for in the seventh, Phillippe came in and "subdued the Cubs with ease" over the final two innings. However, it was way too little, too late as the Pirates fell, 9 to 3.

Four days later Phillippe relieved Irv Young, who had succeeded Al Leifield in the second game of a doubleheader against Philadelphia. Phillippe was quite rusty, permitting six hits in two innings pitched, although he did bang out a double in his only at-bat. C. B. Power of the *Dispatch* remarked, "The Deacon enacted his usual stunt. He spat on the ball, giving the fans the impression that his new fangled saliva slant was the real thing. It was, for the Philadelphia pellet pounders pegged away at a lively rate."[16]

Though it appeared Phillippe just had a bad outing, it was soon apparent that his injured thumb had not healed sufficiently for him to perform at his previous level. The Pirates not only lost Phillippe for the rest of the season, but they may have cost themselves the 1908 pennant with three losses to their cross-state rivals at Exposition Park.

Around the first of July, Sam Leever told Ralph Davis of the *Pittsburgh Press*, "I can't see where the Cubs have anything on us in any department. I believe our team is better balanced and better fortified in every department than ever before since the old pennant winning days.... I think our staff compares favorably with that of the Cubs. We may not have a bunch of stars, but we have an outfit of men who can play the game and who are willing to do all in their power for the team. I can't see how the Cubs are going to beat us out."[17]

On July 15, Leever again tangled with his old teammate Patsy Flaherty, still with the Boston Doves (named after club president George Dovey). Chicago held first place by only .002 percentage points when the sixth-place Doves came to Exposition Park for a four-game series. The 2,342 spectators on hand greeted the announcement that the Boston battery would be the former Pirates, Flaherty and Harry Smith, with applause. Flaherty had already beaten the Pirates twice in the 1908 season, though neither game was pitched by Leever. Over the past two seasons, Flaherty had pitched against the Pirates seven times and won six, Leever coming out on the losing side of the score three times in 1907.

It appeared from the start that the two pitchers were on their game and it would be a low-scoring affair. Pittsburgh scored first, but in the fourth inning, Leever's former battery mate, Frank Bowerman, drove a ball over Clarke's head in left to score a runner and came home himself on Claude Ritchey's timely single. After that, the two hurlers retired the side inning after inning and when the Pirates came up in the ninth for their final swings they were still down to Flaherty, 2–1.

The Pirates got a breath of life when Abbaticchio worked Flaherty for a walk. He was sacrificed to second, but Wilson flied out to deep center field. Down to their final out, the Pirates came through when Leever's roommate, George Gibson, hit a "moon shot" over Ginger Beaumont's head in center field. The Pittsburgh catcher was out at home trying to stretch the hit into a home run, but Abbaticchio had scored to tie the game at 2–2. Leever walked the first batter to face him in the top of the tenth, but avoided any damage by retiring the next three batters.

In the bottom of the tenth inning, reserve catcher Paddy O'Connor pinch-hit for Leever and walked. Roy Thomas was hit by a pitched ball and Leach beat out a little grounder down the first base line to load the bases. With Fred Clarke at the bat, Flaherty hit his second batter of the inning to force pinch-runner Danny Moeller across the plate with the winning run. The Boston players howled that Clarke had not made an attempt to get out of the way of the approaching ball, but their argument fell on deaf ears. Leever and Flaherty would not match up again, but Leever had broken his jinx against the former Pirates spitballer. More importantly, the victory put Pittsburgh into first place by a half-game and the Pirates held on to the top spot for 39 days.

On July 22, Howie Camnitz won a game against Brooklyn, 2–1, but the big news that afternoon was the home run at Exposition Park struck by the Superbas' first baseman, Tim Jordan. Jordan's mighty blast to right field was called the longest home run at the Pirates' home stadium since the major leaguers began playing there in 1890. Reports of the feat surpassed the other baseball news of the day.

Camnitz had allowed only three hits when he faced Jordan with two out in the visitors' ninth inning. "Jordan hit the ball squarely on the nose," reported the wire service, "and everybody knew when it started that it was going over the fence. When the crowd realized what had happened they arose and cheered for five minutes, while Jordan was carried to the bench on the shoulders of his teammates after he had completed the circuit of the bases."[18]

By the first of August it was obvious Deacon Phillippe would be of no help to the team for the remainder of the season, if ever. "Poor Deacon Phil is resting at home," wrote A. R. Cratty. "Sorry to say that his finger may never be right. Bone broken, doesn't seem to heal well. Would be a pity if Charles Phillippe had to give up the spangles. His has been a long and honorable record, marked by earnest loyal endeavor to his employers."[19]

Sam Leever had his own worries. His wife's decision to take a friend on an afternoon drive along the Columbus Pike on August 20 nearly turned into tragedy. When Margaret Leever's automobile stalled at the top of a hill near Goshen it began to roll backward down the incline. The women, paralyzed with fright, were helpless as the vehicle stopped on a bridge at the foot of the hill, where it tottered on the edge for a few seconds. The passenger jumped from the machine just before it plunged, "turning turtle," to the dry creek bed ten feet below. Margaret was pinned beneath the automobile and some men working nearby in a field rushed over to help. It took almost 30 minutes to free her from the wreck. Miraculously, Mrs. Leever suffered no serious injuries though she was badly bruised and had to be removed to her home on a cot.[20] While his wife was pinned in the mangled automobile, Leever was at Exposition Park pitching in a relief role in the Pirates' loss to Brooklyn.

The Giants surged back into the race and on August 20 they took the lead for a day. Pittsburgh quickly regained the top position, but lost it again on August 24 when New York won the first game of what turned out to be a four-game sweep in Pittsburgh. A large crowd of 16,440 jammed Exposition Park for the big doubleheader on Monday. Leever came into the second game with Pittsburgh down to Mathewson, 5 to 1, and pitched one-hit ball over the final two innings.

The next day fewer than 4,500 Pittsburghers came to Expo Park for a game with major implications. The Pirates lost again and the fans' greatest enjoyment came from O'Day's ejection of McGraw and Bresnahan for their actions following a strike call on the latter while he was complaining to the umpire about a pick-off play at third base moments earlier.

It appeared the Pirates were going to salvage the final game of the series on Wednesday. Another disappointing crowd of less than 5,000 watched the Pirates take a 3 to 2 lead into the ninth inning behind the outstanding hurling of Irv Young. The Pirates had scored all three of their runs in the sixth inning after O'Day reversed Charles Rigler's out call on Tommy Leach because the ball had been fumbled by the Giants third baseman before it hit the runner sliding into the base. While the Giants were arguing the call without time being called, the Pirates executed a triple steal with Leach sneaking in to home from third. Abbaticchio then singled home the other two runners.

With one out in the ninth, Doyle singled and Young hit Bresnahan with a pitch. Clarke stuck with Young with Mike Donlin at the plate. After "Turkey Mike" made two wild swings and missed, his wife, the famous Broadway actress Mabel Hite, was heard to yell from President Brush's box, "Hit the ball, Mike! Please, hit it!"

The Giants' captain backed out of the box, nodded his head to his wife and promptly took a pitch that Rigler called a ball, but the Pirates protested it was a strike. The next pitch was knocked through the infield to send the tying run home and Bresnahan to third base. Seymour drove in the winning run with a sacrifice fly. Clarke now summoned Leever to come into the game and get the final out. The move came two batters too late.[21]

The sweep by the Giants pushed the Pirates to three and a half games behind New York. Pittsburgh stayed close by winning three of four games with the Phillies, Leever throwing a masterful 1–0 shutout on August 28.

Philadelphia's ace, George McQuillan, was on his way to a 23-win season, but on that late August afternoon at Exposition Park, the Schoolmaster had something to teach the youngster. Leever allowed only six hits, largely due to some great support by his fielders. In the fifth inning, third baseman Leach made a one-handed stop of a ball off the bat of Kitty Bransfield that was hit so hard it "spun 'the wee' clear round like a top." Leach made a quick throw to first base, which was wild, but the six foot one Warren Gil grabbed it to retire Bransfield. In the seventh, left fielder Spike Shannon, who was playing because Fred Clarke had benched himself for poor play, made a desperate running catch of a line drive off the bat of Fred Osborn to save a run. Leach doubled and scored the only run of the game in the eighth inning.

During August, when it appeared the Pirates had a fair chance to win the pennant, the players began to joke among themselves about what they would do with their share of the World Series receipts. Someone asked Leever what he would take for his share and he offered to sell it for $500. Two weeks later Pittsburgh dropped four in a row to the Giants, who appeared poised to run away with the flag. Leever dropped his offer to $250 and, as Pittsburgh's chances grew less and less, the price for his share fell to $25.

Leever injured his knee in a 9 to 2, complete-game victory in Cincinnati on September 1 and watched the next day's contest from the stands. Then he pitched poorly in a four-inning outing against the Cardinals in the first game of a morning-afternoon doubleheader at Exposition Park on September 7. The game eventually was won by the Pirates, 9 to 7, and Clarke only used Leever as a substitute pitcher for the remainder of the season.

The Giants finally got the Schoolmaster's number in the second game of a doubleheader at the Polo Grounds on September 18, when McGraw's men came from behind to hand Leever the loss in relief of Camnitz. The Pirates lost both games that day to fall five games out of first place.

The first game, started early because of the record crowd seeking to get into the ballpark, was a 7 to 0 Christy Mathewson shutout in an hour and 40 minutes. By the time the second contest began at 3:30, the *Pittsburgh Gazette-Times* estimated that 10,000 of the approximately 35,000 fans that managed to get inside the park stood on the fringes of the baseball field. The Pirates jumped out to a quick lead in the afterpiece with three runs in the top of the first inning, but the Giants came right back with two runs of their own on Cy Seymour's "red-hot liner through the pitcher's box which made Camnitz and umpire O'Day play low-bridge" to escape being hit.[22] With two out and no one on base in the top of the second, Gill pinch-hit for Camnitz and Fred Clarke called on Sam Leever to assume the pitching duties.

The Schoolmaster had been successful against the Giants on many an occasion, but this was not to be his day. He held the Pirates' lead until the sixth inning when the Giants scored three times to take a 6 to 5 advantage. Bob Vail replaced Leever for the seventh and was hit at will in New York's 12 to 7 victory. The city of New York was ecstatic after the double victory that appeared to assure the Giants a National League pennant. The *New York Evening World* even ran a page one banner headline on the day's late edition that read: "Giants Clinch Pennant: Win Twice as Cubs Lose."

Once the disgruntled Leever returned to the team's hotel, Lefty Leifield asked him what he would take for his World's Series share now. "I'll sell for three cents," snapped Leever. Leifield, George Gibson and Tommy Leach quickly produced three pennies and became owners of Leever's potential post-season earnings.[23]

When the club left for its final Eastern trip in mid–September, Phillippe was left at home again. A. R. Cratty noted that Phillippe, the gentleman farmer, "contented himself by trolleying to his pretty country home at Bellevue, Pa.; back to his own, tilling the soil." Cratty added that Phillippe did not waste land or time, producing vegetables on the area around his home not only for his own use but for sale.

When Phillippe appeared downtown at the Farmers Bank Building to pick up his mail, he reported, "Tomatoes fine; potatoes not so great, but expect better luck the next time." He also said any rumor about him taking a job as a minor league manager for next season was news to him and intimated that he might not be done as a major league pitcher. Of course, his friends knew he had thousands of dollars salted away and had revenue from his farm in South Dakota as well as dividends from his interests in Pittsburgh public utilities.[24]

Over the next two weeks, the Pirates reeled off 13 victories in 14 games to move into first place, a half-game ahead of the second-place Cubs, who had passed the slumping Giants in the standings. Leading up to the season's final game in Chicago, Pittsburgh swept six straight games with St. Louis. Though he was seldom called upon down the stretch, Leever made a major contribution to the club on September 30 in the team's final home game of the season. Willis started for the Pirates and was pummeled by the Redbirds for five runs before he was sent to the bench at the end of the third inning.

C. B. Powers of the *Pittsburgh Dispatch* wrote, "At the end of the third inning that sedate old sport, Sammy Leever, jumped into the fray, and right there a change came over the scene. During the six innings in which Samuel took part the Cardinals, who had started out like fiends with the willow, were held to three little plunkers."[25]

While Leever held the Cardinals at bay, the Pirates scored two runs in the bottom of the third and continued to chip away at the lead until they forged ahead, 7 to 5, in the eighth inning. After Leever retired the Redbirds in the ninth, the Pirates were within .004 percentage points of first place. Thursday, October 1, was an off-day on which the Pirates would travel by train to St. Louis for three more games with the Cardinals.

"Never before have the men ran into such a miserable coach for an overnight ride" reported *Sporting Life*. "Going on a high-class road, and on the fastest train operated by the company, fifteen hours Pittsburgh to St. Louis, the treatment of the Pittsburgh players is most amazing."

The players were ushered into an ancient and decrepit Pullman sleeper and Secretary Locke was assured by the company that the correct car was assigned to the ball club. As a precursor to a miserable trip, the car's porter reported for work wearing a fur-collared overcoat. There was no heat, no water, and poor light for the overnight trip to St. Louis, and it was so cold the players could not even play cards.

While the Pirates shivered in their bunks beneath what covers were available, the train's crew tried to start a fire in an old-fashioned stove. They finally got a blaze going, but the smoke blew back into the car where the air became suffocating. Twice the players had to help the porters extinguish fires that were burning in the car. Some players, unable to sleep because of the fumes, dumped water in the stove to douse the ashes. In addition to the smoke and cinders, the Pirates spent the night shaking from the freezing conditions.[26]

"They give us any old car simply because we are ball players," declared Locke after a fruitless complaint to the railroad. "Companies know it is easy money. They hand you anything they want. Ball clubs must travel. The sleeper company knows it."[27]

After their miserable experience during the trip to St. Louis, the Pirates took it out on the Cardinals. The Pirates beat St. Louis three more times to give them 14 straight victories over the Cardinals since Harley Young lost to Bugs Raymond, 8–4, on June 3. Pittsburgh left the Missouri City in first place with only one game left to play.

When the Pirates boarded a train to Chicago for a single game against the Cubs to end the season, they needed a victory to win the National League pennant. The Pirates were confident. After all, Willis had beaten Chicago's ace, Mordecai Brown, 1 to 0, in a ten-inning duel between the two aces at Exposition Park back on September 4. Even a tie or a cancellation would give Pittsburgh the league championship.

During the train ride, Leifield, Leach and Gibson did all they could to torment Leever about their deal for his World Series share, then made him an offer. The trio informed Leever that if he would give them 150 shotgun shells each, win or lose the pennant, they would return his share to him. Leever manufactured the shells himself, so he leaped at the chance. As it turned out, the others would have free ammunition for their fall hunting trip.[28]

A record crowd of 30,247 squeezed into Chicago's West Side Grounds on October 4 to watch the Pirates face Brown. Back in Pittsburgh, 50,000 people watched the progress of the game on telegraph-fed scoreboards at newspaper offices. "Megaphone announcements of play by play is something new in the steel city," wrote A. R. Cratty in *Sporting Life*. "It was followed during the final stages of the league race, also when the world's honor games were on. This indicates the high pitch of excitement reached by the base ball public in Pittsburgh."[29]

The Cubs got an early lead against Vic Willis, but the Pirates tied the score at 2–2 in the sixth inning. When men with megaphones screamed the news of the tying score to the estimated 50,000 people assembled in streets adjacent to two newspaper buildings in Pittsburgh, the throng pushed forward to get closer to the announcers. The situation became so alarming that the police department was telephoned and a score of officers were sent to the scene to restore order.[30]

This very game was the reason Barney Dreyfuss acquired Willis in the first place, but the "Delaware Peach" failed him. Chicago regained the lead in the bottom of the sixth with the opposition pitcher driving home the run with two out. Wagner's error on a routine ground ball cost the Pirates another run in the seventh, and Willis was removed for a pinch-hitter in the top of the next inning. The Pirates trailed, 5 to 2, when Wagner led off the Pittsburgh half of the ninth with a single. Ed Abbaticchio crushed an apparent home run down the right field foul line that would have cut the lead to one run with none out. However, umpire Hank O'Day ruled the drive foul. Players from the Pirates' bench surrounded O'Day in protest and the usually rigid umpire made the concession to consult his cohort Charles Rigler. The call stood. Abbaticchio returned to the plate and eventually struck out to end any Pittsburgh hope of a comeback. *Sporting Life* reported that Rigler originally told Abbaticchio the ball landed fair, but when appealed to by the Pirates, he maintained he did not say where the ball landed.[31]

In the end, the disconsolate Pirates finished the 1908 season tied for second place with the New York Giants, one game behind the Cubs, who had to win a make-up game with New York after the conclusion of the regular season. One can only speculate that had Phillippe been healthy, he might have made the difference between Pittsburgh winning the pennant outright instead of finishing one game out. His performance over the next two seasons makes a strong case for that assumption. Other than the big five of Maddox, Willis, Camnitz, Leifield and Leever, Fred Clarke used seven other pitchers 39 times with a cumulative record of 6 wins and 7 losses. Four of those victories were provided by Irv Young, who did not join the Pirates until late June.

Although he did not start a game in the final four weeks of the season, Sam Leever posted very respectable statistics for 1908: 15 victories, 7 losses and a 2.10 earned run average. However, he struck out only 28 batters in 193 innings pitched. But after that last September start, he would never return to Pittsburgh's regular pitching rotation, starting only 12 games over the next two seasons. Once the baseball season concluded, "Sam Leever went to Goshen, O., in his automobile," reported Ralph Davis, "and (he) will put in the winter handing out Uncle Sam's mail, making gun powder, killing rabbits and otherwise improving his time."[32]

Deacon Phillippe was not a factor in the 1908 season, appearing in only five games because of his sore shoulders and injured thumb. Used only in games where the verdict was all but decided, Phillippe pitched only 12 innings during which he gave up 15 runs.

That October, when Phillippe paid $7,200 for a 109-acre farm 21 miles north of Butler, Pennsylvania, a sportswriter asked Barney Dreyfuss if the "old man" might retire from baseball. "Looks that way," responded Dreyfuss. "He has ever yearned for the Butler county farm. Wants to retire from base ball before being driven out. Has lots of money, is a fine, thrifty man and good citizen. Good luck to him if he means to leave his old pals and employer."[33]

In January of 1909, *The Sporting News* columnist Ralph Davis also speculated that Phillippe might not return to baseball in 1909.[34] However, Phillippe apparently had a change of heart, if Davis' earlier observation had credibility.

Phillippe called on President Dreyfuss in mid–February and said he wanted to pitch another season. He said he was in better shape than any time in the previous two seasons and believed he could deliver the goods. He asked to go South with the advance guard for spring training and if he could get in condition, then he would sign a contract. On the day he left for Hot Springs, word was leaked that Phillippe was one of the owners of a new amusement palace that just opened in Carnegie.[35]

Fred Clarke was glad to see his old friend back with the team and wrote, "If Phil shows anything like his old-time form, he will be a great help to the Pirates."[36]

On February 25, 1909, Barney Dreyfuss received Sam Leever's autograph on a contract for the upcoming season along with a curt letter declining to accompany the other pitchers to West Baden on March 8 as ordered by management. Tommy Leach had been designated leader of the pitching squad with instructions to dry out some of the hard-drinking members of the staff like Willis and Camnitz.

Leever's note to Barney Dreyfuss read, "The water treatment there will be of no particular benefit to me, as I have not played a very extensive engagement with intoxicating drinks during the past winter."

The Pirates owner knew Leever was a teetotaler and decided the veteran's remarks were not designed to slur the other pitchers who had agreed to go to West Baden to "boil out."[37] As the date to report to camp neared, Leever wrote again to his boss in a more conciliatory manner, "I am anxious to show some of the fans who are of the opinion that I am a dead one, that I can still pitch, even though they have ordered a coffin for my arm."[38]

However, the big news of the spring was the holdout by Vic Willis and the absence of Honus Wagner, ostensibly to attend to business. Willis drew $3,500 in 1908 and received a $400 bonus after winning 24 games. The Pirates claimed the pitcher rejected an offer of $4,100, then held out for the $5,000 he wanted. Whereupon, Barney Dreyfuss withdrew the offer and gave Willis the choice of taking or leaving the $3,500 offer for the upcoming season. Willis eventually gave in and reported to camp the last day of March, although he ultimately received an undisclosed raise.[39]

The 1909 Pirates were a juggernaut, winning 110 games, second highest in National League history, to interrupt Chicago's pennant run of three straight. Pittsburgh's pitching staff was so deep, starting assignments for the club's two 37-year-old veterans were hard to come by. Leever and Phillippe did yeoman work, mostly in relief or an occasional start.

Fred Clarke nursed the veteran hurlers Leever and Phillippe along judiciously, picking spots in which to use them. The pair was fresh late in the season and left the league's sluggers frustrated in their attempts to put solid wood on the drops, benders and twisters from the two antique pitchers. Leever started only four games, and six of his eight victories came in relief. Phillippe also won eight games and started 12 times, completing seven. After missing most of the 1908 campaign, Phillippe did not lose his amazing control the following season, walking only 14 batters in 131 innings pitched. Deacon also registered his lowest earned run average in five years.

Manager Fred Clarke's lineup changed considerably for a team that finished only one game out of first place in 1908. Wagner was still the anchor of the club at shortstop, and the durable George Gibson would toil behind the plate in 150 games. Big Bill Abstein, a former St. Louis sandlotter who had a brief trial with the Pirates in 1906, became Pittsburgh's first baseman of the year. John "Dots" Miller, a lanky youngster of German descent who worshipped Honus Wagner, was so impressive in the spring he beat out Abbaticchio for the second base position. Pint-sized French Canadian William Joe "Jap" Barbeau started the season at third base, once again freeing Tommy Leach for center field duty between Clarke in left field and Owen "Chief" Wilson in right. On August 29, Dreyfuss acquired the Cardinals' starting third baseman, Bobby Byrne, for Barbeau, Alan Storke and cash.

Howard Camnitz led the pitchers with 25 victories, Vic Willis won 23, followed by 17-game winner Al Leifield and Nick Maddox with 14 victories. Soon to overshadow them all was a 21-year-old Charles "Babe" Adams, who earned his ticket back to the majors by winning 22 games with Louisville in 1908. The team's old-timers, Deacon and the Schoolmaster, combined to post a record of 16 wins and four losses.

On April 26, Deacon Phillippe started his first game on the mound since a 12–5 loss to Philadelphia on October 1, 1907. He nearly threw a complete game, but St. Louis tied the score at 3–3 with one out in the ninth inning. Leifield replaced him and the Pirates eventually won the game in 12 innings.

"Phil's old raise ball was working finely," noted *Sporting Life*. "His 'teammates' faces wore smiles, for Charley is a most popular man.... 'Sore? No,' said the Deacon. 'Arm's not bothering me.'"[40]

"I feel all right now, but wait until tomorrow," he cautioned. "It did seem a little strange to be back on the rubber after a year's absence, and the game was a tough one as a starter but I feel a real deal of satisfaction out of the fact that I had a good curve. If I can keep that I will be all right as a little more practice will give me control."[41]

May 1, 1909, was a red-letter day in the revitalized baseball career of Phillippe. The Pirates were to leave for Chicago that evening for a short road trip. When Clarke presented the roster of players making the trip to Barney Dreyfuss and Secretary Locke, conspicuous at the top of the list was the name of Deacon Phillippe. "Smiles went round faces of headquarters boys," noted an observer. Three years earlier, when Phillippe was the undisputed ace of the Pirates pitching staff, it became a joke when the writers quipped, "The Pirates, fourteen in number, including Deacon Phillippe, left for the East last night."[42]

On May 14, Phillippe lost to Tully Sparks and the Phillies, 2–0. He gave up only four hits, walked two and hit one batter, but the Pirates managed only four hits themselves and wasted Clarke's triple. The Phillies won the game in the fourth inning when Phillippe's walk to Titus, Bransfield's single, an error by Leach, and an infield out led to the two runs.

The star-crossed hurler lost again by the same score in Brooklyn on May 19. The Pirates managed only two hits off Farmer Bell.

A day earlier, Leever achieved his first victory of the 1909 season as a substitute pitcher. Vic Willis was staked to an early 4–0 lead over the Superbas. Though he gave up only two runs in the first five innings, Willis' deliveries were touched for nine hits and, after the first Brooklyn batter in the sixth inning singled, Leever replaced him. Leever took a 5–3 lead into the ninth inning, but a two-out hit to center field by Tim Jordan tied the game. The big first baseman was out trying for a home run, and the contest was thrown into extra innings. The Schoolmaster's pupils bailed him out with three runs in the top of the tenth, the big blow a two-run triple by Honus Wagner. In Manhattan, the Giants lost to the Reds to plunge McGraw's bunch into last place.

Leever started the first game of a Sunday doubleheader before a huge crowd of 27,000 in Chicago on May 30. He had a 3–1 lead going into the home half of the third, but after retiring the first batter, the Cubs began to hit him at will. Four quick hits and three runs later, he was out of the game. Camnitz came on and held the Cubs at bay until the Pirates came back and eked out a 5–4 win. The victory propelled the Buccaneers past the Cubs into first place and started Pittsburgh on a 14-game winning streak.

After sweeping the Cubs, the Pirates returned home for a Monday doubleheader, and Babe Adams gave the team a glimpse of his future greatness. In the morning game, Adams went to the relief of Maddox and received credit for the victory. After lunch, Adams went out and won the afternoon game, 4 to 2.

Phillippe finally got a break on June 3 in a game against Boston. Camnitz, Powell and Frock all worked from the mound for the Pirates before Phillippe came into the game in the sixth inning with Pittsburgh trailing 8–7. Phillippe threw three scoreless innings and the Pirates won the game with single runs in the sixth and eighth innings.

Phillippe's latest performance led A. R. Cratty to pen, "The old man has steam, control, and also shows his famous curve, a bender that so often cast dismay into the hearts of National Leaguers. Phil's supposed decline in 1907 and 1908 wasn't so much the result of a loss of speed as it was due to poor luck and a severely sore finger. Ask batsmen who have faced Deacon. They will tell you that the sage of Butler County is right 'onto the job again.'"[43]

On Tuesday, June 29, the Pirates played their final game at archaic Exposition Park, defeating Three Finger Brown and the Cubs, 8 to 1. A new baseball park would be dedicated in Pittsburgh the next day.

The opening of the Pirates' new baseball palace, Forbes Field, was a big event in the city. The new park was built in the Oakland District of Pittsburgh at a cost of $1,000,000 and had a seating capacity of 25,000. Two-tiered grandstands were considered the vogue then, but Dreyfuss built three tiers. He was so proud of his new park that he allowed no advertising to spoil the blue-black fences.

Wrote columnist Ring Lardner on the opener, "A throng of 30,338, or ninety-one more than the former record, paid their good money to Messers. Dreyfuss and Murphy, and there were at least 5,000 more who came in on invitations from the president of the Pittsburgh club.... The stands, themselves constructed almost entirely of Pittsburgh steel and concrete, completely surrounded the field and yet were not big enough to hold the mammoth crowd."[44]

At 2:30 Professor Nerillos' military band began the march to the home team's bench. In the line of Pirates adjacent to home plate, Samuel Leever easily held the distinction of longest service with his 13 seasons with the Pirates. The Cubs joined the procession on the opposite side of the diamond. A number of former Pirates, accompanied by National League President Harry Pulliam, Secretary John H. Heydler, National Commission chairman Garry

Main entrance to the grandstand at the new Forbes Field (Library of Congress Prints and Photographs Division).

Herrmann, Charles Murphy of the Cubs and President Dreyfuss passed between the aligned players and marched to the flag pole in the center of the outfield. The Stars and Stripes were hoisted with a pennant bearing the words "Forbes Field" trailing below. The Band played "America," then "Hail, Hail, the Gang's all Here," to which the throng joined in. The Pirates took their positions in the field and when the umpire yelled "play ball!" the *Pittsburg Press* reported, "the scene for the next two or three minutes was simply indescribable. The thousands of fans 'let loose' with one accord, and cheer after cheer made the welkin ring."[45]

After the city's Director of Public Safety threw the first pitch to catcher Gibson, the two teams put on a good game. Despite permitting only four hits, Vic Willis lost a 3–2 decision to Chicago's Ed Reulbach. The Pirates drew 98,000 patrons, including 41,000 on July 5, in the first five games in the new stadium.

After a year and a half of frustration, Deacon Phillippe returned to the mound on a regular basis in July, 1909. He made his Forbes Field debut on July 6 and responded with his only shutout of the season, beating Cincinnati, 5 to 0. A nice Tuesday crowd of 4,024 passed the turnstiles though it was a drastic drop-off from the previous five contests at Forbes Field.

The *Pittsburgh Dispatch* wrote that Phillippe "was in splendid shape at every stage of the game." The Pirates scored four runs off Ewing in the opening frame and Phillippe took it from there. Only in the final two innings were the Reds able to put two hits together. In the eighth a double and a single landed Reds on first and third with two out, but Phillippe fanned the speedy Bob Bescher to retire the side. He struck out Paskert to open the ninth, but centerfielder Leach lost Dick Egan's fly ball in the sun to allow one Red to reach base, and Hoblitzel singled to put two runners on. Mike Mitchell made a bid for the Reds' third straight hit, but Wagner made a great play on the grounder and flipped the ball to Miller for the force out. The final batter grounded to Miller and his toss to first baseman Storke sealed the shutout.[46]

Three days after his whitewash of the Reds, Phillippe started against the Giants in the second game of a doubleheader at the Polo Grounds. Some 40,000 Giants rooters were lucky enough to get into the grounds, and 34,000 of that number were fortunate enough to get a seat. An additional 10,000 watched the contests outside the park from Coogan's Bluff, the viaduct and other vantage points.

"Such an assemblage never before was seen in all the history of the game," recorded *The New York Times*. "It made the great gatherings that witnessed the New York–Philadelphia World Series fade to minor significance. It even eclipsed the famous Chicago–New York game last October, the result of which decided the league championship.... Never before has any sport free of betting interest attracted such a multitude."[47]

In the first game Pittsburgh scored five runs in the first inning, but when it became obvious this was not Maddox's day, Clarke rushed in Camnitz and the Pirates prevailed, 9 to 5. It was expected Mathewson would pitch the second game, but it was Bugs Raymond that McGraw sent out to oppose Deacon Phillippe.

Pittsburgh scored single runs in the first, third and seventh innings. Each time the Giants threatened, Phillippe rose to the task. In the bottom of the first, Larry Doyle singled and made it around to third base with one out. Moose McCormick smacked a ball that appeared to be heading into right field, but first baseman Alan Storke made a fine leaping catch. Red Murray flied out to shortstop and Doyle was stranded at third. To open the sixth, the Giants filled the bases on three successive singles to send the huge crowd into a tizzy. Amid the screams of the Giants' fans for their right fielder to get a hit, Phillippe struck out Murray swinging. Catcher Bill O'Hara popped out to Wagner and Art Devlin flied out to right field to end the threat.

Devlin's triple and a couple of Pittsburgh errors allowed the Giants to pull within a run in the bottom of the seventh. However, Pittsburgh added an insurance run in the ninth, and Phillippe retired the side in the bottom half to give the Pirates a 4–2 victory. Instead of narrowing the pennant race, the Giants finished the day nine games behind the Pirates.

On July 14, Phillippe beat Nap Rucker at Brooklyn's Washington Park. He lost to the Phillies, 3–0, on July 20, the third time during the season that the Pirates did not score in a game started by Phillippe. Wins over Boston and Philadelphia gave the veteran hurler a record of five wins and only one loss for the month of July.

On July 28, 1909, the Pirates family was stunned to learn of the suicide of National League President Harry Pulliam. As secretary of the Louisville club, Pulliam had signed several of the veteran Pirates players and he was held in high regard by many of them. Since his selection as league president in 1903, disputes with owners and players weighed heavily on the 40-year-old Pulliam and he had suffered from severe depression for months. Over the past year he usually stayed secluded in his apartment on the third floor of the New York Athletic Club when not in his office.

It was said that Pulliam's mental problems were exacerbated when he was forced to rule on the 1908 Merkle incident, declaring a crucial Giants-Cubs game a tie that would have to be replayed if it had a bearing on the league championship. Pulliam's decision was condemned by the New Yorkers, especially when the Giants lost the make-up game that decided the 1908 pennant. Pulliam's physician blamed the heated controversy for his patient's severe state of depression.

At the National League's winter meetings after the 1908 season, Pulliam suffered a nervous breakdown and was granted an indefinite leave of absence. After convalescing in the South, he returned to the job in June, 1909, but friends and associates noticed that he was aloof and moody.

President Pulliam came to work the morning of July 28 and went through his mail. At about 1 p.m., he left the office after telling his secretary he did not feel well. He went to his room at the New York Athletic Club and put a pistol to his head. The bullet blew out his right eye, passed through the skull and exited on the left side of his head. Pulliam managed to drag himself to the telephone and knocked the receiver off the hook. At about 10 a.m., a club attendant checked on him because his phone line was tying up the club's circuits. An employee of the athletic club entered the unlocked room and found Pulliam in a pool of blood, but still alive. A physician was summoned and he determined that Pulliam was too badly wounded to be moved to a hospital. The coroner arrived and asked the wounded man how he got shot. Pulliam is said to have moaned with extreme effort, "I am not shot." Then his head fell back and he lost consciousness. Pulliam died at 7:40 the next morning.[48]

The loss of the Pirates' popular ex-secretary was hard on the veteran players left from the years in Louisville and Pulliam's time in Pittsburgh. On the day of his funeral in Louisville on August 2, both the National League and American League games were postponed in tribute.

Sam Leever drew a rare starting assignment on August 13 and he defeated Philadelphia, 2 to 1, in 12 innings at Forbes Field. George McQuillan also pitched a strong game and had only one lapse in regulation when three Pittsburgh singles produced a run. Philadelphia tied it in the fourth inning and threatened to take the lead in the sixth. The Phillies loaded the bases with two out on a safe bunt, an infield hit, and a walk. Leever got out of the jam when second baseman Miller made a diving, one-handed grab of Mickey Doolan's sizzler and flipped to Wagner from "an almost impossible position" to force the runner coming from first.[49] The contest remained tied at 1–1 until the 12th inning.

The 12th frame was filled with drama, in both the top half and the bottom. When the dangerous John Titus came to bat with runners on second and third and two out, Fred Clarke noticed from Leever's body language that the Schoolmaster was in distress. The Buccaneer manager signaled the umpires that he wanted time out. Everyone in the park waited curiously as Clarke walked to the Pirates bench and began to go through a small valise where baseballs were kept. Clarke fiddled with the bag for nearly five minutes and Leever's attention had been deflected from his predicament by the time Clarke headed back onto the field with a pair of smoked glasses. He walked slowly to center field and handed the glasses to Tommy Leach. Tommy handled the glasses for a moment, then laid them on the grass amid cheers from the crowd of nearly 3,000. After the respite that permitted Leever to calm down, Titus took a mighty swing at a pitch but only produced a little bounder to the pitcher. Leever threw Titus out at first to preserve the tie.[50]

With two out in the bottom of the 12th, Clarke beat out a slowly hit grounder to short and scooted to second base when Mickey Doolan's rushed throw sailed over Bransfield's head. McQuillan worked too carefully to Wagner and ran the count to two balls and no strikes. His third pitch bounced before it reached the catcher, glanced off Red Dooin's left shoe and flew toward the grandstand. The speedy Clarke did not hesitate and scored the winning run from second base. Upon retrieving the wayward pitch, Dooin was so incensed he hurled the ball over the top of the pavilion. The crowd's reaction was mixed, many cheering the victory and others jeering the Philadelphia catcher.

Leever walked two and gave up 11 hits in the marathon, but he was at his best with men on base and his fielders helped out with 12 innings of errorless ball. When the Cubs lost to the Giants at West Side Grounds, the first-place Pirates' lead in the pennant race reached six games over Chicago.

Leever drew another starting assignment a week later again against the

Phillies' George McQuillan, this time at the Baker Bowl. Two errors, a botched bunt and a miscue by George Gibson on a play at home plate cost the Schoolmaster two runs. He was replaced by Babe Adams in the sixth inning, but Pittsburgh won the game on Wilson's two-run home run in the seventh.

On August 25, Deacon Phillippe was called on to relieve Nick Maddox after the latter gave up three runs to the Giants in the second inning at the Polo Grounds. Phillippe allowed only three hits over the next six innings, but Mathewson held on to pin a 3–2 loss on the Pirates. A week later Phillippe needed relief himself to get a win in Boston. He was leading 5–3 in the sixth inning when Clarke removed him for a pinch-hitter. Camnitz preserved the victory with four innings of scoreless relief.

Pittsburgh rolled into Chicago late on Saturday, September 4, to begin a key five-game series against the Cubs the following afternoon. The Cubs trailed the Pirates by six games so they desperately needed to win at least four of the games. Frank Chance had his ace, Three Finger Brown, set to pitch the first game, and a loud crowd of 27,000 to cheer them on.

Camnitz held the West Siders without a run until the seventh inning. Schulte started the damage with a single, and up to bat came Frank Chance, who had struck out his previous two times up. With the count two and two, Chance ducked away from a high inshoot and the ball struck his bat. Remarkably, the ball rolled safely down the right field foul line. Frank ran to second and Schulte pulled up at third. Schulte was thrown out trying to score on a grounder to Wagner, but Chance ambled home a few moments later on Hofman's long fly to center field.

Pittsburgh came right back in the top of the eighth inning. With an opportunity to tie the game with a runner on third base, Clarke withdrew Camnitz and sent up Ham Hyatt, who had gained a reputation as a pinch-hitter. Hyatt hit a slow roller to shortstop, and Joe Tinker's throw to the catcher was too late to prevent the tying run. Sam Leever took the mound and retired the Cubs one-two-three in the bottom of the eighth, the ninth and the tenth.

Things turned against Brown in the top of the 11th inning. Bobby Byrne, recently acquired from the Cardinals, opened the frame with a long fly ball into the left field overflow crowd which umpire James Johnstone ruled a ground-rule double. Leach drove a liner out of Chance's reach, but Schulte's throw to home plate held Byrne at third. With the Cubs infield drawn in, Clarke slapped a sharp ground ball to Tinker, who messed it up long enough for Byrne to score and Clarke to reach first safely. The Cubs fell apart after that and Pittsburgh finished the inning up, 5 to 1. Leever retired the side in the bottom of the inning. Even though the Cubs took three of the final four games of the series, it was too little, too late.

Leever defeated St. Louis, 4–1, in his final start of the season on September 13. The victory came in the midst of another long Pirates winning streak that reached 16 before the Giants beat them, 8–7, in the second game of a doubleheader on September 27. The Pirates needed those wins, too, as the second-place Cubs won 104 games.

Pittsburgh clinched the 1909 National League pennant on a Chicago loss shortly after the completion of the Pirates non-championship effort against the Giants at Forbes Field. Before the game, Clarke was presented with a purse of gold amounting to a little over $600 and the Pittsburgh mayor made a speech lauding the work of Clarke and the players.

Phillippe was the second of four Pirates hurlers to work in the game, all of whom were hit freely in a 13 to 9 loss. The Pirates only made the score a little closer with a five-run outburst against Red Ames in the ninth inning. When the Philadelphia-Chicago score went final, much of the crowd that hung around rushed the home team's bench, but the players had already escaped to the dressing room.

Though the two veteran pitchers' 16 victories were crucial in the Pirates' regular season championship, Phillippe and Leever didn't figure to play much of a role in the World Series against the Detroit Tigers. The Buccaneers' big four of Willis, Maddox, Camnitz and Leifield, plus rookie Babe Adams, would handle the pitching duties against baseball's best hitting team. The Tigers' offense was led by right fielder Ty Cobb, who batted .377 for the 1909 season.

The Pirates won two of the first three games of the Series and 17-game winner Lefty Leifield took the ball on October 12 for Game Four in Detroit. A strong, biting wind blew across the field of Bennett Park in varying degrees of gusts. The players jumped up and down in an effort to keep warm as a small World Series crowd of a little more than 17,000 paid to watch. Leifield's body language suggested he was not comfortable in the cold weather and the lefty was pounded for five runs before he was pulled for a pinch-hitter in the top of the fifth. Manager Clarke called for Phillippe to take the mound in the bottom of the frame. He was up to the task, retiring the Tigers the remainder of the contest without allowing a run. The one hit off Phillippe came in the eighth inning when Detroit managed to load the bases, abetted by Phillippe's own error on a bunt. He got out of the jam when he induced Donnie Bush to ground out to end the inning. He faced Cobb only once, and the great one was retired when catcher Gibson quickly fielded the Georgian's bunt and threw him out at first. Unfortunately for Phillippe and the Pirates, Detroit's George Mullin pitched a 5–0 shutout.

Phillippe also pitched in the sixth game after the Tigers built up a 5–3 lead off Willis and Camnitz. He entered the game in the seventh inning and retired six of the seven batters he faced. Only the opposing pitcher, Mullin, hit safely against him. The Pirates rallied in the top of the ninth, loading the bases with no one out. With a run in and two men on base, the game ended abruptly when Abbaticchio, batting for Phillippe, struck out and Chief Wilson was thrown out trying to steal third.

It was left up to Babe Adams to save the Pirates in the deciding seventh game of the Series, and the youngster shut out the American Leaguers to beat them for the third time. Leever and Phillippe were on the bench and out of the picture, but Phillippe said "they were the most nervous onlookers that day."

When Honus Wagner came up in the seventh with two runners on base and smacked a triple to left on the first pitch, "the gang on the bench went wild." Then the left fielder's throw to third was wild and Wagner danced home with the Pirates' seventh run.

"I will not soon forget the demonstration of the Pirates when Honus did his sensational stunt on the bases," recalled Phillippe. "Trainer Ed Laforce, who prayed from start to finish, stopped long enough to let out one of his famous yells, and Sam Leever, who was sitting next to me, punched me so hard that I thought he had fractured my ribs."[51]

Phillippe and Leever finally became World Series champions with the Pirates' victory. Phillippe pitched six innings in the Series, allowing but two hits and no runs. Leever didn't play, but still went home satisfied with a $1,825.00 winners' share.

The Pittsburgh Pirates received a formal welcome home the evening of October 18, beginning with a parade from downtown. Participants included civic bodies, political clubs, and fans in taxis, motor vehicles and some even on horseback. At about eight o'clock the 25,000 bugs marched to Forbes Field, where the formal ceremony was held.

Hippodrome lights illuminated the diamond and the large platform that had been erected. The 50,000 in attendance on the grounds and in the stands watched as Congressman James Francis Burke made a welcome address. The players were called to the stand and each was presented with his World Series check. Tommy Leach and George Gibson made speeches through megaphones, but nobody could hear them because there was so much noise. The crowd held thousands of sticks of red fire throughout the ceremony.

Honus Wagner received a great ovation, but the largest demonstration was reserved for Babe Adams. When Adams was given his check and an additional purse of $1,260, the crowd went wild. Mayor William Magee attempted to restore order for ten minutes, but neither he nor the six massed bands could diminish the crowd's noise.[52]

♦ Eleven ♦

Swan Song

Any rumor that Phillippe and Leever would not be retained by the Pirates was put to rest on January 17, 1910, when Secretary William Locke announced that Phillippe had signed a new contract and Leever's was expected in a few days.

"It makes no difference to me whether these two man ever pitch another league game for my team," said President Dreyfuss. "They can draw a salary from me as long as I am in the business and they want to. When they were in their prime they gave me the best in their stock, and I am for them now."[1]

In its report about Phillippe's 1910 contract with the Pirates, *The Sporting News* added, "Phillippe has said that when he's through with the Pirates he is through with baseball. He is well supplied with this world's goods and is spending the winter on his farm at Keiser (Pennsylvania)."[2]

In mid–March President Dreyfuss received a letter from Sam Leever in which the 38-year-old pitcher said that he had read in some newspaper that the world champion Pirates could get along very well without his services. "I do not want to be a pensioner," wrote Leever, "and I, therefore, decided to remain at home."[3]

Barney Dreyfuss immediately penned a response to Leever assuring the veteran pitcher that had he not been wanted, a contract would not have been mailed to him. Still, Leever failed to report with the advance squad at West Baden and the club's officers had received no word from him. No one knew where he was or what was the matter, but he eventually came around as he always did.

Other than Phillippe and 1909 World Series hero Babe Adams, the Pirates pitching staff flopped a year later and the Bucs fell to a distant third place behind the Cubs. One mainstay of the staff that was long gone well before spring training was the erstwhile ace, Vic Willis. Barney Dreyfuss had grown tired of Willis' disciplinary issues and the pitcher's failures in big games.

Despite his 90 victories in four seasons with the Pirates, the 34-year old pitcher was sent to the Cardinals in a straight cash transaction on February 15, 1910.

"It was not because Clarke thought Willis was all in that he turned him loose," wrote club insider Ralph Davis, "but simply to maintain his policy of punishing, in one way or another, all players who fail to show a proper appreciation of the responsibilities of their position and who refuse to obey the rules of discipline laid down every spring for the government of the Pirates.

"Willis' conduct during part of last summer, and especially during the World's Series, was such as to bring down upon his head the condemnation of his manager. The Pirates were depending on him to win at least two games from the Detroit Americans, but he failed to deliver the goods."[4]

Other than Willis and a different first baseman for the sixth straight season, the Pirates made few changes before opening day. It was expected Babe Adams would easily replace Willis once he moved into the starting rotation on a full-time basis.

On April 21, 1910, the defending world's champions played their opening home game of the season. The day was cold and there was standing water in portions of the outfield following three days of rain, but shortly after two o'clock it was decided to open the gates for the 7,000 enthusiasts that turned out to see the raising of the championship pennant. The club hired a large number of laborers to fill wheel-barrows with mud from inside the park and dump them outside. Meanwhile, other workers scattered sawdust and tanbark into the depressions made by the removal of mud.

During the pre-game ceremonies, the 1909 championship flag was upside-down when it was raised up the staff. The banner had to be hauled down and the process repeated. Mayor William A. Magee pitched the first ball, after which World Series hero Babe Adams took the mound to be honored by the home fans. Unfortunately, the St. Louis Cardinals were not impressed with Adams' World Series success and tagged him for three runs in the third inning. Now a Cardinal, Vic Wills nursed a 4–2 lead into the sixth inning. In that frame, Adams departed for a pinch-hitter and the Pirates tallied four times to take the lead. Deacon Phillippe left his lucky spot on the bench and pitched hitless ball over the final three innings. He also produced the hit that settled the affair in the seventh.

Dreyfuss was delighted that his personal favorite, Deacon Phillippe, got the best of Vic Willis. With two out and two Pirates on base in the seventh inning, Willis elected to walk George Gibson and pitch to Phillippe with the bases loaded. "Let Willis put one in the groove and Phil will show him something," Dreyfuss remarked to a friend in his personal box. "The tall twirler sent up a slow," reported *Sporting Life*. "Phillippe swung on it for a two-bagger down the right-field line, clearing the cushions."[5]

By the rules of baseball, Adams got credit for the victory, but Phillippe was the hero of the day. "Phillippe was in grand form and showed that the good things said about him this season were not exaggerations," reported the *Pittsburgh Dispatch*. "He was the master of the situation at all times and his control was never better."[6]

Though he pitched infrequently, Leever was pretty good when he did take the mound. On April 17, he pitched a complete-game, 4 to 2 victory during a constant drizzle in St. Louis. On May 11, he threw an outstanding game against Brooklyn but lost, 1–0. Brooklyn pitcher "Farmer" George Bell pitched the shutout for the Superbas, singled and scored the winning run himself on a ground out in the sixth inning. In his third start on May 16 before a friendly Forbes Field crowd, Leever blanked the Phillies for five innings, then was removed after allowing four runs on four hits in the sixth. Pittsburgh won the game with a five-run eighth.

A new cork center baseball was introduced in the major leagues during the 1910 regular season. The new, firmer baseball with a solid rubber center was more durable than the older ball. Though the A. J. Reach Company downplayed the resiliency of its new ball, it traveled faster and further when batted than the earlier model. However, the livelier baseball did not affect the performance of Deacon Phillippe as he put together his best statistical season since 1905.

Phillippe blanked the Boston Doves, 3 to 0, at Forbes Field on May 17, 1910, the last of his 27 major league shutouts. Boston's only hits were a pair of singles, both in the fifth inning. With two out Fred Beck sent a line single to right and Bill Sweeney followed with a safety to center. The inning ended when Peaches Graham grounded out to third baseman Byrne. No Hubite reached first base the remainder of the game. Phillippe did not walk anyone and struck out only one of the Bostons, the final batter in the contest. His next start, against the Giants, was not a success as he gave up four hits in two innings before departing.

Pittsburgh was in first place from April 28 until May 25, when they lost to the Giants at Forbes Field. Sam Leever relieved Gene Moore in a 3–3 game and retired the first two Giants to bat in the fifth inning. However, Cy Seymour tripled and scored on Al Bridwell's double to end the scoring for the day. Leever was saddled with the loss.

Three days later, Leifield was knocked out of a game against Chicago in the first inning and Phillippe took over the pitching chores for Pittsburgh. He allowed five hits in seven innings and for good measure hit two Cubs batters.

Deacon Phillippe, circa 1910 (Paul Thompson photographer) (Dennis Goldstein Collection).

The 9–0 thrashing at the hands of Chicago sent the Pirates into fourth place, and the losing streak reached six games the next day before they rebounded with a Decoration Day sweep of Cincinnati.

On June 9, Phillippe picked up a win in relief of Nick Maddox after having pitched an inning against the same Boston club the day before. Maddox took a 5–3 lead into the home half of the ninth inning, but quickly got into trouble and Phillippe was summoned into the game with runners on first and second. The Doves' Bud Sharpe quickly picked out a Phillippe pitch and sent it into right field on a line. One runner scored and when Chief Wilson fumbled the bounding ball, center fielder Vin Campbell had to retrieve it. Campbell's throw into the infield sailed high over Phillippe's head and the tying run scored.

Pittsburgh restored its two-run lead in the 11th inning after Phillippe started the rally with a single, but nearly gave it up again in the bottom of the inning. With one out, Bud Sharpe singled to center field and came around to score on Doc Miller's high fly ball that struck the screen near the top of the left field wall, narrowly missing a home run. Miller landed on second base, but the next batter, Dave Shean, was thrown out by second baseman Dots Miller and Phillippe escaped the jam when he induced Fred Beck to foul out to the first baseman. Though he got the win, Phillippe wasn't sharp in the four innings he pitched and allowed three runs.

The Cubs and Pirates played a close and unusual game at Forbes Field on June 24. During the fourth inning, umpire James Johnstone gave Chicago's Jimmy Sheckard a walk on the count of two balls and one strike. He did it because Howard Camnitz was wasting everybody's time by procrastinating between pitches. After that, Camnitz went to pieces. Schulte smashed a two-bagger to left-center field, after which Fred Clarke announced the Pirates were playing the game under protest. The Cubs went on to touch up the Kentucky Rosebud for five runs, the big blow a two-run triple by Artie Hofman.

Deacon Phillippe replaced Camnitz and shut out the Cubs after that, allowing but three hits in his five innings of work. Pittsburgh won the game in the sixth inning on singles by Gibson and Phillippe, Byrne's safe bunt and Wagner's triple down the third base line.

After his team's 6–5 loss, Chicago columnist Ring Lardner wrote, "After the Cubs had put their mark on the game and had rid themselves of Howard Camnitz, Clarke sent in Deacon Phillippe, who was helping win pennants when Noah was a messenger boy. The one or two Chicago bugs in the stand giggled loudly when the Deacon marched to the pulpit ... and he sailed through like a Mathewson instead of a Methuselah. Deacon may be all in, but he keeps the fact well concealed."[7]

A day later, Leever took the home mound against the Cubs and captured a one-sided victory against Ed Reulbach. The Cubs came into town leading the National League pennant race by a wide margin, and the two losses obviously annoyed Lardner when he penned his column, writing, "It was adding insult to injury to start old man Leever against us. Mr. Clarke did it because Reulbach was named to work for Chicago. He figured that nobody could beat

Reulbach when right and almost anybody could beat him when wrong. He was wrong — not Clarke but Reulbach."[8]

In the second inning, Leever hit Harry Steinfeldt with a pitch and Hofman followed with a double. Pittsburgh elected to purposely walk Johnny Kling to load the bases. With two strikes on pitcher Reulbach, Steinfeldt tried to steal home. Leever threw the ball right at the batter's head and "laid him out for a spell." While Reulbach lay prone on the ground, Steinfeldt and Chance ran out to Leever and launched a verbal assault against the veteran pitcher. Meanwhile, the Pirates argued that Leever had thrown home to get the runner and Reulbach's head had interfered with his throw. Umpire Johnstone insisted the run counted and Reulbach was allowed to take first base. Chance argued that Leever should be removed from the game because his wildness led to the hit batsmen. Umpire Moran ordered Leever to throw several balls over the plate to demonstrate his control, then allowed him to continue in the game. However, Chance and Steinfeldt were ejected from the field for using abusive language to the umpires.

Reulbach made it through the bottom of the second without any damage, but blew up in the third. It was Leever's one-out single that set in motion a rally that led to five runs and chased Reulbach to the clubhouse where he could nurse his headache. Chicago didn't score again off Leever until the ninth, but by then it was way too late as Pittsburgh won, 7–2.

Lardner added to his report that "the surprise of the game was Leever's effectiveness. Pittsburgh can't be counted out of the race as long as Sam and Deacon Phillippe refuse to be taken to the home for the aged and infirm."

His win over the first-place Cubs earned Leever another start four days later, but he was pounded by the Cardinals in the 6 to 2 loss. The use of Leever and Phillippe in important situations on consecutive days said a lot about the state of Pittsburgh's pitching staff.

Howard Camnitz had reported to spring training overweight, was not consistent, and flopped to a 12–13 record. Especially disappointing for the Pirates in 1910 was Nick Maddox, the promising rookie of just three years earlier. He won only two games and was sold to Kansas City (American Association) on September 22, less than a year after winning the third game of the 1909 World Series.

Between their first meeting in 1901 and 1910, Phillippe had won only one of eight starting assignments against Christy Mathewson, that one win a 3–2 decision on Sept 20, 1906. But on Bastille Day, July 14, 1910, Phillippe came out on top in a 4 to 3 decision against Mathewson and won again in another relief role against the great Mathewson two days later.[9]

Phillippe's win over Mathewson on the 14th was an unlikely scenario.

The Giants hurler was vintage Mathewson for eight innings, only two hits allowed going into the ninth inning. After Leifield was pinch-hit for in the eighth, Phillippe pitched a perfect top of the ninth, striking out two of the three batters he faced. The Pirates trailed, 3 to 0, when they came up for their final swings in the bottom of the inning.

Clarke drew a walk to open the Buccaneers' ninth, but Wagner pushed a potential double play grounder to Art Fletcher. However, the young shortstop fumbled the ball and both runners were safe. The next batter was out attempting to beat out a bunt, but successive singles by Jack Flynn and Owen Wilson scored Clarke and Wagner. Flynn was thrown out at the plate on Gibson's grounder for the second out. After Mathewson walked Paddy O'Connor, batting for Phillippe, Bobby Byrne also drew a free pass, forcing Wilson in from third with the tying run. Mathewson threw two balls to Leach and McGraw signaled for Ames, but the relief pitcher completed the walk two pitches later and the 12,000 Pittsburgh fans went delirious as Gibson jogged down and touched the plate with the winning run.

Neither Maddox nor Leever was effective the next day, but Bugs Raymond wasn't sharp either in the early going and by the ninth the score was knotted at 7–7. The Pirates loaded the bases with no one out on a single by pitcher Kirby White, an error by Raymond on Byrne's bunt, and a bunt base hit by Leach. For the second straight day, Pittsburgh beat the Giants on a bases-loaded, ninth-inning walk after Raymond threw four wide ones to Clarke.

Before almost 13,000 Forbes Field fans on July 16, Phillippe pitched the Pirates to their fourth straight victory over the Giants. Babe Adams started, but was down 3–0 when Phillippe was summoned in the third inning. After he took the mound the Giants managed only five baserunners over the final seven innings. "The Deacon was a hot favorite with the noisy crowd and the roars of approval must have done the old fellow's heart good," noted the *Gazette-Times*.[10]

Giants pitcher Doc Crandall ran into trouble in the seventh after Owen Wilson tripled home a run to cut New York's lead to 3–2 with one out. John McGraw called on Christy Mathewson to preserve the lead but George Gibson drove one of his pitches to deep center field. The speedy Wilson tagged up and scored easily. In the top of the eighth, the Pirates scored three runs after two were out and the bases empty. Deacon Phillippe picked up the 6 to 3 victory over the Giants' ace. The Giants had come to Pittsburgh a game and a half behind the first-place Cubs but left town only a game ahead of the Pirates for second place.

On July 22, Phillippe entered the pitcher's box before 2,578 home fans and was the benefactor in a 14–1 rout of the Superbas. He allowed but six hits, one base on balls, and Brooklyn only managed to score their one run on misplays by Bill McKechnie and Chief Wilson. The most dramatic event of the day was the 38-year-old pitcher circling the bases for an inside-the-park home run.

Phillippe's four-bagger was especially special because the bases were loaded. After retiring the Buccaneers in order in the first inning, Brooklyn's Fred "Speedy" Miller ran into trouble in the second. With a run in, Miller walked McKechnie to bring Phillippe to bat with the bases fully stocked. Phillippe watched two bad ones from the left-hander miss the plate. With the pressure clearly on the pitcher, Miller made the next one too good, for Phillippe was still no slouch as a batter. He made solid contact and rifled a sizzler to the opposite field between Jake Daubert and the first base bag. Right fielder Jack Dalton's stab at the sphere came up empty and he had to pursue the bouncing ball all the way to the 25-cent bleachers while the three base runners scored.

As Phillippe approached third base, "the merciless coacher waved him home," reported the *Gazette-Times*, "and Deacon never ran as hard in his life as he did between third and home. He crossed the plate with plenty to spare and went to the bench heaving like an old chap full of health and vigor. He ran to the bench and paid scant attention to the cheers that his singular feat provolked."[11]

The run around the bases did not affect Phillippe's performance on the mound and he wasn't done at the bat for the day either. He added a sacrifice and a surprise bunt down the third base line that he beat out for a hit. It would be 55 years before another major league pitcher would hit a bases-loaded, inside-the-park homer when Mel Stottlemyre of the Yankees accomplished the feat.

Six days later, Clarke sent Phillippe to the firing line again, this time on a brutally hot day in Cincinnati. Clarke decided to remove him despite a two-run lead in the sixth inning and summoned Adams, who had been exercising behind the stands. However, Adams had become ill from the heat and was under the care of the trainer. So it had to be Camnitz who finished the 8 to 4 victory for Phillippe.

Phillippe's success during the summer of 1910 led *The Sporting News* to report, "Manager Clarke is authority for the statement that 'Deacon' Phillippe is one of the best pitchers on his staff, and the Deacon's work bears out the claim. Phil is a veteran but he claims that his good right arm is as strong as ever."[12]

In a game at Forbes Field against Brooklyn in late August, Phillippe picked up one of his seven wins in relief. With the score tied at 3–3 in the bottom of the ninth inning, Lefty Leifield was pulled for a pinch-hitter. When the

Pirates failed to score, Phillippe and George Bell, who went the distance for the Superbas, dueled without further scoring through the top of the 13th inning. Phillippe made an out to open the home 13th, but Bobby Byrne stretched an apparent single to left field into a double. The fleet third baseman made third on a steal as Leach swung at a third strike to protect the runner. Clarke and Wagner were given bases on balls to load the sacks and bring up to bat rookie first baseman Jack Flynn. As Flynn took his place in the batter's box, Byrne suddenly made a dash for home and "scored the winning run on a steal that took away the breath of the spectators," who immediately produced "the fiercest yells heard since the days of the Indians."[13]

Sam Leever's final start in a Pirates uniform came on September 7, 1910, in the second game of a doubleheader against the St. Louis Cardinals. Pittsburgh led 11–0 after the third inning and Leever toyed with the Cardinals batters the rest of the way with his mesmerizing array of benders and twisters. The Bucs triumphed, 11 to 3.

Leever's final victory as a Pirate came on September 20 in the second game of a doubleheader in Boston. When starting pitcher Leifield proved ineffective, Leever relieved him after only two innings, trailing 3–0. He allowed the opposition a fourth run in the third inning, but shut out the Beaneaters thereafter and the Pirates won it with a three-run ninth inning.

Leever started only eight games during 1910 and finished with a record of 6–5. Though he didn't know it at the time, his final appearance on the mound for the Pirates came in the second game of a doubleheader in Brooklyn on September 26, 1910. Leever pitched the bottom of the eighth inning in Pittsburgh's 4 to 1 loss and retired the side in order.

In 1910 Phillippe's tosses were as effective as before his arm injuries; he won 14 games out of 16 decisions and he held the lead in four more. His 2.29 earned run average was well below the Pittsburgh staff's earned run average (2.83) and the league average of 3.02. Phillippe walked nine batters in 121 innings, but his strikeouts declined to only one every six innings pitched.

Samuel Leever, circa 1910 (Dennis Goldstein Collection).

By this time, Phillippe and Belle had tired of country life and decided to return to the city full-time. That November, he sold his 109-acre farm in Butler County, Pa., for $13,000 (a $3,800 profit on his original purchase price two years earlier)[14] and bought a splendid home in Bellevue for $7,500. Considering Phillippe's properties in Western Pennsylvania, a ranch in Redfield, South Dakota, and his block of Philadelphia Traction Company stock, *Sporting Life* speculated that Deacon's worth was around $40,000.[15]

One day in early January, 1911, just after Phillippe had returned from a hunting excursion in Indiana, he decided to call on Barney Dreyfuss and wish him a happy New Year. After pleasantries were exchanged, Dreyfuss asked the veteran, "How would you like to sign a contract while you're here?" "One time suits me as well as another," answered Phillippe.

Phillippe reached for the blank form that was readily made available and affixed his name to it. Dreyfuss added the salary amount to the document that apparently pleased Deacon from the smile as he read it.[16]

Although Deacon Phillippe signed his 13th contract with Barney Dreyfuss well before spring training, Sam Leever did not seem concerned about the upcoming baseball season. That January, Leever won the high honors at the New Year's Day shoot of the Hyde Park Gun Club of Cincinnati, scoring 45 out of 50, and the next day he won the high gun for the leading merchandise prize at the National Cash Register Gun Club grounds at Dayton, Ohio.[17]

Thirty-nine-year-old Sam Leever was disappointed with the salary terms offered by the Pirates and he was a no-show at training camp. Barney Dreyfuss offered to sell Leever to a minor league team and give him a share of the purchase price, but that proposal only annoyed Leever more.

Leever attended the Pirates' opening game of the National League season at Cincinnati on April 12. Ironically, that day was Jesse Tannehill's final appearance in a major league game. Pitching in relief for the Reds, he was pounded for seven runs in just over four innings in his team's embarrassing 14 to 0 loss to Babe Adams. After the game, Jesse asked Reds manager Clark Griffith for his release, and the request was granted.

Following the Pirates' victory, Sam Leever had a conference with Fred Clarke. The Pirates' manager gave the veteran pitcher a salary offer for the 1911 season, but Leever turned it down flat.[18]

It was written that Leever and Dreyfuss parted bitterly, because Leever apparently was insulted by the salary offered and the owner's offer of a "gift" from part of any sale to a minor league club. Leever told "Barney to cut the bunk" and a day later the veteran of 12 campaigns with the Pittsburgh National League Club was unconditionally released—April 27, 1911.[19]

Veteran Pittsburgh baseball scribe A. R. Cratty's take was somewhat different from the official response by Dreyfuss: "There is no doubt that the Pittsburgh management made up its mind last summer to wield the snickersnee on Leever.... With the awakening of spring it was learned that no contract had been mailed to Samuel. Later on a compact was sent his way, but with no response. No one knows the exact amount of salary-slicing, but it must have been a big one, something like $1,500. Pretty soon fans, which had been skeptical, began to believe the Pittsburgh club meant to cast the Ohio man adrift."[20]

During the meetings between the National Commission and the players' union in January, 1914, Barney Dreyfuss reflected on Leever's exit from the Pittsburgh club. "Old Sam Leever had been with me so long I wanted to see him located nicely. I told him I could get $1,000 for his release from Minneapolis and a contract for $450 a month. I made it clear that the Pittsburgh club didn't want a cent of the release money, that he could have it all. Did Sam accept? He said he preferred to conduct his own business, and he did. We gave him his outright release and Minneapolis saved the $1,000 release money the club was willing to give, and got Sam for $350 a month!"[21]

While Deacon Phillippe sat idle on the Pirates' bench in 1911, Leever latched on with the Minneapolis Millers, a top minor league club. On May 19, Manager Joe Cantillon announced that Leever had signed to pitch for the American Association club, and the veteran pitcher joined the team in Louisville on May 27. Also with the Millers that season was Leever's old Pittsburgh teammate, Rube Waddell, who drank himself out of the major leagues two years earlier. For Leever, Waddell was not the only familiar face. Otis Clymer, an outfielder with the Pirates from 1905–07, batted leadoff and patrolled center field for the Millers. Jimmy Williams, the Pirates' star third baseman of 1899–1900, also played for Minneapolis, as did Warren Gill, who played 25 games at first base for Pittsburgh in 1908.

The Millers played their home games at Nicollet Park at 31st Street and Nicollet Avenue, the grounds where Deacon Phillippe made his professional debut in 1897. Leever made his first start for the Millers on June 6 against Kansas City and picked up a complete-game, 10 to 5 victory. Nine days later, he pitched much better in a victory over Indianapolis. A report of the game in the *Indianapolis Star* gave the veteran a good deal of credit. "Samuel Leever, about the oldest one of Cantillon's bunch of baseball relics, probably never used his curve ball pitching better than he did today. He held the Indians to eight hits and three runs and it is reasonable to assume that they would not have had a pair of these but for Cravath's bad play on Getz's speeding hit in the second.... Eleven putouts on fly balls show the manner of game the honorable

Leever threw. The Indians were all but helpless before that curve ball and a couple of their eight hits were of the variety made famous in the Texas League."[22]

The Indians would get their revenge a week later in Indianapolis. *The Star* reported that "The great old Pittsburgh star had his shotgun oiled and his grips packed ready to take the train for Columbus to enter the Grand American Handicap as soon as he bagged the opening game for the champions."

Leever was in command for seven innings. The Indians tied the score in the eighth inning and put runners on first and third with one out in the ninth. It was then that Jimmy Williams, subbing as manager in the absence of Joe Cantillon, decided to pull Leever for a raw southpaw named Smith to pitch to Billy Hallman, a teammate of Leever's with the Pirates in 1906 and 1907. Hallman looked at only one pitch from the lefty before he hammered a fastball off the pitcher's foot and the winning run trotted home.[23]

Leever did have greater success coming into the game as a substitute pitcher than as a starter. He earned a victory in relief on July 11 after he replaced Rube Waddell in the third inning, trailing 5–4 to Milwaukee. Leever allowed only one hit in the remaining six innings and Minneapolis rallied to win, 8 to 6.

Thereafter, Leever rarely pitched well, even when he won. After he had to be relieved in his 16 to 7 win against Milwaukee on July 16, he was regulated to the bullpen. When he did draw a rare start on August 21, H. G. Copeland of *The Indianapolis Star* described Leever as "easy picking" for the Indians and by the third inning he was a "skinned rabbit." The reporter insisted that Leever was lucky the score against him was not worse than 7 to 1.[24]

In a game in Milwaukee on September 13, the Minneapolis starting pitcher, Pug Cavet, was wild in the first inning and was removed in favor of Leever at the start of the second. In perhaps his best effort of the season, Leever scattered six hits, and pitched the Millers a 4 to 1 victory.

Though Leever finished the 1911 season with a 7–4 record for the American Association champions, he allowed 139 hits and 73 runs in only 125 innings pitched. Waddell won 20 and lost 17, but the leading winner on the club was the former American Leaguer, Roy Patterson at 24–10. The popular Otis Clymer batted .342, but that was only third-best on the Millers. Outfielder Gavvy Cravath hit .363 with 29 home runs, a hefty total for that time.

During his 1911 season with the Pirates, 39-year-old Deacon Phillippe appeared in only three games, all in relief. Though seldom used in games, Deacon functioned as an instructor for the club's young pitchers. The last time he pitched in a National League game was in the opener of a doubleheader in Cincinnati on August 13, 1911. He gave up one run in the one inning he pitched in relief of Howie Camnitz.

When the Pirates prepared to leave for a series in Brooklyn three days later, Phillippe was sent on a scouting assignment. His place on the active roster was taken by Marty O'Toole, who had just come to the Pirates from St. Paul after Dreyfuss paid a record purchase price of $22,500 for the left-handed spitballer.

A few days later A. R. Cratty noted in *Sporting Life* that "Deacon Phil, with wide-brimmed Panama hat on head and famous dudeen in his mouth, was encountered on Liberty Avenue. Just back from a scout, the old man was hurrying home. Phillippe is being repaid for some of the loyalty shown Colonel Dreyfuss."[25]

During the game at Brooklyn's Washington Park on August 16, Honus Wagner badly sprained his right ankle while running the bases. When Wagner returned home by rail, his arrival at Union Station resembled that of a returning wounded war hero. All the newspapers had reporters there and numerous photographs were taken before Wagner's entourage departed for Carnegie.

Phillippe met Wagner at the station and A. R. Cratty reported that Phillippe was commissioned to stay with Wagner at his home to assist the fallen star with any of his needs. "Phil had every arrangement for the careful travel of his old pal. Not a cog slipped. Phil's face, with broad-brimmed hat covering that dome of sound reasoning, may be seen in all snap shots, directing matters at station and home."[26]

Oddly enough, Phillippe's job as nursemaid was the last position he held with the Pirates. Upon hearing in September, 1911, that he was not on the Pirates' reserved list for the next season, he appeared unconcerned as he filled his bullhead pipe with tobacco. "I did not know my name had been left off the reserve list, but a little thing like that is not worrying me in the least. I am still on the Pittsburgh club payroll and the high cost of living is giving me no concern."[27]

Phillippe returned to his old pastimes at season's end. "Deacon Phil and Jim Orris took another stroll for grouse," reported *Sporting Life*. "The men averaged 30 miles a day in foot work. Sounds strong but then they hunted from dawn until far into the gloaming, beating brush on all sides in their route. Game bag this trip, twenty-four grouse."[28]

Phillippe's days as a major league pitcher were at an end. He was retired with a record of 189 major league victories and 109 losses for a winning percentage of .634. Phillippe completed 242 of his 288 starts and allowed only 1.25 bases on ball per nine innings pitched over his career—the best ratio among twentieth century pitchers (ninth place on the all-time list).

A few months earlier, Secretary Locke had paid tribute to Phillippe in response to a sportswriter's question. "You cannot say too much about Phillippe's virtues. Here is a ball player who never asked for a raise in salary, never tried to hold up the club, promptly signed his contracts and turned them in with a smile, never growled on being pitched out of his turn, never asked for advance money, never sought spending money on the road, was loyal to the core in war hours, never gave his manager worry as to his whereabouts. Trusted implicitly by all he has world's goods far beyond the limit of scores of base ball men who have drawn larger salaries."[29]

The departure of Leever and Phillippe spelled the end of an era for the Pirates. When Tommy Leach was traded to the Cubs in June, 1912, only manager Fred Clarke and Honus Wagner were left from the great team that won three straight pennants and played in the first World Series.

Before the 1916 season, Fred Clarke resigned as the Pirates manager after second division finishes in consecutive years. Apparently, the verdict was sealed when Barney Dreyfuss reportedly told him that a second division manager couldn't expect a first division manager's pay.

Forty-three-year-old Honus Wagner struggled through his final season in 1917 as a first baseman, batted only .265, then retired. Wagner returned to the Pirates as a coach in 1933, partly out of charity for an aging superstar who was down on his luck. In 1936, Wagner was elected a charter member of the National Baseball Hall of Fame, which was dedicated June 12, 1939, in Cooperstown, New York. Fred Clarke joined him in the Hall upon his election in 1945.

George "Moon" Gibson, who caught 1,113 games for the Pirates from 1905 through 1916, was named the Pirates' manager by Dreyfuss in 1920. Gibson's 1921 team blew a seven-and-a-half-game lead in the final five weeks of the season and lost the pennant to the Giants of

Barney Dreyfuss, president, Pittsburgh Pirates (1900–1932) (National Baseball Hall of Fame Library, Cooperstown, New York).

John McGraw. Gibson quit in mid–1922. He was rehired by Dreyfuss' son-in-law ten years later, guided the Pirates to second-place finishes in 1932 and 1933, then was fired after a slow start in 1934, reportedly because the former catcher could not maintain discipline.

The Pirates returned to the top of the National League in 1925 and also won the World Series with Washington. Only two players remained from the Pittsburgh club that Leever and Phillippe left 15 years earlier. Babe Adams, the hero of the 1909 Series, was nearing the end of a 16-year career which garnered him 194 pitching victories, all with the Pirates. Center fielder Maximilian Caranarius, better known as Max Carey, got three hits in two games for the 1910 Buccaneers, then embarked on a career destined to land him in baseball's Hall of Fame.

On February 19, 1931, Barney Dreyfuss' only son, Sammy, died of pneumonia, four days before his father's birthday. The grief-stricken Pirates owner asked his son-in-law, Bill Benswanger, to assist him in running the club. Benswanger, an insurance man, took over the presidency of the club when Barney, also a victim of pneumonia, died less than a year later. Though Benswanger ran the club, Dreyfuss' widow became chairman of the board. The Dreyfuss heirs sold the Pirates to an investment group that included Bing Crosby and John W. Galbreath in August, 1946. Bernhard "Barney" was inducted into the National Baseball Hall of Fame in 2008.

♦ TWELVE ♦

With the Outlaws

During the winter of 1912, a group of investors from eight eastern cities formed a professional league that would employ players unaffiliated with clubs in Organized Baseball. The new United States League (U.S.L.) would have franchises in Pittsburgh, Chicago, Cincinnati, Cleveland, New York, Reading, Pa., Richmond, Va., and Washington. Without recognition by the National Association of Professional Baseball Leagues that governed the minor leagues, the newcomers would be considered "outlaws."

Organizers of a U.S.L. club in Pittsburgh met on January 31 to form the Pittsburgh Park Athletic Association. The officers of the new club were Marshall Henderson, president; William T. McCullough, secretary; and A. J. Henderson, vice-president.[1] The novice baseball executives contacted Charles "Deacon" Phillippe about managing their team, but the savvy ex-baseball player put off a decision until he was sure the new league would get off the ground.[2]

According to Secretary McCullough, the team would most likely play games at Exposition Park, vacant since the Pirates abandoned it for Forbes Field in 1909. However, old Expo Park was in disrepair and the famous grandstand had been razed. The fences and bleachers were standing, but they were not in the finest of fettle due to water damage from the river's overflow. However, the bleachers had a capacity of close to 8,500 and were repairable at a moderate expense.

On March 1, the backers of the local U.S.L. club received a charter from the Common Pleas Court for a corporation titled the Pittsburgh Athletic Park Association, with $10,000 of capital stock of which Messrs. Henderson and McCullough each owned over 540 shares at $50 apiece. Although the Pittsburgh National League Club officially retained the lease on Exposition Park until its agreement expired on April 1, 1912, the corporation was able to secure use of the grounds in early March. The Association was also granted permission by city officials to erect a wooden grandstand that would seat 2,800 persons, and it could be completed within 28 days after the contractors began work.³

Alfred R. Cratty commented on the return of baseball to Exposition Park. He pointed out that a man could walk from downtown to Expo Park in about 12 minutes and wrote, "It's more than likely that the U. S. League will draw back Allegheny people who gave up game going when the Corsairs moved to old Pittsburgh and four miles away from their old lair. These folks prior to 1909 watched ball games at Expo Field and then hurried to the railroad stations four squares away, catching trains for early dinners."⁴

In his column a week later, Cratty added, "In Pirate days the near presence of the ball park was splendid revenue to hotel men. Several licensed houses within a stone throw of Expo field surrendered their licenses when the Corsairs pulled up stakes for Forbes Field. That neighborhood now is but a wreck of its former self, activity being reduced to the minimum. If the new league is to be a go, property owners surrounding the park will be a joyous set."⁵

The U.S.L. would employ several managers with major league playing experience: George Browne, once a member of the New York Giants, was named manager of the Washington club; Jack O'Connor, the former Pirates catcher and manager of the St. Louis Browns in 1910, was hired by Cleveland; longtime Cubs third baseman Harry Steinfeldt would captain in Cincinnati; and Deacon Phillippe decided to cast his lot with the Pittsburgh franchise.

Phillippe had developed strong ties in Pittsburgh by the end of his 12-year career on the diamond there. He owned a home in Bellevue, a Pittsburgh suburb, and it did not hurt that the recently retired ball player was still very popular in the city. On March 2, 1912, Phillippe signed a contract to manage the Pittsburgh United States League team at a salary said to be $3,500, which was placed in a local bank account to Phillippe's credit.⁶

Sporting Life noted in its March 23, 1912, issue that manager Phillippe had established an office in the Columbia Bank Building and "Deacon Phil has a stenographer at his elbow and his correspondence runs into a score of communications every day."⁷

When the Pittsburgh U.S.L. team assembled its players for spring training at Newport News, Virginia, they were for the most part a gang of unknowns other than manager Phillippe and his old pinochle partner, Claude Ritchey, who was named team captain. Ritchey had been the second baseman at Louisville in Phillippe's very first major league game in April, 1899. Ritchey played his final games in the major leagues with the Boston Nationals in 1909 and had been retired from Organized Baseball since his release by Louisville only two weeks into the American Association's 1910 season.

The United States League recruited a handful of ex-major league players, mostly pitchers. The Chicago club had the well known spitballer but alcoholic "Bugs" Raymond, and manager/pitcher Burt Keeley spent 1908 and part of the next season with Washington. The Washington U.S.L. entry signed Frank Owen, who won 79 games while in the American League, and Big Jeff Pfeffer, a six-year National League veteran who last pitched in the majors with the Boston Rustlers in 1911.

It is questionable whether Deacon Phillippe had the intensity to be a successful manager. When the new U.S.L. Pittsburgh team returned to the Smoky City that April, they put on a practice game at Exposition Park for about 500 curious onlookers. Phillippe took the mound for four innings despite his bad back. He rarely attempted to throw a fast ball and mostly used his slow outcurve that was quite successful against the minor leaguers.

Phillippe was pitching for the Yanigans (substitutes) in the seventh inning when the "regulars" landed runners on first and second with two out. The next batter drove one of Phillippe's slow ones over left fielder Red Blackstone's head. After a long run and just as he was about to spear the ball, Blackstone slipped in the mud and fell flat on his face. By the time the ball was recovered the two baserunners had scored. After firing the ball back to the infield, an annoyed Blackstone yelled at Phillippe, "What's the matter with you in there — been pitching in a bush league? Why did you put it over for that fellow for when you had two strikes on him — think I am out here to run my young legs off?"

Phillippe collapsed in laughter and when he went to the bench was holding his side. "I have, during my experience in baseball, received some pretty fair call downs, but that was the limit. At that the young man was right — I had no business putting the ball right over the plate when I had two strikes on the batsman."[8] It would be incomprehensible to imagine that Fred Clarke, Frank Chance or John McGraw would absorb such a public rebuke.

The U.S.L. Pittsburgh club, dubbed the "Filipinos" for their manager, opened the season in Cleveland with an 11 to 7 victory. Pittsburgh won three of their first five games on the road before the Filipinos played their home opener. Manager Phillippe announced in advance that he would pitch against the Cleveland Buckeyes in the club's first game at renovated Exposition Park on May 8, 1912.

On the day of the opener, players and officials of the two U.S.L. teams were en route to the ball park from the Colonial Annex Hotel in automobiles and proceeded by a band when their procession was subjected to a torrential downpour. After a period of wind, rain and lightning, the clouds parted and the sun emerged just as the parade arrived at the Exposition Park shortly after three o'clock. Phillippe and umpire Louis Fyfe held a conference and, despite the muddy condition of the field, it was decided to proceed with the game. The flag flying on the Diamond Bank Building notified the public that the game would be played as scheduled.

Despite the rainstorm, a crowd estimated at 7,500 gathered at the stadium to welcome baseball back to downtown Pittsburgh and cheer the return of a city baseball icon, Deacon Phillippe. Though not yet completed, the grandstand was packed and the bleachers were filled for the most part. Since there would be no game at Forbes Field that day, National League umpire Klem, his wife and fellow umpire Garnet Brush attended the U.S.L. game. A large box of American beauty roses from members of the Pittsburgh Pirates was presented to Phillippe and the crowd gave the presentation a grand round of applause.

Deacon Phillippe, manager, Pittsburgh club, United States League (Chicago History Museum, SDN-009766; photograph by *Chicago Daily News*).

The Filipinos made two early runs and held the lead until the ninth inning when Cincinnati tied the score on a lead-off triple and a one-out sacrifice fly. Phillippe pitched the entire game, and the contest was decided in the 11th inning on a bad call by the umpire and a trio of errors. The first Buckeye to bat in the 11th reached base when Phillippe's shortstop messed up a ground ball because of the mud. The next batter attempted to sacrifice and the Pittsburgh catcher, Goes, picked up the ball just as it rolled into foul territory. He tossed it over the first baseman's head to allow the runners to advance to second and third. According to the *Pittsburgh Dispatch*, the ball should have been dead when Goes picked it up in foul territory, but umpire Fyfe ruled it was fair. When the Filipinos' second baseman made yet another error on another grounder, the runner from third scored the lead run and it held up in the 3 to 2 Cincinnati victory.[9]

Phillippe would have better luck ten days later. On May 18, he took the mound with his club leading Chicago, 8–4, in the seventh inning and "made the locals eat out of his hand, eight of the nine men facing him grounding out on infield wallops."[10]

Poor organization, bad spring weather and poor attendance, primarily in New York, plagued the United States League's first and only season. The Cincinnati club postponed its game against Cleveland on May 21 because of dismal attendance for home games, and a day later the Forest City Ball and Amusement Company surrendered the Cleveland franchise to the league. The same day, members of the Washington club issued an ultimatum that they would not play in any more games unless they were paid what was owed them.

"All that we have received for our services during the present season is $20 apiece," declared the veteran pitchers Owen and Pfeffer, "and unless (owner) Mockabee comes across with the full amount the players will leave for their homes."[11]

Although Pittsburgh played the opener of a three-game series in New York before only 200 patrons on May 23, Phillippe's team had drawn reasonably well for games at Exposition Park. However, the club made a significant cost-cutting move in early May. It was obvious early in the season that Claude Ritchey was washed up and it wasn't worth the expense to keep him as an occasional back-up infielder, so he was released.[12] A few days later, Chicago cut Bugs Raymond.

After winning only two of its first 17 games, the New York club, which played its games at a semi-pro park called the Bronx Oval, became the first U.S.L. club to fold, dropping out when it could not provide enough players to field a team for a game on May 27.

On May 30, three doubleheader sweeps — Chicago over the Richmond Rebels, Cincinnati over Reading, and Pittsburgh over Cleveland — ended the United States League's one abbreviated season. A day later, the league collapsed. The problem wasn't with Pittsburgh. The Filipinos drew an announced crowd of 5,000 to Exposition Park for their Memorial Day doubleheader.

On June 1, league president William Wittman's own club in Reading filed for bankruptcy. Pittsburgh's Marshall Henderson assumed the league's presidency and the remaining four clubs, Pittsburgh, Chicago, Richmond and Cincinnati, elected to play an informal schedule as long as they could hold out. Only two days later, the Cincinnati Buckeyes became the next club to fail. On June 3 their game with Chicago was cancelled, and a day later the bank account of owner John J. Ryan was garnished for $1,200 after 14 players filed separate suits for a month's salary.

Deacon Phillippe took the mound against Chicago at Exposition Park on June 8 and pitched a complete game, but lost 7 to 5. His assortment of breaking pitches did not fool the young "Uncle Sams," who reached him for 14 hits. Pittsburgh played its last league game on Sunday, June 22, in Chicago, losing to the Uncle Sams, 9 to 4.

In order to pick up an additional paycheck, the Filipinos played an exhibition game in Chicago on June 24 and lost, 9–1, to Rube Foster's powerful African-American baseball club, the American Giants. The minor leaguers were no match for an American Giants' line-up that included some of the best baseball players of the era, Pete Hill, Bruce Petway, Bill Monroe, and manager Rube Foster himself, who pitched and held the homeless Filipinos to only four hits. Though the papers had advertised Phillippe vs. Foster, Phillippe did not play.

Manager Deacon Phillippe's Pittsburgh club of the United States League did fairly well in 1912. When the league ceased operation in June, the "Filipinos" were in first place with 19 victories. The team's success convinced its owners, principally William Tice McCullough, that Pittsburgh could be a two-baseball-team town.

Stuck with the lease on Exposition Field, the ex–U.S.L. owners were not about to give up on professional baseball just yet and worked to revive the outlaw league for 1913. "Expo Field, according to rumor, isn't idle this winter," reported *Sporting Life* that November. "A firm made up of some Pittsburghers who were in the base ball movement have established a factory for the manufacture of butter making machines. Deacon Phillippe is said to be special traveling agent of the concern and is meeting with success. A soccer base ball league also uses Expo field."[13]

In January, 1913, 41-year-old Charles Phillippe went to work on the night shift at Tarentum Steel Works. Declaring that he was "through with baseball" and it killed him to just loaf, Phillippe said he was going to learn the steel business. A report in *The Philadelphia Enquirer* noted that "His years as big league pitcher, combined with his thrifty ways, made him the possessor of a comfortable fortune. He has a beautiful home in Bellevue and a daughter in high school. But he says he wants to qualify to go before a steel investigation committee and give expert testimony some day."[14]

Reported *Sporting Life* in its February 1, 1913, issue, "Phillippi is not going to grind away his life as a common laborer, for he has saved ample cash to be comfortable in his remaining days. The Deacon aspires to thoroughly learn the steel business, so that he can go into the trade as a part owner of a furnace with some local men."[15] His employment options were about to widen.

That same month, John T. Powers, former head of the Wisconsin-Illinois League, announced the formation of a new independent baseball league in the Midwest that would be called the Federal League. Again Marshall Henderson and W. T. McCullough became principle backers of the Pittsburgh club in an outlaw league.

Better organized and financed than the United States League, the Federal League planned to begin play in 1913, with clubs in Pittsburgh, Chicago,

Cleveland, Indianapolis, St. Louis, and Covington, Kentucky. In the beginning, no attempt was made to sign established major league players, and the Federal Leaguers chose to recruit players from the ranks of free agents, semi-pros and amateurs. The league opted for a 120-game schedule, the season to begin on May 6 and end September 14. Phillippe would again manage in Pittsburgh and his old foe Cy Young signed on to pilot the Cleveland club.

Covington's chances for success seemed remote when it replaced Cincinnati for a Federal League franchise in March of 1913. A plan to put the team across the Ohio River at Cincinnati's Hippodrome Park fell through so the club reverted back to Covington, where businessmen William Reidlin, president of the Bavarian Brewery, and R. C. Stewart, president of Stewart Iron Works, raised $12,500 in capital stock for a park. With financing in place for a ballpark, Covington was officially granted a Federal League franchise.

With the start of the baseball season less than a month away, the Covington backers selected part of Riverbreeze Park for a new ball yard. On April 16 ground was broken at 2nd and Scott streets and bleachers were built to hold 4200 patrons. The site restricted the distance from home plate to 267 feet to the centerfield wall, 194 feet down the right field line and 218 feet in left. The business manager of the Covington Club was John A. Spinney, who knew Samuel Leever well from the 1890s when the sporting goods store owner arranged schedules for the numerous amateur and semi-pro leagues in the Cincinnati area. On April 17 the Blue Sox named Sam Leever the Covington Club's manager.

Leever had been out of baseball since the end of the 1911 Minneapolis Millers season. Millers manager Joe Cantillon owned a 30-acre farm outside Hickman, Kentucky, and adjacent to the property were lakes and woods full of wild game. He built several houses on the property and often invited players and baseball people to his place. While on a hunting trip to Hickman with Cantillon after the 1911 baseball season, Leever was thrown from a horse and badly injured his knee. When his knee was still ailing the following January, Leever wrote the Cantillons from Goshen that he would not be able to join the Millers for the upcoming season. Since he was assured Leever would not be able to start the season, Joe Cantillon gave the 40-year-old pitcher his unconditional release on January 27, 1912.[16]

Leever was well regarded in the Cincinnati area, and an important factor in his decision to take the job in Covington was its proximity to his home town. Since Leever would be expected to perform occasionally on the mound, he assured the owners his pitching arm was as good as it was ten years earlier. When he signed his contract in the clubroom of the Industrial League Club, it contained a clause that the manager would forfeit part of his salary if the team did not land in first or second place. Business manager Spinney immediately announced an open tryout before manager Leever at Crowe's ballpark, the last stop on the Elberton streetcar line in Price Hill.[17]

The first game played between Federal League teams took place May 3, 1913, between Cy Young's Cleveland club and Leever's Blue Sox at Luna Park in Cleveland. The game ended in a ten-inning tie.

On Opening Day in Covington six days later, thousands of people lined up to see the game against St. Louis. The headline in the local newspaper read "Covington Goes Crazy, Baseball Crazy." A parade commenced at Scott and 12th Street and made its way to the Riverbreeze Park where the bands played while bombs containing tiny American flags burst overhead.[18] Manager Leever posed for a rather uncomfortable looking photograph with St. Louis manager Jack O'Connor, the same O'Connor who had served as an American League agent in raids on the Pirates in 1902 while still employed by Barney Dreyfuss.

The crowd was too big for all the fans to sit in the stands so they lined up all the way around the edge of the playing field. Balls hit into the spectators became ground-rule singles. Covington pitcher Walter Justus shut out St. Louis, 4 to 0.

As it had the year before, Exposition Park served as the home field to a team from a new league in 1913. The opening day game was threatened when Expo Park flooded following a heavy rainfall on March 31. However, the club had the park in shape for the first home game on May 6 and the event was preceded by a downtown parade, a tradition from earlier years that had since been discarded by major league clubs. Along the route to the ball park cries of "Go to it, Phil," "Good luck, Phil" and similar shouts of adulation came from the thousands that greeted the popular manager. A big crowd announced at 7,225 assembled in Exposition Park, but Indianapolis ruined the festivities with a 9 to 5 win over Phillippe's club, again known as the "Filipinos."[19]

On May 14, a day after he jumped to the Pittsburgh Federals, left-handed pitcher Roy Ashenfelder took the mound at Exposition Park before about 1,400 bugs for the game against the St. Louis Terriers. Ashenfleder had displayed a lack of control of his pitches at Indianapolis of the American Association so the Indians farmed him out to Terre Haute. However, he quarreled with his manager there and jumped to the Pittsburgh Federal League club.[20]

Ashenfelder not only won the game against St. Louis, 5–0, he came within one scratch hit of pitching a no-hitter. That hit was made by the Terriers' first batter of the game and witnesses said that either second baseman Menosky or first baseman Eddie Sabrie could have fielded the roller.[21] Ashenfelder won his first three games for Pittsburgh in grand fashion. Two of his victories came against the first-place Keeleys of Chicago.

The Federal League only had to wait two more days for its first no-hitter when a St. Louis pitcher named Chief Reymer used a baffling slow ball to no-hit the Filipinos — sort of. Actually, Pittsburgh had a hit on the scorebook for a few minutes. In the fourth inning, Henry Warren of the Filipinos hit a clean single to center field. Immediately after the next batter flied out, St. Louis manager O'Connor rushed out and informed umpire Franklin that the Pittsburgh third baseman had batted out of turn. Upon checking Phillippe's official lineup card, it was discovered that Warren had indeed batted out of order and he was promptly called out.[22]

Despite the seven walks issued by starting pitcher Ashenfelder, the Filipinos staggered to a 5 to 3 victory over St. Louis later that month thanks to a home run and a double by second baseman Mike Menosky, an 18-year-old western Pennsylvania native. When the Pittsburgh pitcher was called out on strikes in the sixth inning, he threatened to bean umpire Franklin with his bat, but he was not ejected.

The Pittsburgh Gazette Times explained, "Umpire Franklin lost his eyesight during the contest and could not see whether the ball was over the pan or not and for kicking so hard on some of his decisions, Manager Phillippe, Pitcher Bridges, and Manager O'Connor of the St. Louis team were banished from the grounds."[23]

Phillippe tried to pull his club out of the doldrums by taking the mound himself in a game on May 31, but he got no run support, his fielders' errors cost him two runs, and he lost to St. Louis, 3 to 0. He tried again and again, but his pitching luck was no better each time.

After Indianapolis pounded the Filipinos' starting pitcher, Buck Ramsey, for six runs in the second inning of a game on June 1, Phillippe took the mound and allowed only three hits and no runs over the remainder of the contest with the best-hitting team in the Federal League. Pittsburgh still lost, 6 to 1. Five days later in Chicago, Phillippe relieved an erratic Ashenfelder in the fourth inning with the Filipinos trailing 3 to 2. He shut out the Keeleys for the next six innings on only one hit but lost that game, 4 to 3, on a pair of two-out hits in the tenth inning. He finally got a win on June 9 though he departed in the sixth with a 6–5 lead against O'Connor's bunch in St. Louis. Despite shaky control, Ashenfelder retired the Terriers over the final three innings without allowing further scoring.

The game in Indianapolis on June 14 was a microcosm of Phillippe's season when he pitched 12 heroic innings in the opener of a doubleheader. Despite sloppy play by his infielders that allowed cheap runs in the first and third innings, he took a 4 to 3 lead into the ninth inning, but Indianapolis tied the game on a double and a one-out single.

Phillippe no longer had a strikeout fastball and used an assortment of "foolers" and a change of pace to keep the Indy batters off-balance. He pitched in and out of trouble all day, allowing 13 hits, but he allowed the Hoosiers only one run from the fourth through the 12th inning. He also made three of his club's seven hits. With one out in the home half of the 12th, Rube Sellers, playing shortstop for the Filipinos, fielded a ground ball and heaved it well over the first baseman's head to allow the batter to reach third base. Moments later the contest ended with a hit off Phillippe that split the outfielders to easily score the deciding run. The Filipinos also lost the second game to drop their record to 13 wins and 24 losses.[24]

Sam Leever didn't have any better luck on the mound than his old teammate with the Pirates. After appearing only in short stints as a relief pitcher, he made his first start as a pitcher in nearly two years in the game against the Chicago Federals at DePaul Field on June 16. "Whatever chance the Schoolmaster had to show the fans he was still in the game went up when his fielders started booting the ball," reported the *Chicago Daily Tribune*. Three errors in the first inning contributed to five Chicago runs and set the course for a 12 to 1 rout. Leever stuck to his guns for five rounds, but a volley of three singles in the fifth sent the manager back to the bench.[25]

On June 20 the 41-year-old Phillippe lost a pitching duel with Henry Miller of Cy Young's Cleveland club, 2 to 0. One play cost him the game. In the fourth inning he intercepted a throw from the center fielder, permitting one run to score, then the third baseman let Phillippe's throw to him get away and a second runner raced home.[26]

The Pittsburgh Federal League club received an infusion of talent on June 14 when former major league pitcher Elmer "Baron" Knetzer, infielder Jack Lewis, recently farmed out to St. Paul by the Boston Red Sox, and Tom Murray, a catcher who had been suspended by the St. Paul team, joined Phillippe's last-place team. Knetzer became the first player bound to a major league club under the reserve clause to jump to a Federal League club. The acquisition of Knetzer was largely due to the manipulations of manager Phillippe, who had been after the Allegheny County native since the season began.[27]

Knetzer had started 55 games during four seasons with the Brooklyn Dodgers before he left the club during the 1912 season because of illness in his family. Instead of playing for less money, Knetzer refused to sign a contract to play for Brooklyn in 1913. Because he was bound to that club due to baseball's reserve rule, Knetzer had no choice but to play for Brooklyn, retire, or play with an "outlaw" team outside of the National Agreement. In addition to inserting Knetzer into his starting rotation, Phillippe moved the youngster

Mike Menosky to right field and installed Lewis at second base. However, nothing seemed to help.[28]

On June 26, Knetzer made his debut for the Filipinos and defeated St. Louis, 8 to 4, to end a nine-game Pittsburgh losing streak. That same afternoon, Covington beat Cleveland, 6 to 1, to run the Blue Sox's record to 22 wins against 20 losses.

That evening the Federal League magnates met in Indianapolis, where President Powers announced that Covington's franchise had been awarded to Kansas City. League Secretary Lloyd Rickart was assigned to proceed to Cleveland and take over the club during the remainder of its road trip.[29]

Sam Leever was having more success as a manager than Phillippe, but after the large opening day crowd in Covington, the locals lost interest and stopped going to Blue Sox games almost immediately. *The Kentucky Post* posted a letter begging fans to come out and support the Blue Sox, but all efforts to save the franchise failed.

A businessman associated with the Covington enterprise told a *Sporting Life* correspondent the club lost $12,000 before the franchise transfer and proclaimed, "Some of the base ball experts who said that park was big enough are responsible for the fizzle." The baseball tabloid chimed in that the venture was doomed to failure from the start. "No real lover of the game would go out often and see the sport massacred in a band-box. Curiosity would draw the elect once or twice, but there was no chance on the Covington field for real fast play."[30]

The inevitable happened on June 28, 1913, when the newly christened Kansas City Federal League club visited Exposition Park. The local club advertized a pitching match-up between Pittsburgh manager Deacon Phillippe and his ex-teammate, Sam Leever. It would be the first time the pair of ex–Pirates opposed one another in a regulation game since the 1899 season. A large Pittsburgh crowd turned out to watch the two former war horses go against one another, though they were only shells of what they had been in the previous decade.

Pittsburgh jumped out to a two-run lead off 41-year-old Leever in the first inning. With Menosky on first base, Rube Sellers hit a line drive that went under the left field bleachers. The Pirates argued that it should have been a home run, but the umpire ordered Menosky back to third base and put Sellers on second. The Filipinos got the runs anyway on a sacrifice fly and another single. Kansas City got one of the runs back in the top of the second when Hicks' line drive bounced over the center fielder's head and he was able to circle the bases while Rosser was chasing the ball in the spacious Expo Park outfield.

Neither team scored again until the top of the sixth when Phillippe was tagged for three runs. Leever left for a pinch-hitter during the rally and Phillippe departed after giving up the three runs. When the Filipinos tied the game in the bottom of the seventh, neither of the veterans would get the decision. Kansas City eventually won, 7–5, with single runs off Ashenfelder in the eighth and ninth innings.[31]

On July 2 Manager Phillippe suspended pitcher Roy Ashenfelder and the Pittsburgh club indicated it would try to work out a trade for him with another Federal League club. Phillippe's stated reason for the action was Ashenfelder's repeated refusal to exert himself and the hurler's performance in the July 1 game against Kansas City when he made several wild throws and failed to field a bunt. When Ashenfelder went to the bench at the end of the second inning, he was called to account by Phillippe. Ashenfelder responded in kind and was suspended without pay.[32]

The Pittsburgh Federal League club failed to meet payroll on the first of July, nor were paychecks distributed the next day. Roy Ashenfelder watched from the grandstand in street clothes as his teammates played their game of July 2 against Kansas City. The Pittsburgh players declared they would not play another game unless paychecks were issued. The players were finally paid and a crisis was averted.[33] Two days later Marshall Henderson resigned as president of the Pittsburgh club although he remained on board as a significant shareholder.[34]

On July 9 Kansas City began a series on a rainy day in Chicago, but Sam Leever managed to escape the elements early by getting tossed by the umpire in the second inning. The game was called after four innings. The next day, Chicago's Whitey Timmerman pitched one of two one-hitters he threw that season, but that one hit cost him the game against the visitors. Two walks, two sacrifices, and a home run by Leever's third baseman gave Kansas City a 3 to 0 lead, and it held up. Timmerman allowed only two base runners on two walks over the next eight innings, but the visitors' hurler, Hogue, was also up to the task, permitting only four singles and one run. Kansas City won, 3 to 1.[35]

The transition of the Covington club to Kansas City went remarkably smoothly. The team secured an adequate ball park at 47th and Tracy and there were only a few scheduling conflicts with the American Association Blues to work out. The ownership of the transplanted club was transferred to a group headed by Charles C. Madison, a local attorney.[36] The club would be dubbed the "Packers," after the city's main industry.

On July 12, 1913, the Kansas City Federal League team played its first game on the home grounds against Jack O'Connor's St. Louis aggregation. Preceding the game at Gordon and Koppel Field, there was a parade through the downtown streets with the mayors of Kansas City, Missouri, and Kansas City, Kansas, as well as officials of the Federal League, riding in cars. Riley & Kelly's band, followed by the Kansas City and St. Louis players, marched across the field when the procession reached the grounds. With approximately 5,000 looking on, Kansas City right hander Pete Henning was the master of the St. Louis crew, allowing but three hits and striking out 11 of O'Connor's men in Kansas City's 3 to 1 win.[37]

Sam Leever was attracted to the Covington job because he was able to work close to his home, but this all changed when the club was transferred to Kansas City. After only two-thirds of a season Leever gave up his aspirations as a baseball manager. After four straight losses to Cleveland left the Packers record at 41–45, Leever was given his release on August 11, a little over a month after the team was transferred to Kansas City. Hugo Swartling, a defector from Steubenville (Ohio) in the Inter-State League, was named manager for the remainder of the season and the team performed even worse for him than it did for Leever.[38] The Covington/Kansas City job was his final hurrah in Organized Baseball. He retired to his farm near Goshen, Ohio, and never returned to baseball on a professional basis.

Meanwhile, the frustrations for Deacon Phillippe were manifest in a game before a large crowd at Exposition Park on July 14. Elmer Knetzer allowed only one run to Chicago, but the Filipinos were completely frustrated by opposing pitcher Whitey Timmerman, who pitched his second successive one-hitter. The only Pittsburgh hit was made by Knetzer himself in the seventh inning when he beat out a slow roller to second baseman Farrell, who was slow in fielding the ball before he made the throw to first base.

On July 20, the unhappy Roy Ashenfelder lost a game to the Chicago Federals at DePaul Field, dropping the lowly Filipinos' record to 27–43. When the Pittsburgh club left town two days later, Ashenfelder wasn't with them, because he stayed in the Windy City as a member of the Chicago Federal League squad.

Unlike Leever, Deacon Phillippe stuck it out until the end of the Federal League season despite the dire financial situation of the club. He later described the travails of managing in the bush leagues during a road trip to Kansas City that August. He was sent on the road with train tickets and $15 in expense money for himself and his players. The club would play a pair of exhibition games along the way to raise addition money to cover expenses for the final leg of the trip.

"One of the exhibition games netted $22.25 and the other $25.75," he recalled, "And I had to dig down in my own pocket for the reminder of the expense money."

When the club reached Kansas City, Phillippe telegraphed the club for more money. He was sent $50.[39] After losing both ends of a Sunday doubleheader, the Filipinos snapped an eight-game losing streak the next day.

In an otherwise miserable season for Deacon Phillippe as a moundsman, the highlight of his season had to be the 8 to 7 victory against Sam Leever's Packers on August 5. Elmer Knetzer started for the Filipinos, but after he allowed two runs in the first inning and hits to the first three Kansas City batters in the second, Phillippe decided to take matters into his own hands and took the mound for Pittsburgh. Phillippe only had one bad inning, the sixth, when Kansas City reached him for three runs. Pittsburgh tied the game at 7–7 in the ninth, then Phillippe and Kansas City's George Hogan battled for seven more innings.

Kansas City only threatened to score once in the extra frames. With two out in the bottom of the 11th, center fielder Dawson tripled to right but was thrown out trying to stretch the hit into a home run. Pittsburgh won it in the 17th inning on a strange play. With one out the Filipinos' Tommy Sheehan swung at a third strike that was missed by catcher Hicks. While Sheehan ran to first, the ball rolled to the Pittsburgh team's bat boy, who tossed it into the diamond. Umpire "Eagle Eye" Beckley ruled the ball "dead" and awarded the runner second base. The Kansas City players swarmed around Beckley, protesting his decision. While this was going on, Sheehan sneaked over to third base and was allowed to remain there since "time out" had not been called. The former Pirates third baseman scored moments later when the Kansas City shortstop erred on Sellers' grounder. Phillippe retired the Packers in order in the bottom half for his 11th consecutive scoreless inning.[40]

Phillippe still had to get his players back to Pittsburgh at minimal expense. He recalled, "We were not drawing anything and all we got was the guarantee money. I got all the railroad agents in the town to help me to figure out the cheapest way home. I found that by paying 75 cents per ticket more than a certain road wanted I could get home twelve hours sooner than by going over the cheaper route, but we did not have the coin, so we had to take the long route."[41]

Phillippe's Pittsburgh club finished in last place for the 1913 Federal League season, posting a record of 49 wins and 71 losses. That fall, the Federal League declared open warfare on the existing major leagues and began to sign players much in the fashion of the American League in 1901. The Pittsburgh Federals announced shortly after the end of the season that Phillippe would not be returning as manager the next year.[42] In the spring of 1914 Phillippe accepted the position of baseball coach at historic Allegheny College, a school affiliated with the United Methodist Church, located in Meadville, Pa.[43]

The Cubs' Tommy Leach snubbed the Feds' offer to manage in Pittsburgh after Chicago owner Charles Murphy told his player about Deacon Phillippe's bitter experience with the outlaws. Said Murphy, "According to President Dreyfuss of the Pirates, Manager Phillippe is still trying to get $1,700.00 salary alleged to be due him from 1913."[44]

In January, 1914, the former manager of the Filipinos prepared papers for the filing of a suit against the Pittsburgh Athletic Park Association, the title under which the local Federals did business. The suit was designed to recover $1,555.40, with interest at six per cent due him after July 15, 1913, which he claimed as unpaid salary for the previous year.

Pittsburgh's Exposition Park was again remodeled and expanded when the Federal League became a "major" in 1914. The improvements expanded the park's seating capacity to 16,000. When the Federal League folded after the 1915 season, Exposition Park's day as home to major league baseball was over. Three Rivers Stadium was built on the former site of Exposition Park and served as the Pirates' home field from 1970 through 2000.

After the demolition of Three Rivers Stadium in 2001, members of the Forbes Field Chapter of the Society for American Baseball Research surveyed the area and marked the bases of Exposition Park. Exposition Park was on what is now Gold Lot 2 between the Pirates' current home, PNC Park, and Heinz Field, although it sat much lower.

◆ THIRTEEN ◆

Life After Baseball

The Sporting News reported in October 1915 that Deacon Phillippe had decided to sell his place near Meadville, Pennsylvania, and move back to Pittsburgh. "He has no idea of re-entering baseball, but just wants to be around where there is a bit of excitement."[1] A month later, Phillippe was named manager of the Colonial-Annex Hotel's cigar stand.[2]

Phillippe wasn't involved in professional baseball after his Federal League experience, but he did remain close to his hunting buddy, Honus Wagner. On February 24, 1916, he attended the 42nd birthday fete for Wagner at the second annual banquet of the Pittsburgh Hot Stove League. He also became financially involved in the "Honus Wagner Sporting Goods Company" on Wood Street in Pittsburgh.

Deacon Phillippe's life after baseball was unremarkable. He and his wife Belle lived in the Pittsburgh area for the rest of their lives. Mrs. Phillippe suffered a disabling hip fracture that plagued her for much of of her life.[3] The 1920 Federal census taker found the ex-pitcher and wife Belle residing at 5006 Friendship Avenue in Pittsburgh, and his occupation was described as proprietor of a cigar store. Belle's 61-year-old mother Mary Kennedy was residing with the couple at the time. The Phillippes' daughter Mary Isabelle had married Julian Ivan Byers a year earlier in a ceremony performed by a Presbyterian minister in the family's living room. A beaming Deacon Phillippe had the honor of giving the bride away.[4]

By 1922 he had grown restless and sought to get back into Organized Baseball as a scout. He talked with Pat Moran, manager of the Cincinnati Reds, who said he didn't need any "ivory hunters," but would speak to some of the club owners about a job. Barney Dreyfuss admitted that Phillippe would be an ideal man to go to the bushes and find the latest "phenom," but he too was well-stocked with scouts.[5]

Phillippe was invited to participate in Pittsburgh's celebration of the

National League's Golden Jubilee on June 6, 1925, before the National League game between the Phillies and Pirates at Forbes Field. The evening before the game, Barney Dreyfuss entertained the former players, current Pirates and Phillies, as well as visiting moguls and dignitaries at the Hotel Schenley. Fifteen former Pirates, including the 1901 batboy J. W. Watson, attended. Sam Leever was among only a few of the survivors from the Pirates' first pennant winner not to attend.

The next morning the players assembled at Wagner's sporting goods store, in which Phillippe still held a financial interest. A vintage horse-drawn omnibus with a moustached driver was provided for the players' ride to the ballpark. The old-time players marched alongside the current team to the Forbes Field outfield for the raising of the Stars and Stripes and the National League Jubilee flag.

The highlight of the day was a special three-inning contest pitting the group of Pirates' "old timers" against the current team. The old-timers' batting order consisted of Beaumont, Leach, Clarke, Wagner, Bransfield, Ritchey, McCreedy and Zimmer. Deacon Phillippe, "as trim as he was in 1901," pitched the first inning, Jesse Tannehill the second and Jack Chesbro threw the third stanza for the old-timers while the rarely used Babe Adams hurled for the 1925 club. The 1925 team won, 5 to 3, before about 20,000 at Forbes Field. Phillippe did not fare very well in his one inning on the mound. After Ginger Beaumont dropped Max Carey's fly ball, Phillippe fanned Eddie Moore for the first out. Then four successive singles led to three runs. Phillippe admitted that the old ball didn't "break" for him like it used to.[6]

The festivities of World Series that year between the Pirates and the Washington Senators were dampened by news of Christy Mathewson's death from tuberculosis on October 7, the date of the opening game. Both teams wore black arm bands throughout the Series.

In his article describing Honus Wagner's attendance at the Series opener in Pittsburgh, Richards Vidmer added, "There were other ghosts of former Pirate cruises to Pennant Island. Deacon Phillippe, Wagner's lifelong friend and business partner ... Tommy Leach, Ed Abbaticchio, Lefty Leifield, Schoolmaster Sam Leever — these were others whom age had forced to sit and watch while their successors played the game and earned the plaudits of the crowd."[7]

Phillippe was a frequent participant at "old-timers" events in the Pittsburgh area, and on June 9, 1933, 61-year-old Phillippe attended "Honus Wagner Day" at Forbes Field. "Marching bands, drum-and-bugle corps and more than 800 vehicles wound their way past hundreds of thousands of spectators who had lined downtown thoroughfares for a glimpse of (Wagner) the legendary Pirate." In addition to Wagner and Phillippe, several teammates from the glory days who were present included Fred Clarke, Claude Ritchey, George Gibson and Ed Abbaticchio. Phillippe's old nemesis from the 1903 World Series, Cy Young, was also in attendance. Following the festivities, the graybeards participated in a two-inning old-timers game in the grueling summer heat.

In November, 1935, Phillippe received the appointment as tipstaff for the county court in Pittsburgh. The 63-year-old Phillippe was elected to fill a vacancy out of more than 625 applicants for the $215 a month position that was usually good for life. Following the swearing-in ceremony a month later, he was assigned to Judge Frank A. Piekarski's court. He would hold the position of bailiff the remainder of his life.[8]

Reminiscing 51 years later, Harry M. Montgomery said that upon his appointment as judge for the Allegheny County Court in 1944 he had to share the limelight with his aide, or tipstaff, Charles "Deacon" Phillippe. Honus Wagner was an Allegheny County deputy sheriff at the time.

"These two old baseball players would meet in my outer office and talk baseball," Montgomery said. "They'd meet with more people than I'd see in my office."[9]

Charles "Deacon" Phillippe, tipstaff, Allegheny County Court, Pittsburgh (National Baseball Hall of Fame Library, Cooperstown, New York).

Just as Phillippe had defended the pitchers in his era from the old underhand flingers of the 1800s, he promoted the brand of baseball played in his day. In 1946 a reporter caught up with Phillippe at a fanning bee in Pittsburgh, and Deacon echoed the sentiments many of his era's players when the 74-year-old ex-pitcher observed, "Babe Ruth was the biggest drawback to smart baseball the game has ever known.

"When Ruth broke in, he pioneered the long ball. He hit for distance. Instead of outfielders having plenty of room to roam for fly balls and help pitchers, the magnates built stands in the outfield to aid Ruth's home runs and take care of the overflow fans. They brought the fences in.

"All this hurt the pitchers and produced the cheap home runs. Teams quit playing smart baseball and went in for slugging.... I think that's what's wrong with baseball today. Everybody is aiming for the fences."[10]

Though Phillippe's hypothesis was off-base as far as the popularity of baseball was concerned, his comments about cheap home runs achieved ironic credence when the use of steroids by the game's biggest home run hitters cast a dark cloud over the game in the first decade of the twenty-first century.

In his later years, Phillippe and Belle lived in apartment across the hall from their only child, Isabella Byers, on California Avenue in Avalon, a borough of Bellevue. One of Phillippe's last personal appearances was at Ginger Beaumont's induction into the Wisconsin Athletic Hall of Fame in Milwaukee on November 28, 1951.

Charles Louis "Deacon" Phillippe died while watching television late in the evening of Sunday, March 23, 1952, at his home in Avalon. At the time of his death, he was still employed as tipstaff in the court of Judge Homer Brown, who said Phillippe was in court the Friday before his death and noted that the former pitcher was in good spirits and was looking forward to the upcoming baseball season.[11]

Al Abrams, sports editor of the *Pittsburgh Post-Gazette*, wrote in his column, "Although 79 years of age, Deacon Phillippe, the former pitching great, appeared to be in excellent health and stood as straight as a ramrod."[12]

Following a late-evening ceremony at an Avalon funeral home, Charles Louis Phillippe was buried the following morning in the Allegheny County Memorial Park Cemetery, 4734 Butler Street, Pittsburgh. Reports from the time noted that he was survived by his wife; a daughter, Mrs. Julian (Isabelle) Byers of Avalon; two grandchildren[13]; his youngest sibling, Ellis, who was living in Canada; and a sister, Mrs. J. H. Mair of Riverside, California.

Belle Phillippe died at the age of 80 on April 14, 1961, in a Pittsburgh suburb hospital. She was survived by her daughter, two grandchildren and four great-grandchildren.

Deacon Phillippe was posthumously elected to both the Virginia Sports Hall of Fame and the South Dakota Sports Hall of Fame. In 1969, the Pittsburgh Pirates fans voted him the number one right-handed pitcher in the team's history.

Phillippe returned to the public consciousness during 2003, the 100th anniversary of baseball's first World Series. During the 2003 baseball season, *The Pittsburgh Post Dispatch* ran daily retrospectives of each Pirates corresponding game from 100 years earlier all the way up through the World Series. Three books on the 1903 Series were released during the centennial anniversary in which Phillippe, of course, was a principle character. On the day of the fifth game of the 2003 World Series a baby boy was born to prominent motion picture actors Ryan Phillippe and Reese Witherspoon. Their child was named "Deacon Phillippe," which immediately generated the curiosity of Hollywood tabloids and baseball history buffs. Though the immediate family released no information on the name, relatives let it be known that the boy was named after the pitcher, who was baby Deacon's ancestor.

Like Deacon Phillippe, Sam Leever was one of the few players in the first decade of the century who left baseball with money. Leever was not only renowned for his serious demeanor, he was also known to be somewhat of a tightwad. Hugh Fullerton referred to him as "careful with his money" in an article written in 1928. Even Leever's own niece referred to him as "tight."

When the 1915 Phillies drew about $500 more as losers in the World Series than the Pirates got per man for winning in 1909, one wise-cracking newspaper writer penned, "We will wager a hat that Sam Leever's cut is still drawing interest."[14]

Upon retiring from the game, Leever used the money he and Margaret saved from his years with the Pirates to purchase a 70-acre farm near Goshen, and the ex-pitcher became a full-time farmer. Of course, he also remained active in trapshooting competitions.

On November 3, 1924, the nation's wire services ran a report that "Sam Leever ... well-known pitcher of the Pittsburgh Nationals, it has just become known, died last week at his home near Goshen, Ohio."[15] The problem was that Sam Leever, the former baseball pitcher, was not the Samuel Leever who had died.

The Sporting News reported that Leever "had a great deal of enjoyment out of reading his own obituary and he appreciates all the nice things that were said about him, but he insists that he is not even half-dead. In fact, Sam says he never felt better in his life, and he has no thought whatever of cashing in.

"Leever has lived a quiet life ever since he retired from baseball a number of years ago," continued the retrospective. "He served a term or two as postmaster at Goshen, and is today one of the town's leading citizens. Always a frugal liver, Sam didn't worry much about income when his baseball days were over, although he certainly never drew the immense salaries which baseball pitchers get today."[16]

Following retirement, Leever rarely participated in activities relating to his baseball career. However, in 1925 Sam accepted an invitation to come to Forbes Field for a celebration of the Pirates' first appearance in the World Series since 1909. One reporter noted that Leever, John McGraw and Bill McKechnie were seen talking over "old times" on the Pirates bench before the World Series game on October 13.[17]

In August 1937, 65-year-old Samuel Leever finished third in a shoot-off for first place at the Vandalia, Ohio, North American trap championships. His obituary mentioned his passion and expertise at trapshooting, reporting that he had fired a score of 99 (out of 100) as late as age 71. Wrote Mark Armour in his short biography of Leever, "Though that passion may have cost him greater fame (in the 1903 World Series), it also kept him active and entertained long after his baseball career had ended."[18]

When the Leevers retired from farming, the childless couple moved to his in-laws' old place nearer to town. One Goshen native described Leever as a "good man who became crotchety in his old age." A writer from the *Cincinnati Enquirer* noted that Leever refused to attend his wife's family (the Malloys) annual Christmas dinner because he was a Republican and didn't want to break bread with "a bunch of Democrats."[19]

Leever became a regular at "Sunday ball" in Goshen, but he rarely talked about his own baseball career and did not socialize with the players unless there was one that showed a lot of promise. The Leevers' house was across from the school baseball field, but the ballplayers did not get any breaks from "Old Man Leever." A foul ball back of third base would often land in the Leevers' big garden. "If Sam was out there working and he got to the ball before we could, he'd keep the ball," remembered Bill Glancy, captain of the Goshen varsity baseball teams in 1944 and 1945. "Can you believe that? A former big-league player keeping our baseball because he was mad it went in his garden? We beat him to it most of the time, though."[20]

Leever always wore a big straw hat when he worked outside in his garden and rarely removed it except indoors. Those not close to Leever were surprised at the old ball player's bald plate when it was rarely displayed.

Sam Leever died at home, at age 81, on May 19, 1953. Some 50 years after his death, the Leevers' old white house on Old State Road 28 was still standing, though it was boarded up. Gone was the shed where he manufactured the ammunition for his trap shoots and hunting trips. Three quarters of a mile up the road is the graveyard where Sam and Margaret (she died in 1959) are buried on a slight rise near a huge, 100-year-old maple tree. In 1995 the Ohio House of Representatives passed a resolution promoting the induction of Sam Leever into the National Baseball Hall of Fame.[21]

For a pitcher, the main statistical qualification for National Baseball Hall of Fame election appears to be the number of major league victories. Both Leever and Deacon Phillippe are handicapped in their bids for the baseball Hall of Fame because they each reached the major leagues at a late age and just missed reaching the 200 plateau in major league victories. Phillippe was a month shy of his 27th birthday when he debuted for Louisville in 1899. Leever had only five major league games and only one victory under his belt at age 27. Although pitchers in their era racked up more decisions than modern players because pitchers back then finished what they started, both Leever and Phillippe were further hampered because their best years came when the National League used a 140-game schedule and postponed contests were often not rescheduled.

Many of the early 20th century pitchers were overworked at various times during their career. Leever was so over-utilized in his first full major league season he suffered a chronically sore arm. During that 1899 season he led the National League with 51 games(39 of them starts with 35 complete games) and 379 innings pitched (he never came close to that again).

Leever's 194 career victories compare favorably with several contemporary pitchers in the Hall of Fame: Rube Waddell, 193–143, .574; Jack Chesbro, 198–132, .600, and Ed Walsh, 195–126, .607. Additionally, Leever's career won-lost percentage was .660, good enough for sixth place on the all-time list of post–1893 pitchers with 200 or more decisions. Whitey Ford, Lefty Grove and Christy Mathewson, the three twentieth century pitchers ahead of Leever in career winning percentage that are eligible for induction, are in the Hall of Fame. During the Pirates' glory years (1901–1909), Leever's winning percentage in his 210 decisions was an amazing .711. Leever also has more victories than several other pitchers in the Hall of Fame, including Sandy Koufax, Dizzy Dean, Candy Cummings, and Addie Joss.

Bill James, author of *The Politics of Glory: How Baseball's Hall of Fame Really Works*, wrote that Leever is more deserving than a dozen inductees, including three since 1984: Catfish Hunter, Don Drysdale and Jim Bunning. According to James' "win points" rating system for pitchers, Leever was tied for 28th place in the history of major league baseball.[22]

James observed, "the four pitchers who were the Pirates' rotation when they won the National League in 1901 (Chesbro, Tannehill, Leever and Phillippe) all had extremely similar career records. Chesbro had probably the poorest career record of the four, Sam Leever the best, yet Chesbro is the only one who is in the Hall of Fame. Why? You all know the answer. He had the big year."[23]

Comparing Leever's record with his teammate who is in the Hall of Fame and pitched in approximately the same number of games, Jack Chesbro won four more games, but the Schoolmaster's winning percentage was 50 points higher than the spitballer's. Leever pitched 38 shutouts, Chesbro 35. When the earned run averages for that era were computed, Leever came out on top, 2.47 to Chesbro's 2.68. Chesbro's credentials are simply enhanced because he had that remarkable record of 41 victories for the New York Highlanders in 1904.

Leever's case for the Hall of Fame was damaged because of his poor performance in the 1903 World Series and by the fact he didn't pitch in a glamorous media city like New York. He was a control pitcher who had low strikeout totals even for the period in which he pitched. (Big strikeout totals are obviously an asset in Hall of Fame balloting).

Though Leever and Phillippe are still eligible for election to baseball's Hall Of Fame, there appears to be little support within the veterans' committee for their selection. Neither was flashy, controversial or verbose; they did not have descendants who campaigned for them; and neither remained in baseball as an executive or coach. Several other pitchers on the list, including Pittsburgh's Babe Adams, have similar credentials and it is doubtful the two forgotten hurlers of the early 1900s will gain induction any time soon. At the very least, they should be part of the discussion.

Appendix: Career Pitching Summaries

(See note next page)

Sam Leever's Major League Pitching Summary

YEAR	TEAM	W	L	PCT	G	SHO	IP	ERA	BB	K	SV	BA
1898	PGH(NL)	1	0	1.000	5	0	33	2.45	5	15	0	.250
1899	PGH(NL)	21	23	.477	51	4	379	3.18	122	121	3	.226
1900	PGH(NL)	15	13	.536	30	3	233	2.71	48	84	0	.205
1901	PGH(NL)	14	5	.737	21	2	176	2.86	39	82	0	.183
1902	PGH(NL)	15	7	.682	28	4	222	2.39	31	86	2	.178
1903	PGH(NL)	25	7	.781	36	7	284	2.06	60	90	1	.165
1904	PGH(NL)	18	11	.621	34	1	253	2.17	54	63	0	.263
1905	PGH(NL)	20	5	.800	33	3	230	2.70	54	81	1	.102
1906	PGH(NL)	22	7	.759	36	6	260	2.32	48	76	0	.211
1907	PGH(NL)	14	9	.609	31	5	217	1.66	46	65	0	.151
1908	PGH(NL)	15	7	.682	38	4	193	2.10	41	28	2	.148
1909	PGH(NL)	8	1	.889	19	0	70	2.83	14	23	2	.167
1910	PGH(NL)	6	5	.545	26	0	111	2.76	25	33	2	.065
Major League Totals		194	100	.660	388	39	2661	2.47	587	847	13	.184

Deacon Phillippe's Major League Pitching Summary

YEAR	TEAM	W	L	PCT	G	SHO	IP	ERA	BB	K	SV	BA
1899	LOU(NL)	21	17	.553	42	2	321	3.17	64	68	1	.203
1900	PGH(NL)	20	13	.606	38	1	279	2.84	42	75	0	.181
1901	PGH(NL)	22	12	.647	37	1	296	2.22	38	103	2	.230
1902	PGH(NL)	20	9	.690	31	5	272	2.05	26	122	0	.221
1903	PGH(NL)	25	9	.735	36	4	289	2.43	29	123	2	.210
1904	PGH(NL)	10	10	.500	21	3	167	3.24	26	82	1	.123
1905	PGH(NL)	20	13	.606	38	5	279	2.19	48	133	0	.093
1906	PGH(NL)	15	10	.600	33	3	219	2.47	26	90	0	.244
1907	PGH(NL)	14	11	.560	35	1	214	2.61	36	61	2	.185
1908	PGH(NL)	0	0	...	5	0	12	11.25	3	1	0	.250
1909	PGH(NL)	8	3	.727	22	1	132	2.32	14	38	0	.071
1910	PGH(NL)	14	2	.875	31	1	123	2.29	9	30	4	.220
1911	PGH(NL)	0	0	...	3	0	6	7.50	2	3	0	1.000
Major League Totals		189	109	.634	372	27	2607	2.59	363	929	12	.189

Because of the erratic nature of scoring rules in baseball around the turn of the century, records have been adjusted over time. Deacon Phillippe has been credited with three additional victories (one in 1899 and two in 1900 to increase his career win total from 186 to 189. Leever gained an additional victory for the 1899 season, but lost one for 1902. *(Baseball Reference.com)*

Chapter Notes

Preface

1. *Sporting Life*, March 21, 1903, 5.
2. "Phillippe as Great as Alexander," *Pittsburg Press*, October 3, 1915, 4.
3. "He Fooled 'em All," *Syracuse Post Standard,* February 22, 1910, 12.
4. "Gossip of the Players," *The Sporting News*, December 19, 1903, 2.
5. Lawrence S. Ritter, *The Glory of Their Times* (New York: Macmillan, 1966), 33.
6. "Religions of World's Champion Ball Tossers," *Charleroi (Pa.) Mail*, March 26, 1910. This article gave the religious denominations of the 1909 Pittsburgh Pirates. Wagner was the only Lutheran, Leach and Clarke were Catholic, and Leever was a Methodist. "Deacon Phillippe is not a member of any church," the article concluded.
7. *The Sporting News*, December 19, 1903, 2.
8. "Gossip of the Players," *The Sporting News*, March 12, 1904, 2.
9. *The Sporting News*, May 6, 1905, 3. "Phillippe Finds Spit Ball," *The Daily News* (Frederick, MD), July 6, 1908, 4.
10. *The Sporting News*, March 12, 1904, 2.
11. "Are Not Willing," *The Sporting News*, July 22, 1899, 4.

Chapter One

1. Louis P. Masur, *Autumn Glory: Baseball's First World Series* (New York: Hill & Wang, 2003), 183.
2. Honus Wagner, "Hans Wagner's Story," *Los Angeles Times*, January 13, 1924, 15.
3. "Gossip of the Players," *The Sporting News*, December 19, 1903, 2.
4. In each census report from 1870 through 1910 the spelling "Phillippe" was used by Deacon's father. Blacklick Township, Wythe County, VA, 1870 census, p. 57; Sulphur Springs District, Carroll County, VA, 1880 census, p. 24. *Compiled Service Records of Confederate Soldiers Who Served in Organizations from the State of Virginia* for "Andrew J. Phillippe" enlisted from Wythe County, VA, January, 1862, Company B, 29th Infantry Regiment. There actually were two Andrew Jackson Phillipp(i)e's in Wythe County at the same time. There was Andrew J. Phillippe (born 1838), son of John Phillippi; and there was Andrew J. Phillippi (born 1843), son of Joseph Phillippi (1860 and 1870 Wythe County, VA, Census).
5. "Charles Louis Phillippi (Deacon), Legend of the Game" (web site); by Joe Cameron; http://www.serve.com/smythgen/Deacon.htm.
6. "National League News," *The Sporting News*, July 4, 1903, 7.
7. Ottie Padgett, "Rock throwing in Carroll helped Charlie Phillippe become a Great Pitcher," uncredited article (November 1962) in Deacon Phillippe file in National Baseball Hall of Fame Library.
8. "Phillippe Brothers Hold Reunion," *Pittsburg Press*, April 5, 1908, 19.
9. Cullen Cain, "Looking Back in Baseball," *Miami News*, November 30, 1957, 11.
10. "How Deacon Phillippe Broke into Baseball," *Pittsburg Press*, December 13, 1907, 26. (Bar-

ney Dreyfuss related how Charles Phillippe got his start in professional baseball to Henry Mauss who, in turn, gave the story to the *Press*.) Also "Phillippe's Progress," *Sporting Life*, November 7, 1903, 9.
  11. *Mankato Daily Free Press*, April 25, 1896, 1.
  12. "Twelve to Five," *Mankato Daily Free Press*, April 27, 1896, 1.
  13. *Mankato Daily Free Press*, Saturday, April 25, 1896, 1.
  14. "Well Fought Game," *Mankato Daily Free Press*, April 30, 1896, 1.
  15. "Childish," *Winona Daily Herald*, May 21, 1896, 1.
  16. "Six Signed," *Mankato Daily Free Press*, July 22, 1896, 1.
  17. *Ibid.*, 1.
  18. "Excellent Playing," *Winona Daily Republican*, August 10, 1896, 1.
  19. "Tigers Were Mad," *Mankato Daily Free Press*, September 3, 1896, 1.
  20. "Connor a Fast Player," *Chicago Daily Tribune*, March 29, 1897, 6.
  21. "Took the Last One," *St. Paul Globe*, May 18, 1897, 5.
  22. "One Lone Tally," *St. Paul Globe*, May 21, 1897, 5.
  23. "Minneapolis Mourns," *Sporting Life*, May 29, 1897, 15.
  24. *Morehead Independent*, June 25, 1897, 1.
  25. "Lost by Roat et al," *Minneapolis Journal*, July 19, 1897, 10.
  26. "The Best Game Ever," *Minneapolis Journal*, September 4, 1897,16.
  27. *Chicago Daily Tribune*, July 14, 1897, 4.
  28. "A Triple Play in It," *St. Paul Globe*, September 10, 1897, 7.
  29. *Sporting Life*, January 8, 1898, 6.
  30. "First Mill City Game," *St. Paul Globe*, April 29, 1898, 5.
  31. *Minneapolis Tribune*, April 29, 1898, 5.
  32. "Like Old Times," *Minneapolis Tribune*, May 24, 1898.
  33. "'Twas Won but Lost,"*Minneapolis Tribune*, July 4, 1898, 6.
  34. "Western League Patronage," *Sporting Life*, November 19, 1898, 3.
  35. "Wilmot Redivivus," *Sporting Life*, July 30, 1899, 17.
  36. "Western Work: The League's Official Averages for 1898," *Sporting Life*, October 29, 1898, 9.
  37. *Sporting Life*, October 8, 1898, 8.
  38. "Western Star Players," *Sporting Life*, September 3, 1898, 13.
  39. "The Rise of Barney Dreyfuss," *Washington Post*, April 26, 1908, 33.
  40. Bill Lamberty, "Harry Clay Pulliam," from *Deadball Stars of the National League*, edited by Tom Simon (Washington, D.C.: The Society for American Baseball Research, Brassey's, 2004), 22.
  41. "Baseball Outlook in the National League," *Chicago Daily Tribune*, April 14, 1899, 4.
  42. *Sporting Life*, February 25, 1899, 2.
  43. *Sporting Life*, January 14, 1911, 4.
  44. "Trusts Dreyfuss," *The Sporting News*, January 19, 1907, 2.
  45. *The Sporting News*, October 18, 1902, 4.
  46. "News and Comments," *Sporting Life*, April 15, 1899, 3.
  47. "Louisville Lines," *Sporting Life*, April 15, 1899, 6.
  48. "Clark's Bad Break," *The Sporting News*, April 29, 1899, 1.
  49. *Washington Post*, May 6, 1899, 8.
  50. *Washington Post*, May 9, 1899, 8.
  51. *New York Times*, May 26, 1899, 4. Only one other no-hitter was spun that season, Boston's Vic Willis claiming the honors against Washington on August 7.
  52. "Balky Colonels," *Sporting Life*, June 3, 1899, 6.
  53. *Boston Daily Globe*, August 17, 1899, 2.
  54. *Washington Post*, July 30, 1900, 8.
  55. *The Sporting News*, September 9, 1899, 4.
  56. "Colonels Beat Garvin," *Chicago Daily Tribune*, October 2, 1899, 18.
  57. C. L. Moore, "Colonels Ahead," *The Sporting News*, October 21, 1899, 7.
  58. Roger I. Abrams, *The First World Series and the Baseball Fanatics of 1903* (Boston: Northeastern University, 2003), 53.
  59. "Gigantic Deal," *The Sporting News*, December 16, 1899, 3.

Chapter Two

1. *The Sporting News*, February 10, 1906, 2.
2. *Sporting Life*, October 9, 1909, 9; December 11, 1909, 7.
3. Clermont County, OH, marriage record of Edward C. Leever and Amerideth Ardelia Watson (2 September 1864). Clermont County, Ohio, Probate Court, Certificate of Birth, Samuel Leever (National Baseball Hall of Fame Library).
4. "Leever One of Grand Old Men of Diamond," *Mansfield News*, January 9, 1913, 10.
5. "The Initial Game at Mayville's Handsome New Park in the Presence of Big Crowd," *Daily Public Ledger* (Maysville, KY), May 31, 1895, 1.
6. *Ibid.*, 1.
7. Terry Simpkins, "Norman Elberfeld," in *Deadball Stars of the American League*, ed. David Jones (Dulles, VA: Potomac Books, 2006), 704.
8. "Down They Went Again!" *Daily Public Ledger* (Maysville, KY), July 11, 1895, 1.
9. *Daily Public Ledger* (Maysville, KY), July 19, 1895, 1.
10. *Daily Public Ledger* (Maysville, KY), July 24, 1895, 1.
11. "Earle the Discoverer of Professor Sam Leever," *Pittsburg Press*, December 2, 1902, 16.
12. *Daily Public Ledger* (Maysville, KY), September 24, 1895, 1.
13. *Daily Public Ledger* (Maysville, KY), July 23, 1896, 1.
14. "Well-Well-Well!" *Daily Public Ledger* (Maysville, KY), July 23, 1896, 1.
15. *Portsmouth Times*, June 27, 1896, 2.
16. "Those Twenty 0's," *Daily Public Ledger* (Maysville, KY), June 29, 1896, 4.
17. "Has a Star Pitcher: Leever of Maysville, Is the Man," *Richmond Dispatch*, March 9, 1897, 1.
18. *Daily Public Ledger* (Maysville, KY), August 10, 1896, 1.
19. *Daily Public Ledger* (Maysville, KY), September 9, 1896, 1.
20. "Editor Barney Dreyfuss Interviews Magnate Dreyfuss," *Pittsburg Press*, November 23, 1901, 24.
21. "Has a Star Pitcher: Leever of Maysville, Is the Man," op. cit.
22. W. Harrison Daniel and Scott P. Mayer, *Baseball and Richmond* (Jefferson, NC: McFarland, 2003), 38–39.
23. "Leever's Pitching Record," *The Sporting News*, December 1, 1906, 6.
24. "Sam Leever Did It," *Richmond Dispatch*, April 29, 1897, 3.
25. *Ibid.*
26. "Here We Go Again: The Johnny Rebs Once More in First Place," *Richmond Dispatch*, May 15, 1897, 3.
27. "They Tied Twice," *Richmond Dispatch*, July 15, 1897, 3.
28. "Great Is Leever: Professor Sammy Shut Hartford's Players Out," *Richmond Dispatch*, September 4, 1897, 3.
29. *Washington Post*, September 16, 1897, 8.
30. "Taken into Camp," *Richmond Dispatch*, September 18, 1897, 3.
31. *Sporting Life*, April 9, 1898, 8.
32. *Sporting Life*, July 23, 1898, 5.
33. "No Wonder at All," *Sporting Life*, September 24, 1898, 4.
34. "Rosy Richmond," *Sporting Life*, September 25, 11.
35. *Sporting Life*, February 19, 1898, 2.
36. *Pittsburg Leader*, April 3, 1898, 2.
37. *Sporting Life*, April 9, 1898, 8.
38. *Pittsburg Leader*, April 3, 1898, 2.
39. *New York Times*, April 16, 1898, 10.
40. "Pittsburg Points," *Sporting Life*, May 7, 1898, 9.
41. *New York Times*, May 27, 1898, 10.
42. "Leever Goes Back to Richmond," *Sporting Life*, June 4, 1898, 4.
43. *The Sporting News*, June, 25, 1898, 1.
44. "Richmond's Triumph," *Sporting Life*, September 17, 1898, 17.
45. *New York Times*, September 16, 1898, 5.
46. *Sporting Life*, October 1, 1898, 8.

47. *Pittsburg Leader*, October 10, 1899, 4.
48. *Pittsburg Leader*, October 13, 1898, 4.
49. *Chicago Daily Tribune*, April 20, 1899, 6.
50. *Pittsburg Leader*, May 7, 1899.
51. "Like Patsy of Old," *Pittsburg Leader*, May 7, 1899.
52. "Luck Fails Senators," *Washington Post*, May 31, 1899, 8.
53. *Chicago Daily Tribune*, July 9, 1899, 7.
54. "Pittsburg Points," *Sporting Life*, July 15, 1899, 6.
55. Locke wrote a column about Pittsburgh baseball in *The Sporting News* under the pseudonym "Pirate."
56. "Are Not Willing," *The Sporting News*, July 22, 1899, 4.
57. "The Tables Turn," *Pittsburg Leader*, August 12, 1899, 6.
58. "Baseball Notes," *Washington Post*, August 17, 1899, 8.
59. "The Baseball War," *Washington Post*, October 26, 1902, 23.
60. "Baseball Gossip," *Pittsburg Press*, September 23, 1899, 5.
61. "Won His Own Game," *Pittsburg Leader*, September 29, 1899, 14.
62. "Ended in a Row," *Pittsburg Leader*, October 14, 1899, 6.
63. Ralph Davis, "Leever's Work," *Sporting Life*, April 4, 1908, 9.
64. "Pittsburg Points," *Sporting Life*, November 18, 1899, 6.

Chapter Three

1. Honus Wagner, "Hans Wagner's Story," Chapter XXXII, *Los Angeles Times*, June 14, 1924, B2.
2. "Baseball Notes," *Pittsburg Press*, July 18, 1903, 10.
3. *The Sporting News*, February 10, 1900, 3.
4. *Sporting Life*, March 31, 5.
5. "The Two Teams Here," *The Sporting News*, April 14, 1900, 7.
6. "Caught on the Fly," *The Sporting News*, July 13, 1901, 5.
7. "Pittsburgh Pirates—1902," *Baseball Library* (web site), www.baseballlibrary.com.
8. *The Sporting News*, May 5, 1900, 5.
9. "Schriver's Swat," *Pittsburg Leader*, May 3, 1900, 10.
10. "Baseball By-plays," *The Sporting News*, December 20, 1923, 4.
11. *The Sporting News*, June 2, 1900, 4; *Chicago Daily Tribune*, May 27, 1900, 17.
12. "Pittsburg went all to pieces in afternoon game..." *New York Tribune*, May 31, 1900, 5.
13. *New York Sun*, June 12, 1900, 4.
14. *Chicago Daily Tribune*, June 19, 1900, 6.
15. "Leever Pitches a Great Game," *Pittsburg Post*, June 29, 1900, 6.
16. "Higginsport Is Avenged" *Chicago Daily Tribune*, July 16, 1900, 8.
17. *Ibid.*, 8.
18. *Ibid.*, 8.
19. Daniel Ginsburg, "Jack Taylor," http://bioproj.sabr.org.
20. *The Sporting News*, August 25, 1900, 4.
21. "Reds Had All the Luck," *Pittsburg Press*, August 27, 1900, 3.
22. "Pittsburgers Are Hustling," *Pittsburg Press*, September 12, 1900, 3.
23. "Big Betting on the Brooklyn-Pittsburg Series," *The Sporting News*, October 27, 1900, 2.
24. *Ibid.*
25. *The Sporting News*, October 27, 1900, 5.
26. *The Sporting News*, October 27, 1900, 2.
27. "Tannehill Says a Few," *Sporting Life*, December 29, 1900, 7.
28. J. G. Taylor Spink, "Clark Griffith's 50 Golden Years," *The Sporting News*, August 4, 1952, 11.
29. Arthur D. Hittner, *Honus Wagner: The Life of Baseball's "Flying Dutchman"* (Jefferson, NC: McFarland, 1996), 86.
30. *Ibid.*, 87.
31. "Baseball Notes," *Pittsburg Press*, October 16, 1903, 20.
32. "Sam Leever Is Chopping Wood," *Pittsburg Press*, February 21, 1904, 19.

Chapter Four

1. *The Sporting News*, February 23, 1901, 2; March 2, 1901, 4.
2. *The Sporting News*, February 9, 1901, 1,3.
3. *The Sporting News*, March 16, 1901, 2.
4. Dixie Tourangeau, "Jimmy Williams," Bioproj.sabr.org.
5. Mike Sowell, *July 2, 1903* (New York: Macmillan, 1992), 22.
6. "Pirates Like Training Place," *Pittsburg Press*, April 7, 1901, 16.
7. Alan H. Levy, *Rube Waddell* (Jefferson, NC: McFarland, 2000), 75.
8. *Sporting Life*, January 18, 1902, 3.
9. Levy, 75.
10. *Pittsburg Leader*, April 20, 1901.
11. "Pirates Down the Reds in Opening Game," *Pittsburg Leader*, April 21, 1901, 14.
12. Masur, 77.
13. "Beau's Smash," *Pittsburg Leader*, April 25, 1901, 12.
14. "Donahue Picks the Pirates," *Chicago Daily Tribune*, May 27, 1900, 17.
15. *Pittsburg Press*, May 3, 1901, 8.
16. *The Sporting News*, May 4, 1901, 4.
17. *The Sporting News*, May 11, 1901, 3.
18. *The Sporting News*, May 4, 1901, 5.
19. "Beat Pirates Easily," *Chicago Daily Tribune*, May 2, 1901, 6.
20. Levy, 77.
21. *Ibid.*
22. *Chicago Daily Tribune*, May 4, 1901.
23. "Umpire Put Out of the Grounds," *New York Daily Tribune*, May 22, 1901, 8.
24. "Great Pitching and Fielding by Pirates...," *Pittsburg Press*, June 11, 1901, 8.
25. "Game Saved by Many Rooters," *Pittsburg Press*, June 12, 1901, 8.
26. "Victory at Last for the Pirates," *Brooklyn Eagle*, June 29, 1901, 8.
27. "Giants and Pirates Fighting Second Battle for the Lead on Muddy Grounds," *The Evening Sun*, July 4, 1901, 1,4.
28. *New York Evening World*, July 5, 1901, 1.
29. *Ibid.*
30. *The Sporting News*, July 13, 1901, 4.
31. *Washington Post*, August 14, 1901, 8.
32. "Philadelphia Beat Pittsburg in Fourteen Rounds," *Pittsburg Press*, July 13, 1901, 3.
33. "Hank O'Day Lacks Humor," *Pittsburg Press*, July 25, 1901, 8.
34. "Doheny to Return," *The Sporting News*, August 8, 1901, 4.
35. *Sporting Life*, April 18, 1908, 9.
36. "Caught on the Fly," *The Sporting News*, July 13, 1901, 5.
37. "Baseball's Stormy Days Are Recalled by Barney Dreyfuss," *Pittsburgh Post Gazette*, April 18, 1931, 14.
38. *The Sporting News*, June 29, 1901, 4.
39. *The Sporting News*, August 3, 1901, 4.
40. "Pittsburg Points," *Sporting Life*, April 6, 1901, 2.
41. *The Sporting News*, August 10, 1901, 5.
42. *The Sporting News*, August 31, 1901, 4.
43. "Baseball Notes," *Washington Post*, August 22, 1901, 8.
44. *Pittsburg Leader*, August 23, 1901, 8.
45. William R. Cobb, ed., *Honus Wagner: On His Life & Baseball* (Ann Arbor, MI: Sports Media Group, 2006), 145.
46. *The Sporting News*, September 7, 1901, 4.
47. "Flag Is Clinched," *Pittsburg Leader*, September 28, 1901, 8.
48. *Ibid.*
49. *Ibid.*
50. "Proud Pittsburg," *The Sporting News*, October 5, 1901, 5.
51. *The Sporting News*, October 12, 1901, 5.
52. Frederick G. Lieb, *The Pittsburgh Pirates* (New York: G. P. Putnam's Sons, 1948).

53. "Celebration Successful," *Pittsburg Press*, October 5, 1901, 4.
54. *The Sporting News*, October 12, 1901, 2.
55. *The Sporting News*, October 19, 1901, 5.
56. *Oakland Tribune*, April 28, 1908, 27.
57. *Sporting Life*, January 18, 1902, 11.
58. *The Sporting News*, February 15, 1902, 3.

Chapter Five

1. "Girls Throw Straight," *Sporting Life*, February 8, 1902, 25.
2. *Sporting Life*, June 21, 1902, 9.
3. *The Sporting News*, May 3, 1902, 3.
4. *The Sporting News*, May 30, 1903, 5.
5. Start Was a Wonder," *Pittsburg Leader*, April 18, 1902, 14.
6. *Pittsburg Leader*, April 18, 1902, 14; *Pittsburg Press*, April 18, 1902.
7. "Prof. Sam Leever Reports to Clarke," *Pittsburg Press*, April 6, 1902, 20.
8. "Champion Flag Unfurled," *Washington Post*, April 23, 1902, 8.
9. "Day Will Never Die," *Pittsburg Leader*, April 23, 1902, 12.
10. "Thumping for Ewing," *Pittsburg Leader*, April 24, 1902, 12.
11. "Check Pace of Colts," *Chicago Daily Tribune*, April 27, 1902, 9.
12. "Coat of White for the Colts," *Chicago Daily Tribune*, April 28, 1902, 6.
13. *New York Evening Sun*, May 22, 1902, 8.
14. "Colts Shut Out Champions," *Chicago Daily Tribune*, May 31, 1902, 5.
15. "Pirates in Panamas," *Sporting Life*, June 14, 1902, 3.
16. *New York Evening World*, June 7, 1902, 4.
17. "Pittsburg's Owner Responsible for the Panama Hat Epidemic," *Sporting Life*, June 28, 1902, 3.
18. *Sporting Life*, June 28, 1902, 9.
19. "Colts Capture 19 Inning Game," *Chicago Daily Tribune*, June 23, 1902, 6.
20. *Ibid.*, June 23, 1902, 6.
21. "Grand Contests," *The Sporting News*, June 28, 1902, 6.
22. "Notes of the Colts," *Chicago Daily Tribune*, June 24, 1902, 6.
23. "Mix Base Hits with Fisticuffs," *Chicago Daily Tribune*, June 24, 1902, 6.
24. *Ibid.*, 6.
25. *Sporting Life*, July 5, 1902, 5.
26. *Ibid.*
27. Charles Alexander, *John McGraw* (Lincoln, NE: University of Nebraska, 1988), 90–92.
28. *The National Police Gazette*, New York, November 8, 1902, 3.
29. *New York Evening World*, July 11, 1902, 4.
30. "Davis Is Missed," *Sporting Life*, July 26, 1902, 5.
31. Craig R. Wright, "Evolution of the Spitball," from *A Page from Baseball's Past*, www.baseballspast.com/samplespitball.htm.
32. *Sporting Life*, June 21, 1902, 6.
33. *The Sporting News*, August 2, 1902, 4.
34. *Ibid.*, 4; *Sporting Life*, August 2, 1902, 9.
35. "Pittsburg Points," *Sporting Life*, August 16, 1902, 3.
36. *Ibid.*, August 16, 1902, 3.
37. *Sporting Life*, August 23, 1902, 9.
38. "Raid on Pittsburg Club," *Washington Post*, August 21, 1902, 8.
39. *Sporting Life*, August 23, 1902, 9. "The Singular Manner in Which the Pittsburgh President Discovered the Conspiracy in His Own Team," *Sporting Life*, November 20, 1902, 9.
40. "Pittsburg Points," *Sporting Life*, September 13, 1902, 2.
41. *Pittsburgh Post-Dispatch*, April 18, 1931, 16. *Sporting Life*, August 30, 1902, 2.
42. *Ibid.*, 16.
43. *Sporting Life*, January 13, 1906, 9.
44. A. R. Cratty, "Pittsburg Points," *Sporting Life*, September 13, 1902, 2.
45. "Johnson, Tempter," *Sporting Life*, September 6, 1902, 6.

46. *Pittsburg Press*, September 3, 1902, 10.
47. *Sporting Life*, August 30, 1902, 2.
48. *Sporting Life*, September 13, 1902, 2.
49. *Sporting Life*, August 30, 1902, 2.
50. *Pittsburg Press*, September 3, 1902, 10.
51. "Afternoon Game Won by Pittsburg," *Brooklyn Eagle*, September 2, 1902, 11.
52. *Sporting Life*, September 20, 1902, 3.
53. *Sporting Life*, August 9, 1902, 5; September 6, 1902, 21.
54. Bob Smizik, *The Pittsburgh Pirates: An Illustrated History* (New York: Walker & Company, 1990), 197.
55. "Pittsburg Points," *Sporting Life*, September 13, 1902, 2.
56. *The Sporting News*, April 4, 1903, 6.
57. "Some Fun Ahead," *Sporting Life,* June 14, 1902, 2.
58. "Champions Win First Game," *Pittsburg Chronicle Telegraph*," October 8, 1902, 20.
59. "Pittsburg Points" *Sporting Life,* October 18, 1902, 7.
60. "Grand Pitching by Mr. Phillippe," *Pittsburg Press*, October 9, 1902, 16.
61. "Phillippe Is Admired by Cleveland's Star," *Pittsburg Press*, March 9, 1911, 50.
62. "A Treat for Cleveland Fans," *Pittsburgh Chronicle Telegraph*, October 12, 1902, 10.
63. "Pirates Beaten by a Single Run," *Pittsburg Leader*, October 12, 1902, 14.
64. *The Sporting News*, October 18, 1902, 4.
65. *Pittsburg Chronicle Telegraph*, October 14, 1902.
66. "Deacon Phillippe Here for the Winter," *Pittsburg Press,* November 17, 1902, 10.
67. "How Deacon Phillippe Broke into Baseball," op. cit.
68. Masur, 61.

Chapter Six

1. "Giants Are Up Against It," *New York Evening World*, June 2, 1903, 1.
2. *Newark Daily Advocate*, September 2, 1903.
3. *Mansfield (OH) News*, February 27, 1904, 10.
4. *The Sporting News*, March 28, 1903.
5. *The Sporting News,* April 25, 1903, 2.
6. *Los Angeles Times*, April 22, 1903, 5.
7. "Leever Shut St. Louis Out," *Pittsburg Press*, April 30, 1903, 18.
8. "Why Ball Pitchers Are Not Good Batters," *Mansfield (OH) News*, February 27, 1904, 10.
9. "Played Like Real Champs," *Pittsburg Press*, May 11, 1903, 10.
10. *The Sporting News,* June 6, 1903, 1.
11. "Giant Punches Captain Clarke," *New York Evening World,* June 26, 1903, 1.
12. Masur, 144.
13. *New York Evening World*, June 11, 1903, 12.
14. Sowell, 245–47; Masur, 145–46.
15. "Ten Thousand Cheer Giants and Pirates," *New York Evening World,* June 26, 1903, 1.
16. "Given but One Run in Two Games," *Pittsburg Press*, July 5, 1903, 18.
17. *Ibid.*
18. "Phillippe Is Coming Home," *Pittsburg Press*, August 4, 1903, 10.
19. "Kennedy Knew It," *Pittsburg Press*, August 3, 1903, 10.
20. "Eddie Doheny Deserts Team," *Pittsburg Press*, July 29, 1903, 12.
21. "Wilhelm's Plucky Wife," *The Sporting News*, August 8, 1903, 1.
22. "Left an Egg in Beantown," *Pittsburg Press*, August 19, 1903, 10.
23. "The Baseball War," *Washington Post*, October 26, 1902, 23.
24. "Lee Landed by Pirates," *Pittsburg Press*, March 30, 1904, 10.

Chapter Seven

1. *The Sporting News,* October 5, 1903, 4.
2. *Sporting Life*, September 19, 1903, 6.
3. *Pittsburg Dispatch,* September 24, 1903; Masur, 17.

4. *The Sporting News*, November 15, 1902, 2.
5. *Pittsburg Press*, September 29, 1903, 14.
6. "Final Score 7 to 3 — Easy All the Way," *Pittsburg Post*, October 12, 1903, 12.
7. "Pirates Points," *Sporting Life*, October 10, 1903, 7. Masur, 26.
8. Abrams, 30.
9. "Fans Crows the Streets," *Pittsburg Leader*, October 2, 1903.
10. "Praise from Pulliam," *Pittsburg Press*, October 2, 1903, 20.
11. "The Pirates Were Blanked," *Pittsburg Press*, October 3, 1903, 11.
12. "Phillippe Is Likely to Pitch in Today's Game," *Pittsburg Press*, October 3, 1903, 11.
13. Masur, 82.
14. "Phillippe Says He Will Pitch Two More," *Pittsburg Press*, October 4, 1903, 19.
15. "Pittsburg Fans are Wild," *Chicago Daily Tribune*, September 23, 1903, 6.
16. "Collins Men Are Fighters," *Pittsburg Press*, October 5, 1903, 10.
17. *Pittsburg Press*, October 9, 1903, 20.
18. *Ibid.*, 20.
19. "Game Today Postponed by Clarke," *Pittsburg Press*, October 9, 1903, 1.
20. "Unprecedented Attendance Is Expected at Today's Baseball Contest," *Pittsburg Press*, October 10, 1903, 1. Abrams, 140.
21. "Champs Beaten Early," *Pittsburg Press*, October 11, 1903, 1.
22. *Ibid* 1.
23. "Pittsburg's Pride," *The Sporting News*, October 17, 1903, 1.
24. Masur, 202.
25. "Doheny Demented," *Sporting Life*, October 17, 1903, 6.
26. Abrams, 169.
27. Masur, 219.
28. "Clarke Reveals Wagner Was First to Pitch the Blooper," *The Sporting News*, March 21, 1951, 16.
29. "The Aftermath," *Sporting Life*, October 24, 1903, 4.
30. "What the Players Got," *Sporting Life*, October 24, 1903, 4.
31. "Knocking Leever," *The Sporting News*, October 24, 1903, 3.
32. James Jerpe, "Second Pirate Squad Will Depart Tonight," *Pittsburgh Gazette Times*, March 9, 1912, 35.

Chapter Eight

1. *The Sporting News*, March 5, 1904, 3.
2. *Daily Kennebec Journal*, April 18, 1904, 4.
3. *The Sporting News*, March 5, 1904, 3.
4. *Daily Kennebec Journal*, April 18, 1904, 4.
5. "Pitcher Leever's Arm," *Los Angeles Times*, March 27, 1904, B2.
6. "Pirates in Shape," *The Sporting News*, April 16, 1904, 4.
7. *Pittsburg Leader*, April 16, 1904, 8.
8. "Balk Rule Made Leever Mad," *Pittsburg Leader*, April 25, 1904, 10.
9. "Ovation Given Leever and Champions Yesterday Has No Local Precedent," *Pittsburg Press*, May 17, 1904, 14.
10. *Ibid.*
11. *Sporting Life*, June 11, 1904, 5.
12. "Storm Fails to Stop Game; Players' Protests Are in Vain," *Washington Post*, March 4, 1917, S2.
13. *The Sporting News*, July 2, 1904, 4.
14. "Hart's Side of the Scandal," *Chicago Daily Tribune*, January 18, 1905, 8.
15. *The Sporting News*, July 2, 1904, 4.
16. "The Pirates Win and Lose," *Pittsburg Press*, July 30, 1904, 8.
17. *The Sporting News*, July 23, 1904, 6.
18. *The Sporting News*, June 11, 1904, 6.
19. *The Sporting News*, July 23, 1904, 6.
20. *The Sporting News*, July 9, 1904, 4.

21. "Sebring's Slide," *Sporting Life*, August 13, 1904, 3.
22. *Sporting Life*, August 13, 1904, 3. Donlin was traded back to New York (for McCormick) after he was originally sent into exile for striking an actress and serving a jail sentence. *The Sporting News*, August 13, 1904, 1.
23. *Sporting Life*, August 20, 1904, 3.
24. "Champs Hurt in a Dangerous Section," *Pittsburg Chronicle Telegraph*, August 9, 1904.
25. *Sporting Life*, February 11, 1911, 7.
26. *Pittsburg Leader*, August 10, 1904, 8.
27. "'Deacon Phil' to the Rescue," *Pittsburg Chronicle Telegraph*, August 16, 1904, 11.
28. "Deacon Phil's Arm Very Sore," *Pittsburg Press*, August 26, 1904, 12.
29. *Sporting Life*, October 1, 1904, 4.
30. *Sporting Life*, September 24, 1904, 9.
31. *Sporting Life*, October 1, 1904, 6.
32. "Phil Goes Home," *Sporting Life*, November 5, 1904, 8.
33. *The Sporting News*, December 24, 1904, 3.
34. "May Let Leever Go" *Sporting Life*, April 8, 1905, 5.
35. "Sam Leever Liked Little Game," *Fort Wayne Sentinel*, March 22, 1912, 7.
36. *Sporting Life*, March 24, 1906, 6.
37. *Sporting Life*, October 26, 1907, 3.
38. "Phillippe Had Narrow Escape," *Pittsburg Press*, March 16, 1905, 14.
39. "Pirates Now in Good Form," *Pittsburg Press*, March 26, 1905, 19.
40. *The Sporting News*, April 22, 1905, 7.
41. "Baseball Notes," *Pittsburg Press*, May 9, 1905, 14.
42. "Leever Far from Being a Dead One," *Pittsburg Press*, April 20, 1905, 14.
43. "Superb Work Brought Victory to Pirates," *Pittsburg Press*, April 30, 1905, 18.
44. "Hard Luck Begins," *The Sporting News*, May 20, 1905, 2.
45. Hittner, 139.
46. *New York Times*, May 19, 1905, 7.
47. *Sporting Life,* June 10, 1905, 8.
48. *The Sporting News*, May 27, 1905, 1.
49. *Washington Post*, May 29, 1905, 6; Hittner, 140.
50. "Pirates Win Slugging Bee," *Pittsburg Press*, June 10, 1905, 10.
51. Hittner, op. cit, 142.
52. *New York Times*, July 18, 1905, 5.
53. Bozeman Bulger, "Giants Play a Scrappy Game," *New York Evening World*, July 19, 1905, 1.
54. *New York Times*, July 20, 1905, 5.
55. "Streak of Yellow," *The Sporting News*, August 12, 1905, 5.
56. Alexander, 115.
57. *Washington Post*, July 18, 1905, 5.
58. "Klem Makes a Record," *Sporting Life*, August 19, 1905, 10.
59. "Gamblers After Klem," *Sporting Life*, August 19, 1905, 10.
60. "Champions Walk Away from Pittsburgs," *New York Times*, August 22, 1905, 5.
61. "Arndt Steals Home and Wins Game for Cardinals," *St. Louis Star*, September 13, 1905.
62. *Sporting Life*, October 14, 1905, 15.
63. *The Sporting News*, October 7, 1905.
64. *Ibid.*, 2.
65. *The Sporting News*, November 4, 1905, 5.
66. *The Sporting News*, November 18, 1905, 5.
67. "The Rich Have Their Troubles, Too." *Ibid.*, 5.
68. *Sporting Life*, January 20, 1906, 8.
69. "Tessie Is Out Hunting," *Sporting Life*, November 11, 1905, 6.
70. *The Sporting News*, November 25, 1905, 4.
71. *The Sporting News,* December 9, 1905, 7.
72. *The Sporting News*, November 25, 1905, 4.
73. *The Elyria* (OH) *Reporter*, December 29, 1905, 6.

Chapter Nine

1. *The Sporting News*, March 17, 1906, 7. (Boston received third baseman Dave Brain, first baseman Del Howard and pitcher Vive Lindaman in the Willis deal.)
2. *Ibid.*
3. *Ibid.*
4. *The Sporting News*, April 28, 3.
5. *Ibid.*
6. Bozeman Bulger, "Pittsburgs Cackle Over McGraw's Team," *New York Evening Sun*, May 18, 1906, 1. "McGraw Goes Free in Assault Case," *Washington Times*, May 20, 1906, 9.
7. *The Sporting News*, July 7, 1906, 3.
8. *Washington Post*, June 28, 1906, 8.
9. *The Sporting News*, July 7, 1906, 3.
10. *Boston Daily Globe*, June 29, 1906, 13.
11. "Sale of Seymour," *The Sporting News*, July 21, 1906, 3.
12. *The Sporting News*, May 4, 1907, 3.
13. *Sporting Life*, June 23, 1906, 9.
14. *The Sporting News*, June 9, 1906, 4.
15. *Chicago Daily Tribune*, July 25, 1906, 8.
16. *The Sporting News*, August 4, 1906, 1.
17. *Sporting Life*, February 23, 1907, 8.
18. *Ibid.*
19. *Washington Post*, October 19, 1906, 8.
20. "Trusts Dreyfuss," *The Sporting News*, January 19, 1907, 2.
21. *New York Times*, January 22, 1907, 7.
22. "Have the Goods," *Sporting Life*, April 20, 1907, 12.
23. *Sporting Life*, January 19, 1907, 14.
24. "A Pittsburgh Story," *Sporting Life*, October 13, 1906, 18.
25. Hittner, 157.
26. "Honus Wagner's Own Story, Forty Years Young," *Atlanta Constitution*, February 20, 1916, A4.
27. *The Sporting News*, March 23, 1907, 3.
28. *Ibid.*
29. *Sporting Life*, September 28, 1907, 9.
30. "Honus Wagner's First Autocar Toys with Him and Sammy Leever," *Pittsburg Gazette Times*, August 4, 1907, 1.
31. *The Sporting News*, December 8, 1948, 29.
32. *Washington Post*, August 25, 1907, S1.
33. *Sporting Life*, November, 9, 1907, 8.
34. Application for Marriage License, Allegheny County, PA, Department of Court Records: Wills/Orphans' Court Division (filed October 21, 1907); "Decree of Divorce, Frank Perry vs Belle Perry," Allegheny County, PA, Department of Court Records: Wills/Orphans' Court Division, granted 30 June 1903. *Sporting Life*, September 29, 1906, 11.
35. U.S. Federal Census, Allegheny City, 5th Ward, District No 18, Enumeration District 53, Sheet 14. Belle Perry and daughter Isabel M. Perry were found in the household of William E. Kennedy and Mary E. Kennedy. The census reflected that Belle had been married three years at that time
36. "On Equal Footing," *The Sporting News*, November 28, 1907, 6.
37. Hittner, 162.
38. John Erardi, "Goshen Cemetery Holds Hidden Treasure," *Cincinnati Enquirer*, January 14, 2001, www.enquirer.com/editions/2001/01/14/spt_goshen_cemetery.html.
39. "Honus Wagner's Own Baseball Story," *Atlanta Constitution*, January 16, 1916, A4.

Chapter Ten

1. "Pitcher Leever Is Regarded a Humorist," *Sporting Life*, February 29, 1908, 10.
2. *Ibid.*

3. National Teams Are Getting in Shape," *Pittsburg Press*, March 26, 1905, 20.
4. *Sporting Life,* January 18, 1908, 8.
5. "Phillippe Brothers Hold Reunion," *Pittsburg Press*, April 5, 1908, 19.
6. "The Best Ever," *Sporting Life*, May 2, 1908, 7.
7. *Pittsburg Press*, April 8, 1908, 14.
8. *The Sporting News*, March 26, 1908, 3.
9. *Sporting Life*, May 11, 1908, 5.
10. "An Innovation," *Sporting Life*, May 2, 1908, 2.
11. *Chicago Daily Tribune*, April 28, 1908, 8.
12. *Sporting Life*, May 30, 1908, 7.
13. *Sporting Life*, June 6, 1908, 6.
14. *Pittsburg Dispatch,* June 11, 1908, 6.
15. "Pirates Shut Out New York Giants and Leever Shows Mid-Season Form," *Pittsburg Post*, June 11, 1908, 10; *Pittsburg Dispatch,* June 11, 1908, 6.
16. *Pittsburg Dispatch*, July 9, 1908, 10.
17. *The Sporting News*, July 9, 1908, 2.
18. "Tim Jordan's Long Blast," *Boston Daily Globe*, July 23, 1908, 4.
19. *Sporting Life*, August 8, 1908, 5.
20. "Wife of Veteran Pirate Twirler Was Pinioned Under Overturned Machine," *Pittsburg Press*, August 22, 1908, 22.
21. "Brilliant Finish Wins for Giants," *New York Times*, August 27, 1908, 5.
22. "Pirates Pennant Aspirations Jolted by the Giants," *Pittsburg Gazette Times*, September 19, 1908, 9.
23. "Sold Chance for Big Sum for Three Cents," *Fort Wayne Journal Gazette*, August 15, 1909, 20.
24. A. R. Cratty, "Pittsburg Points," *Sporting Life*, October 3, 1908, 12.
25. "Pirates Capture Closing Contest," *Pittsburg Dispatch*, October 1, 1908, 10.
26. *Sporting Life*, October 24, 1908, 11; "Clarke Threatens Big Suit," *Chicago Daily Tribune*, October 3, 1908, 8.
27. *Sporting Life*, October 24, 1908, 11.
28. "Sold Chance for Big Sum for Three Cents," *Fort Wayne Journal Gazette*, August 15, 1909, 20.
29. *Sporting Life*, October 28, 1908, 11.
30. "Police Called Out to Restrain Crowd Near Bulletin Boards," *New York Times*, October 5, 8.
31. *Sporting Life*, October 17, 1908, 10.
32. "Pirates Scatter," *The Sporting News*, October 22, 1908, 6.
33. "Phil's Farm Purchase," *Sporting Life*, October 31, 1908, 7.
34. *The Sporting News*, January 7, 1909, 3.
35. *Sporting Life*, March 28, 1909, 6.
36. *The Sporting News*, March 11, 1909, 2.
37. *New York Times*, February 25, 1909, 8.
38. *The Sporting News*, March 11, 1909, 2.
39. *The Sporting News*, March 4, 1909, 6; March 11, 1909, 2.
40. "Phil's Good Start," *Sporting Life*, May 15, 1909, 3.
41. "Deacon Phillippe Is a Happy Man Today," *Pittsburg Press*, April 27, 1909, 14.
42. *Sporting Life,* May 15, 1909, 3.
43. *Sporting Life*, June 19, 1909, 7.
44. "Record Crowd Opens New Park in Pittsburg," *Chicago Daily Tribune*, July 1, 1909, 10.
45. "35,000 Fans Help to Dedicate Ball Park," *Pittsburg Press*, June 30, 1909, 1–2.
46. "Brush Wielded by Phillippe on Reds," *Pittsburg Dispatch*, July 7, 1909, 7.
47. "Record Crowd Sees Pirates Win Twice," *New York Times*, July 10, 1909, 5.
48. Bill Lamberty, "Harry Clay Pulliam," from *Deadball Stars of the National League*, edited by Tom Simon (Washington, D.C.: The Society for American Baseball Research, Brassey's, 2004), 23.
49. *Pittsburg Dispatch*, August 14, 1909, 6.
50. *Pittsburg Gazette Times*, August 14, 1909, 7.

51. "Phillippe Talks About Lengthened Schedule and the Cigarette Habit," *Pittsburg Press*, January 30, 1910, 9.
52. "Pirates Welcomed by 50,000," *Chicago Daily Tribune*, October 19, 1909, 8.

Chapter Eleven

1. *Fort Wayne Daily News*, May 7, 1910, 14.
2. *The Sporting News*, January 27, 1910, 6.
3. *The Sporting News*, March 24, 1910, 1.
4. "Why Willis Went," *The Sporting News*, February 24, 1910, 2.
5. *Sporting Life*, May 7, 1910, 20.
6. *Pittsburg Dispatch*, April 22, 1910, 10.
7. *Chicago Daily Tribune*, June 25, 1910, 12.
8. *Chicago Daily Tribune*, June 26, 1910, C1.
9. Warren N. Wilbert, *What Makes an Elite Pitcher* (Jefferson, NC: McFarland, 2003), 59.
10. "For the Fourth Time Pirates Beat Giants," *Pittsburg Gazette Times*, July 17, 1910, III,2.
11. "Deacon Phillippe the Hero of the Ball Game," *Pittsburg Gazette Times*, July 23, 1910, 9.
12. *The Sporting News*, July 28, 1910, 1.
13. "Unusual Baseball Games," *Washington Post*, February 4, 1917, S2.
14. *Sporting Life*, November 26, 1910, 17.
15. *Sporting Life*, February 25, 1911, 10.
16. "Signs Queen Contract," *Los Angeles Times*, January 8, 1911, VII6.
17. *Sporting Life*, January 14, 1911, 13.
18. *The Sporting News*, April 20, 1911, 5.
19. *Galveston Daily News*, May 7, 1911, 9.
20. "Pirate Points," *Sporting Life*, May 13, 1911, 7.
21. "Where Gossip and Reminiscence Rubbed Elbows," *Sporting Life*, January 17, 1914, 16.
22. *Indianapolis Star*, June 16, 1911, 10.
23. *Indianapolis Star*, June 22, 1911, 8.
24. *Indianapolis Star*, August 22, 1911, 8.
25. *Sporting Life*, August 26, 1911, 2.
26. *Sporting Life*, September 2, 1911, 3.
27. "Phillippe Off List," *Boston Daily Globe*, September 26, 1911, 6.
28. "Holiday Squibs," *Sporting Life*, December 30, 1911, 2.
29. A. R. Cratty, "How 'Deacon' Phillippe Served His Own Interest, While Doing His Best Always for His Club," *Sporting Life*, February 25, 1911, 10.

Chapter Twelve

1. *Sporting Life*, February 10, 1912, 11.
2. "Phillippe for Manager," *Boston Daily Globe*, March 3, 1912, 14.
3. "Those New Leagues," *Sporting Life*, March 9, 1912, 7; *Sporting Life*, March 23, 1912, 14.
4. "Pirate Points," *Sporting Life*, March 23, 1912, 14.
5. *Sporting Life*, March 30, 9.
6. "Phillippe for Manager," op. cit.
7. "Bits of News," *Sporting Life*, March 23, 1912, 14.
8. C. B. Power, "Lively Practice on Expo Field," *Pittsburgh Dispatch*, April 17, 1912, 17.
9. "Cincinnati Buckeyes Win Opener from Filipinos," *Pittsburgh Dispatch*, May 9, 1912, 2.
10. *Chicago Daily Tribune*, May 19, 1912, 7.
11. "Senators Quit Unless Paid," *Washington Post*, May 23, 1912, 8.
12. *Sporting Life*, May 11, 1912, 9.
13. *Sporting Life*, November 30, 1912, 8.
14. Loose article dated January 22, 1913, in Deacon Phillippe file, National Baseball Hall of Fame Library.
15. *Sporting Life*, February 1, 1913, 16.
16. *Evening Post* (Frederick, MD, February 7, 1912, 6. *Racine Journal-News*, January 19, 1912, 9; *Fort Wayne Sentinel*, March 22, 1912; *Indianapolis Star*, January 28, 1912, 38.

17. Loose clipping, Sam Leever file, National Baseball Hall of Fame Library.
18. "Covington Blue Sox," www.cincysports.net/BlueSox.htm.
19. Samuel Sivitz, "Deacon Phillippe Remembered by Admirers," *Pittsburgh Chronicle Telegraph*, May 7, 1913.
20. "Deacon Suspends Red Ashenfelter," *Pittsburgh Gazette Times*, July 3, 1913, 10.
21. "Filipinos Hand Out Blank to St. Louis," *Indianapolis Star*, May 15, 1913, 10.
22. "Fils Fail to Secure a Hit," *Pittsburgh Gazette Times*, May 17, 1913, 9.
23. "Filipinos Start Series with Victory," *Pittsburgh Gazette Times*, May 29, 1913, 11.
24. "Whoa Bill's Squad Now Leads Federal," *Indianapolis Star*, June 15, 1913, 41.
25. "Covington Easy for 'Feds,'" *Chicago Daily Tribune*, June 17, 1913, 14.
26. *Chicago Daily Tribune*, June 21, 1913, 13.
27. *Sporting Life*, June 21, 1913, 1.
28. *The Sporting News*, July 17, 1913, 1; July 24, 1913, 1.
29. "Kansas City Gets Federal League Franchise," *Chicago Daily Tribune*, June 27, 1913, 13.
30. Ren Mulford, Jr., "A Federal Echo," *Sporting Life*, July 26, 1913, 9.
31. "Kansas City Beats Filipinos; Phillippe and Leever Pitch," *Pittsburgh Gazette Times*, June 29, 1913, section 3, 3.
32. "Deacon Suspends Red Ashenfelter, *Pittsburgh Gazette Times*, July 3, 1913, 10.
33. *Washington Post*, July 3, 1913, 8.
34. *Pittsburgh Chronicle Telegraph*, July 5, 1913.
35. "One Hit Beats Keeleys, 3 to 1," *Chicago Daily Tribune*, July 10, 1913, 14.
36. Marc Okkonen, *The Federal League of 1914–1915: Baseball's Third Major League* (Garrett Park, MD: Society for American Baseball Research, 1989), 5.
37. "Couldn't Hit Henning," *Kansas City Star*, July 13, 1913, 8A.
38. *New York Times*, August 12, 1913, 6.
39. "Phillippe Says the Pittsburgh Fed Club Owes Him $1,555.40," *Indianapolis Star*, January 19, 1914, 8.
40. "Packers Lose to Fils in Seventeen Innings," *Pittsburgh Gazette Times*," August 6, 1913, 9.
41. "Phillippe Says the Pittsburgh Fed Club Owes Him $1,555.40." *Indianapolis Star*, January 19, 1914, 8.
42. "Federal League Figuring on Managers," *Sporting Life*, November 1, 1913, 8.
43. *Pittsburgh Press*, April 17, 1914, 36; *Pittsburgh Press*, April 29, 1914, 29.
44. *Chicago Daily Tribune*, May 15, 1914, 15.

Chapter Thirteen

1. *The Sporting News*, October 21, 1915, 6.
2. "On and Off the Field," *Pittsburgh Press*, November 15, 1915, 8.
3. Ottie Padgett, "Rock Throwing in Carroll Helped Charlie Phillippe Become a Great Pitcher," op. cit.
4. "To Meet Recent Bride," *Pittsburgh Press*, April 12, 1919, 3.
5. "Phillippe Is Willing to Be Baseball Scout," *Oakland Tribune*, September 12, 1922.
6. "Pirates of 1901 Beaten by 1925 Bucs," *Pittsburgh Press*, June 7, 1925, 15–16.
7. "Heroes of the Past Among the 46,000," *New York Times,* October 8, 1925, 2.
8. *Pittsburgh Press*, November 20, 1935, 7.
9. "Judge, 94, Hears Final Arguments," *The Intelligencer* (Doylestown, PA), December 15, 1995, A-5.
10. "Ruth Blamed by Phillippe for End of Smart Plays," *The Sporting News*, February 28, 1946, 14.
11. "Deacon Phillippe Dies: All-Time Pirate Great," *Pittsburgh Post Gazette*, March 25, 1952, 1.
12. *Pittsburgh Post Gazette*, April 2, 1952, 18.
13. The grandchildren were John Byers and Jane Hodgson.
14. "Can't Make Sam Leever Angry," *Washington Post*, October 21, 1915, 8.
15. *Washington Post*, November 3, 1924, S1.
16. "Sam Leever Denies He Is Dead," *The Sporting News*, November 20, 1924, 1.
17. *New York Times*, October 14, 1925, 21.
18. Mark Armour, "Sam Leever," in *Paths to Glory*; 2003; http://www.pathstoglory.com/mark writings.html.

19. John Erardi, "Goshen Cemetery Holds Hidden Baseball Treasure," http:www.enquirer.com/editions/2001/01/14/spt_goshen_cemetery.html.

20. *Ibid.*

21. Copy of resolution, Representative Dan Bateman, House District #71 of Milford, February 1, 1995; National Baseball Hall of Fame Library.

22. James, Bill. *The Politics of Glory: How Baseball's Hall of Fame Really Works* (New York: Macmillan, 1994), 269–70.

23. *Ibid.*, 78.

Bibliography

Newspapers

Boston Daily Globe
Brooklyn Eagle
Charleroi (PA) Mail
Chicago Daily News
Chicago Daily Tribune
Daily Kennebec Journal (Augusta, ME)
Daily Public Ledger (Maysville, KY)
Elyria (OH) Reporter
Fort Wayne Sentinel
Galveston Daily News
Indianapolis Star
The Intelligencer (Doylestown, PA)
Kansas City Star
Liberty Magazine
Los Angeles Times
Mankato Daily Free Press
Mansfield (OH) News
Minneapolis Journal
Minneapolis Tribune
Morehead Daily News
New York Evening World
New York Times
New York Tribune
Oakland Tribune
Pittsburg Chronicle Telegraph
Pittsburg Dispatch
Pittsburg Leader
Pittsburg Gazette
Pittsburg Post
Pittsburg Press
Pittsburgh Gazette Times
Pittsburgh Post Dispatch
Pittsburgh Tribune Review
Racine Journal-News
Richmond Dispatch
St. Louis Star
St. Paul Globe
Sporting Life
The Sporting News
Syracuse Post Standard
Washington Post
Washington Times
Winona Daily Herald
Winona Daily Republican

Books

Abrams, Roger I. *The First World Series and the Baseball Fanatics of 1903.* Boston: Northeastern University, 2003.
Alexander, Charles. *John McGraw.* Lincoln: University of Nebraska, 1995.
Cobb, William R., ed. *Honus Wagner: On His Life & Baseball.* Ann Arbor, MI: Sports Media Group, 2006.
Cohen, Richard M., and David S. Neft. *The World Series.* New York: Dial Press, 1979.
Daniel, W. Harrison, and Scott P. Mayer. *Baseball and Richmond.* Jefferson, NC: McFarland, 2003.
Fleming, G. H. *The Unforgettable Season.* New York: Holt, Rinehart and Winston, 1981.
Hittner, Arthur D. *Honus Wagner: The Life of Baseball's "Flying Dutchman."* Jefferson, NC: McFarland, 1996.
James, Bill. *The Politics of Glory: How Baseball's Hall of Fame Really Works.* New York: Macmillan, 1994.
Jones, David, ed. *Deadball Stars of the American League.* Dulles, VA: Potomac, 2006.
Levy, Alan H. *Rube Waddell.* Jefferson, NC: McFarland, 2000.
Lieb, Frederick G. *The Pittsburgh Pirates.* New York: G.P. Putnam's Sons, 1948.

Masur, Louis P. *Autumn Glory: Baseball's First World Series*. New York: Hill & Wang, 2003.
McCollister, John. *The Bucs: The Story of the Pittsburgh Pirates*. Kansas City, MO: Addax, 1998.
Murphy, Cait. *Crazy '08*. New York: Smithsonian Books, 2007.
Okkonen, Marc. *Baseball Memories: 1900–1909*. New York: Sterling Publishing, 1992.
_____. *The Federal League of 1914–1915*. Garrett Park, MD: Society for American Baseball Research, 1989.
Reichler, Joe L., ed. *The Baseball Encyclopedia*. New York: Macmillan, 1979.
Ritter, Lawrence S. *The Glory of Their Times*. New York: Macmillan, 1966.
Ryan, Bob. *When Boston Won the World Series*. Philadelphia: Running Press, 2003.
Seymour, Harold. *Baseball: The Golden Age*. New York: Oxford University Press, 1971.
Simon, Tom, ed. *Deadball Stars of the National League*. Dulles, VA: Brassey's, 2004.
Smizik, Bob. *The Pittsburgh Pirates: An Illustrated History*. New York: Walker, 1990.
Sowell, Mike. *July 2, 1903*. New York: Macmillan, 1992.
Spink, J. G. Taylor. *Daguerreotypes of Great Stars of Baseball*. St. Louis, MO: Charles C. Spink, 1961.
Wiggins, Robert P. *The Federal League of Base Ball Clubs*. Jefferson, NC: McFarland, 2009.
Wilbert, Warren N. *What Makes an Elite Pitcher*. Jefferson, NC: McFarland, 2003.

Articles

Abrams, Al. "Baseball's Stormy Days Are Recalled by Barney Dreyfuss," loose article in Barney Dreyfuss file, National Baseball Hall of Fame Library.
Armour, Mark. "Deacon Phillippe," *Paths to Glory*; 2004; http://www.pathstoglory.com/markwritings.html.
_____. "Sam Leever," *Paths to Glory*; 2003; http://www.pathstoglory.com/markwritings.html.
Cameron, Joe. "Charles Louis Phillippi (Deacon), Legend of the Game," http://www.serve.com/smythgen/Deacon.htm.
Erardi, John. "Goshen Cemetery Holds Hidden Baseball Treasure," http:www.enquirer.com/editions/2001/01/14/spt_goshen_cemetery.html.
Fullerton, Hugh. "The Sad Plight of Sam Leever," *Liberty Magazine* (Vol. 5, Issue 30), July 28, 1928, p. 71.
Ginsburg, Daniel. "Jack Taylor," http://bioproj.sabr.org.
Padgett, Ottie. "Rock Throwing in Carroll Helped Charlie Phillippe Become a Great Pitcher," non-credited article (November 1962) in Deacon Phillippe file, National Baseball Hall of Fame Library.
Reis, Jim. "Blue Sox Sang the Blues," *Kentucky Post Online*, April, 3, 2000.
Tourangeau, Dixie. "Jimmy Williams," bioproj.sabr.org.
Youngblood, Jeff. "Early Life and Times of Barney Dreyfuss: Paducah and the World Series" Loose article (2002) in Barney Dreyfuss file, National Baseball Hall of Fame Library.

Web Sites

www.baseball-reference.com/.
www.baseball-fever.com/showthread.php?57538-Meet-The-Sports-Writers.
Charles "Deacon" Phillippe, South Dakota Sports Hall of Fame (web site), www.sdshof.com.
http://chroniclingamerica.loc.gov/.
"Covington Blue Sox," http://www.cincysports.net/BlueSox.htm.
"Historic Pittsburgh," http://digital.library.pitt.edu/pittsburgh/news.html.
"Photographs from *The Chicago Daily News*, 1902–1933"; The Chicago Historical Society; http://memory.loc.gov/ammem/ndlpcoop/ichihtml/cdnhome.
"Pittsburgh Pirates" (1900–1911 seasons), http://www.baseballlibrary.com/teams/.
http://www.retrosheet.org/.

Index

Abbaticchio, Ed 170, 171, 188, 190, 203, 205, 209, 220, 252, 253
Abrams, Al 254
Abstein, Bill 211
Adams, Charles "Babe" 194, 211, 213, 218, 219, 220, 221, 227, 228, 230, 252, 258
Alexander, Grover Cleveland 2
All-Americans team 107–11
Allegheny City 34, 83, 87, 185
Allegheny College 249
Allegheny County Memorial Park Cemetery 254
American League war 61, 99–102
Anderson, Edward "Goat" 189, 191
Anson, Cap 12
Armour, Mark 256
Arndt, Harry 174
Ashenfleder, Ray 243, 244, 247
Ashton, South Dakota 9
Auten 64

Baltimore American League Club 61
Bancroft, Frank 44
Barbeau, William "Jap" 211
Barclay, George 98
Barrow, Ed 32
baseball: in the "dead ball era" 3, 4, 19, 46, 48, 52; gambling 34, 57, 59, 134, 163, 171, 172, 182, 163, 171, 172, 182; pitching 2, 3; rowdyism in 61; rules 1, 19, 59; schedule 48, 150; on Sunday 49; umpires 35, 48, 151
baseball war *see* American League war
Baseball's National Agreement 113
Baseball's National Commission 113, 160, 163
Bauswine, Umpire George 164, 170, 171
Beaumont, Clarence "Ginger" 26, 39, 40, 44, 48, 49, 50, 53, 62, 67, 78, 80, 82, 86, 89, 92, 94, 98, 102, 103, 106, 108, 111, 121, 122, 123, 125, 126, 128, 130, 138, 139, 140, 141, 142, 150, 153, 171, 173, 179, 184, 185, 186, 188, 189, 192, 203, 252
Beck, Fred 227

Beckley, Jake "Eagle Eye" 43, 57, 65, 66, 105, 121, 153, 249
Bell, George "Farmer" 223, 229
Benswager, William E. 235
Bergen, Bill 88
Bernhard, Bill 107, 110
Bernheim, Bernard 18
Bernheim, Isaac 18
Bescher, Bob 215
Birdwell, Al 190, 201, 223
Blackstone, Red 238
Blankenship, Cliff 164, 165
Bloomer Girls baseball team 20
Boston American League Club 133–45
Bowen, Cy 33
Bowerman, Frank 43, 44, 119, 121, 124–25, 127, 130, 169, 193, 203
Bradley, Bill 107
Brain, Dave 169, 175, 190, 192, 270n
Bransfield, Kitty 66–67, 72, 80, 82, 88, 91, 92, 93, 99, 102, 104, 108, 109, 119, 120, 123, 125, 135, 141, 142, 150, 158, 161, 199, 205, 212, 252
Breitenstein, Ted 38
Bresnahan, Roger 96, 124, 174, 181, 186, 190, 193, 194, 201, 205
Briggs, W.E. 9
Broad Street Park, Richmond 30–31
Brown, Judge Homer 254
Brown, Mordecai "Three-Finger" 2, 116, 154, 164, 180, 202, 208, 213, 218
Brown, Umpire Thomas 91, 98
Browne, George 119, 168, 170, 237
Brush, Garnet 239
Brush, John T. 95, 96, 157, 167, 182, 205
Buckenberger, Al 122
Buelow, Charlie 75
Bunch, Al 194
Bunning, Jim 257
Burke, Frank 186
Burke, Congressman James 220
Burke, Jimmy 82, 90, 98, 100, 102, 103, 105
Burkett, Jesse "Crab" 50, 77

277

Bush, Donnie 219
Byers, John 273n
Byers, Julian I. 251
Byers, Mary Isabelle 195, 251, 254, 270n
Byrne, Bobby 211, 218, 223, 225, 227, 229

Callahan, Nixey 52
Camnitz, Howie 150, 191, 193, 200, 202, 204, 206, 209, 211, 212, 212, 215, 218, 219, 225, 226, 228, 233
Campbell, Vin 225
Cantillon, Joe 87, 93, 107, 231, 232, 242
Carey, George "Scoops" 107, 109, 235, 252
Carey, Max 235, 252
Carish, Fred 150, 158, 179
Carney, Pat 158
Carr, Charlie 179
Carr, Lew 74, 76
Carrick, Bill 33
Case, Charlie 149, 155, 162, 163, 169, 170, 172, 175–76
Casey, Doc 118, 164
Cassady, Harry 158
Cavet, Pug 232
Chadwick, Henry 82
Chance, Frank 89, 91, 123, 180, 184, 191, 218, 170, 172, 175–76
Chesbro, Jack 24, 25, 31, 37, 38, 41, 44, 47, 54, 57, 69, 70, 72, 73, 75, 77, 79, 81, 82, 90, 91, 92, 97, 99, 100, 101, 102, 104, 106, 108, 109, 112, 113, 114
Chicago American Giants 241
Chicago Federal League Club 244, 247, 248
Chicago U.S.L. Club 239, 240
Childs, Pete 71
Chronicle-Telegraph Cup Series 58–60
Clancy, Bill 162, 168
Clarke, Fred 6, 16, 20, 23, 25, 26, 39, 45, 48, 49, 50, 51, 52, 53, 54, 60, 61, 66, 67, 68, 72, 73, 73, 74, 76, 80, 82, 83, 84, 86, 89, 91, 92, 93, 98, 100, 101, 102, 103, 104, 105, 108, 110, 111, 118, 119, 120, 121, 124–25, 126, 128, 129, 130, 140–44, 149, 150, 153, 155, 156, 158, 162, 163, 164, 165, 167, 169, 171, 172, 173, 177, 184, 185, 187, 188, 190, 191, 192, 193, 198, 199, 201, 202, 203, 205, 206, 209, 211, 212, 215, 217, 219, 222, 225, 227, 228, 229, 230, 234, 238, 252, 253
Clarkson, John 40
Clemente, Roberto x
Cleveland American League Club 161
Cleveland National League Club 20, 21, 37
Clingman, Billy 21, 24, 39
Clymer, Otis 162, 164, 165, 169, 173, 186, 231, 232
Cobb, Ty 17, 219
Colgan, Umpire Harry 74
Collins, Jimmy 23, 61, 135, 136, 141, 142, 143
Columbus Western League Club 15
Congalton, Bunk 89, 94
Connolly, Umpire Tom 24, 135

Conroy, Wid 86, 91, 93, 94, 95, 97, 98, 99, 101, 102, 112, 113
Considine, George 182
Cooley, Duff 49, 52
Copeland, H.G. 232
Corbett, James J. 32
Corcoran, Tommy 42
Cork center baseball 223
Courtney, Ernie 187
Covington Federal League Club 242–43, 246
Crandall, Doc 227
Cratty, Alfred R. ix, 1, 35, 78, 97, 101, 174, 187, 200, 204, 207, 208, 213, 231, 233, 237
Cravath, Gavvy 231, 232
Crawford, Sam 43, 112
Criger, Lou 135, 140
Cronin, John 37
Crosby, Bing 235
Cross, Lave 60
Cross, Monte 107, 108, 109, 111
Cummings, Candy 257
Cunningham, Bert 21, 25

Dahlen, Bill 60, 103, 169, 174, 175, 182
Dalton, Jack 227
Daly, Tom 60, 73
Daubert, Jake 228
Davis, Alfonzo "Lefty" 74, 76–77, 80, 82, 88, 89, 92, 95, 97, 100, 101, 102, 112
Davis, George 72, 74
Davis, Harry 107, 109, 110
Davis, Ralph 44, 57, 121, 126, 143, 146, 156, 161, 164, 166, 175, 176, 179, 183, 195, 197, 209, 222
Dean, Dizzy 257
Delahanty, Ed 1, 41, 42, 54, 99
DeMontreville, Gene 40
Detroit Western League Club 11–12, 14, 16
Devlin, Art 171, 172, 181, 194, 215
Dexter, Charlie 71, 88, 89, 90
Diehl, Ernie 150, 157
Dillon, Frank "Pop" 42, 43, 48, 49, 50, 53
Dinneen, Bill 39, 137, 140, 141, 144, 147
Doheny, Ed 21, 76, 78, 79, 82, 90, 92, 95, 98, 102, 108, 114, 116, 119, 121, 127–28, 130, 131
Dolan, Cozy 71, 103, 170
Donahue, Tim 68
Donlin, Mike 61, 105, 170, 169, 174, 205, 269n
Donovan, Patsy 21, 35, 39, 42, 44, 50, 77, 78, 116
Dooin, Red 200, 217
Doolan, Mickey 217
Dougherty, Patsy 136, 137, 140
Douglass, Klondike 42, 122
Dovey, George 187, 203
Dovey, John 187
Doyle, Conny 25
Doyle, Jack 70

Doyle, Larry 193, 205, 215
Dreyfuss, Barney 4, 78, 104, 105, 131, 151, 158, 209, 243; background 18; bonus to Phillippe 146; death 235; Exposition Park and 73, 115–16; feud with Giants 166, 167, 175, 193; Forbes Field and 213, 214; gamblers and 183; Hall of Fame 235; Herrmann and 182–83; joke on 188; Kerr dispute 48; Leever and 6, 30, 47, 196, 197, 221, 230–31; on Leever 47, 165, 183, 196, 221, 231, 197; Louisville owner 18–19, 23, 25, 69–70; McGraw and 96, 166–67; owner of farm with Phillippe 112; Panama hats and 51, 92; players union 86; on Phillippe 103, 210, 221, 262n; Phillippe and 19, 112, 161, 187, 230; Phillippe favorite of 222, 230; photograph 106, 234; players acquired 115, 149, 155, 160, 177, 212, 233, 251; post season series (1902) 106, 107; president of Pirates 25, 44, 63–64; relations with players 69–70, 200, 211; tarpaulin introduction 199; trades of players by 69–70, 157, 187–88; Wagner on 45; war with American League 65, 76, 85, 99–102, 104, 108, 112–13; World Series and (1903) 133, 136, 139, 142, 145
Dreyfuss, Sammy 235
Dryden, Charles 92
Drysdale, Don 257
Duffy, Hugh 23
Duggleby, Bill 192
Dwyer, Frank 104

Earle, Billy 28, 29
Edwards, Henry P. 110
Egan, Dick 215
Egan, Rip 12
Elberfield, Norman "Kid" 28, 29, 30, 33
Ely, Fred "Bones" 42, 48, 49, 51, 54, 55, 57, 59, 65, 68, 71, 73
Emslie, Umpire Bob 37, 58, 90, 127, 153, 155, 167, 181
Evans, Roy 90, 92, 103, 126
Everett, Bill 24
Evers, Johnny 118, 123
Ewing, Bob 55, 88, 165, 186
Exposition Park, Pittsburgh 21, 34–35, 43, 48, 56, 73, 74, 97–98, 115–16, 142, 179, 204, 222, 236–37, 238–39, 241, 250; flooding 34, 67–68, 96, 189

Face, Elroy x
Falkenberg, Fred "Cy" 93, 115, 116, 128
Farrell, Duke 140
Farrell, John 86, 87
Federal League 241–49
Ferris, Hobe 138
Fisher, Tom 158
Flaherty, Patsy 25, 43, 47, 55, 153, 162, 163, 169, 172, 173, 188, 190, 192, 203
Fleischmann, Mayor Julius 66
Fletcher, Art 227

Flick, Elmer 41
Flynn, Jack 227, 229
Forbes Field, Pittsburgh 213, 214, 252, 256
Ford, Whitey 2, 257
Foster, Rube 241
Fox, George 25
Franklin, Umpire 244
Fraser, Chick 54, 126
Freedman, Andrew 71, 95, 96, 99
Freeman, Buck 136
Frisk, Emil 43
Fullerton, Hugh S., Sr. 94
Fyfe, Umpire Louis 238, 239

Galbreath, John W. 235
gambling *see* baseball, gambling
Ganley, Bob 173, 179, 180, 181, 187
Ganzel, John 53
Gardner, Jim 36
Geir, Phil 158
Gibson, George "Moon" 168, 169, 171, 172, 174, 180, 182, 191, 199, 203, 206, 211, 214, 218, 220, 225, 227, 234, 235, 253
Gilbert, John H. 135
Gill, Warren 200, 205, 206, 231
Glancy, Bill 256
Goes, Eddie 239
Gould, William 25
Graham, Peaches 223
Grand Rapids (Western League) 13
Green, Danny 71
Grey, Reddy 120
Griffith, Clark 61, 230
Grove, Lefty 2, 257

Haddix, Harvey x
Hahn, Frank "Noodles" 38, 39, 57, 118, 120
Halladay, Roy 2
Hallman, Billy 186, 232
Hanlon, Ned 51, 58
Harley, Dick 107, 108, 110, 118, 123
Harper, Jack 116
Hart, Billy 37, 38
Hart, Jim 154, 155
Hartzell, Tully 16, 107, 108, 110
Heidrick, John 68, 69
Henderson, Marshal 236, 240, 241, 247
Henning, Pete 248
Herrmann, Gerry 113, 157, 159, 160, 182, 213
Hershmann, O.S. 115
Hickman, "Piano Legs" 56, 72, 74
Hill, Pete 241
Hillebrand, Homer 171, 175, 198–99
Hite, Mabel 205
Hoblitzer, Dick 215
Hodgson, Jane Byers 273n
Hoffer, Bill 38
Hofman, Artie 173, 218, 225
Hogan, George 249
Holliday, Umpire "Bug" 118
Honus Wagner Sporting Goods Company 251

Hot Springs, Ark., spring training site 12, 64–65, 149, 162–63, 178, 188
Howard, Del 161, 162, 165, 167, 169, 172, 173, 174, 190, 270n
Howell, Harry 9, 59, 60
Hughes, Jimmy 73
Hughes, Tom 138
Hulen, Bill 3
Hunter, Catfish 257
Huntington Avenue Baseball Grounds 135, 138
Hurst, Umpire Tim 51, 60, 100
Hutchinson, Bill 12, 13, 14
Hyatt, Ham 218

Jackson, Joe 17
James, Bill 6, 257–58
Jennings, Hughie 59, 61
Johnson, Ban 16, 61, 96, 100, 101, 102, 112, 133
Johnson, Grant "Home Run" 10
Johnstone, Umpire James 151, 165, 166, 169, 170, 173, 181, 218, 225
Jones, Cowboy 67
Jones, Davy 91, 94, 123
Jones, Fielder 107, 108, 110
Jones, Sheriff 90
Jordan, Dutch 123
Jordan, Tim 204, 212
Joss, Addie 107, 109, 257
Justus, Walter 243

Kane, Jim 200, 201
Kansas City Federal League Club 246
Kansas City Western League 14, 15
Karger, Ed 180
Keeler, Willie 1, 61, 73, 81, 103
Keeley, Burt 238
Keliner, Punch 29
Kelley, Joe 52, 59, 73, 96, 105, 118
Kennedy, Mary 251, 270n
Kennedy, William "Brickyard" 141
Kerr, William W. 25, 41, 63, 64
Killen, Frank 35
Killilea, Henry 133
Kirschler, Mayor Charles 185
Kitson, Frank 57, 80, 81, 103
Kittredge, Malachi 21
Klem, Umpire Bill 163, 169, 170, 171–72, 194, 195, 201, 239
Kling, Johnny 94
Knetzer, Elmer 245, 248, 249
Knowles, Fred 124, 185
Koufax, Sandy 257
Krueger, Otto 68, 87, 117, 118, 120, 121, 125, 127, 134, 150, 158, 161

LaChance, Candy 140
Laforce, Ed 131, 220
Lajoie, Nap 41, 54, 58, 61, 107, 110, 111
Landreth, Clementine Phillippe 9

Landreth, Sen. Sidney Floyd 8
Lardner, Ring 213, 225, 226
Latham, Arlie 57
Latimer, Cliff 25
Lauder, Bill 42, 90
Law, Vernon x
Leach, Tommy 2, 3, 16, 22, 25, 34, 49, 51, 71, 72, 76, 82, 87, 88, 90, 92, 94, 98, 101, 102, 103, 104, 107, 110, 111, 112, 113, 117, 120, 125, 130, 133, 135, 140, 141, 145, 150, 151, 169, 179, 180, 181, 184, 186, 187, 188, 191, 194, 199, 203, 205, 206, 208, 211, 212, 215, 217, 220, 227, 229, 250, 252
Lee, Wyatt 149, 151, 153, 234
Leever, Amerideth 27, 263n
Leever, Edward 27, 263n
Leever, Maggie 54
Leever, Margaret Malloy 148, 196, 204, 255, 256, 257
Leever, Samuel 17, 25, 80, 90, 92, 103, 105, 114, 128, 186, 191, 211, 219, 235; vs. All-Americans 108, 110; amateur baseball 55; automobile and 176, 187, 192; baldness 27, 256; barnstorming 44, 83, 111; batting 37, 39; Beaumont, Ginger, friendship 26, 78; against Brown, Three-Finger 180, 202; businesses 176; *Chronicle-Telegraph* series 59, 60; Clarke, Fred and 26, 201, 217; coaching by 46, 75; comments about 116, 164, 165, 178, 187, 189, 197, 206, 226, 256; contract negotiations 230–31; with Covington (F.L.) 242–43, 246; criticism 99, 146–47; death and burial 256, 257; death, false reports 79, 255; description 26–27, 30, 40; Dreyfuss, Barney and 47, 196, 230–31; education 27; ejections and suspensions 151, 167; family 27, 198; farm 255–56; fiddle played by 78; against Flaherty, Patsy 190, 192, 203; friends 26, 78, 188–89, 196; frugality 255; gambling by 141, 162, 206, 208; hitting 37, 70; hunting by 62, 146; illnesses 29–30; injuries 68, 75, 78, 133, 139, 157, 158, 200, 206, 242; as manager 87, 242, 245, 246, 247, 248; marriage 148–49; against Mathewson 72, 102, 119, 125, 152, 165, 204, 206; with Maysville, Ohio, team 27–28; against McGinnity, Joe 60, 121, 126–27, 130, 167, 168, 170, 173, 181, 185, 193, 200; with Minneapolis (A.A.) 231–32, 242; nicknames 26; with the Norwoods 28; one hitters by 98;123; against Phillippe 21, 22, 38–39, 246–47; photographs 2, 27, 106, 117, 150, 189, 229; pitching style 3, 5, 35, 42, 57, 129; as postmaster 255–56; post season series 161; practical jokes on 51, 196; quoted 156, 203; record 1, 2, 58, 81, 131, 175, 195, 229, 257, 258, 259, 260; relief pitcher as 169, 171, 204, 207, 212, 218, 223; religion 24, 261n; retirement threatened 178; with Richmond 31–33, 36–37; as school teacher 8, 36, 37, 39, 40, 67, 111;

scoreless inning streak 122–24, 181, 183; sense of humor 197; shutout streak and 123–126; shutouts by 54, 88, 104, 110, 153, 194, 205; Smith, Harry, friendship with 188–89; sore arms 36, 40–41, 44, 131, 146–47, 149, 155; at spring training 34, 65, 197; against Taylor, Jack 55, 129, 154–55, 159, 183; trap shooting by 62, 65, 131, 230, 256; as umpire 57, 155; against Waddell 71; Wagner, Honus friendship 26, 196; World Series (1903) 134, 137, 141–42 (1909) 220 (1925) 252; against Young, Cy 37, 38, 49, 50, 58, 108
Leever, William 27, 48
Leifield, Al "Lefty" 173, 182, 183, 184, 191, 200, 202, 206, 208, 209, 211, 219, 223, 227, 228, 229, 252
Lewis, Jack 245, 246
Lieb, Frederick x
Lobert, Hans 191
Locke, William H. 6, 40, 201, 114, 124, 187, 197, 198, 207, 208, 212, 234, 264n
Long, Herman 23
Louisville Colonels 4, 16–24, 30, 32, 38, 43, 45
Lowe, Bobby 23, 93, 94
Lumley, Harry 194
Lynch, Mike 89, 155, 158, 162, 165, 167, 172, 173, 191, 193

Mack, Connie 32, 86, 107
Maddox, Nick 194, 195, 200, 209, 211, 213, 215, 218, 219, 224, 226, 227
Madison, Arthur 25
Madison, Charlie C. 247
Magee, Billy 20, 37
Magee, Mayor William 220, 222
Magoon, Topsy 118
Mair, Mrs. J. H. 254
Malarkey, John 104
Malloy, James 148
Mankato Maroons 9–11
Martinez, Pedro 2
Mathewson, Christy 2, 49, 55, 70, 71, 72, 73, 74, 75, 97, 99, 104, 119, 121, 127, 130, 150, 152, 165, 166, 167, 168, 169, 170, 171, 172, 173, 181, 182, 185, 193, 194, 195, 201, 205, 206, 227, 235, 238, 256
Maupin, Harry 20
Maysville Maroons 27–28, 165
Mazeroski, Bill x
McCarthy, Jack 44
McCarthy, Tom 202
McCormick, Barry 53, 70
McCormick, Harry "Moose" 161, 215, 269n
McCreedy, Tom 22, 39, 50, 51, 103, 252
McCullough, William Tice 236, 241
McFarland, Charles 153
McGann, Dan 27, 50, 67, 79
McGinnity, Joe 38, 52, 57, 59, 60, 61, 62, 96, 119, 125, 126, 130, 150, 152, 154, 158, 167, 170, 173, 181, 185, 193, 200
McGraw, John J. 1, 38, 61, 65, 95–96, 101, 102, 127, 150, 151, 161, 165, 166, 172, 173, 181, 182, 185, 193, 194, 195, 201, 205, 206, 227, 235, 238, 256
McKean, Ed 37
McKechnie, Bill 228, 256
McLean, Larry 154
McLoskey, John 184
McNichol, Ed 158
McQuillan, George 205, 217, 218
McQuiston, Frank 122, 134
Menefee, Jack 90, 123, 129
Menosky, Mike 243, 246
Mercer, Win 107, 109
Merkle, Fred 216
Merritt, George 79, 82, 102, 111, 118, 120
Mertes, Sam 13, 53, 174, 175
Messerley, Jack 9, 10, 11
Meyer, Leo 182
Miller, Dankin 89
Miller, Doc 225
Miller, Fred "Speedy" 228
Miller, George "Doggie" 14
Miller, Henry 245
Miller, Jack "Dots" 211, 215, 225
Miller, Kid 10
Miller, Roscoe 127, 139, 149, 150, 152, 153, 158, 159
Minneapolis Millers American Association 231–32
Minneapolis Millers Western League 12–16
Mitchell, Mike 215
Moeller, Danny 203
Monroe, Bill 241
Montgomery, Judge Harry M. 253
Moore, C.C. 20
Moore, Eddie 252
Moran, Lew 150, 151
Moran, Pat 158, 251
Morrissey, Jack 118
Mullin, George 219, 220
Murphy, Charles 213–14
Murphy, Ed 77
Murphy, John 146
Murray, Red 215
Murray, Tom 245

Nash, Billy 71
National Baseball Hall of Fame 6, 234, 235, 257–58
Nealon, Joe 179, 180, 181, 184
New Richmond baseball team 28, 29
Nichols, Art 68, 98
Nichols, Kid 1, 153

O'Brien, Jack 140
O'Conner, Paddy 203, 227
O'Connor, Jack 2, 52, 53, 58, 59, 65, 68, 71, 75, 76, 77, 82, 86, 87, 91, 98, 99–101, 102, 112, 237, 243, 244, 247
O'Day, Umpire Hank 72, 75, 77, 93, 108, 122, 135, 185, 201, 205, 206, 209

Odwell, Fritz 164
O'Hagan, Hal 91
O'Hara, Bill 215
Ohio House of Representatives 257
O'Loughlin, Umpire Silk 108
O'Neil, Jack 154
O'Neil, Mike 155
Orris, James L. 233
Orth, Al 80
Osborn, Fred 205
Otey, Bill 205
O'Toole, Marty 233
Overall, Orval 164
Owen, Frank 238, 240

Padden, Dick 79
Page Fence Giants 10
Parent, Freddy 135, 138, 141
Paskert, Dode 215
Paterson Atlantic League Club 32
Patterson, Roy 232
Payne, Harley 39
Peitz, Heinie 39, 88, 161, 164, 172, 184
Perry, Belle *see* Phillippe, Belle
Petway, Bruce 241
Pfeiffer, Jeff 238, 240
Pfeister, Jack 149
Phelps, Ed 86, 103, 104, 120, 123, 126, 136, 141, 152, 156, 161, 182
Philadelphia Athletics Atlantic League 32, 33
Phillippe, Andrew J. 8, 261n
Phillippe, Belle 195, 230, 251, 253, 270n
Phillippe, Charles "Deacon" 40, 45, 50, 52, 53, 74, 77, 79, 91, 102, 108, 115, 127, 152, 173, 182, 183, 188, 191, 216, 231, 234, 257; Alexander, Grover, compared to 2; All Americans and 109–11; baseball card 20; batting 117, 119, 128; character 7, 85; *Chronicle-Telegraph* Cup series 60; and Clarke, Fred 83–84; Clarke, Fred on 137, 143, 145; coaching 46, 115; comments about 7, 9, 109, 169, 212, 213, 234, 241; contract negotiations 19, 178, 187, 221; control of pitches 4; death and burial 254; description 83; Dreyfuss, Barney and 19, 161; early baseball 9; ejections 163, 171, 172; exhibition games pitched 93; family 8; family life 198, 230, 251; Fargo, played in 13; farm 19, 111–12, 207; Forbes Field debut 214–15; halls of fame in 255; home runs by 92, 228; hunting 176, 177, 233; ice hockey played 84; illnesses 64, 154, 155–56; injuries 15, 96, 126, 128, 129, 163, 165, 158, 200, 204, 209; Lefty Davis and 101; with Louisville 16–24; as manager (Allegheny College) 249, (Federal League) 242–49, (U.S.L.) 236–41; Mankato, played in 9–12; marriage 195; against Mathewson, Christy 71, 167, 170, 172, 174–75, 186, 193, 226–27; with Minneapolis (Western League) 12–16; name misspelled 8, 9, 12, 14, 261n; nickname origin 4, 7, 9; no hitter by 21–22; old timers games 252; as opening day pitcher 66, 86–87, 116, 150–51, 179, 189, 222–23; opposed by Leever; 21, 22, 38–39, 246–47; as outfielder 47, 120; pennant clinching win 80; photographs 5, 17, 82, 106, 139, 150, 224, 239, 253; on pitching 7; Pittsburgh (F.L.) 236–41; Pittsburgh (U.S.L.), 242–49; popularity 22, 139, 140, 143, 239, 243, 254; quoted 134, 135, 148, 177, 210, 212, 220; record 1, 4, 58, 81, 92, 132, 160, 186, 209, 211, 229, 233, 259, 260; relief pitcher 202, 218, 225, 232; religion and 49, 261n; retirement rumor 210; on Ruth, Babe 254; shutout streak 122–26; shutouts by 55, 60, 89–90, 109, 121, 168–69, 172, 223; snowball fight 114; sore arms 6, 76, 131, 159; spitball thrown by 5–6, 163, 164, 202; spring training 47, 64, 65, 199, 210; Sunday, pitching on 57, 118; against Taylor, Jack 93–94, 97, 118, 123, 124, 153, 174, 184; as Tipstaff 253, 254; trade rumors 187; traded 25; twentieth victory 24, 105, 130; as umpire 122; Wagner, Honus and 17, 83–84, 176, 233; wealth 207, 230, 237, 241; winning streak 126; World Series (1903) 7, 134–47 (1909) 219–20; against Young, Cy 24, 58, 110–11, 135–36, 138, 142, 143
Phillippe, Deacon Reese 255
Phillippe, Ellis 254
Phillippe, Margaret Hackler 8
Phillippe, Mary Isabelle *see* Byers, Mary
Phillippe, Ryan 255
Phillippe, Sidney 198
Phillippi, Andrew J. 261n
Phyle, Bill 72, 74
Piatt, Wiley 126
Piekarski, Judge Frank 253
Pittinger, Togie 122, 153, 165
Pittsburgh Athletic Park Association 250
Pittsburgh Federal League Club 241–49
Pittsburgh United States League Club 147, 236–41
Players' Protective Association 61, 86
PNC Park, Pittsburgh 250
Poole, Eddie 79, 82, 120, 126, 151
Portsmouth, Ohio, club 29
Power, C.B. 202, 207
Powers, John T. 241, 246
Protective Association of Baseball Players 61, 86
Pulliam, Harry 18, 25, 30, 48, 64, 78, 79, 92, 95, 101, 102, 103, 112, 118, 125, 151, 160, 166, 171, 182, 185, 213, 216–17

Ramsey, Buck 244
Raymond, "Bugs" 208, 215, 227, 238
Reach & Company 244
Reese, John "Bonesetter" 131, 137
Reidlin, William 242
Reidy, Bill 134
Reilly, Charles 15, 16

Reulbach, Ed 56, 168, 191, 214, 225, 226
Reymer, Chief 244
Rhines, Billy 38
Richmond Atlantic League club 29, 30–33, 36
Rickart, Lloyd 246
Rigler, Charles 205, 209
Ritchey, Claude 22, 25, 48, 49, 54, 65, 77, 79, 81, 82, 98, 102, 108, 117, 119, 121, 123, 127, 128, 133, 135, 140, 141, 150, 167, 168, 170, 171, 186, 188, 190, 203, 237, 240, 252, 253
Riverbreeze Park 242–43, 246
Robison, Frank de Haas 77, 87, 98, 103
Robitaille, Chick 162, 172
Roosevelt, Pres. Theodore 37, 96
Rough Riders 37
Royal Rooters 137, 140
Rucker, Nap 194, 216
Rural Retreat, Va. 8
Ruth, George Herman "Babe" 254
Ryan, John J. 240

Sabrie, Eddie 243
St. Paul Western League 12, 13
St. Vrain, Jimmy 89
San Francisco earthquake 179–80
Saulpaugh, Clarence 16
Saunders, John J. 22
Scanlan, Doc 150
Schaefer, Germany 93
Schmidt, Henry 31
Schulte, Frank "Wildfire" 180, 218, 225
Sebring, Jimmy 104, 105, 112, 116, 118, 128, 136, 138, 143, 150, 156–57
Selbach, Kip 72
Sellers, Rube 245, 246
Sentelle, Paul 187
Seybold, Ralph "Socks" 31
Seymour, Cy 96, 105, 179, 182–83, 186, 201, 205, 206, 223
Shannon, Spike 185, 186, 205
Sharp, Bud 225
Sharsig, William 32
Shean, Dave 225
Sheckard, Jimmy 63, 73, 81, 225
Sheehan, Tommy 180, 191, 192, 193, 249
Shriver, William "Pop" 51, 68
Smith, Elmer 76
Smith, Hal x
Smith, Harry 26, 86, 93, 101, 102, 103, 112, 120, 128, 150, 158, 172, 182, 188–89, 190, 194, 195, 203
Smith, Walter 101
Society for American Baseball Research 250
Soden, Arthur 160
Somers, Charles 100, 101, 102
South Dakota Sports Hall of Fame 255
Sparks, Tully 21, 37, 38, 97, 172, 212
Speaker, Tris 17
Spinney, John A. 242, 243

Stahl, Chick 54
Steinfeldt, Harry 184, 191, 226, 237
Stewart, W.C. 242
Stockdale, Otis 31
Storke, Alan 190, 191, 193, 200, 211, 215
Stottlemyre, Mel 228
Strang, Sammy 169, 170, 181
Strickett, Elmer 183
Sudhoff, Willie 68
Sullivan, Billy 107, 108, 110
Sullivan, Sport 134
Swacina, Harry 200
Swartwood, Umpire Ed 39, 43, 53
Sweeny, Bill 223

Tannehill, Jesse 30, 31, 35, 36, 37, 38, 41, 44, 54, 58, 60, 67, 70, 71, 74, 80, 82, 88, 91, 92, 93, 94, 98, 100, 102, 103, 106, 109, 110, 111, 122, 123, 124, 125, 129, 160, 230, 252, 257
Taylor, Judge Harry 61
Taylor, Jack 55–56, 93–94, 97, 118, 123, 124, 126, 153, 154–55, 159, 160, 168, 174, 182, 183–84, 189, 191
Taylor, Luther "Dummy" 71, 74, 130, 150, 152, 169, 185
Tebeau, Patsy 13
Teineham, Art 12
Tenner, John 64
Tenny, Fred 23, 190, 192, 201
"Tessie" 137, 147, 151, 176
Thomas, Roy 203
Thomasville, Ga. 19, 47
Thompson, Gus 134, 150
Three Rivers Stadium, Pittsburgh 250
Timmerman, Whitey 247
Tinker, Joe 89, 91, 93, 94, 95, 97, 123, 184, 218
Titus, John 187, 212, 217

Union Depot (Station) Pittsburgh 139, 233
United States League 236–41

Vail, Bob 206
Van Haltren, George 72, 90, 92
Veil, Bucky 115, 116, 128, 137, 150, 156
Vickers, Rube 105
Vidmer, Richards 252
Villa, Joe 175
Virginia Sports Hall of Fame 17, 255

Waddell, Rube 16, 24, 25, 49, 50, 53–54, 59, 60, 62, 66, 67, 69, 71, 78, 83, 107, 231, 232, 257
Wagner, Al 146
Wagner, Honus 1, 16, 21, 22, 25, 39, 48, 74, 88, 92, 93, 94, 100, 102, 103, 107, 122, 123, 124, 125, 148, 165, 168, 172, 174, 180, 190, 193, 211, 215, 217, 218, 229; acting manager 121, 128, 129, 156; All-American series 109–111; American League courted by 100; automobile 192,

195; bats left handed 56; batted against Leever 32, 43; on Dreyfuss 45; friendship with Leever 26, 62, 196; friendship with Phillippe 17, 83–84, 117, 176, 253; Hall of Fame induction 234; hidden ball trick 182; hitting heroics by 71, 80, 169, 212, 220, 225; holdout 197, 199, 200; and hunting 146; injuries 66, 133, 175, 233; nickname 49; old timers games 252; on Phillippe 177; photographs 82, 198; religion 17, 261n; shortstop 76, 77, 79; stolen base record 195; suspensions 98, 118, 167, 170–71; wealth 187; World Series (1903) 135, 138, 140, 141, 143, 145, 147 (1909) 220 (1925) 252
Wallace, Bobby 49, 68, 107, 109, 110
Walsh, Ed 257
Ward, Piggy 31
Warner, John 71, 121
Warren, Henry 244
Washington National League Club 20, 26, 39
Watkins, Bill 34, 35, 37, 39
Watson, J.W. 252
Weaver, Art 126, 127
Weimer, Jake 179
Wells, Jake 29, 30, 31, 32, 40–41
Wicker, Bob 173, 180, 181
Wilhem, Irwin 36, 37, 115, 116, 120, 121, 122, 128–29
Williams, Art 91
Williams, Jimmy 22, 24, 39, 40, 41, 48, 49, 50, 51, 53, 57, 58, 59, 64, 65, 76, 101, 231, 232
Willis, Vic 23, 126, 178, 181, 183, 184, 185, 191, 193, 200, 208, 209, 210, 211, 212, 214, 219, 221, 222, 262n, 270n
Wilmot, Walter 12, 13, 14, 16
Wilson, Owen "Chief" 199, 201, 203, 211, 220, 225, 227, 228
Wiltse, George 150, 185, 201
Wiltse, Lewis 70
Winona, Minnesota, baseball club 10, 11
Wisconsin Athletic Hall of Fame 254
Witherspoon, Reese 255
Wittman, William 240
Woods, Walt 21, 25, 47
World Series: (1903) 133–45; (1909) 219–20; (1925) 252, 256; (1960) x–xi

Yeager, George 82
Yerkes, Stan 87
Young, Denton True "Cy" 24, 37, 38, 49, 50, 58, 61, 107, 110, 111, 135, 136, 138, 141, 142–43, 147, 242, 243, 245, 253
Young, Harley 202, 208
Young, Irving "Young Cy" 167, 170, 201, 202, 205
Young, Nick 74

Zimmer, Charles "Chief" 25, 48, 49, 52, 54, 61, 71, 74, 77, 81, 82, 86, 88, 89, 102, 103, 122, 123, 252

www.ingramcontent.com/pod-product-compliance
Ingram Content Group UK Ltd.
Pitfield, Milton Keynes, MK11 3LW, UK
UKHW041927140426
5217IPUK00014B/357